W9-AQL-626

The Constitution in Conflict

The Constitution in Conflict

ROBERT A. BURT

THE BELKNAP PRESS OF
HARVARD UNIVERSITY PRESS
Cambridge, Massachusetts
London, England   1992

Copyright © 1992 by the President and Fellows of Harvard College
All rights reserved
Printed in the United States of America
10 9 8 7 6 5 4 3 2 1

This book is printed on acid-free paper, and its binding materials
have been chosen for strength and durability.

Library of Congress Cataloging-in-Publication Data

Burt, Robert, 1939–
The Constitution in conflict / Robert A. Burt.
p.   cm.
Includes bibliographical references and index.
ISBN 0-674-16536-5
1. Judicial power—United States—History.   2. United States.
Supreme Court—History.   3. United States—Constitutional law—
Interpretation and construction—History.   4. Separation of powers—
United States—History.   I. Title.
KF5130.B87   1992
347.73'12—dc20
[347.30712]
91-28107
CIP

To Linda,
da capo al fine

Contents

The Constitution in Conflict

Introduction:
White Bosses

ABRAHAM LINCOLN entered Richmond on April 4, 1865, just one day after the city had fallen to the Union army. As he walked through the streets with a small escort, he was recognized by a group of black people. "Bless the Lord! The great Messiah! He's been in my heart four long years. Come to free his children from bondage. Glory, Hallelujah!" they called, as they pressed around him. "I know I am free," an elderly woman said, "for I have seen Father Abraham and felt him." One black man fell to his knees. Lincoln, visibly overcome, responded, "Don't kneel to me. That is not right. You must kneel to God only, and thank Him for the liberty you will enjoy hereafter."[1]

This response is the heart of Lincoln's democratic creed. He had stated this same ideal earlier, in more formal terms: "As I would not be a slave, so I would not be a master. This expresses my idea of democracy. Whatever differs from this, to the extent of the difference, is not democracy."[2] Based on this ideal, he had evaluated the Supreme Court of the United States, in his first inaugural address:

> I do not forget the position assumed by some, that constitutional questions are to be decided by the Supreme Court; nor do I deny that such decisions must be binding in any case, upon the parties to a suit, as to the objects of that suit, while they are also entitled to very high respect and consideration in all parallel cases by all other departments of the Government. . . . [But] if the policy of the Government upon vital questions, affecting the whole people, is to be irrevocably fixed by decisions of the Su-

preme Court, the instant they are made, in ordinary litigation between parties in personal actions, the people will have ceased to be their own rulers, having to that extent practically resigned their government into the hands of that eminent tribunal.[3]

The specific impetus of Lincoln's observation was the Supreme Court's decision in the *Dred Scott* case, which held that no black person could be a citizen of the United States and that a congressional act—the Missouri Compromise of 1820 restricting territorial slavery—violated the Constitution. There was, however, a larger implication in Lincoln's critique—that the Court's claim to supremacy over the Congress in constitutional interpretation made it, in effect, a slavemaster and imposed a form of involuntary servitude on the people.

My aim in this book is to explicate this evaluation of the concept of judicial supremacy. In the 1930s, when the Supreme Court was eviscerating the New Deal, this position would have had a strong leftward political inclination (and, indeed, Franklin Roosevelt himself cited Lincoln's inaugural passage to justify his own attack on the Court).[4] Fifty years later, in the wake of the Warren Court's activism and the Burger Court's decision in *Roe v. Wade*, this evaluation of judicial supremacy would have borne the markings of right-wing politics (and, indeed, Edwin Meese—who served Ronald Reagan as attorney general, among other capacities—also relied on this same passage from Lincoln's inaugural in his condemnation of judicial activism).[5] Today, however, the politics of Supreme Court criticism suddenly has become quite muddled. The commitment of liberals to the principle of judicial supremacy has been increasingly strained, and may soon be shattered, under the accumulated number of new appointments to the Court from four successive Republican presidents. Contemporary conservatives similarly might soon find an atavistically rekindled fervor for judicial supremacy now that the Court has come once again to its senses.

Perhaps nothing more than this crude partisanship explains the shifting currents of opinion throughout our history regarding the status of judicial authority in the American constitutional scheme. I am reluctant, however, to endorse this conclusion; and this very moment of transition in the Court's composition may provide an unusual impetus for reflection about the idea of judicial suprem-

acy among political partisans of all stripes, precisely because memory of their grievances is still so vivid among the newly triumphant Right, and nostalgia for their victories is still so strong among the newly beleaguered Left.

The clearest support after Lincoln that I have found for this re-examination is in an observation that Thurgood Marshall made just before his greatest triumph of advocacy in the Supreme Court. Marshall was preparing for his argument in *Brown v. Board of Education* during the summer of 1953. The case had already been argued once, but the Court ordered reargument on several specific questions regarding the meaning of the Fourteenth Amendment. The central question posed by the Court was, "Is it within the judicial power, in construing the Amendment, to abolish segregation in public schools?"[6] After weeks of exhausting research and discussion, Marshall proposed to his associates at the NAACP Legal Defense Fund that they offer this answer to the Justices' question: "White bosses, you can do *any*thing you want 'cause you got de power!"[7]

Marshall did not reiterate this argument in his brief or his oral presentation before the Court; and he was content to rely on judicial supremacy after the Court's favorable ruling. But in this bitter joke, Marshall implicitly acknowledged what Lincoln had explicitly identified—that the very judicial power which he invoked to overturn centuries of oppression itself rested on an oppressive conception of social authority. Insofar as the Justices claimed supremacy in constitutional interpretation, they could not say as Lincoln had said: "Don't kneel to me. That is not right." They could not say, "As I would not be a slave, so I would not be a master."

Lincoln's egalitarian creed is the foundation for the central claim of this book: that judicial supremacy in constitutional interpretation is inappropriate and that a different conception of judicial authority—the Supreme Court as equal, not hierarchically superior, to other branches—is preferable in principle and in practice. The central example for this claim is the Supreme Court's decision in *Brown v. Board of Education*—which, I maintain, can best be understood in both its underlying principle and its practical application as an institutional claim by the Court of equal, not supreme, authority in constitutional interpretation.

Part I of this book explores the justifications in democratic

principle for judicial authority in constitutional interpretation. Chapter 1 provides a preliminary examination of *Brown* to show how the currently prevalent schools of jurisprudence—all of which are based on the premise of judicial supremacy in constitutional interpretation—fail to provide an adequate justification for that decision. Chapter 2 explores the founders' views of judicial authority, focusing particularly on James Madison. Madison sharply differed in his views about judicial authority in constitutional adjudication from Alexander Hamilton, whose support for judicial supremacy (most notably in *Federalist* 78) is the cornerstone of the currently prevalent conception. In this chapter, I reconstruct Madison's conception that the federal branches should be equal in their authority to interpret the Constitution, and I set his disagreement with Hamilton in the context of general attitudes toward social conflict and political authority within the founding generation. My goal in this chapter is not to establish that Madison's view was the true intention of the founders and is accordingly binding on us; I claim only that his view is as plausible a candidate as Hamilton's for the honorific status of "original intent" and that we remain free today to choose between them.

Chapter 3 identifies the fundamental reason why Madison's conception of judicial authority is, in my opinion, preferable. Though Madison did not himself fully develop it, this principled justification was most clearly expounded by Abraham Lincoln in his complex vision of egalitarianism. Lincoln claimed that the Constitution embodied the egalitarian creed in the Declaration of Independence.[8] In this chapter, I will show how Madison's institutional conception of equality among the three branches of government in interpreting the Constitution provides the practical framework for the realization of Lincoln's egalitarian ideal.

But Hamilton's competing conception of judicial supremacy has been dominant in our constitutional jurisprudence. The critical events in the evolution of this dominance occurred during the nineteenth century. Part II of this book provides an extended historical narrative of this evolution, setting the decisions of the Supreme Court in the political and social context of their time. My purpose here is not to write a comprehensive history of the Court but to focus selectively on one important strand in its jurisprudence—its claim for supremacy in constitutional interpretation

and the reasons for the initial resistance to and ultimate acceptance of this claim in the American political community during the nineteenth century.

Chapter 4 begins this narrative by addressing the evolution of John Marshall's jurisprudence from his adroit appropriation of Madisonian tenets in the famous lawsuit that William Marbury brought against Madison, to his embrace of Hamiltonian supremacy in his later jurisprudence. To understand the rationale for Marshall's supremacy claim, this chapter explores the significance of his conviction that American society was so deeply divided by irreconcilable conflicts that mutual respect for equality among individuals or political institutions was inconceivable. Chapter 5 shows how this Hobbesian vision of irreconcilable social hostility came to pervade all aspects of American political life during the Jacksonian era—relations between whites and Indians, whites and black slaves, and the white North and South. I suggest that this increasingly stark view of inevitable, irremediable conflict gave impetus and imagined plausibility to the institutional claims of the Court to stand "above politics" as the supreme expositor of the Constitution.

Chapter 6 depicts the dramatic force of the Civil War in confirming that American society was torn by irreconcilable conflicts and that judicial authority might promise some transcendent resolution. Chapter 7 completes this historical narrative by showing how this wish for transcendence of conflict found fullest expression in the apotheosis of judicial authority at the end of the nineteenth century. I then briefly sketch the challenge to judicial supremacy that took hold during the first third of this century, culminating in the New Dealers' assault on the Court. I explore specifically the significance of the premise for this challenge among Progressive thinkers that American society was not fundamentally and irreconcilably divided but that mutual accommodation was a plausible goal.

In Part III I return to the initial claim of principle in this book—that in constitutional interpretation, an egalitarian conception of authority among the branches is preferable—and I illustrate the application of this principle in several contemporary litigated conflicts. My central example of egalitarian adjudication, which I extensively reconsider in Chapter 8, is the Supreme Court's decision in *Brown v. Board of Education*. I will show how the egalitarian principle justified the distinction drawn by the Court between its bold proclamation in *Brown I* that school segregation was unconstitutional and its deliberately delayed enforcement of this ruling in *Brown II*. Chapter 9 addresses three additional decisions—in the 1974 *Nixon Tapes* case and in the series of death penalty and abortion cases during the past twenty years—in which, I maintain, the Court fell away from the egalitarian jurisprudence of *Brown* and returned to an essentially authoritarian conception of its role. In each case the Court was driven by the same concerns about irreconcilable social conflict that had led to the triumph of judicial supremacy during the nineteenth century. For all of these cases, I identify the alternative results that an egalitarian conception of judicial authority would dictate. Chapter 10 looks to the future, to show how this egalitarian conception would reshape judicial interventions in other deeply divisive contemporary social disputes, particularly in race relations.

If I have come close to achieving my goal by the end of this book, I will have demonstrated the sterility of the debate that has long been waged between proponents of judicial activism and proponents of judicial restraint—a debate that I do not resolve but simply displace. Because this debate has been conducted within the framework of the Hamiltonian conception of judicial supremacy, it offers only a choice between majoritarian or judicial autocracy—both equally unsatisfying. There is a better choice.

I

JUDICIAL AUTHORITY IN PRINCIPLE

1

The Constitutional Question

ASK THE WRONG QUESTION, you get the wrong answer. This is the problem with the great bulk of the theorizing that goes on in constitutional law today. And it is a great bulk—a virtual torrent of books and articles clustered around the same wrong question: "When the Supreme Court interprets the Constitution, how can it ensure that its interpretation is unimpeachably legitimate?" This question is at the core of contemporary constitutional theorizing, however, only because it starts from the premise that the Court is the final, authoritative interpreter of the Constitution. From this premise the demand for an unquestionable basis for judicial interpretation ineluctably arises: so Justice Robert Jackson implied in his quip that the Court was not final because it was infallible but infallible because it was final.[1]

Roughly four different answers have been offered to this erroneous question. The "originalists" maintain that strict fidelity to the original intention of the authors of the constitutional document provides the only justifiable basis for interpretation. Judge Robert Bork is the most prominent exponent of this position.[2]

The "interpretationists" claim that original intention is an unhelpful, and probably also unknowable, guide but that constitutional interpretation can be rooted in judges' reading of the "fundamental values" of American culture.* There are almost as many

---

*In current legal commentary, my designations of "originalist" and "interpretationist" schools have been labeled "interpretivists" and "noninterpretivists," respectively. See Thomas Grey, "Do We Have an Unwritten Constitution?" 27 *Stanford L. Rev.* 703 (1975); John Hart Ely, *Democracy and Distrust: A Theory of*

formulations of fundamentality—from "republican virtue" to "morality" (transcendent or conventional), "truth" and "integrity"—as there are members of this school.[3]

Adherents of the "process" school claim that it is never proper for judges to invalidate laws based on "fundamental values," however defined, and that the only legitimate ground for judicial review is to ensure that access to influence in political institutions is adequately open to all contenders. John Hart Ely has been the leading proponent of this view. A fourth position has been staked out by the Critical Legal Theory school, whose members claim that none of the other schools provides a legitimate basis for judicial review because no such basis can possibly be provided. The Critical Legal theorists have not, as a group, focused their attention on constitutional law with the same single-mindedness that characterizes the advocates of the other three schools. Their impeachment of constitutional adjudication is part of their general criticism of the rule of law, which asserts that any claim to the legitimate exercise of authority is inevitably nothing more than question-begging verbiage trying to mask the unprincipled (or nonprincipled) social reality that the strong dominate the weak.[4]

Three of these schools claim to solve the problem of constitutional interpretation, though by mutually inconsistent routes. The fourth, the Critical Legal scholars, agree with the others that the central question is "What gives legitimacy to the Supreme Court's interpretation of constitutional issues?" Their answer is "nothing." (This response is the basis for the fierce attacks on this group as "nihilists," even extended by some to argue for their exclusion from the legal academy and relocation in humanities departments such as political or perhaps even military science.)

For a brief moment in the late 1950s and mid-1960s, a different question emerged as the central inquiry for constitutional law. It erupted with almost elemental force from the Supreme Court's 1954 decision in *Brown v. Board of Education*, though it was identified and elaborated only by Alexander Bickel in 1962 in his book *The Least Dangerous Branch*.[5] The question was "How can the Su-

---

Judicial Review 1–2 (Cambridge: Harvard Univ. Press, 1980). These labels have always confused me; my designations seem to me more clearly descriptive.

preme Court properly adjudicate constitutional disputes, notwithstanding its questionable legitimacy to do so?"

Each of the four schools I have sketched would view this formulation as a nonsense question, a category error such as "How can a woman be a man?" Each would say it can't be done. The Court's decision in *Brown,* however, coupled with Bickel's explication of it, fundamentally challenged the sharp dichotomy between legitimacy and illegitimacy in constitutional adjudication. This was jurisprudential androgeny; and like current efforts to transcend polarized gender classification, the Court's decision in *Brown*—and Bickel's account of it—discomforted many people.

Today, a generation after *Brown,* efforts to domesticate the decision through the conventions of the four jurisprudential schools have marched forward relentlessly. *The Least Dangerous Branch* remains, however, a considerable obstacle in this course. Most observers today treat *Brown* as an easy case for legitimacy: whatever difficulty they see in the Court's decision they ascribe to "politics," to the fierce resistance that the Court confronted from the wrongdoing segregationists, and not to the illegitimacy of the Court's warrant to identify race segregation as wrong. Bickel's account makes clear, however, that at the time of the *Brown* decision not only the Justices themselves but a considerable number of the sophisticated jurisprudential observers of the day had considerable difficulty in justifying the decision by the criteria confidently invoked today by the adherents of the four schools. It is important to recapture the contemporaneous uncertainty and unease that *Brown* inspired even among jurisprudents inclined to applaud the decision, in order to grasp the fundamental challenge that *Brown* still represents for the four conventional theories of constitutional legitimacy.

Start with the originalist school. It is clear (as clear as historical records can ever be) that the framers of the Fourteenth Amendment—guaranteeing, among other things, equal protection under the law—did not intend to invalidate racial segregation in schools. At the time of the amendment's ratification in 1868, public schools were segregated in several northern states, but there was no indication in congressional or state ratification debates that the new amendment would affect these practices. Even more significantly, the same Congress that passed the Fourteenth Amendment almost immediately thereafter enacted legislation establishing racially segregated public schools in the District of Columbia. No one at the time suggested that the then-pending constitutional amendment was relevant to this action.*

When he was nominated to the Supreme Court in 1987, Judge Bork tried to defend *Brown* on originalist grounds by arguing that while the framers did not directly intend to overturn public school segregation, they did mean to proscribe state-imposed inequalities on blacks. In his testimony before the Senate Judiciary Committee, Bork maintained that by 1954, when public education had attained much greater social importance than in 1868, these two original intentions became inconsistent and the Court was obliged to choose between them. He also claimed that the framers themselves had provided clear direction for choosing between these inconsistent intentions: to prefer the protection of racial equality.[6]

This is an ingenious attempt to legitimize *Brown* by the originalist lights, but it just won't float. The basic premise of the originalist position, as Bork tirelessly explained to the Committee in other contexts, is to constrain the exercise of judicial discretion in adding latter-day glosses to the constitutional text. If judges take on the task of "up-dating" the document to account for problems that the original authors did not directly anticipate, the entire discipline of the originalist position is undermined. From an originalist perspective, the proper resolution of an unanticipated interpretive problem is to insist on ratification of a new constitutional amendment directly.**

---

*In its decision in *Plessy v. Ferguson*, 163 U.S. 537 (1896), the Supreme Court upheld state laws requiring race segregation in transportation facilities in part by invoking these facts to establish the unquestioned legitimacy of public school segregation at the time the Amendment was enacted—ironically enough, citing (id. at 544) an antebellum decision by the Massachusetts Supreme Court finding racially segregated schools consistent with its state constitutional guarantee of equality, Roberts v. City of Boston, 59 Mass. (5 Cush.) 198 (1849). See Leonard Levy, *The Law of the Commonwealth and Chief Justice Shaw* 109–17 (New York: Oxford Univ. Press, 1957).

**Bork's account of the intentions expressed in the Fourteenth Amendment is inadequate, surprisingly so in light of his proclaimed commitment to precise historical reconstruction of original intent. Bork stated, "The ratifiers probably assumed that segregation was consistent with equality but they were not address-

Bork's eagerness to endorse *Brown* is a measure of the centrality of this decision in our jurisprudence. No aspirant to judicial office who openly doubts the legitimacy of the Court's decision in *Brown* can expect Senate confirmation today. William Rehnquist understood this proposition when he emphatically disavowed in his confirmation hearings a memorandum he had written as a law clerk to Justice Jackson in 1954. In it he had suggested that *Plessy v. Ferguson*—upholding race segregation laws—"was right and should be re-affirmed."[8] *Brown v. Board of Education* has become a lodestar by which contemporary political actors chart their course.

Bork's rejection by the Senate provides indirect confirmation for this proposition. Opposition from black leaders, based on their doubts about Bork's commitment to the use of judicial authority on behalf of racial equality, was a crucial factor in his defeat. In the Senate vote, Southerners were more united in opposing him than the Senators from any other region; and of the southern Senators, opposition was concentrated among the Democrats, all of whom were white men who had depended on black votes for their electoral victories. Of the twenty-two Senators from the former states of the Confederacy, sixteen were Democrats in 1987; of these, only Hollings of South Carolina voted for Bork's confirmation. Of the six Republican southern Senators, all but Warner of Virginia supported him. Bork was defeated by a vote of 58 to 42.[9]

The superior capacity of the interpretationist school to justify *Brown* gives it a theoretical edge over its contemporary rivals. Advocates of the process school have not been willing, however, to concede this advantage; they argue that race segregation laws were illegitimate because of the wholesale exclusion of southern blacks from electoral participation. But if they restrict their cri-

---

ing segregation. The text itself demonstrates that the equality under law was the primary goal." Bork failed to acknowledge, however, that many framers had a different conception of "equality" from the version he invoked; many of them distinguished between "social" or "civil" and "political" equality, and it would have been incoherent for them to conclude that "equality as such" was relevant to the validity of race segregation. Bork's formulation that "equality under law was the primary goal" rests on an anachronistically univocal conception of equality.[7]

tique to this failure of the political process, two consequences follow, and neither adequately accounts for *Brown.* First, the proper judicial remedy for the segregation laws would have been to overturn the various measures excluding blacks from the electorate, rather than directly to invalidate the segregation laws themselves. This remedy would also have more easily satisfied originalist strictures because of the explicit prohibition against race barriers to voting in the Fifteenth Amendment. A second, and even more disturbing, consequence might have been the reenactment of segregation laws even in a cleansed electoral process wherever blacks were a minority of the electorate. John Ely, in his influential explication of the tenets of the process school, strove mightily to overcome this latter consequence by claiming that any majority actions directed toward an outcast group, based on "we/ they" distinctions, unfairly excluded the minority from political participation.[10] But like Bork's effort to squeeze an originalist justification for *Brown* from a barren historical record, Ely's attempt to identify a process flaw at the heart of *Brown* relies on barely disguised substantive interpretationist premises.[11]

Although the interpretationists are thus the leading candidates among the contemporary schools for justifying *Brown,* their account ultimately falls short as well. It is much more difficult today to appreciate the problems in the interpretationist account than it was when *Brown* was decided. The moral repugnance of race segregation, and the consequent correctness of *Brown,* has by now become an article of faith in our polity. But it was not always so— and certainly not in 1954 when the Justices struggled with this issue. Some might rely on the subsequent history to validate the Court's judgment—pointing out that the Justices correctly predicted the future in condemning race segregation. But this kind of *post hoc* validation does not give much guidance to the Justices themselves when a question appears hotly contested before them in litigation. At that moment, moreover, the Justices do have an indication of public opinion in the enactments challenged by the aggrieved litigants. Some weight—but how much weight?—should be given to this indicator if the Justices see themselves as riding the wave of future moral convictions.

In *Brown* itself, the Justices were visibly uncomfortable with the role of fundamental moralist, in any of the guises offered by the various exponents of interpretationism. The clearest indication of this discomfort was the reluctance of the Justices to issue a clear moral denunciation of race segregation in their opinion in the case. They came closest in this observation: "To separate [school-children] from others of similar age and qualifications solely because of their race generates a feeling of inferiority as to their status in the community that may affect their hearts and minds in a way unlikely ever to be undone." But the Justices immediately qualified the moral force of their stance with this pronouncement: "Whatever may have been the extent of psychological knowledge at the time of *Plessy v. Ferguson,* this finding is amply supported by modern authority."[12] Footnote eleven follows this sentence— perhaps the most controversial footnote in the entire United States Reports—citing published works by various social scientists as the "modern authority" on which the Court purports to rely for ample support. In retrospect, this reliance was clearly a tactical error not only because the footnote helped protesters portray *Brown* as a vendetta masterminded by ivory-tower liberal intellectuals but, more interestingly, because the cited studies were themselves methodologically flawed. The basic criticism of the studies was that the data collected about the psychological harm inflicted by school segregation as such was equivocal, and that the researchers based their "scientific" condemnation on their own moral repugnance toward segregation.[13]

There is considerable irony here, since the Court cited this scientific authority in an attempt to rest their condemnation of segregation on some basis that transcended their own merely subjective morality. The Justices themselves were probably not much influenced in reaching their decision by the publications they cited in footnote eleven; the citation was most likely intended to invoke the public prestige of science and to add the weight of its supposedly impersonal authority to the Court's judgment.

The proposition that authority should be impersonal, transcending the merely idiosyncratic or subjective, is deeply engrained in our constitutional tradition. The interpretationists' acceptance of this tenet is the Achilles heel of that school. Proponents of both the originalist and the process persuasions basically part with the interpretationists on this score, arguing that judges who chart their constitutional course by nontextual "fundamental values" of the society inevitably will confuse those values with their own personal predilections. The interpretationists accordingly have spent much energy and ink in asserting the objectivity and impersonality of their enterprise. This was the impetus behind Herbert Wechsler's claim in 1958 that constitutional adjudication must be grounded in "neutral principles"—a claim that led him to find *Brown* an illegitimate exercise of judicial authority.[14]

Wechsler's charge came at a time when the white southern segregationist forces had embarked on a campaign of massive resistance to the Court's decision. Their opposition was obviously self-interested and narrowly partisan, but Wechsler's criticism could not be so readily dismissed. He spoke from the podium of the Holmes Lectures at the Harvard Law School, the bastion of Langdellian legal science, and his critique had the structure and trappings of objectivity. After spending most of his lecture establishing the imperative of neutrality and attempting to define this imperative in general terms, he then reluctantly and even mournfully—against his personal inclinations, he assured his listeners, thus credibly establishing his own objectivity—applied the syllogism to *Brown*. The Court did not apply a neutral principle, Wechsler concluded, because it upheld the rights of blacks freely to associate with whites but did not acknowledge that this same principle of free association equally supported the claims of whites to refuse association with blacks. *Brown* therefore failed the test of neutrality, he claimed, because there was no single overarching general principle on which the decision could rely.

Wechsler's criticism invited, and quickly received, a refutation within the terms of his own premises of "neutral principle." The true principle upheld in *Brown*, so went the rejoinder, was not to protect free association; the true principle was that state authorities are forbidden to impose racial subordination.[15] This was the premise underlying the Civil War amendments to the Constitution, and even if this premise was not understood at that time to forbid school segregation, in our own time such segregation had become a centrally important instrument of racial subordination and was therefore unconstitutional. Stated in this way, *Brown* did appear to rest on an overarching general principle consistently applied.

This is certainly the dominant vision of *Brown* today, a vision within the distinctive province of the interpretationist school rather than its rivals. As attractive as this vision is in our time, however, it obscures the fundamental difficulty that *Brown* confronted but could not immediately overcome in its day. This difficulty was identified by two of the Justices who participated in *Brown,* in memoranda that were never published but may have been intended as drafts for possible opinions. Justice Frankfurter wrote,

> The outcome of the Civil War, as reflected in the Civil War Amendments, is that there is a single American society. Our colored citizens . . . [cannot] be denied the right to grow up with other Americans as part of our national life. . . . The legal problem confronting this Court is the extent to which this desirable and even necessary process of welding a nation . . . can be imposed as a matter of law upon the States in disregard of the deeply rooted feeling, tradition and local laws, based upon local situations to the contrary.[16]

Justice Jackson made the same point in his private musing, and with his customary pungent clarity:

> Since the close of the Civil War the United States has been "hesitating between two worlds—one dead, the other powerless to be born." War brought an old order to an end but as usual force proved unequal to founding a new one. . . . In the South the Negro not only suffers from racial suspicions and antagonisms present in other states and in other countries, but also, I am convinced, has suffered great prejudice from the aftermath of the great American white conflict. The white South retains in historical memory a deep resentment of the forces which, after conquest, imposed a fierce program of reconstruction and the deep humiliation of carpet bag government. The Negro is the visible and reachable beneficiary and symbol of this unhappy experience, on whom many visit their natural desire for retaliation.

Having set out this historical context, Jackson then stated (but at the same time backed away from) the central difficulty in *Brown*: whether the "real abolition of segregation will be accelerated or retarded by what many are likely to regard as a ruthless use of federal judicial power is a question that I cannot and need not answer."[17] This was, in other words, what Frankfurter had called "the legal problem confronting this Court."

In what sense, however, is this a *legal* problem? To interpretationists today, this seems a misnomer: the legal problem is to identify the proper principle, in this case forbidding state-imposed racial domination. The problem identified by Frankfurter and Jackson is real enough, but it is a "political" or "tactical" problem, not a "legal" one.[18] By this definitional compartmentalization, the *Brown* discussion is legitimate in principle, whatever its difficulties in actual implementation.

But this compartmentalization is false. The difficulties of implementation that Frankfurter and Jackson privately identified are not just a matter of choosing the correct adjective; they are at the very heart of the principle of nonsubordination at stake in *Brown*. This principle could not be invoked to invalidate segregation laws in the South without falling into an internal contradiction, for the reasons that Justice Jackson saw: "The white South retains in historical memory a deep resentment of the forces which, after conquest, imposed a fierce program . . . [and] deep humiliation." *Brown* today seems an easy case in principle only because the vast destructiveness and bitter hatreds of the Civil War have faded from living memory.[19] The War now, at long last, has become a distant historical event; but it was not yet so in 1954. For white Southerners then, the War was a past injustice with vivid current consequences, an old but persisting blood feud with scores still to be settled. From the perspective of the white South, their defeat in the Civil War was itself an imposition of race domination.[20]

The forced abolition of slavery did not, as the white South saw it, rest on a principle of racial equality, any more than forced preservation of the Union honored the principle of the equality of states. In both matters, black–white or federal–state relations, equality was a meaningless principle for white Southerners; the operative norm was to rule or to be ruled. The heart of the issue for them in 1954, as in 1864, was not avoiding association with blacks; they wanted association, but only on the basis of domination. The issue for the white South was still in 1954, as in 1864, their right to withdraw from the Union to protect their practices of race subordination.

The Civil War had been settled by force of arms, but the legitimacy of this northern domination had not been resolved, even by 1954. To be sure, the Union had persisted as a result of the War. But the white South grudgingly acquiesced in this persistence, and only on the basis of an implicit understanding reached in 1877 when the northern occupying troops were withdrawn from southern soil: the understanding that the white South would be left free to impose subordinated status on blacks.[21] Southern blacks did not embrace this understanding; for them it was a betrayal of the promises of the Civil War amendments. But for the white South, those promises were extracted by military force and were therefore illegitimate. So the matter remained in 1954.

Wechsler's invocation of the principle of free association was a pale version of this problem. Although he did not adequately formulate the principles in conflict, he did correctly see that no "neutral" or "objective" resolution was possible. This was because the principle available to the Justices to overturn race segregation laws—that of nonsubordination—also justified these laws, from the point of view of white Southerners. Segregation laws did embody racial subordination of blacks by whites; but for an arm of the federal government to overturn these state laws was, for white Southerners, a direct recapitulation of the subordination they experienced during the Civil War and Reconstruction at the hands of white Northerners and blacks.

Today, we may be prepared to say that the white South had a distorted view and should have understood that racial equality, not domination or subordination, was the moving principle behind the abolition of both segregation laws and slavery itself. But this prescriptive vision had the same plausibility for white Southerners in the hundred years following the Civil War as the advice offered in 1948 by the American ambassador to the United Nations that the warring Arabs and Jews in Palestine should settle their differences in the spirit of "Christian charity."[22]

So Wechsler was right as far as he went: no neutral principle was available to overturn race segregation laws. Whether the governing principle was, as he said, to protect free association or, as his critics maintained, to eschew racial domination, segregation laws were both legitimate and illegitimate with reference to the identical principle. From this paradox Wechsler drew the conclusion that the judiciary should have done nothing. The role of courts for Wechsler was to declare authoritative resolutions of disputes; in this case, the Supreme Court could not properly discharge this role because there was no neutral principle to yield a single correct resolution.

"Neutrality" is no longer a fashionable word for the current proponents of interpretationism, but they share with Wechsler the same underlying view of the courts as a forum for the authoritative resolution of disputes, and therefore they share his quest for an unimpeachably legitimate basis for judicial intervention. As I suggested earlier, the other three jurisprudential schools also demand an unimpeachably legitimate basis for judicial interpretation of the Constitution, and this demand also follows from the same view of the dispute-resolving character of courts. These assumptions are as true for the Critical Legal theorists as for the others, except that these lineal descendants of the 1930s Legal Realists deny that any overarching principle can ever be found for the legitimate resolution of disputes. All judicial interventions are for them what *Brown* was for Herbert Wechsler: instances of judges commanding obedience based on an illegitimate confusion of their personal values with universally applicable and acceptable principle.

In *The Least Dangerous Branch,* Alexander Bickel set out to reformulate these conventional premises. His response to Wechsler's criticism and his justification for the Court's action in *Brown* formed the centerpiece of a larger critique of the received wisdom in constitutional jurisprudence. As he stated, "I have adverted repeatedly, at about every decisive point in the argument of this book, to the *School Segregation Cases,* for they at once epitomize and challenge all that I have tried to say about the role of the Supreme Court in American government."[23]

Bickel was quick to dismiss Wechsler's claim that freedom of association was the basic principle at issue. Rather, he agreed with others that racial equality was the core principle, but he did not claim that the Court consistently applied this principle in *Brown.* Bickel accordingly was prepared to acknowledge and confront Wechsler's fundamental challenge to the decision: his argument that no internally consistent constitutional principle was available to the Court as a basis on which to adjudicate the constitutionality of race segregation laws.

The most important and illuminating inconsistency that Bickel identified in the Court's action was its refusal, in its second *Brown* decision, to demand immediate enforcement of the constitutional right to nonsegregated education proclaimed in its first ruling.* Critics, then and now, claimed that if the 1954 declaration in *Brown I* was a correct interpretation of the Constitution, then there could be no legitimate reason for delayed enforcement of the black schoolchildren's constitutional rights. In 1955, however, the Court announced that delay—"all deliberate speed"—was permissible. The conventional view, then and now, was that *Brown II* was "politics"—an illegitimate derogation from principle by the Court, though an understandable and perhaps (or perhaps not) wise one. Bickel had a different view.

He started with the conventional premises of the interpretationist school. Quoting Justice Frankfurter, Bickel said that Supreme Court judgments "must 'rest on fundamental presuppositions rooted in history . . . *to which widespread acceptance may fairly be attributed.*'" He then continued,

> The qualifying clause is the thing. And it is, indeed, a component of the judicial judgment that is easily dealt with, at least in theory—causing the other pieces of the puzzle to fall readily into place as well—if what is meant is that the Court is restricted to declaring an existing national consensus . . . so widely shared that they can be said to have the assent of something like Calhoun's concurrent majorities. But this would charge the Court with a function to which it is, of all our institutions, least suited. Surely the political institutions are more fitted than the Court to find and express an existing consensus. . . . What is meant,

---

*Bickel also identified inconsistencies in the Court's refusal to overturn a state miscegenation law notwithstanding *Brown* and the status of supposed "benign racial quotas" in the teeth of the apparent endorsement in *Brown* of "colorblindness" as a constitutional norm. *Least Dangerous Branch* at 59–65, 174. Bickel's support for the Court's embrace of these seeming inconsistencies, though a characteristic expression, is less important for understanding his jurisprudence than his treatment of the enforcement delay in *Brown II*.

rather, is that the Court should declare as law only such principles as will—in time, but in a rather immediate foreseeable future—gain general assent.*

This is the core of Bickel's jurisprudence: "general assent" is the
only legitimate derivation for judicial principle, but the Court can
endorse a principle that lacks such consensus if, assisted by the
Court's very endorsement, the principle might "foreseeably" become generally accepted. As he capsulized the proposition: "the
Court's principles are required to gain assent, not necessarily to
have it."[24] This is radically different from the conventional account, which demands a legitimate *prior* basis for judicial action.
By Bickel's account, the Court can properly act without prior
legitimation so long as it can anticipate obtaining subsequent ratification: in the vernacular, it can properly "bootstrap" itself to
legitimacy.

From this perspective, the Court's enforcement delay in *Brown
II* was indeed inconsistent with its earlier pronouncement of the
unconstitutionality of race segregation laws. But this inconsistency
was not simply "political"; it was a proper exercise of judicial
authority that "fits precisely . . . the unique function of judicial
review in the American system."[25] In *Brown II*, the Court directly
acknowledged that the principle enunciated in *Brown I* was not
yet constitutionally sanctioned but that this principle should proceed "with all deliberate speed" toward that legitimized status.
Bickel saw nuanced doubletalk in the Court's directive in *Brown
II*: implementation would come in a deliberately methodical and
unhurried manner, but only after extensive deliberation about the
wisdom of thus proceeding.

---

*Least Dangerous Branch at 239 (emphasis in original). Bickel was adding his
own gloss about "what is meant" by Frankfurter's statement, more than discerning
the Justice's original intent; as Bickel subsequently observed, Frankfurter "never
successfully identified sources from which [the Court's] judgment was to be drawn
that would securely limit as well as nourish it, he never achieved a rigorous
general accord between judicial supremacy and democratic theory, so that the
boundaries of one could be described with some precision in terms of the other,
and he was thus unable to ensure that the teaching of a duty of judgment would
be received as subordinate to the teaching of abstention." *The Supreme Court and
the Idea of Progress* 34 (New York: Harper & Row, 1970).

Bickel's approval of this ambiguous instruction, with its possible internal inconsistency, grew from his vision of the purposeful ambiguity in the process of constitutional adjudication: the Supreme Court standing "at the Bar of Politics." This was both the subtitle of his book and the title of its final chapter extolling *Brown II*: the Supreme Court was both barred from engaging in "politics" and pleading at this Bar so as to transform "mere politics" into enduring constitutional principle. This perspective on the judicial process meant, among other things, that courts must not engage in the authoritative resolution of constitutional disputes; courts properly participate in, even provoke, but do not independently and conclusively resolve such disputes. As Bickel put it,

> Over time, as a problem is lived with, the Court does not work in isolation to divine the answer that is right. It has the means to elicit partial answers and reactions from the other institutions, and to try tentative answers itself. When at last the Court decides that "judgment cannot be escaped—the judgment of this Court," the answer is likely to be a proposition "to which widespread acceptance may fairly be attributed," because in the course of a continuing colloquy with the political institutions and with society at large, the Court has shaped and reduced the question, and perhaps because it has rendered the answer familiar if not obvious.[26]

Thus, according to Bickel, the principle of racial equality that *Brown* invoked was not an accepted norm of constitutional law in 1954 and was just barely so by 1963 when he wrote. (I would say, by Bickel's own criteria, that he anticipated the event by at least a year, when the grip of the southern filibuster was broken by two-thirds vote of the Senate in passing the Civil Rights Act of 1964, and perhaps not even then but only when this signal event had been reiterated by the 1965 and 1968 Civil Rights Acts.)[27] Whatever the precise date of its ratification, the principle in *Brown* that seems today so right and so inevitable was neither at the time, according to Bickel's contemporary observations and his jurisprudence. The difficulty came from the near-success of the southern campaign of massive resistance. This difficulty was not, again, "merely political"; it was, in Bickel's imagery, at the intersection where politics and principle blend to become constitutional law.

Southern resistance carried its own possibility of foreseeable legitimation:

> When the law summons force to its aid, it demonstrates, not its strength and stability, but its weakness and impermanence. The mob, like revolution, is an ambiguous fact. The mob is bad when it is wrong; it may be heroic when it is right. It is surely a deeply ingrained American belief that mobs of our people do not generally gather to oppose good laws, and the very fact of the mob, therefore, puts the law in question. Fear of the mob, moreover, the interest in good order, is an ambivalent feeling, for it is more easily satisfied, everything else being equal, by conceding what the mob wants, by redressing its grievances, than by fighting it. And so a few enforcement crises like Little Rock, rather than hurting their cause, might well have gone far to win the southern leaders' battle for them. The Court's integration principle would have been in train of being reversed, directly or by desuetude.[28]

Bickel's justification for *Brown* thus rested on a conception of constitutional law and the judicial role that was a bold and original break with conventional premises. His treatment of *Brown* was, however, more radical in its implications than even he was prepared to acknowledge in explicit theoretical terms. He was ultimately unwilling to generalize in a thoroughgoing way the jurisprudence that he fashioned to account for *Brown*. In his subsequent work, Bickel moved *Brown* from the center of his jurisprudence to the sidelines; it became an exceptional exercise of judicial authority rather than an enterprise that illuminated the core function of judicial review.[29] He also appeared disenchanted with *Brown*—not with the Court's initial actions in 1954 and 1955, not with *Brown I* or *II,* but with the Supreme Court's increased energy and adamancy in demanding "less deliberation and more speed" toward desegregated schools in the mid-1960s.[30] Bickel did not adequately consider the possibility that the burst of judicial enforcement energy in the mid-6os was a response to the ratification of *Brown* by the independent actions of Congress and the Executive, especially in the Civil Rights Acts of the time; he did not, that is, apply his own criteria for discerning when the Court must seek or has obtained legitimation for its interventions.

By 1969, Bickel saw *Brown* as merely "the beginning"[31] of a larger trend toward judicial activism in a wide range of matters, such as voting reapportionment, criminal procedure, and sexual privacy, and he linked this activism, with its judicial elocutions of high-minded moral certainty, to the inflamed rhetoric and self-proclaimed rectitude in the public combat of the late 1960s. This turmoil and incivility in public discourse were anathema to Bickel; and he blamed the Supreme Court: "In the end the highest price will be exacted for sounds of unreason made by 'the voice of reason.'"[32]

The late 6os were indeed a tumultuous time in American life: the Vietnam War unaccountably escalated to its destructive heights, domestic protests against the War were aimed with greatest ferocity by students at universities (so that Bickel found himself directly on the frontline embattlements), race riots spread from city to city, and a terrifying wave of assassinations—of Robert Kennedy, Martin Luther King, Jr., and Malcolm X, as well as the crippling attempt against George Wallace—changed the calculus of political action.

To blame the Supreme Court for any part of this turbulence seems almost perverse. Bickel's censure of the Court blames the messenger for bringing bad news. In fact, the bad news was already embedded in *Brown I*: in 1954 a substantial part of the American population was clearly unwilling to acknowledge the legitimacy of the claims adamantly and even desperately asserted by another part. Ordinary political institutions were thus unable to address, much less ameliorate, this polar conflict; and the rule of law was thereby endangered, whether ideally conceived as commitment to shared principles of justice or minimally viewed as the maintenance of social order.

This was the American South in 1954, as the Court saw it; by acknowledging the justice of the southern black grievances and by provoking the southern white campaign of massive resistance, the Court gave widespread credence to this stark social vision. It was, however, an article of faith in 1954, among both the Justices and more generally, that this polarized conflict was restricted to the South and that the rest of American society was fundamentally harmonious—not simply in race relations but in virtually all social affiliations. Of course there were disagreements, sometimes quite heated, but these conflicts could readily be contained and even resolved by the ordinary politics of bargaining and compromise among different "interest groups." The South was supposedly a deviation from this national norm. This was the American story according to the most vocal American storytellers circa 1954.

This was not always the received version. From one generation to the next, the dominant accounts have alternated in characterizing America as fundamentally united or divided, as a society whose momentary disagreements rest on a deeper base of consensus or whose momentary agreements only mask deeper class, race, ethnic, gender conflict.[33] In 1954 the doomsayers of the conflict school were in popular and academic disfavor: the country had emerged from the Great Depression, the worst in our history, with worker and capitalist more harmonious than the most panglossian vision imaginable in the mid-1930s. And we had come through the most destructive war the world had known not only as victor but as the strongest, most prosperous nation on earth.

The dominant attitude of the mid-1950s was epitomized, as if he were writing lyrics to accompany the melody of this upbeat mood, by Louis Hartz, a Harvard political scientist, in his immensely influential book *The Liberal Tradition in America*.[34] Hartz took his text from Alexis de Tocqueville: "The great advantage of the Americans is, that they have arrived at a state of democracy without having to endure a democratic revolution; and that they are born equal, instead of becoming so."[35] Here, Hartz said,

> is the master assumption of American political thought . . . : the reality of atomistic social freedom. . . . There has been only one major group of American thinkers who have dared to challenge it frontally: . . . [those] of the pre-Civil War South. . . . But American life rode roughshod over them. . . . They were soon forgotten, massive victims of the absolute temper of the American mind, shoved off the scene by Horatio Alger.[36]

Hartz acknowledged that many observers, beginning with the founding generation, had seen fundamental conflict in America where he now saw unity; but their vision, he said, was flawed, even "neurotic."[37] The reality was that "a hidden and happy accident has lain at the bottom of the American constitutional experience. The Founding Fathers devised a scheme to deal with conflict that could only survive in a land of solidarity. The truth is, their conclusions were 'right' only because their premises were wrong."[38] Hartz accordingly discounted the gravity of "the classic problem of American thought"—the difficulty of protecting minority rights from majority tyranny.[39] From this perspective, Hartz had no trouble accommodating judicial authority: "judicial review as it has worked in America would be inconceivable without the national acceptance of the Lockian creed, ultimately enshrined in the Constitution, since the removal of high policy to the realm of adjudication implies a prior recognition of the principles to be legally interpreted."[40]

Hartz was a political scientist, not a lawyer; most lawyers, legal academics, and judges were not so complacent about the successful working of judicial review. Indeed, it was virtually agreed ground by 1954 within the legal subculture that from the 1890s until the end of the 1930s the Supreme Court had not worked properly, that there had been no adequate "prior recognition of the principles" invoked by the Justices to overturn an array of economic and social regulatory measures. But from this criticism of judicial conduct, the post-New Deal generation drew a conclusion—that courts should ordinarily defer to legislative majorities—based on the same vision of a basically unified American society that Hartz held aloft.[41] The proper occasions for judicial intervention to protect minorities were exceptional, by this theory, because fundamental conflict was the exception, not the rule, in American society.

This was the framework of Bickel's analysis in *The Least Dangerous Branch,* and this framework led him to discount the general significance of *Brown.* Bickel began his book by asserting that because judicial review is a "counter-majoritarian force," it is "a deviant institution in the American democracy."[42] This premise coupled with his vision of America as basically united led him to regard *Brown* itself, and the underlying imperative for judicial intervention that arose from the character of the dispute over race segregation, as deviant events in American experience. But he was wrong: *Brown* represented a recurrent and prototypical problem for the American democracy. The problem was not race conflict as such but more fundamentally what race conflict signified.

To abstract this problem, imagine you, me, and a third person in the same room. Two of us decide that you should give your life to serve us. Is our decision legitimate, do you have an obligation to obey, simply because we were a majority within the room? Even if we had all previously agreed that the three of us were "a group"—that is, we were members of the same society—does that prior agreement bind you to accept a decision that so extensively denigrates you, or are you thereby entitled to withdraw from the social group in order to preserve your equal status?

On the face of it, you can claim that our decision "enslaves" you and denies you "equal status" with us. We can claim that your equal status is not impaired because our voting rule—one person, one vote—gave you an equal opportunity at the outset to prevail. This is the basic theoretical justification, the *ex ante* argument, for majority rule as the instrument for honoring the democratic norms of equality and self-determination. But you can plausibly respond that the *ex ante* perspective is not self-evidently exclusive or correct and that the majority decision viewed in retrospect, in light of its actual impact on our social relations, is such an excessive deprivation of your status as to beggar your claims to equality and self-determination. We in turn can reply that we need your life to serve the common cause in which you have previously shared and benefitted (the cause, let's say, is the defeat of a foreign enemy threatening our shores, and you, whom the two of us have previously raised and sheltered, are the youngest, strongest, and thus best qualified soldier among us).

Stated in these terms, this could be an argument in the 1960s between draft resisters and their elders responsible for waging the Vietnam War; but the argument is hardly unique to this issue or time. A recognizable version of this abstract argument has recurred many times in American history: in the conflict between the American colonists and the British Mother Country in the 1760s, between the white South and the white North in the 1860s, between workers and capitalists through the first half of this century, repeatedly between native Americans and whites and between other groups divided in polar terms by such characteristics as race, gender, age, and sexual orientation. The argument regarding the legitimacy of race segregation by majority vote was simply another conflict where, because the antagonists each regarded defeat as intolerable enslavement, the fundamental democratic principles of equality and self-determination were necessarily traversed for the loser. No matter who wins, the principle of self-rule is defeated; in such disputes no scheme of governance, no system of aggregative social decisionmaking, can find "ultimate self-consistency."[43]

This does not mean that some neutral third party, like a judge standing aloof from the immediate antagonists, can resolve this dispute so as to vindicate the democratic principles of equality and self-determination. It means that these principles cannot be vindicated by any means, in any institutional setting, so long as the disputants remained locked in polarized conflict. The dispute can only be resolved by authoritarian imposition of the victory of one antagonist over the other: by force of arms. This coercion can occur on the battlefield, in a legislature, or in a courtroom; in all of these settings, such resolution is contrary to democratic principle. But it is misleading to say that judicial review is therefore a deviant institution in a democracy. More accurately, judicial review—that is, the resort to some coercive instrument extrinsic to the disputants—is a logical response to an internal contradiction in democratic theory between majority rule and equal self-determination. It is not a deviation from that theory. A sharply polarized dispute, where neither antagonist is willing to accept defeat, brings forward this internal contradiction and consequently destroys the legitimacy, in the terms of democratic theory, of any authoritative resolution of this dispute—whether this resolution is effected by majority vote or by judicial override on behalf of the previously defeated minority.

In *Brown,* the Supreme Court stepped between the poles of this contradiction with extraordinary agility, even artistry, though it was guided more by intuition than explicit understanding. In *Brown I* the Court unsettled the previous resolution of the racial conflict that had been imposed by the southern legislatures; and in *Brown II,* the Court refused to impose its own authoritative resolution. The Court thus dramatically signified, first, that race segregation laws were illegitimate impositions because they hurtfully enslaved the black antagonists; and, second, that no legitimate resolution could be imposed on either antagonist, that legitimacy could come only with the "general assent"[44] of both blacks and whites, and that the pursuit of this accommodation should proceed, guided and prodded by local federal judges, "with all deliberate speed."[45] The Court's action signified all of this, but it was Bickel in *The Least Dangerous Branch* who clearly saw and said it.

Bickel's account of *Brown* thus provides an illustrative answer to the question posed at the outset of this chapter, "How can the Supreme Court properly adjudicate constitutional disputes, notwithstanding its questionable legitimacy to do so?" Bickel did not grasp, however, that the question itself arose from an intrinsic contradiction in democratic theory; he did not acknowledge that the polarized racial dispute in *Brown* both pointed to this contradiction and was only one instance among many such disputes in American political history. Bickel was too intent on insisting not only that judicial review was a deviant institution but also that *Brown* was a deviant dispute in the fundamentally unified American democracy.

In maintaining this stance, Bickel was half-right but he was also half-wrong. This is the paradox of the American polity: that historically it has been a place both of fundamental unity and of intense polar conflict. At different times one or the other characterization seems most plausible; but even when one appears dominant, the other waits almost visible in the background: the *yin* and *yang* of our national life or, more precisely, the image of figure/ground ambiguity, like a picture that viewed from one angle is a vase and from another is two profiled faces confronting one another. Looking at this ambiguous image, you cannot see the vase simultaneously with the two faces, even though you know that with a slight shift in visual perspective one depiction will disappear and the other will emerge. So with our national history: from one perspective it is "our" land, united in commitment to principles of freedom and equality, often falling short but never abandoning the pursuit of these high ideals; and from a slightly different angle of vision, it is a land where the only "us" are some who oppress and exploit others, systematically mocking and degrading them while invoking formal ideals of freedom and equality. The paradox and the tragedy of American history are that each image is true.

Judicial review trades on the image of unity; but courts are regularly invoked to address polar conflict. Indeed, they are institutionally situated so as to invite the invocation. Unless the

Court can convincingly shift the litigants' perspectives from the profiled confrontation to the reversed image of unity, the dispute cannot legitimately be resolved. This shift in perspective is the underlying goal of all the schools of jurisprudence—originalist, process, and interpretationist—so that the Court can transform and transcend the litigants' dispute by invoking universally shared resolving propositions.

Among the contemporary proponents of the interpretationist school, Ronald Dworkin's extensive account most clearly identifies this unifying goal at its core.[46] Dworkin argues that the process of legal interpretation rests on an assumption that there is a single correct answer to all disputed questions, notwithstanding the difficulty or the disagreements that may arise in identifying this answer. Dworkin is correct in claiming that our legal system has this univocality at its conceptual core to justify the legitimacy of its claim for binding authority. But he glides too quickly over two problems that obstruct the attainment of this univocality.

The fundamental difficulty, as we have seen, is in the contradiction between the two root democratic principles of majority rule and equal self-determination. This contradiction is deeply anarchic in its implications; unless it can be overcome, no organized communal life is possible that is not based on the coercion of some over others. The task of identifying some alternative, superseding basis for communal relations—a basis that denies the existence of irreconcilable conflicts of interest and perspective— may thus seem necessary to avert frightening consequences; but it is not therefore necessarily achievable in principle, as Dworkin maintains.

Because Dworkin insists that univocality is possible in principle within the internal premises of democratic jurisprudence, he glosses over a second difficulty: the practical problems that confront flesh-and-blood judges in persuading equally real, and intensely antagonistic, litigants that the judges can find, and have found, the one right answer to the conflict that divides them. Dworkin's half-playful appellation of Hercules for his ideal judge revealingly, though probably unintentionally, conveys the admixture of awe and fear that his judge must inspire to bring the antagonists to defer to any answer as *the* answer to their conflict. Dworkin is not concerned, however, with the practice of persuasion; his judge is a remote ratiocinator who views social relations from an excessive distance.*

In his later writings, Bickel discussed the social need for the perspectival shift from fundamental conflict to unified allegiance, but he emphatically denied that courts could serve any proper role toward this end. Indeed, at times he seemed even to claim that there were no realistic reasons for any American political institution to address this need because we were a basically unified society. In his 1969 Holmes Lectures he approvingly cited Learned Hand's observation that "a society so riven that the spirit of moderation is gone, no court *can* save, [and a society] where that spirit flourishes, no court *need* save."[47] In 1974, he found his apostle of the moderating spirit in Edmund Burke:

> For Burke a politics of theory and ideology, of abstract, absolute ideas was an abomination, whether the idea was the right of the British Parliament to tax the American colonies or the rights of man. Such a politics . . . begins and ends by sacrificing peace, and it must proceed from one bloodbath to another and from one tyranny to another. Ideas are the invention of men and are as arbitrary as their will. The business of politics is not with theory and ideology but with accommodation.[48]

Bickel's explicit historical model in *The Least Dangerous Branch,* however, was not Burke but Lincoln; and Lincoln was a better model for thinking about American institutions and social history. When Burke wrote, he could rely on widespread habits of deference in British society to support the social allegiance crucial to the realization of his politics of accommodation; when Lincoln spoke, his appeal to this social allegiance was more guarded. "We are not enemies, but friends," he said in his first inaugural address. "We must not be enemies. Though passion may have strained, it

---

*Thus in Dworkin's treatment of *Brown,* he can portray it as an easy case because the "condemn[ation of] officially sponsored racial segregation in schools . . . [was] consistent, in 1954, with ethical attitudes that were widespread in the community" (*Law's Empire* at 388); and he can say, as Bickel never would, that he "will not pursue the history of *Brown*'s [implementing] progeny . . . because [this] story is [not] particularly important to the constitutional wardrobe of law as integrity" (id. at 393). Dworkin's Hercules reports for work only after the stable has been cleaned.

must not break, our bonds of affection."[49] Those bonds did break, leaving open wounds and unresolved issues that are still vivid emblems of the tenuousness of social allegiance in American life.

Bickel's ultimate conclusion may be correct, that the judiciary cannot reliably serve a constructive role in fostering the social bonds that alone can legitimate political authority. We must, however, acknowledge that if our contemporary jurisprudence demands that the Supreme Court have an unimpeachable source of legitimacy before it may intervene in any dispute, then there is no role for the judiciary in addressing the fundamental challenges to democratic principle repeatedly presented by polarized social conflict in American life.

This observation is, of course, no argument for the relevance of judicial authority. There is a fact of history, however, that our jurisprudence should not ignore: the fact that the Supreme Court has recurrently intervened in the intensely polarized conflicts that have regularly erupted in our social life. We may ultimately conclude that this has always been a mistake. But I prefer at least to explore the possibility that there are better and worse ways to explain why the Justices themselves so regularly are drawn into these conflicts, and, once in, that there are better and worse ways for them to act. That is why I choose to pose the constitutional question, "How can the Supreme Court properly adjudicate constitutional disputes, notwithstanding its questionable legitimacy to do so?" The lessons that Alexander Bickel drew from *Brown* have a general significance in answering this question. On this rock, a jurisprudence can be built.

2

Madison's Institutional Answer

IN 1968 the President of Columbia University, Grayson Kirk, returned to his office after it had been occupied for six days by protesting students. He found a shambles—cigarette butts and orange peels scattered about, his furniture soiled and torn. "My God," he said, "how could human beings do a thing like this?" Erving Goffman, citing this event, observed that President Kirk had asked the wrong question: "The great sociological question . . . [is,] how is it that human beings do this sort of thing so rarely. How come persons in authority have been so overwhelmingly successful in conning those beneath them into keeping the hell out of their offices?"[1]

Goffman's puzzlement was anticipated, with equally ironic penetration, by David Hume in 1758:

> Nothing is more surprising to those, who consider human affairs with a philosophical eye, than to see the easiness with which the many are governed by the few; and to observe the implicit submission with which men resign their own sentiments and passions to those of their rulers. When we enquire by what means this wonder is brought about, we shall find, that as Force is always on the side of the governed, the governors have nothing to support them but opinion. 'Tis therefore, on opinion only that government is founded; and this maxim extends to the most despotic and most military governments; as well as to the most free and most popular.[2]

Hume's influence on James Madison, in particular among the founders, has been documented.[3] But even if Madison and his colleagues had not read Hume, they could not have avoided the unsettling lesson of this passage from his work. They themselves had changed from loyal though aggrieved subjects of the King to rebels. Hume's observation that "Force is always on the side of the governed" might have seemed a bit glib to the rebellious colonists while they were directly engaged in the Revolutionary War with its hardships and uncertainties. But in retrospect, it seemed clear that royal authority could not have been sustained indefinitely once the "opinion" of the governed had resolutely turned against it.

After the former colonists had thrown off the royal yoke, the great question for them was what might replace its social authority, on what "opinion" might these rebels base a new government. In retrospect, we know the answer: "popular sovereignty" replaced the royal prerogative in the American pantheon. We also know— or imagine that we know—that the history of the American enterprise from its founding has been the progressive expansion of this ideal of popular sovereignty from its cautious and even ambivalent endorsement by the gentlemen who met in Philadelphia in 1787. Thus, we know, the electorate has been dramatically expanded from the minority of the adult population in 1787 who were white, male property holders, to all white males by 1840 or so, then to black men following the Civil War, and finally to all women in 1919. And popular sovereignty has expanded from the original provision of Senators chosen by state legislatures to direct popular election in 1916 (and, less well-known but consistent with this trend, from the original practice of selection of presidential electors by state legislatures to direct popular choice by 1840).

This historical progression appears to underwrite the proposition that distrust of majority rule, though deeply embedded in the original structure of the Constitution, is now only a minor feature of our system. Accordingly, it might be argued that judicial review, which has been only one of many antimajoritarian elements in our governance scheme, should itself be re-examined and more narrowly confined. As I suggested in the first chapter, however, this panglossian view of majority rule ignores its inherent contradiction with the premise of self-determination in the inequality imposed on majoritarian losers. This contradiction in democratic theory is an underlying reason why the founding moment holds such fascination for American constitutional lawyers. It stands precisely at the intersection where solitary individuals try to unite, to find any common ground for organized social action. The contradiction is accordingly easiest to contemplate at the founding moment.

The Founders and Polarized Conflict

Professional historians are often bemused by constitutional lawyers' obsession with the founding moment, pointing to the many vast differences in outlook between the founding generation and ours that limit any sensible capacity to transport lessons from one era to the next. But constitutional lawyers have grasped one continuing, unsettling parallel between us and the founders, a parallel that illuminates a persistent feature of our social life: the founders stared fixedly into the face of social anarchy because they were required to build their scheme of social organization from ground zero. This prospect of anarchy remains today always just barely visible in the premises of popular sovereignty, equality, and self-determination on which the founders' structure rests.

We lawyers, in our professional concerns with practical questions of social action, can thus find lessons in the founding moment that historians, approaching these events with different purposes, would not find. Lawyers' lessons should, however, be carefully confined to this purpose. It is inappropriate for us to conclude, for example—as some interpretationists today have done—that concepts of "republican virtue" which historians have identified at the core of the founders' social thought can be carried across the generations to guide the decisions of today's Supreme Court Justices. Assumptions of social deference owed to gentry and the moral superiority of "public, disinterested" pursuits versus "private, self-seeking" behavior colored the founders' conception of republican virtue in ways that are fundamentally alien to our current conceptions of social life.[4] Lawyers can appropriately draw contemporary lessons, however, from the founders' reliance on "republican virtue" by identifying the role such an organizing concept played for the founders in addressing a problem that persists for us: the problem of identifying a basis for organized social action that answered, or at least appeased, the anarchic impulse that their Revolution had starkly revealed.

Erving Goffman's way of formulating this problem—how persons in authority con those beneath them into keeping the hell out of their offices—has a distinguished lineage in American historiography. It was at the heart of Charles Beard's debunking of the founders' motives, by reducing their concerns to the protection of their direct economic interests. Beard wrote *An Economic Interpretation of the Constitution* in 1913, at an extreme moment in the pendular swing of American historical attention toward social conflict, and his analysis was quickly put to service as a weapon against the pretensions of the Supreme Court of his day to rule by the light of disinterested principle refracted through the founders' example.[5] But Beard inflated a half-truth to the whole story.

The founders' era was itself a moment of heightened attention to social conflict. The founders were fearful about the implications of such conflict; and, as Beard clearly saw, they had more to lose than their less favorably endowed contemporaries. But it is misleading to assume that they cared only for their own economic well-being. From their direct experience, some of them—James Madison most notably—glimpsed what Burke later saw in the French Revolution and what Lincoln saw in our Civil War: that unrestrained conflict can devour all its children, both the immediate antagonists and the bystanders then living and yet to be born. The founders thus saw themselves working on their own behalf but also on behalf of others, including us—intending to speak as "We, the People of the United States . . . for ourselves and our Posterity." We miss most of what they can teach us if we approach them only in a debunking spirit.

There is, however, another kind of piety toward the founders that also hides them from us: the adulatory enshrinement of their work that was the staple of bicentennial oratory. So, for example, Chief Justice Warren Burger observed that "our Constitution has had as great an impact on humanity as the splitting of the atom."[6] The quick rejoinder to this pretentious praise is to recall the status of black slavery in the Constitution. Thus Justice Thurgood Marshall observed that the Constitution "was defective from the start" because it sacrificed "moral principles for self-interest" in the "perpetuation of slavery," that " 'We the people' no longer enslave, but the credit does not belong to the Framers" and, accordingly, "in th[e] bicentennial year, we may not all participate in the festivities with flag-waving fervor."[7] This is a powerful and appropriate antidote to unction; but it offers only the limited lesson that the founders' work, like ours, will inevitably be judged and found wanting by later generations.

Perhaps the founders should have aggressively and immediately attempted to eradicate the abomination of black slavery; they demurred for reasons that they, though not succeeding generations, found persuasive. It is more devastating, however, to criticize people for failing in the enterprises that they actually set for themselves; and even on this score the founders deserve criticism. In the one task that they self-consciously identified as their central mission—forging a lasting, peaceable union—they ultimately failed, totally and terribly, with the outbreak of the American Civil War.

The increasingly bitter estrangement between the white North and South, the unilateral withdrawal of the South from political relations, and the coercive rejoinder undertaken by the North represented, in their fundamental outlines, a reenactment of the deteriorating relations between Great Britain and the American colonies that the founders themselves had experienced. The South indeed draped itself in the revolutionary mantle of the founders, invoking both the time-honored vocabulary of colonial oppression and the remedy of secession. The North could repossess these hallowed symbols of the American revolutionary past only by transforming its war aims from the initial goal of preserving an unwanted Union to abolishing slavery and thereby universally vindicating the earlier promises of the Declaration of Independence. Wherever justice lay between these competing claims of abolition and revolutionary secession, the Constitution was designed to avert precisely this modality of conflict resolution, and it is in this sense that the founders failed in the enterprise they set for themselves.

We must understand how deeply the Civil War signified the failure of the founders' ambitions in order to grasp the central problem of social organization as they saw it. The fact is that the founders were haunted by the prospect of civil warfare—not necessarily between North and South, but generally—and they designed the Constitution fundamentally to avert it, based on their analysis of the latent causes of civil war in all social relations. With this understanding, we can see why a case like *Brown v. Board of Education*—a polar conflict between apparently irreconcilable antagonists poised at the edge of civil war—was not a deviant problem but was the modal problem addressed in the initial design of our constitutional system. And we can ultimately return to an enriched consideration of the constitutional role of the judiciary in addressing a case like *Brown.*

The founders' attitude toward black slavery is a key to this understanding. From their perspective, it was not a "peculiar" social institution. For them black slavery exemplified, albeit in an intense and (for some) even horrific way, the general problem they saw in designing a legitimate and effective governance mechanism. The most direct indication of the political significance the founders ascribed to black slavery is the fact that throughout the escalating dispute with Great Britain, at least from the early 1760s, the American colonists explicitly accused the imperial authority of attempting to "enslave" them.[8] To our ears, this endlessly repeated charge has a hollow ring: not only for its hypocrisy (as Samuel Johnson observed at the time, "How is it that we hear the loudest yelps for liberty from the drivers of Negroes?")[9] but even more for its hyperbole. King George did not attempt to sell any white children away from their parents, to separate husband from wife, to transport whites from one colony to another without their consent. But for the American colonists, these features were the details (however grievous) of black slavery, not the essence of its political and moral signification. The essence of slave status was the subjection of one man to the unconstrained and therefore endlessly self-aggrandizing will of another.

This was the yoke of British enslavement as the colonists defined it that led them to violent and ultimately successful resistance. Almost immediately after this emancipation, the former colonists used this same template to identify new threats to their freedom, this time from their compatriots. Jefferson's *Notes on Virginia,* published just a year after the British surrender at Yorktown, sounded the alarm. Evaluating the structure of his state's new constitution, Jefferson observed:

> All the powers of government, legislative, executive, and judiciary, result to the legislative body. The concentrating these in the same hands is precisely the definition of despotic government. It will be no alleviation that these powers will be exercised by a plurality of hands, and not by a single one. 173 despots would surely be as oppressive as one. . . . As little will it avail us that they are chosen by ourselves. An *elective despotism* was not the government we fought for.[10]

Barely four years later, the delegates meeting in Philadelphia concurred in Jefferson's premise that, having cast off the enslaving British, the successor regime was repeating this same cycle of selfish pursuit by allowing the strong to unjustly oppress the weak. The new villain was the tyrannical majority in state legislatures leveling unjust oppressions against men of property.

The specific issues of contention in these legislative measures, such as issuance of paper money and debt moratoria, were not, however, the core of the problem for the founders. These issues were illustrative of the more general characteristic of the repetitive cycle of oppressive enslavements by self-aggrandizing governmental power. Thus Madison, in a Convention speech that anticipated the argument in his *Federalist* 10, maintained that

> all civilized societies would be divided into different Sects, Factions, and interests, as they happened to consist of rich and poor, debtors and creditors, the followers of this political leader or that political leader, the disciples of this religious Sect or that religious Sect. In all cases where a majority are united by a common interest or passion, the rights of the minority are in danger.

This was true not simply for democracies organized around voting majorities but for "every Country antient and modern." Madison then cited two telling examples in immediate succession:

> Why was America so justly apprehensive of Parliamentary injustice? Because G[reat] Britain had a separate interest real or supposed, and if her authority had been admitted, could have pursued that interest at our expense. We have seen the mere distinction of colour made in the most enlightened period of time, a ground of the most oppressive dominion ever exercised by man over man.[11]

Black slavery for Madison is thus a subcategory (even though especially horrifying) of the oppression of the strong against the weak.[12]

This oppression was not simply morally wrong, as Madison saw it; it was also socially dangerous. As the vivid example of the American Revolution instructed, this kind of oppression fomented disorder and ultimately armed rebellion. And such civil warfare unleashed passions on all sides that would overwhelm the proper influence of reason in human affairs. Madison even expressed misgivings about the American Revolution on this ground, though with tactful indirection, in *Federalist* 49: "Notwithstanding the success which has attended the revisions of our established forms of government . . . the experiments are of too ticklish a nature to be unnecessarily multiplied."[13]

Madison made this observation in the course of rejecting a proposal that Thomas Jefferson had advanced in his *Notes on Virginia*. The proposal was designed to guard against majority despotism by providing for recurrent popularly elected conventions for "altering . . . or correcting breaches" of a state's constitution. For Madison, this proposal raised an excessive "danger of disturbing the public tranquillity by interesting too strongly the public passions. . . . " Directly echoing Hume's observation, Madison stated that

> frequent [popular] appeals would, in great measure, deprive the government of that veneration which time bestows on everything, and without which perhaps the wisest and freest governments would not possess the requisite stability. If it be true that all governments rest on opinion, it is no less true that the strength of opinion in each individual, and its practical influence on his conduct, depend much on the number which he supposes to have entertained the same opinion. The reason of man, like man himself, is timid and cautious when left alone, and acquires firmness and confidence in proportion to the number with which it is associated.[14]

In this passage, Madison appears to apply a version of the maxim "divide and conquer"—divide the populace, that is, by withholding opportunities from them for massed activities, such as Jefferson envisioned.

Here too we can see direct parallels in the founding generation's thinking regarding black slavery and social relations generally. Jefferson shows the linkage in another portion of his *Notes on Virginia* where he discussed the "influence on the manners of our people produced by the existence of slavery among us":

> The whole commerce between master and slave is a perpetual exercise of the most boisterous passions, the most unremitting despotism on the one part, and degrading submissions on the other. . . . Permitting one half the citizens thus to trample on the rights of the other, transforms those into despots, and these into enemies, destroys the morals of the one part, and the amor patriae of the other.[15]

Jefferson envisaged the possibility of emancipating the slaves, but with the proviso that they should then be "colonized" elsewhere: "It will probably be asked," he continued,

> Why not retain and incorporate the blacks into the state, and thus save the expence of supplying by importation of white settlers, the vacancies they will leave? Deep rooted prejudices entertained by the whites; ten thousand recollections, by the blacks, of the injuries they have sustained; new provocations; the real distinctions which nature had made; and many other circumstances will divide us into parties, and produce convulsions, which will probably never end but in the extermination of one or the other race.[16]

This is a stark and frightening vision, all the more so that it was made public when Jefferson was serving as Governor of Virginia.* These observations also reveal an implicit parallel in Jefferson's mind between racial antagonisms and the colonial conflict between

---

*Jefferson wrote *Notes on Virginia* for private circulation while he was Minister to France in 1781; it was published without his consent in 1785. See David Brion Davis, *The Problem of Slavery in the Age of Revolution, 1770–1823* at 177 (Ithaca: Cornell Univ. Press, 1975). Madison's similar views on slavery were never publicly broadcast; he spoke out in the secret sessions of the Constitutional Convention, for example, but never put in print the parallels he drew there between black slavery and factional oppression generally.

the American and the British. This was the widely shared analysis of the growing estrangement between blacks and whites in the 1760s. Even Jefferson's imagined solution of colonization for the emancipated slaves suggests a parallel with the final resolution of the conflict with Britain: political separation made effective and safe by geographic separation. Indeed, colonization was embraced not just by Jefferson but by Madison, John Marshall, and a host of similar revolutionary-generation notables.

The underlying conviction in the minds of the founding generation thus was that black slavery was not a unique instance of social conflict but was the modal expression of all social conflict, and the dangers that Jefferson acknowledged in the slave relationship—moral corruption of the oppressor, bitter resentments by the oppressed, which "will divide us into parties, and produce [exterminative] convulsions"—were generally seen as the likely consequences of all social conflict. Where, in this feverish imagining, would the faultline break apart into schismatic, violent confrontation: In conflict between rich and poor (as Shays's Rebellion augured for many at the Constitutional Convention)?[17] Between North and South (as Madison implied in a Convention speech)?[18] Between black and white (as Jefferson prophesied)? Addressing these anarchic impulses on all sides was the task that the founders defined for themselves in Philadelphia.

When John Locke imagined social life "in the beginning," before the institution of government, he said that "all the world was America."[19] When the newly freed Americans constructed their government, they imagined that all the world was the Civil War, all the world was *Brown v. Board of Education*: that is, a place of conflict populated by irreconcilable antagonists, none of whom could conceive any outcome but to rule or be ruled.

The entire political experience of the founders in the thirty years after the adoption of the Constitution was essentially devoted to testing this fearful vision. When James Monroe, the last member of the founding generation to hold the presidency, took office in 1817, he appeared to proclaim its disproof: "Harmony of opinion . . . pervades our Union. . . . Discord does not belong to our system. . . . The American people have encountered together great dangers and sustained several trials with success.

They constitute one great family with a common interest."[20] As if to confirm his point, the American electorate returned Monroe for a second term in 1820 by one vote short of unanimity in the electoral college; and that vote was withheld from him only because the elector believed that George Washington alone deserved the honor of unanimous selection.

But even if this fearful, generalized anticipation of civil conflict was unrealistic (a "vast neurotic fear," as Louis Hartz alleged)[21] and even if it was effectively dispelled in subsequent national experience, we must not dismiss this fear or attempt to marginalize it (for example, by characterizing the Civil War or the racial conflict over segregation laws as "deviations" from the mainstream American experience of consensus) if we want to understand the constitutional scheme that the founders established. This is so for two reasons. First, we cannot grasp the founders' own understanding of the Constitution unless we see the pervasiveness and importance of this fear of civil conflict for them. And second, this fear—whether realistic or not—was so deeply written into the interstices of the Constitution that it has pervasively (if subliminally) influenced the decisions of Supreme Court Justices, who have seen themselves as the special custodians of the integrity of the document.*

Acknowledging the depth of the founders' fears of civil conflict creates several acute difficulties for the originalist school of constitutional interpretation. It first of all underscores the great gulf in worldview between us and the founders. Their fears led them to an intense distrust of partisan political conflict that we today consider strange and dangerous to civil liberty. None of the founders would have given unqualified endorsement to the Supreme Court's finding in 1964 that the American polity has had "a pro-

---

*Indeed, the best way to understand judicial interpretations of the Constitution at various critical junctures of our history may be by taking seriously Hartz's charge of a "neurotic" belief in the imminent perils of social conflict; in its clinical usage, that is, a neurotic belief is not only fiercely resistant to disproof by experience but also influences its adherents to shape their conduct so as to prove its reality. We will return to this speculation in considering such landmark decisions as *Dred Scott v. Sandford* (in Chapter 5), *Lochner v. New York* (in Chapter 7), *Roe v. Wade* (in Chapter 9), and even John Marshall's effort in *McCulloch v. Maryland* (in Chapter 4).

found national commitment to the principle that debate on public issues should be uninhibited, robust and wide-open."[22] Consider, as one measure of the vast difference from our understandings, the fact that the debates in the Philadelphia Convention regarding the drafting of the document were all conducted in secret sessions. Not only did the founders agree to bar any public disclosure of their deliberations but the secretary of the Convention, James Madison, withheld publication of the official notes of the proceedings until, with his death in 1836, there were no surviving participants. This rigorously observed secrecy was not simply a response to the extraordinary sensitivity of the task but reflected the founders' more general conviction that politically conflictual questions should be debated only "in doors" among men of virtue, who were then obliged to unite in supporting the resolutions reached.[23]

In a different sense, however, the founders' hostility to openly waged political conflict does suggest that the originalist perspective could yield insights relevant to judicial interventions in polarized disputes such as *Brown*. The founders' distrust of majority rule, like their aversion to partisan political conflict, was not explicitly based on the contradiction between equal self-determination and majority rule as revealed by polarized disputes; but their attitude loses nothing in translation when applied to such disputes.

Indeed, the founders' opposition to majoritarian democracy generally was premised on the belief that all social conflict was polarized dispute, with the self-aggrandizing winner likely to oppress the loser. The solution they embraced, in their opposition to organized parties, was to seek political unanimity. This goal was not simply rhetorical for the founders, and it meant much more than grudging or temporary acquiescence by the losers. For the founders, actual—not simply symbolic or ceremonial—unanimity was their goal.[24] We know of course that unanimity as a formal voting rule is a paradoxically crippling requirement for social decisionmaking. Actual unanimity is, however, the only voting rule that consistently vindicates the democratic principles of equality and self-determination.

The constitutional scheme that the founders designed did not, of course, rest explicitly on working rules of unanimity; the founders were not fools. But their deep aversion to partisan conflict did lead them to aim toward unanimity as an ideal;[25] and in thus trying to solve the problem of partisan conflict, as they saw it, the founders were effectively, albeit inadvertently, trying to solve the central problem of democratic theory. By exploring the ways that their constitutional scheme was designed to approach the unanimity ideal, we might see how their solutions have direct relevance to our problem of finding a legitimate basis for the exercise of judicial authority.

The founders did not envisage a special role for the judiciary in pursuit of the ideal of unanimity. Rather, their overall conception of institutional authority, both within the federal structure and between state and federal government, aimed toward this goal. By our time, every institutional element in this interlocking scheme except for the federal judiciary has become more directly open to partisan conflict than the founders had envisaged (or would ever have approved). Accordingly, it is plausible to say that the task of buffering and transcending partisan conflict for which the founders designed their entire scheme has today, by a process of elimination, become focused on the judiciary. Put another way, insofar as their general institutional design was aimed toward unanimity and is thereby relevant to solving the contradiction we have identified in democratic theory, the federal judiciary is the only element of their scheme that remains adapted to implement their solution on our behalf.

This is a much more convoluted path toward applying the intention of the founders to a contemporary constitutional problem than most originalists would follow. It is, however, a way to leap across the differences in understanding that separate long-dead generations from us—to acknowledge, as James Madison warned, "the silent innovations of time on the meaning of words and phrases"[26] and accordingly to search for, rather than assume the existence of, common ground that can yield a true meeting of our minds with theirs.

In this particular pursuit, moreover, we will quickly encounter an insuperable obstacle to the possibility of applying the founders' intention to solve our problem, even in the modified version of originalism that I have applied. The obstacle is that the founders disagreed among themselves about how to design institutions so as to achieve or approach unanimity, and they did not resolve but rather implicitly embedded this disagreement in their constitutional scheme. Indeed, this disagreement directly complicates the specific task I have identified, to find in their intentions relevant guidance for the exercise of judicial authority. At the end of this chapter, when we have identified the bases of the founders' disagreement and their specific application of that disagreement in their competing conceptions of judicial authority, we will not have authoritative directives from them but rather a set of alternative possibilities they held out for us, and from among which we must find some way to choose.

Publius and Judicial Review

The broad strokes of the founders' disagreement regarding institutional response to the problem of partisan conflict have been set out in Richard Hofstadter's superb book, *The Idea of a Party System*. Hofstadter identified three fundamentally different conceptions. One was to embrace such conflict as a "necessary and, on balance, good" means to check abuse in the exercise of governmental authority by the persistent political activity of a "loyal opposition" prepared to supplant the existing government. In the 1770s, Hofstadter found, Edmund Burke espoused this view in England but "no one" among the founding generation in America agreed.[27] It was not until the early 1820s that this view gained any respectable adherents here, becoming dominant only after Andrew Jackson's presidency.[28] Among the founders, there were two different views, both of which were fundamentally hostile to political conflict. There was what Hofstadter identifies as "the orthodox view . . . [which] despite its general currency, may be called for convenience the Hamiltonian view—that parties are evils that can be avoided or abolished or suppressed, even if this must be done, paradoxically, through the temporary agency of a party of national unification."[29] And there was the view "which in America could be called Madisonian, in England Humean—that though parties are indeed evil, their existence is an unavoidable by-product of a free state, and that they must therefore be endured with patience by all men who esteem liberty."[30]

For originalists accustomed to appealing to the guiding authority of the *Federalist Papers*—consisting of essays variously written by Hamilton, Madison, and Jay, and jointly issued as the unitary work of "Publius"—Hofstadter's schematic must be unsettling. There has been considerable historical controversy about whether the *Federalist* has a fundamentally unified outlook or a "split personality"[31] and indeed whether Hamilton wrote almost all of the work himself—a claim that gained mistaken credence in the late nineteenth century when Madison was inaccurately viewed as an early apologist for slavery and southern secessionist impulses.[32] No one can dispute the existence of fundamental disagreements between Hamilton and Madison after the adoption of the Constitution. Their estrangement on many issues regarding the proper scope of national power finally culminated in disagreement over the status of partisan conflict, in precisely the terms that Hofstadter identified. Hamilton became a leading proponent of the Sedition Act, which imposed criminal penalties against political criticism of the national government, and Madison (in alliance with Jefferson) became a leading opponent (and, not incidentally, a possible target of application). But before this bitter falling out, both men were united in supporting adoption of the Constitution, and their joint effort in the *Federalist* was bent to that end. The central question for reading the *Federalist,* therefore, is whether the disagreements between Madison and Hamilton that subsequently erupted in public battle also led them either toward conflicting positions in the drafting of the Constitution or toward conflicting interpretations of the document in the *Federalist* itself.

The question of initial drafting is easiest to answer. There was stark disagreement between Hamilton and Madison (indeed, between Hamilton and most members of the Convention) regarding the structure of authority to be provided in the Constitution. The disagreement was evident from Hamilton's first and most extended speech at the Convention on June 18. "All the passions . . . we see, of avarice, ambition, interest, which govern most individuals, and all public bodies, fall into the current of the States," Hamilton observed. "How then are all these evils to be avoided? only by such a compleat sovereignty in the general Government as will turn all the strong principles [and] passions . . . on its side."[33] To accomplish this, Hamilton suggested, it would be preferable to "extinguish" the state governments altogether, on the ground that "two Sovereignties can not coexist within the same limits." He acknowledged that such a proposal would "shock the public opinion" but suggested nonetheless that opinion might yet change on this subject and come to agree with him that the British Constitution was "the best in the world." The delegates should copy it, he said, in order to "attain stability and permanency" by providing life terms for the Executive and one branch of the Legislature. "Is this a Republican Government," Hamilton asked, and he answered, "Yes if all the Magistrates are appointed . . . by the people, or a process of election originating with the people," notwithstanding the life tenure of those officials. Hamilton then concluded by recurring to the problem of popular opinion:

> He was aware that [his plan] went beyond the ideas of most members. But will such a plan be adopted out of doors? In return he would ask will the people adopt the other plan [i.e., the Virginia plan, drafted by Madison and submitted to the Convention by Edmund Randolph]? At present they will adopt neither. But he sees the Union dissolving or already dissolved—he sees evils operating in the States which must soon cure the people of their fondness for democracies—he sees that a great progress has been already made [and] is still going on in the public mind. He thinks therefore that the people will in time be unshackled from their prejudices; and whenever that happens, they will themselves not be satisfied at stopping where the plan of Mr. R[andolph] would place them, but be ready to go as far at least as he proposes.[34]

Hamilton's proposal grew from premises about political authority that he had set out in 1775, in a pamphlet extolling the British monarch as embodying in his "person and prerogative" the "connecting, pervading principle" of the Empire that "conjoins all these individual societies into one great body politic . . . preserve[s] their mutual connexion and dependence . . . and make[s] them all co-operate to one common end [,] the general good."[35] This praise of the King, coming at the very eve of the American Declaration of Independence, is not as odd as it might appear; even at this late date, it was common among the patriot colonists to honor, even to exalt, the King in sharp contradistinction to the British Parliament. This was not simply a strategy by the colonists but apparently a sincere belief that their grievances were caused by the actions of a corrupt Parliament and that the King, once alerted to this corruption, would protect them (one might say, to jump ahead in the argument, by declaring the unjust laws unconstitutional). Hamilton wrote his panegyric within this patriot consensus at the time, but his views were nonetheless the "most comprehensive claims" put forward for this role of "imperial unifier."[36] He explicitly derived this conception of royal authority from this premise: "In every government, there must be a supreme absolute authority lodged somewhere . . . to which all the members of that society are subject; for otherwise there could be no supremacy, or subordination, that is, no government at all."[37]

This is the same premise that Hamilton invoked in his June 18 speech to the Philadelphia Convention as the basis for his proposal that they should recreate the British Constitution in an American garb. Here too Hamilton was not so far from the predominant views of his contemporaries as we today might think.[38] In later years, the charge of "monarchism" had become so opprobrious in American politics that Hamilton ostentatiously backed away from, and even apparently misrepresented, the specifics of his Convention proposal.[39] But though the members of the Convention rejected Hamilton's specific scheme, almost without further mention, they had much more difficulty coming to terms with his basic premise about the necessary indivisibility of sovereignty.

On this issue, our contemporary schoolbook understanding of the Constitution is misleading. We come too quickly to the proposition that the founders honored the idea of indivisible sovereignty by locating it in "We the People" and then proceeding to divide the governmental attributes of sovereignty both vertically and horizontally, between state and federal governments and among the federal branches. This is of course the formal organizational chart of the founders' work. But the founders did not expect that the direct commandatory voice of the sovereign People would be heard very often in the daily affairs of governance. The People would assemble in the initial ratifying conventions, to serve as a kind of jump-start mechanism to launch the constitutional enterprise, but then would recede into the remote background. This was the clear purpose of the cumbersome formal processes for constitutional amendments to ensure, in Madison's words, that "the ticklish experiment" of "interesting . . . the public passions" in revising "established forms of government" would not be "unnecessarily multiplied."[40] This expectation has been realized in practice; setting aside the first ten amendments, which were adopted as part of the initial ratifying endeavor, the sovereign voice of the People has been heard in the land only sixteen times in two hundred years.[41]

With the sovereign People thus safely ensconced, the question remained for the founders as to the locus of sovereignty in the ordinary affairs of governance. Hamilton's premise that "there must be a supreme absolute authority lodged somewhere" in every government was not satisfied by this remote icon of popular ratification; his conception of the authoritarian role demanded easy and regular access, if for no other reason than (as he put it in *Federalist* 9) "to repress domestic faction and insurrection."[42] Whatever the attractions of Hamilton's premise for the other delegates, they were not prepared to adopt his specific implementing proposals.* But when the Constitution was completed, Hamilton stepped forward as its principal proponent in New York. He solicited the participation of Madison and John Jay in preparing a series of newspaper articles as part of the ratification campaign in New York; this was the origin of the *Federalist Papers*. Eighty-five separate articles were written between October 1787 and May 1788, fifty-one by Hamilton, twenty-six by Madison, and only five by Jay (with three jointly authored by Hamilton and Madison).[43]

These articles are conventionally used today by lawyers as an authoritative guide to the intention of the founders as a group and accordingly as a preferred source for construing the meaning of the Constitution.[44] But the articles can be used with greatest assurance only as evidence for the conception that each author had of the Convention's workproduct. Even for this use, some caution is required, since it is possible that each author might have shaded or even distorted his true belief regarding his colleagues'

---

*Hamilton himself left the Convention on June 29, perhaps because he was annoyed that his views were not accepted or perhaps because, as he said, he had more pressing business affairs and clients to tend. He returned in mid-August to participate in the final drafting process. See Richard Morris, *Witnesses at the Creation: Hamilton, Madison, Jay, and the Constitution* 211 (New York: New American Library, 1985).

purposes in order to make the document most acceptable to the ratifying public. This kind of partisan presentation seems to me, however, less likely than another, less self-conscious distorting influence on the authors of the *Federalist Papers*.

Both Hamilton and Madison were disappointed with important aspects of the ultimate constitutional document. Both suffered defeats at the Convention for different proposals that seemed to each man crucial for the success of the endeavor. Each nonetheless wholeheartedly believed that the Constitution was markedly superior to the extant Articles of Confederation. In setting out arguments for the virtues of the new Constitution, however, it was inevitable that each should approach the analysis from within his own criteria of excellence.

Thus Hamilton, convinced that an actively available locus of indivisible sovereign authority was necessary in any government worthy of the name, was likely to find such authority in order to commend the enterprise to the citizens of New York. This finding may reflect Hamilton's honest appraisal of his fellow delegates' intentions; it may reflect his own construction of their intentions to fit his cherished goals; or it may be some indistinguishable mixture of both elements.[45]

Hamilton found his sovereign in two aspects of the Constitution. The first was in the supremacy awarded to the laws and treaties of the national government, as well as the Constitution itself, over state actions. Thus, by Hamilton's lights, between the state and national government, the latter was sovereign (even though the Constitution had not "extinguished" the former governmental structures and reduced the states to mere administrative units, as he had preferred). But placing the locus of authority in the national government was not sufficient to satisfy Hamilton's basic premise because the national government itself was divided. This apparent division posed a question that, for Hamilton, must be answered consistent with the very definition of government: where, within this supreme national government, was the single locus of supreme national authority? Without an identifiable, and available, superior, the Constitution would have committed the solecism of an *imperium in imperio*—the absurdity of multiple sovereigns in a governmental structure that requires unity by its nature.

Hamilton answered his question in *Federalist* 78: the supreme locus of authority within the national government was the Supreme Court of the United States, through the existence of its "duty . . . to declare all acts contrary to the manifest tenor of the Constitution void."[46] Hamilton's conception of the Court's status is evident from his discussion whether this invalidating authority "would imply a superiority of the judiciary to the legislative power." Hamilton denied this proposition on the ground that "the power of the people is superior to both." But, he said, "the courts were designed to be an intermediate body between the people and the legislature in order . . . to keep the latter within the limits assigned to their authority."[47] His hierarchical pyramid is thus clear: the people are at the pinnacle; but in their (ordinarily anticipated) silence, the Court speaks as their intermediary, as the delegated repository of ultimate sovereignty from the People.

This is not an implausible reading of the constitutional document, and Hamilton was not the first such reader. Indeed, it appears that *Federalist* 78 was written partly as a response to newspaper letters published several months earlier under the pseudonym Brutus by Robert Yates, an opponent of ratification. Brutus concluded that "the supreme court under this constitution would be exalted above all other power in the government, and subject to no controul."[48] However much Hamilton might want to find a single exalted power within the government, he was also eager to refute the accusation of uncontrollable authority. To this end, he claimed that notwithstanding their authority to pronounce legislative acts void, the judiciary "will always be the least dangerous to the political rights of the Constitution":

> The judiciary . . . has no influence over either the sword or the purse; no direction either of the strength or of the wealth of the society, and can take no active resolution whatever. It may truly be said to have neither FORCE nor WILL but merely judgment; and must ultimately depend upon the aid of the executive arm even for the efficacy of its judgments.[49]

This, Hamilton concluded, "proves incontestably that the judiciary is beyond comparison the weakest of the three departments; that it can never attack with success either of the other two," appending a footnote that "the celebrated Montesquieu . . . says, 'Of the three powers . . . , the JUDICIARY is next to nothing.' "[50]

This is an effective rhetorical response to Brutus's charge, but it surely raises questions about the internal coherence of Hamilton's general claim that "the courts of justice are to be considered as the bulwarks of a limited Constitution against legislative encroachments . . . as faithful guardians of the Constitution."[51] What kind of guardian is so toothless as to be disabled from ever attacking with success the object of its surveillance, what kind of bulwark can sensibly be characterized as next to nothing?

Hamilton's description of the inherent weaknesses in judicial authority was faithful to the constitutional scheme. He might have added that Article III explicitly gave Congress such extensive authority to make "exceptions" and "regulations" regarding the Court's jurisdiction as to raise the possibility that questions of legislative constitutionality might be withheld altogether;[52] or that the Constitution made no provision regarding the size of the Supreme Court, so that the legislative and executive branches together might enlarge or contract its membership at will to avoid adverse judgments;[53] or that the Constitution is also silent regarding the voting rules of the Court, inviting the possibility that a congressional enactment might require even unanimity among the Justices to declare legislation void.[54]

All of this does not necessarily cast doubt on Hamilton's claim that the Constitution gives judges authority to declare legislative acts void. The institutional vulnerabilities of the Court, however, are so obvious on the very face of the document as to suggest that Hamilton's depiction of the pyramidal hierarchy of authority— from the People to the Court to the lesser breeds under the law— misses a crucial aspect of the constitutional scheme. Even from the weaknesses cited by Hamilton, it appears that the Constitution applied David Hume's maxim regarding governance generally: that "Force is on the side of the governed" and that the Court's authority depends on "opinion," on the continuously volunteered submission of those who are to be governed by the Court's construction of the Constitution.

It is not surprising that no one at the Convention cited Hume for this theoretical perspective on the role of judicial authority in the structure of the Constitution. It is surprising that there was hardly any discussion of any sort at the Convention, at least as appears in the surviving minutes, regarding the theoretical basis for judicial invalidation of unconstitutional laws. The few recorded observations about the existence of this judicial authority took place in the course of debates about other matters, most notably Madison's proposal for a Council of Revision to join the Justices and the President with veto authority over congressional acts. The existence of a separate judicial authority to determine constitutionality was invoked by several delegates as a ground for opposing the inclusion of the Justices in this added role.[55] In the course of this debate, one delegate expressed opposition to the existence of such independent judicial authority; the rejoinder, by John Dickinson of Delaware, seems to me to capture the essence of most delegates' concerns on this issue: "*Mr. Dickinson* was strongly impressed with the remark of Mr. Mercer as to the power of the Judges to set aside the law. He [also] thought no such power ought to exist. He was at the same time at a loss what expedient to substitute. The Justiciary of Arragon he observed became by degrees, the lawgiver."[56] I read this remark as an ambivalent, even a reluctant, endorsement of judicial review, though an endorsement nonetheless.

Dickinson was not an influential member of the Convention; but on this matter I believe his ambivalence captures the general sentiment, for at least one reason: that judicial authority to overturn unconstitutional laws is not expressly inscribed in the text of the Constitution.* The existence of this authority may have been assumed by most delegates at the Convention; it may follow logically (as Hamilton argued in *Federalist* 78) from the proposition

---

*The only explicit textual directive to judges regarding their duty to invalidate laws inconsistent with the Constitution is limited to state judges and state laws; Article V provides, "This Constitution, and the Laws of the United States which shall be made in Pursuance thereof . . . shall be the supreme Law of the Land; and the Judges in every State shall be bound thereby, any Thing in the Constitution or Laws of any State to the Contrary notwithstanding." This provision implicitly suggests that state judges are not equally bound by federal laws not "made in Pursuance" of the Constitution; but this is surely a less direct way of instructing judges—and only state judges, at that—regarding their authority to invalidate unconstitutional federal laws, as compared to the clear command regarding inconsistent state laws.[57]

that the Constitution is a "law" (albeit a "fundamental law") that judges are obliged to enforce like any law,[58] or from the fact that no explicit provision of the Constitution vests this enforcement authority elsewhere. But the delegates certainly understood the importance of the location of ultimate authority in interpreting the meaning of their handiwork, and they surely had the verbal facility to address this issue explicitly if they had chosen to do so.

Their failure may have been inadvertent, a lapse of attention on this (not insignificant) issue that somehow persisted throughout the five months of their deliberations. Or, as I am inclined to believe, their silence may have reflected the same reasoning that led the delegates to refuse to include the word "slave" in their constitutional document, notwithstanding that several provisions addressed and effectively endorsed the institution of slavery. Practical considerations, an inability to imagine "what expedient to substitute," led the founders to accept the continuation of slave status, but they would not acknowledge its legitimacy.[59] As reluctant as they were to speak the word "slave," I would say that they were equally unwilling to identify a "master" in the constitutional document who would have final, effectively unreviewable authority to enforce his will on all other institutional actors.[60] And yet they were at the same time at a loss what expedient to substitute.

James Madison, the most "systematic, deliberate and profound thinker" at the Convention and among his generation,[61] himself took no clear position at the Convention regarding the existence of judicial review. Madison was occupied both at the Convention and before with large questions about the overall design of the constitutional structure. He did not turn to an intensive consideration of the guardianship role of the judiciary until after the Convention had adjourned, and he did not arrive at a settled view until long after the Constitution had been ratified. His final view was radically different from Hamilton's—though from Madison's perspective, this final view was not a change from the position he had held at the Convention but a consistent application of the principles that he had espoused and that had been adopted in designing the general structure of the Constitution. In this sense, Madison's position on judicial review deserves the encomium of a "founder's original intent" as much as Hamilton's subsequent elucidation of the underlying logic of the Constitution in *Federalist* 78.

At the Convention itself, Madison's own notes contain only one direct reference by him to the practice of judicial review in the context that Hamilton later elaborated. On August 27, when the Convention finally turned to a direct consideration of the judicial branch, Madison observed that "he doubted whether it was not going too far to extend the jurisdiction of the Court generally to cases arising under the Constitution [and] whether it ought not to be limited to cases of a Judiciary nature. The right of expounding the Constitution in cases not of this nature ought not to be given to that Department." The notes record that a motion was then adopted, "it being generally supposed that the jurisdiction given was constructively limited to cases of a Judiciary nature."[62] Madison's meaning here is not exactly pellucid, as subsequent disputes attest in construing the Article III limitation of judicial power to "cases and controversies."

Aside from this doubting observation, Madison's principal attention to judicial authority at the Convention had been his repeated effort to join the judges with the executive in constituting a Council of Revision with veto power over congressional acts.* The Convention rejected this proposal with several delegates maintaining, as I noted earlier, that it would in effect give judges a double negative regarding legislation. In private correspondence much later, Madison stated that if the Convention had accepted his proposal, this would have eliminated any subsequent judicial review of legislation for constitutional validity.[63] At the Convention

---

*Madison made one other remark that might be construed as a reference to Hamiltonian-style judicial review. On July 23, in the course of discussing whether the Constitution should be submitted to state legislatures or specially convened conventions for ratification, Madison observed that legislative ratification might lead judges to regard subsequent violating enactments "as a law, though an unwise or perfidious one" whereas with direct popular ratification, a "law violating the constitution established by the people themselves, would be considered by the Judges as null and void." *Notes of Debates* at 352–53. It is, however, most likely that Madison was referring here only to violative laws enacted by the states themselves, and not to federal laws; he reasoned that judges would treat a state-ratified constitution as a treaty and that subsequent violative enactments would be judicially respected notwithstanding that they were treaty violations, which clearly implies that he was referring to laws enacted by the states as parties to the treaty rather than to laws enacted by Congress, a creature of the treaty. At the Convention and thereafter, Madison consistently maintained that the federal judiciary had authority to strike down state laws that violated the Constitution.

itself, however, Madison did not explicitly draw this conclusion and, at least according to his notes, he said nothing about the need for choosing between anterior and posterior judicial review of legislation.

Immediately after the Convention adjourned, however, Madison did express his misgivings about post hoc judicial review, somewhat indirectly but I believe unmistakably in his contributions to the *Federalist Papers*. Madison's essays are not read by most commentators as addressing judicial review,[64] which leaves the field apparently clear for Hamilton's *Federalist* 78 and misses the differences between the two men on this issue.[65]

Madison directly addressed the questions of remedies for unconstitutional laws in *Federalist* 47 through 51. In *Federalist* 47, he stated his initial premise, the maxim that "the legislative, executive, and judiciary departments ought to be separate and distinct," and he observed that in the various state constitutions, "no . . . competent provision [has] been made for maintaining in practice the separation delineated on paper."[66] In *Federalist* 48, Madison identified his "next and most difficult task[:] to provide some practical security for each [branch] against the invasion of the others."[67] He then proceeded to explore various possible devices for enforcing this fundamental principle of the Constitution; it is in this exploration that his underlying resistance to Hamiltonian-style judicial review can clearly be discerned.

First, Madison asked, is it sufficient to mark precise delineations of authority in the constitutional document and "to trust to these parchment barriers against the encroaching spirit of power?"[68] No, he answered in *Federalist* 48, citing experience under various state constitutions to make the point. Madison then moved, in *Federalist* 49, to consider the merits of Jefferson's proposal, advanced in his *Notes on Virginia*, for "correcting breaches" of a constitution by providing for popularly elected conventions to be convened by two-thirds vote of "any two of the three branches of government."[69] Madison rejected this proposal on various grounds: one, noted earlier, was "the danger of disturbing the public tranquillity" by too frequent involvement of "popular passions" in "constitutional questions";[70] a second, more revealing for present purposes, was that the legislature, as Madison saw it, would be the most likely constitutional transgressor and that any popularly elected convention would probably be composed of popular legislators who "would [therefore] be constituted themselves the judges" of their own transgressions.

At this point we might expect the logic of Madison's argument to lead him to judicial review, to an impartial group of judges, neither popularly elected nor drawn from the legislature, duty-bound to guard the "parchment barriers" of a constitution. Sure enough, Madison opened *Federalist* 50 with this possibility: "that instead of *occasional* appeals to the people . . . *periodical* appeals are the proper and adequate means of *preventing and correcting infractions of the Constitution.*"[71] By "periodical appeals," Madison envisioned some regularly constituted tribunal that would meet at assigned intervals only "for *enforcing* the Constitution" and not "for *altering*" it[72]—the precise role that Hamilton subsequently assigned to the Supreme Court in his *Federalist* 78. Madison rejected this.

Though he did not refer directly to the Supreme Court, Madison drew his negative lesson principally from examining the workings of an apparently equivalent tribunal for correcting constitutional breaches that had been convened in Pennsylvania in 1783–84, the so-called Council of Censors. First, he noted, many of the Council members had been, within the preceding seven years, "active and leading characters" in "parties" or "influential members of the legislative and executive branches"; and the proceedings of the Council showed the effect of persistent partisanship in their deliberations.[73] Second, it appeared that the Council "misconstrue[d] the limits prescribed for the legislative and executive departments . . . " Finally, "the decisions of the council on constitutional questions, whether rightly or erroneously formed, have [not] had any effect in varying the practice" of the legislative or executive branches.[74] Though Madison did not explicitly draw parallels to the likely composition, conduct, or practical efficacy of the United States Supreme Court, I find unmistakable links following from his analysis.

Having thus rejected these three alternatives—the text standing alone, occasionally elected conventions, or regularly constituted enforcement tribunals—as means for enforcing constitutional limitations, Madison then identified his preferred "expedient" in *Federalist* 51. This essay is justly famous for setting out the heart of

Madison's vision that the Constitution had "so contriv[ed] the interior structure of the government . . . that its several constituent parts may, by their mutual relations, be the means of keeping each other in their proper places."[75] The fundamental technique that Madison identified for this purpose was division of authority in order to supply "opposite and rival interests" throughout the governmental structure.

Thus, the legislature, which "necessarily predominates" in republican government, is divided in two and rendered "by different modes of election and different principles of actions, as little connected with each other as the nature of their common functions and their common dependence on the society will admit." Legislative authority is then further divided by the executive's qualified veto which permits "this weaker department" to augment the strength of the "weaker branch" of the legislature.[76] Beyond these internal divisions within the national government, Madison observed, the federal scheme provides two additional safeguards. First:

> In the compound republic of America, the power surrendered by the people is first divided between two distinct governments, and then the portion allotted to each subdivided among distinct and separate departments. Hence a double security arises to the rights of the people. The different governments will control each other, at the same time that each will be controlled by itself.[77]

Second, reiterating the analysis he had set out in *Federalist* 10:

> Different interests necessarily exist in different classes of citizens. If a majority be united by a common interest, the rights of the minority will be insecure. . . . In the federal republic of the United States the society itself will be broken into so many parts, interests and classes of citizens, that the rights of individuals, or of the minority, will be in little danger from interested combinations of the majority.[78]

Madison thus answered the question he posed in *Federalist* 48: how would power be "effectively restrained" in the Constitution? His answer, in *Federalist* 51: by dividing and then by subdividing authority within and among the various institutions of governance.

For our purposes, it is striking that in *Federalist* 51 Madison does not directly list the judiciary in his catalogue of the effective checks on the abuse of power. Indeed, Madison nominates every other governmental institution—the bicameral congress, the executive with its veto, the states—and omits the judiciary. This omission does not seem inadvertent. In the middle of his analysis in *Federalist* 51, Madison noted the need to protect minorities against oppressive majorities and observed,

> There are but two methods of providing against this evil: the one by creating a will in the community independent of the majority—that is, of the society itself . . . . [This] method prevails in all governments possessing an hereditary or self-appointed authority. This, at best, is but a precarious security; because a power independent of the society may as well espouse the unjust views of the major as the rightful interests of the minor party, and may possibly be turned against both parties.[79]

This is a concise critique of the conception of judicial review that Hamilton put forward later in *Federalist* 78. Madison went no further than this indirect criticism in his contributions to the *Federalist Papers*. But his disagreement with Hamilton clearly emerged almost immediately following the publication of *Federalist* 78.

The *Federalist Papers* were written separately, not as a unified work, and with limited direct collaboration among the three authors. Madison ended his writing and left New York in March 1788. Hamilton did not write *Federalist* 78 until the following month; it first appeared on May 28 in a single volume collecting *Federalists* 37 through 85, and then was published separately in a New York newspaper on June 14.[80] Madison was occupied at the time in the Virginia ratifying convention, which met throughout June; the New York convention began in mid-June and concluded with its ratification on July 26.[81] Just three months later, in October 1788, with the arduous ratification effort successfully concluded, Madison addressed Hamilton's analysis of the judicial role in *Federalist* 78.

In private correspondence urging that draftsmen of the Kentucky state constitution adopt a provision similar to his initial proposal for an Executive–Judicial Council of Revision, Madison stated that if the state legislature overrode this Council veto, "it should not be allowed the Judges or the Executive to pronounce a law thus enacted unconstitutional and invalid." He then continued:

In the state Constitutions and indeed in the Federal one also, no provision is made for the case of a disagreement in expounding them; and as the Courts are generally the last in making their decisions, it results to them by refusing or not refusing to execute a law, to stamp it with its final character. This makes the Judiciary Department paramount in fact to the Legislature, which was never intended and can never be proper.[82]

This is no latter-day recantation of a previous position; this is a clear contemporary joinder of issue by Madison against Hamilton and his glib assurance in *Federalist* 78 that his "doctrine [of judicial review] would [not] imply a superiority of the judiciary to the legislative power" because "the power of the people is superior to both" and the judiciary is thus the "intermediate body between the people and the legislature."[83] For Madison, this spatial locus of judicial authority contradicted his central premise in *Federalist* 51, rejecting "exterior provisions" to enforce constitutional limits and relying exclusively on the multiple, mutually interlocking divisions of authority within "the interior structure of the government."

It was deceptively easy for Madison's contemporaries, and equally easy for us today, to miss the pervasive significance of this central premise of *Federalist* 51. This premise was the second of the stunningly original contributions to political theory that Madison made in his *Federalist* essays. His first achievement was to refute the conventional republican precept that liberty can be protected only in a small *polis* where citizens can directly control their own affairs. Madison turned this idea on its head to show, in *Federalist* 10, why a large republic comprehending a multitude of conflicting interests is a preferable governance structure. Madison's second achievement was in *Federalist* 51, where he took the conventional precept that every government by definition must have a single locus of sovereign authority and turned this idea upside down to maintain that a well-designed government could and should divide and then subdivide all authority. Madison maintained that the mutual competition among these multiple divided authorities would effectively check abuses of power; and by this means, no single sovereign could be found.

The full import and originality of Madison's view in *Federalist* 10 was clear at the time because the Constitution obviously encompassed a larger field for governance than the state-dominated Articles of Confederation. The significance of his analysis in *Federalist* 51 was obscured, however, because there appeared to be a single, supreme sovereign in the scheme, a sovereign that Madison himself appeared to accept as such: the People. This was not, however, Madison's precise position, as a careful reading of *Federalist* 51 would indicate.[84]

In fact, Madison's scheme for divided and subdivided authority applied with equal force to the exercise of popular authority over government and to the interior organization of governmental institutions. The capstone of his scheme in *Federalist* 51 referred back to his analysis in *Federalist* 10 regarding the necessity of dividing the populace itself into multiple competing "parts, interests and classes of citizens" by encompassing a large republic. Madison was thus as hostile to a readily accessible, unitary locus of ultimate governmental authority in the sovereign people as he was opposed to the creation of "a will in the community independent of the majority," such as a monarch or a life-tenured Court with effectively unreviewable, supreme authority "to stamp [law] with its final character." In writing his *Federalist* essays, however, Madison was not eager to emphasize his reservations regarding popular sovereignty. He intended the essays to win tenure, but not in an academic department of political philosophy.[85]

Whether or not Madison had grasped the full theoretical implications of his position when he wrote *Federalist* 51, he systematically developed these implications during the remainder of his life in both his public and private papers, and most notably in the context of considering the role of the judiciary in enforcing constitutional limitations against the other branches of the federal government. His first occasion for this consideration after the ratification of the Constitution was in drafting the Bill of Rights. In an October 1788 letter to Jefferson, Madison discussed his misgivings about the intrinsic usefulness of adding a Bill of Rights to the Constitution and finally concluded that two "precautionary" purposes might be served: "the political truths declared in that solemn manner acquire by degrees the character of fundamental maxims of free Government, and as they become incorporated with the national sentiment, counteract the impulses of interest and passion"; and "a bill of rights will be a good ground for an appeal to the sense of the community" in response to "usurped acts of the Government."[86] Jefferson responded,

> In the arguments in favor of a declaration of rights, you omit one which has great weight with me, the legal check which it puts into the hands of the judiciary. This is a body, which if rendered independent, and kept strictly to their own department merits great confidence for their learning and integrity. In fact what degree of confidence would be too much for a body composed of such men as Wythe, Blair, and Pendleton?[87]

Madison's omission of the judiciary was clearly intentional; he had written Jefferson in the same month, and perhaps even on the same day, that he wrote his Kentucky correspondent criticizing judicial review.

When Madison turned from these private expressions to the performance of his public duty, as he saw it, regarding the proposed Bill of Rights, he tempered his previous misgivings, however, not only about the utility of the amendments but even about the judicial enforcement role. Thus, in his speech introducing the amendments in the House of Representatives on June 8, 1789, Madison deferred to Jefferson's view in this frequently cited passage:

> [The proposed amendments] may have, to a certain degree, a salutary effect against the abuse of power. If they are incorporated into the constitution, independent tribunals of justice will consider themselves in a peculiar manner the guardians of those rights; they will be an impenetrable bulwark against every assumption of power in the legislative or executive; they will be naturally led to resist every encroachment upon rights expressly stipulated for in the constitution by the declaration of rights.[88]

Notwithstanding this bow toward judicial review, however, Madison immediately added the following observation (which is never cited by modern proponents of judicial supremacy):[89]

Beside this security, there is a great probability that such a declaration in the federal system would be enforced; because the state legislatures will jealously and closely watch the operations of this government, and be able to resist with more effect every assumption of power than any other power on earth can do; and the greatest opponents to a federal government admit the state legislatures to be sure guardians of the people's liberty.[90]

In this significant addendum, Madison anticipated the formulation of an enhanced role for state legislatures in the enforcement of constitutional limitations that he and Jefferson would subsequently put forward in the Virginia and Kentucky Resolutions of 1798. These Resolutions were the strongest challenge issued in our entire history to the supremacy of the federal judiciary in interpreting the Constitution. By 1798, moreover, Jefferson had abandoned the views he expressed to Madison and become a more adamant and thoroughgoing opponent of judicial review. In any event, it is ironic and unjustified that current proponents of judicial supremacy find support by isolating from its full context Madison's depiction of the judiciary as an "impenetrable bulwark" for enforcing the Bill of Rights.

We need not wait until 1798 to confirm the full context of Madison's thinking about judicial review when he proposed these amendments. Just nine days later, on June 17, 1789, Madison spoke in the House of Representatives to argue that the Constitution vested sole authority in the President to remove executive officials from office, even if these officials had been subject to Senate confirmation. Madison concluded his speech by addressing the objection that the Congress must defer to the courts for the authoritative interpretation of legislative powers under the Constitution. Madison responded,

I acknowledge, in the ordinary course of government, that the exposition of the laws and constitution devolves upon the judicial. But, I beg to know, upon what principle it can be contended, that any one department draws from the constitution greater powers than another, in marking out the limits of the powers of the several departments. The constitution is the charter of the people to the government; it specifies certain great powers as absolutely granted, and marks out the departments to exercise them. If the constitutional boundary of either be brought into question, I do not see that any one of these independent departments has more right than another to declare their sentiments on that point.

Perhaps this is an omitted case. There is not one government on the face of the earth, so far as I recollect, there is not one in the United States, in which provision is made for a particular authority to determine the limits of the constitutional division of power between the branches of the government. In all systems there are points which must be adjusted by the departments themselves, to which no one of them is competent. If it cannot be determined in this way, there is no resource left but the will of the community, to be collected in some mode to be provided by the constitution, or one dictated by the necessity of the case.[91]

The tenor of Madison's remarks regarding judicial authority seems radically different between June 8 and June 17, 1789.[92] In these two contemporaneous speeches, I believe, Madison still had not crisply formulated his view of the judicial role in enforcing the Constitution. He anticipated his ultimate view, however, in the final sentence I quoted from his June 17 speech: that if no one governmental institution may finally determine the meaning of the Constitution, "there is no resource left but the will of the community, to be collected in some mode to be provided by the constitution, or one dictated by the necessity of the case." On the face of this remark, Madison might appear to refer primarily to the formal amendatory process in Article V of the Constitution as the preferred mode for "collect[ing] the will of the community." In succeeding decades, however, Madison developed a vision of extensive alternative means for discerning the "will of the community" in authoritatively construing the Constitution, as "dictated by the necessity of the case." In this vision, judicial interpretation played an important but not dispositive role. By exploring Madison's vision in some detail, we will see a role for the judiciary that is different from the conventional conception of judicial supremacy planted by Hamilton.

Madison's conception is not a truer version of the founders' intent than Hamilton's; it is, however, an equally plausible rendition which accentuates one side of the founders' initial ambivalence, just as Hamilton pressed on the other. My goal in recapturing the full dimensions of Madison's alternative conception is not to discern the founders' "true intentions." My goal is to identify an institutional structure which—unlike Hamilton's conception—can give practical realization to the egalitarian ideal that Madison himself ambivalently espoused, an ideal that found fullest expression in Lincoln's thought and example.

Madison's conception of the judicial role in constitutional interpretation was deduced from the premises that he set out in *Federalist* 51, premises that systematically addressed the underlying bases for the ambivalence toward judicial review that was evident in the work of the Philadelphia Convention. There is, however, no single text where Madison sets out a comprehensive statement of his jurisprudence, no equivalent for him of Hamilton's *Federalist* 78. This makes Madison's jurisprudence hard to read, a difficulty compounded by the fact that his important writings after the *Federalist* essays were all essentially reactions to some specific public controversy. Madison never responded to these events in an ad hoc fashion—he was always guided by a consistent set of overarching principles. But it is easy to misread him and to see inconsistency where he saw none.

Some historians thus maintain that at the outset of his career, Madison was a strong nationalist but that by 1800 he had changed his views to become a strong proponent of state's rights.[93] This characterization makes sense only in narrow political terms: the great disputes of the day pitted partisans of national and state power against one another, and Madison allied himself first with the protagonists on the nationalist side and then, in response to later events, with their antagonists on the state side. Nonetheless, a close reading of Madison's positions throughout reveals that his nationalism was always more modest and carefully qualified than that of his erstwhile early allies[94] and that this guarded nationalism persisted in his later advocacy for state prerogatives, when he was accordingly also more modest and carefully qualified than his firebrand latter-day allies.

Madison's moderation was, moreover, not simply temperamental but was a contextually sensitive application of the guiding principals that he had enunciated in *Federalist* 51. Wherever Madison saw the vortex of social power, he leaned against its force.[95] Thus, in 1787, state legislatures were the most active claimant, and Madison worked to check those claims. In the first decade of the new national government, assertions of executive predominance led him first to stand against Hamilton in the House of Representatives, most notably in opposing creation of the first Bank of the United States, and then in the Alien and Sedition Act controversy of 1798 to bolster state legislative authority in countering the Federalist Party's efforts to keep control of the national government. And near the end of his life, when the proponents of state sovereignty claimed authority to nullify federal acts and sought to rely on Madison's 1798 position, he refuted their reliance and reasserted his support for the prerogatives of the national government.

In all of this Madison applied the premise he had set out in *Federalist* 51, that the "great security" against abuse of power

> consists in giving to those who administer each [instrumentality of government] the necessary constitutional means and personal motives to resist encroachments of the others. . . . Ambition must be made to counteract ambition. The interest of the man must be connected with the constitutional rights of the place. . . . This policy of supplying, by opposite and rival interests, the defect of better motives, might be traced through the whole system of human affairs, private as well as public.[96]

Among the "necessary constitutional means" that Madison saw for this protective purpose was the authority to construe the meaning of the Constitution itself. To vest this authority in a single fixed locus, as Hamilton envisioned in *Federalist* 78, would defeat an essential aspect of Madison's vision.

This position creates an apparent paradox: there is only one constitutional document; if there are multiple authorized interpreters, each in fact strongly motivated to oppose the others, how is any determinate reading of this one document possible? Madison's answer rested on two related principles. His first principle was that constitutional interpretation takes place over time, not in a single instant at a fixed and privileged institutional locus of interpretive authority. His second principle was that the institutional competitors for interpretive authority must be linked together in an inextricably nested relationship, so that each would clearly see its interdependence with the others and all would accordingly work toward mutual accommodation.

This second principle was the basis for his rejection of the states-rights claim, during the Nullification Crisis of 1828–1830, that an individual state could authoritatively determine the constitutionality of congressional acts. This rejection led the nullifiers to accuse Madison of inconsistency (and even senility);[97] they asserted that Madison was betraying the position he took in 1798 when he drafted the Virginia Resolution declaring the unconstitutionality of the federally enacted Alien and Sedition laws.

The nullifiers were wrong, though their confusion was understandable. Two state legislatures had enacted resolutions in 1798, Kentucky and Virginia. The Kentucky Resolution was drafted by Jefferson and did indeed provide support for the states-rights nullifiers of 1828–1830; the Resolution recited that the Constitution was a compact entered by the states and that the national government was not "the exclusive or final judge" of its powers but that each state had a "right to judge for itself." On this premise, the Kentucky legislature declared that the Alien and Sedition Acts were "altogether void and of no force."[98]

Madison drafted the Virginia Resolution, which was enacted a month after Kentucky's; and Madison was much more cautious in his claims for state authority. The Virginia Resolution began by reciting, in apparent tandem with Kentucky, that "the powers of the federal government . . . result[ ] from the compact, to which the States are parties," and the State parties "have the right and are in duty bound, to interpose for arresting the progress of the evil" of an unconstitutional act. But unlike Jefferson's Kentucky Resolution, these premises did not lead the Virginia legislature to a unilateral declaration; the Virginia Resolution ended thus:

> The General Assembly doth solemnly appeal to the like dispositions of the other States, in confidence that they will concur with this Commonwealth in declaring, as it does hereby declare, that the [Alien and Sedition Acts] are unconstitutional, and that the necessary and proper measures will be taken by each, for cooperating with this State, in maintaining the Authorities, Rights and Liberties, reserved to the States respectively, or to the People.[99]

The legislatures of Delaware and six New England states responded critically to these resolutions, maintaining that the federal judiciary alone had authority to determine the constitutionality of congressional acts.[100] The Kentucky legislature then responded, in a resolution again drafted by Jefferson, that since the states "who formed the Constitution" were "sovereign and independent," they had an "unquestionable right to judge" infractions and "*a nullification by those sovereignties . . . is the rightful remedy.*"[101] By contrast, Madison wrote a lengthy report, adopted by the Virginia legislature in 1800, that made no claims to state sovereignty or independence but instead characterized the declaration of unconstitutionality in its original resolution as "expressions of opinion, unaccompanied with any other effect, than what they may produce on [others'] opinion, by exciting reflection."[102]

Though the overheated politics of 1798 may have blurred contemporaries' vision, a careful reader would have seen clear differences between the Kentucky and Virginia Resolutions and (when the secret of their authorship was much later exposed) between Jefferson and Madison. These differences arose, moreover, from more than a dispute about the authentic derivation of the Constitution, whether from the people standing apart from or within the states. From Madison's perspective there was a functional concern about governance structure that lay beneath, and was the moving force for, resolving this question of constitutional cosmology. Madison clearly stated this functional concern in a letter to Jefferson in 1823:

> A paramount, or even a definitive, authority in the individual States [to invalidate congressional acts] would soon make the Constitution and laws different in different States, and thus destroy that equality and uniformity of rights and duties which form the essence of the compact. . . . To leave conflicting decisions to be settled between the [federal and state judiciaries] could not promise a happy result. The end must be a trial of strength between the posse headed by the marshal and the posse headed by the sheriff.

Madison then identified the critical difference between federal–state relations, which required a unitary arbiter in the federal judiciary, and relations among the branches of the federal government, where such arbiter would be inappropriate:

> Nor would the issue be safe if left to a compromise between the two Governments [federal and state]: the case of a disagreement between different Governments being essentially different from a disagreement between branches of the same Government. In the latter case neither party being able to consummate its will without the concurrence of the other, there is a necessity on both to consult and to accommodate. Not so with different Governments, each possessing every branch of power necessary to carry its purpose into compleat effect. It here becomes a question between Independent Nations, with no other *dernier* result than physical force. Negotiation might, indeed, in some instances, avoid this extremity; but how often would it happen, among so many States, that an unaccommodating spirit in some would render that resource unavailing?[103]

Madison's functional concern here would have led him not simply to the conclusion that a unitary arbiter for federal interbranch conflict would be unnecessary but that it would be undesirable. A unitary interbranch arbiter would have no motive "to consult and to accommodate" the other branches and, in the very assertion of sovereign authority over the others, would likely provoke pitched battle, the warfare between rival posses that he colorfully envisioned as the consequence of Jefferson's views. By contrast, in Madison's view, the existence of a unitary arbiter in federal–state conflicts was desirable not because it ensured federal supremacy but precisely because it fostered motives of consultation and accommodation between both the state and federal antagonists.

Madison's explanatory Report on the Virginia Resolution made this paradoxical claim: because the state of Virginia was not constitutionally authorized to act alone against the Alien and Sedition Acts, it was forced to solicit the support of other state legislatures; and "if the other states had concurred in making a like declaration . . . it can scarcely be doubted" that the federal government would be moved to an accommodation.[104] After all, he observed, the state legislatures were "the immediate constituents of one of [the] branches" of the Congress;[105] and even judicial opinion might be directly swayed by this expression of state legislative opinion since, as he explicitly noted in his later letter to Jefferson, "the Senate, chosen by the State Legislatures, [must concur] in appointing the Judges."[106] By Madison's lights, moreover, the President would also likely be swayed by the massed sentiment of state legislatures since they dictate the means for choosing presidential electors, and in 1798 these electors were directly chosen by legislatures in all but two states.[107]

Thus, as Madison saw it, the supremacy of the federal judiciary over the acts of individual state legislatures did not create a unitary sovereign with hierarchically superior authority over states considered as a group. If some federal act infringed state prerogatives sufficiently to provoke united, or even majority, action among the states, the intertwined character of the federal and state governments would virtually guarantee that effective "consultation and accommodation" would occur. This is the assurance that Madison gave in 1821 to Judge Spencer Roane of Virginia, an adamant opponent of federal judicial supremacy: "such a trust [to invalidate individual state laws] vested in the government representing the whole [nation], and exercised by its [judicial] tribunal . . . would be controllable by the States, who directly or indirectly appoint the trustees."[108] By contrast, giving final interpretative authority to individual state legislatures would denominate a unitary sovereign with clear authority over all other institutional actors in the constitutional scheme. This status as the single authoritative interpreter of the Constitution was for Madison as much an anathema if vested in individual states (as Jefferson proposed in 1798 and the nullifiers reiterated in 1828) as it was if vested in the United States Supreme Court (as Hamilton proposed in *Federalist* 78).

Madison thus depicted a complex scheme: the federal judiciary was supreme as against the states but was only co-equal as against the other branches of the federal government, which meant that the other branches could effectively contest judicial constructions of the Constitution, when prompted to do so by state remonstrances. This intrabranch contest would be constrained, however, by a spirit of consultation and accommodation because, as Madison observed to Jefferson, none of the federal branches would be "able to consummate its will without the concurrence of the other."

This is the practical application of the premises Madison articulated in *Federalist* 51: that sovereignty should not be unitary but divided and subdivided so that ultimate governance authority would be dispersed and shared.

Madison's own position, first as a member of Congress and then as President, regarding the constitutionality of the Bank of the United States provides an illustration of the process of consultation and deliberation that he envisioned in such interpretative disputes. Madison opposed the first Bank bill when it was proposed in the House of Representatives in 1791; he argued that there was no express constitutional authority for Congress to grant charters and that the construction of implied authority necessary to support the Bank bill would "go to the subversion of every power whatever in the several States."[109] The bill was enacted over his objections, and the Bank operated for the next twenty years, with annual recognition of its existence from the Congress. This subsequently meant for Madison that the Bank had obtained "the uniform sanction of successive legislative bodies, through a period of years under the varied ascendancy of parties." Moreover, during this time, the Bank's operations had been extended into new states and generally had received "the entire acquiescence of all the local authorities."[110] The Bank's charter was not renewed in 1811, but Congress approved a second Bank after the financial dislocations of the 1812 War. Madison, now President, concluded that his earlier constitutional objections had been "precluded . . . by repeated recognitions under varied circumstances of the validity of such an institution . . . accompanied by indications, in different modes, of a concurrence of the general will of the nation."[111]

No fixed formula for adjudicating constitutional disputes can be drawn from this illustration: no requisite numbers of separate institutional approbations multiplied by time elapsed. The closest encapsulation of Madison's thinking on this score might be the Supreme Court's formulation in *Brown v. Board of Education*: that various institutional actors had considered the constitutional issues in various modes "with all deliberate speed." (My own reckoning in the first chapter that the Court's 1954 construction of the Constitution in *Brown* became clearly accepted law with the enactment of the Civil Rights Act of 1968 closely enough tracks

Madison's account of the twenty-year deliberation on the Bank issue.) The formulation of positivist rules by which the law of the Constitution might be authoritatively identified at some predictable fixed moment was not Madison's enterprise. He was concerned with designing techniques of governance that could adequately address polarized factional conflict—not only in social relations generally but also as such conflicts were refracted through disputes about the meaning of the Constitution. Successful "accommodation and consultation" in such fractious matters adheres to no single unyielding organizational or time chart.

The touchstone for Madison's governance technique, as revealed in this microcosm of the Bank controversy, was the pursuit of unanimity among governmental actors (but not directly among the populace at large)[112] in institutions whose interlocking authority and overlapping constituencies would tend to promote accommodation rather than fixed confrontation. Madison always viewed the Supreme Court as an important participant in this pursuit; toward the end of his life he was more enthusiastic about the Court's contributions than at earlier times.[113] But he never wavered from his position that the Court was "co-ordinate" with rather than hierarchically superior to the other federal branches in interpreting the Constitution.[114]

Hamilton's view of judicial superiority was also an attempt to address polarized factional conflict and to secure unanimity by providing clear governance mechanisms for conclusive termination of conflict—or, as he vividly put it in *Federalist* 9, "to repress domestic faction and insurrection."[115] Hamilton's conjunctive rendering of partisan conflict as faction and insurrection was the motive force for his central role in securing passage of the Sedition Act of 1798, which criminally punished "defamatory" criticism of the Government.[116] Madison had a markedly different attitude toward social conflict. As he stated in *Federalist* 10, "the latent causes of faction are . . . sown in the nature of man," and "it is in vain to say enlightened statesmen will be able to adjust these clashing interests and render them all subservient to the public good."[117] And in *Federalist* 51, he stated that although factional oppression by a majority might be checked "by creating a will in the community independent . . . of the society itself," this would be "but a precarious security," since this power could itself readily be abused.[118] Thus, Madison sought to divide and diffuse sovereign authority, while Hamilton worked to consolidate it; thus, Madison opposed vesting the Supreme Court with final constitutional interpretive authority, while Hamilton embraced this.

Their differences in principle are clear; the practical consequences of these differences are less clear. But if ideas guide conduct, then Hamilton's conception of sovereignty led directly to the outbreak of the American Civil War. The proposition that every government must have one supreme sovereign was common ground between North and South; and on this ground the Union split, because each side asserted a unitary but mutually inconsistent locus of sovereignty. These terms of war were, moreover, already clearly established in the dispute over the constitutionality of the Sedition Act. Jefferson astutely observed, in his Kentucky resolution, that the claim for national supremacy implicit in the Act would "tend to drive the States into revolution and blood, and will furnish . . . new pretexts for those who wish it to be believed, that man cannot be governed but by a rod of iron." Jefferson did not clearly see, however, that his counter-claim for state sovereignty rested on a claim for unitary supremacy that carried the same implications and ultimate consequences.

Madison understood this at the time. But most of Madison's contemporaries in the founding generation could hardly imagine a world without a unitary ruling sovereign. By 1830 this imaginative possibility had vanished for virtually all Americans, a social fact revealed by the eruption of the Nullification Crisis, the "rehearsal for disunion." Madison, the last survivor of the Philadelphia Convention, saw this and despaired.[119]

The confidence of the Supreme Court in claiming the Hamiltonian role of final authoritative expositor of the Constitution also grew in these later years. The intellectual links between the growth of this judicial authority and the outbreak of Civil War are more tenuous than for the general conception of political sovereignty; but some linkage can be seen. In the application of this authoritarian role, the Supreme Court certainly exacerbated sectional conflicts—not only in its infamous *Dred Scott* decision but in others, as Chapters 4 and 5 will recount. Though the specific holding of *Dred Scott* was overturned by the War, as Chapter 6 will tell, the underlying claim for judicial supremacy was ironically ratified by the Civil War amendments, which represented an untrammeled embrace of the Hobbesian sovereign, impelled by the trauma of battle.

Throughout these events, Madison's jurisprudence was eclipsed, misunderstood by his contemporaries and hidden from us, his posterity. Eclipsed but not lost—because his jurisprudence was embedded in the interlocking, mutually interdependent structure of our governance institutions he had designed. Madison's jurisprudence still occasionally appears in the work of the Supreme Court, though unacknowledged as such. It usually emerges in the best of times, only to be resubmerged in the worst.

3

Lincoln's Egalitarian Answer

ABRAHAM LINCOLN, more than any other leader in American political history, joined a visionary commitment to universal equality with painstaking attention to the practical techniques of statescraft in order to approach this ideal. Madison had envisaged an egalitarian structure of governance, but one that applied only to relations among a narrow band of men who would effectively rule others. For these happy few, the scheme that Madison devised in 1787 and embellished throughout his long life was based on mutually acknowledged equal status in principle and in practice. He did not see, however, how this scheme could be generalized for all political relations and did not strive toward this end, even though he privately acknowledged the injustice of all impositions of unequal status. Lincoln, by contrast, was committed to a universal equality; and the very depth of his commitment led him to confront difficulties in its attainment that Madison had only glimpsed from a distance.

The central effort in Lincoln's career was to contain, and to aim toward the elimination of, black slavery without subjugating the white slaveholders. Lincoln failed in this effort. But in the struggle itself, he provided a model for the role of political authority generally, and of judicial authority specifically, in combating majoritarian tyranny. Taking the two men together, we might find a guide toward reaching Lincoln's visionary egalitarian ideal through the institutional means that Madison designed.

There is a special difficulty, however, in reconstructing Lincoln's political thought. He is, in an odd way, less accessible to us than Madison. This is not because Madison was more systematic than

Lincoln, either in his thinking or his exposition. The most extensive source for Madison's thought, the *Federalist Papers,* were, like the basic source for Lincoln in his debates with Stephen Douglas, campaign documents, not treatises on political philosophy. The full dimensions of Madison's thought cannot be apprehended from this initial source but must be traced through his later state papers and private correspondence as he developed and refined the implications of his premises in the *Federalist Papers.* So too for Lincoln, as he tested in office the basic premises that he had enunciated in his quest for popular approval.

The real difficulty in understanding Lincoln is that he seems more familiar to us than Madison. Lincoln looms in our imagination as a popular icon, while Madison's image, notwithstanding his sobriquet as "father of the Constitution," is so indistinct that our few preconceptions about him can be readily stripped away. Indeed, Madison's importance in drafting the Constitution had almost disappeared even from scholarly attention until after World War II, when his reputation was revived, most notably in the work of Douglass Adair.*

The comparative advantage over Lincoln that Madison obtained from his long eclipse can be seen in the work of Richard Hofstadter. In 1969, Hofstadter described Madison as "the philosopher of the Constitution," as "a more systematic . . . more deliberate and profound thinker" than Jefferson and, by extension, than any among the founding generation.[1] In 1948, however, when he published his most widely read book, *The American Political Tradition and the Men who Made It,* Hofstadter virtually ignored Madison.** Lincoln was not so fortunate; Hofstadter devoted a full chapter in that book to unmasking his popular reputation as the Great Emancipator.

---

*Until publication of Adair's essay, "The Authorship of the Disputed Federalist Papers," 1 *Wm. & Mary Q.* 97 (1944), dominant scholarly opinion had awarded all of the disputed papers to Hamilton notwithstanding, as Adair adroitly demonstrated, the implausibility of these claims.

**Of the twelve chapters in this book, ten were dedicated to specific men—including Jefferson, Jackson, Calhoun, and Wendell Phillips; Madison was briefly mentioned only in the cursory opening chapter on the Founding Fathers generally and as a tagalong in the chapter on Jefferson.

Thus Hofstadter eviscerated the Emancipation Proclamation itself:

> It contained no indictment of slavery, but simply based emancipation on "military necessity." It expressly omitted the loyal slave states from its terms. Finally, it did not in fact free any slaves. For it excluded by detailed enumeration from the sphere covered in the Proclamation all the counties in Virginia and parishes in Louisiana that were occupied by Union troops and into which the government actually had the power to bring freedom. It simply declared free all slaves in "the States and parts of States" where the people were in rebellion—that is to say, precisely where its effect could not reach.[2]

The Proclamation, Hofstadter concluded, "had all the moral grandeur of a bill of lading."[3]

Hofstadter also called attention to a passage in Lincoln's first inaugural address that was even more inconsistent with the popular image. Just two days before Lincoln's inauguration, in an effort to avert secession, Congress had passed a proposed constitutional amendment that not only protected the existing institution of slavery but specified that this amendment was perpetually irrevocable; if it had been ratified, this ironically would have been the Thirteenth Amendment.[4] Hofstadter stated:

> In his Inaugural Address Lincoln repeated with pathetic vehemence his several earlier assurances that slavery would not be attacked in the states. He went further. . . . Although it was no part of his constitutional function, Lincoln did what he could to speed the *proposed* amendment toward ratification by announcing that he considered it only an explicit statement of what was already implicit in the Constitution—"I have no objection to its being made express and irrevocable."[5]

Hofstadter also pointed to other statements customarily omitted from the Lincoln canon—his "pathetic" idea of black colonization,[6] his opposition to "social and political equality" for blacks as proclaimed in his debates with Douglas.[7] "It is impossible to avoid the conclusion," Hofstadter said, "that so far as the Negro was concerned, Lincoln could not escape the moral insensitivity that is characteristic of the average white American."[8]

The debunking spirit behind Hofstadter's account unfortunately obstructed his capacity to gauge Lincoln's full measure. One hint of these broader dimensions briefly emerged in an additional inconsistency that Hofstadter identified: "There was," he observed, "a tremendous incongruity in Lincoln as a war leader. He did not want war; he wanted Union, and accepted war only when it seemed necessary to the Union. He had always been preeminently a man of peace."[9] This "incongruity" was indeed at the heart of Lincoln's political thought: not only the man of peace who waged war but the advocate for political freedom who imposed an involuntary bondage on southern rebels, the apostle of equality who subjugated the secessionists. These were authentic tensions in Lincoln's thinking, and they were linked to the inconsistencies in his actions regarding slavery. But these tensions were not evidence of Lincoln's "moral insensitivity," contrary to Hofstadter's charges or to the harsher revisionist account of Lincoln and of the supposed "needlessness" of the Civil War that had become dominant by the beginning of this century.

The pervasive contradictions in Lincoln's thought and actions have misled, moreover, even fundamentally sympathetic observers. Alexander Bickel, for one, saw these inconsistencies and he applauded them; indeed, he placed what he called "the Lincolnian tension" at the ideological center of his own jurisprudence in *The Least Dangerous Branch*.[10] But Bickel misconceived the nature of the tension in Lincoln's thought: it was, he said, a "tension between principle and expediency."[11] This is incorrect. The Lincolnian tension exists within the principle of democratic self-governance itself—whether that principle is defined as "equality" in Lincoln's terms, as "liberty" in the secessionists' vocabulary, or as "republican community" in the current version of the founders' conception.

Bickel's account implies a hierarchical moral ordering and thus reinforces rather than refutes Hofstadter's debunking enterprise—that Lincoln regularly (and pathetically) succumbed to "expediency" and thus abandoned "principle." This depiction virtually invited the critical jibe that Bickel's own jurisprudence was "100% insistence on principle, 20% of the time" and was accordingly incoherent.[12] Bickel's account, moreover, betrayed the impetus in his own thinking that led him in his later work to temper his enthusiasm for *Brown,* at least as a precedent for the exercise of judicial authority, because "principle" appeared to be a more reliable guide than "expediency." Bickel thus ultimately missed the central lesson of Lincoln's tension: that the principle of democracy contains an inherent contradiction between the concepts of equal self-determination and majority rule and can therefore provide no univocal guidance for the resolution of social conflict or even for determining which institutions should address it.

Lincoln's own account of his political thought occasionally obscured this central contradiction. Most notably, in his first inaugural address, he appeared to demand ultimate deference to majority rule: "Unanimity is impossible; the rule of a minority, as a permanent arrangement, is wholly inadmissable; so that, rejecting the majority principle, anarchy or despotism in some form is all that is left."[13] Bickel followed the same reasoning to his conclusion that because "judicial review is a counter-majoritarian force in our system," it is a "deviant institution in the American democracy."[14] But Lincoln was more fundamentally at odds with the majority-rule principle than this passage from his first inaugural suggests. His invocation of majoritarianism was one aspect of his appeal against the course of secession; but even in this context it was neither the only nor the most important basis for his appeal to avert "anarchy or despotism."

The core of Lincoln's opposition to majority rule was expressed in his Illinois senatorial election debates with Stephen Douglas. Lincoln unequivocally rejected the claim that majority rule (or "popular sovereignty," as Douglas put it) should determine whether slavery might exist in the territories. In his 1854 Peoria address, which anticipated the later face-to-face debates and was the most comprehensive statement of his opposition to Douglas, Lincoln stated,

> The doctrine of self-government is right—absolutely and eternally right, but it has no just application, as here attempted. Or perhaps I should say that whether it has such application depends upon whether the negro is not or is a man. If he is not a man, why in that case, he who is a man may, as a matter of self-government, do just as he pleases with him. But if the negro is a man, is it not to that extent a total destruction of self-government, to say that he too shall not govern himself? When the

white man governs himself that is self-government; but when he governs himself and also governs another man, that is more than self-government—that is despotism. If the negro is a man, why then my ancient faith teaches me that "all men are created equal;" and that there can be no moral right in connection with one man's making a slave of another.

Judge Douglas frequently, with bitter irony and sarcasm, paraphrases our argument by saying: "The white people of Nebraska are good enough to govern themselves, but they are not good enough to govern a few miserable negroes!!"

Well I doubt not that the people of Nebraska are, and will continue to be as good as the average of people elsewhere. I do not say the contrary. What I do say is, that no man is good enough to govern another man, without that other's consent. I say this is the leading principle—the sheet anchor of American republicanism.[15]

This is no brief for majority rule, except in those limited circumstances where one man might consent to acquiesce in others' wishes; and the hallmark for such limited consent must be others' commitment to acquiesce in his wishes for different matters or at different times.[16] There is, however, a suggestion of anarchy in this prescription, a connotation of unbridled individualism at odds with sustained communal attachments.

From the outset of his political life, Lincoln was aware of and apprehensive about these implications. In his first significant address, to the Springfield Lyceum in 1838, Lincoln warned of threats from two directions that could destroy "the attachment of the people" and "alienat[e] their affections from the government." One threat was the "mobocratic spirit which all must admit is now abroad in the land"[17]—a distortion of popular sovereignty, one might say, in which vigilante mobs dispense their own justice. The second threat arose from the possibility of a new "Alexander, a Caesar, or a Napolean . . . some man possessed of the loftiest genius, coupled with ambition sufficient to push it to its utmost stretch, [who] will at some time spring up among us"[18]—a distortion of individualism, one might say. To counter these twin threats, Lincoln offered an "answer [which] is simple . . . Let reverence for the laws be breathed by every American mother . . . Let it become the political religion of the nation; and let [everyone] sacrifice unceasingly upon its altars."[19]

A direct connection can be traced from this 1838 address to Lincoln's confrontation in 1861 with "the essence of anarchy" that he discerned as "the central idea of secession."[20] In his inaugural address, Lincoln also searched for ways to strengthen "the attachment of the people" and to remedy "the alienation of their affections from the government." He ended his inaugural address with a similar spiritual invocation: "The mystic chords of memory, stretching from every battle-field and patriot grave to every living heart and hearthstone all over this broad land, will yet swell the chorus of the Union when again touched, as surely they will be, by the better angels of our nature."[21]

But Lincoln also offered a more secular rationale to underwrite the "political religion" he invoked in 1861. To the seceding Southerners, he insisted that, as a practical matter, it was impossible for them to sever political relations with the rest of the Union:

> Physically speaking, we cannot separate. We cannot remove our respective sections from each other, nor build an impassable wall between them. A husband and wife may be divorced and go out of the presence and beyond the reach of each other; but the different parts of our country cannot do this. They cannot but remain face to face, and intercourse, either amicable or hostile, must continue between them. Is it possible, then, to make that intercourse more advantageous or more satisfactory after separation than before? Can aliens make treaties easier than friends can make laws? Can treaties be more faithfully enforced between aliens than laws can among friends? Suppose you go to war, you cannot fight always; and when, after much loss on both sides, and no gain on either, you cease fighting, the identical old questions as to terms of intercourse are again upon you.[22]

Four months later, when secession and civil war were accomplished facts and he was justifying his unilateral enforcement actions to Congress, Lincoln added another argument for the impossibility of severing political ties—not a practical but a moral impossibility:

> The nation purchased with money the countries out of which several of these [seceding] States were formed. Is it just that they shall go off without leave and without refunding? The nation paid very large sums (in the aggregate, I believe, nearly a hundred millions) to relieve Florida of the aboriginal tribes. Is

it just that she shall now be off without consent or without making any return? The nation is now in debt for money applied to the benefit of these so-called seceding States in common with the rest. Is it just either that creditors shall go unpaid or the remaining States pay the whole? A part of the present national debt was contracted to pay the old debts of Texas. Is it just that she shall leave and pay no part of this herself?

Again, if one State may secede, so may another; and when all shall have seceded, none is left to pay the debts. Is this quite just for creditors? Did we notify them of this sage view of ours when we borrowed their money? If we not recognize this doctrine by allowing the seceders to go in peace, it is difficult to see what we can do if others choose to go or to extort terms upon which they will promise to remain.[23]

There are, then, three arguments that Lincoln set out to oppose the disintegrative consequences not simply of secession but of his own insistence on the individual consensual basis of political relations. These arguments, moreover, can be read in the varying vocabularies of republican community, liberty, and equality. For community, Lincoln reverentially invokes common memories of battlefields and patriot graves. For liberty he insists that no one is in practical fact free to disengage from others. And for equality, Lincoln cites indivisibly shared past burdens. The central premise underlying all of these arguments is to acknowledge mutual respect as the bond that not only joins but gives reliable political content to the virtues of community, liberty, or equality, and to understand that without mutuality, "anarchy or despotism in some form is all that is left."

Of these three vocabularies, Lincoln clearly preferred the language of equality. The "central idea" of the American republic, he said, is not "that 'all States as States are equal' nor yet that 'all citizens as citizens are equal,' but . . . the broader, better declaration, including both these and much more, that 'all *men* are created equal.' "[24] Among the many reasons that we today should also share this preference, equality conveys—as liberty does not—that no social value exists as an abstraction apart from its specific realization in a political relationship. And equality necessarily denotes—as community does not—that mutual consent is the only proper basis for communal relations.

This concordance between equality and mutual consent was also central to Lincoln's thinking. As he stated in Peoria, "No man is good enough to govern another man, without that other's consent. I say this is the leading principle—the sheet anchor of American republicanism." It was this concordance, however, that forced Lincoln to equivocate in his attitudes toward blacks—not necessarily because he shared, as Hofstadter charged, "the moral insensitivity that is characteristic of the average white American" but because the consent principle demanded that he work from within the perspective of average moral sensibilities. Hofstadter's specific accusation was that "Lincoln could not escape the moral insensitivity"; but Lincoln would say that he must not escape it, that he must persuade others to come with him or be guilty of despotism in the imagined service of equality.[25]

Lincoln never retreated from his dedication to persuasion and his aversion to coercive imposition, even while presiding over this country's most destructive war. This is a considerable paradox; but it follows from the paradoxical implications of Lincoln's commitment to equality and mutual consent in all political relations. This commitment excludes all coercion, except as a defensive response to others' unilateral use of force. This response, moreover, can hold true to the principle of equality and mutuality if the defensive coercion is aimed not at the subjugation of the original aggressor but only at the restoration of an equal, mutually consensual relationship. This finely calibrated response is exceedingly difficult to put into practice, especially when the aggressor adamantly insists that his goal is subjugation rather than equality. But this calibration is the only way that coercion can be justified within the democratic ethos. The true measure of Lincoln's stature, as a statesman and political thinker, was the rigorous consistency of his efforts to achieve this goal even as commander-in-chief of the Union army.

As Lincoln saw it, the North's use of force in the Civil War was justified because the South's secession was a unilaterally imposed aggression inconsistent with the prior, mutually acknowledged relationship of equality within the Union. Secession was not, however, the first aggressive act. The breach began for Lincoln with the southern states' insistence that slavery be extended to the territories. His view of the aggressive implications of secession was shaped by this immediate context.

Lincoln had not been an abolitionist; he had not insisted on ending slavery in the South or on repealing the Missouri Compromise so as to ban slavery from all future territories. He viewed both southern slavery and the Missouri Compromise as existing arrangements in the world as he found it. Though he might disapprove of these arrangements, he acknowledged that others endorsed them; and his conjunctive commitments to equality and consent required him to acquiesce in these existing arrangements unless they could be altered on the basis of mutual consent.[26] At the same time, however, Lincoln insisted that the proponents of slavery must honor, in their dealings with him, the same principle of equality and mutual consent that led him to acquiesce in their claims. This meant that black slavery must not be extended beyond the existing arrangements—specifically, into territories north of the Missouri Compromise line—without *his* consent; that is, majority rule, either in the territories or in Congress, was not an acceptable basis for this extension.

This was, of course, an impossibly demanding condition which not only doomed any imaginable extension scheme but, more fundamentally, seemed inconsistent with the general workings of majority rule in a democracy. This was the basis for Douglas's criticism of Lincoln's position. But Lincoln responded that American democracy rested on equality, not on majority rule as such; that, although the very existence of slavery was inconsistent with this principle, it was not endorsed but merely tolerated by the founders;[27] and that, if slavery were now extended beyond prior limits, this would constitute an axiomatic break with the founding premise that equality was the norm and slavery was a disfavored exception.[28]

Lincoln insisted, moreover, that the enslavement of blacks as such was not at the core of his concern, but that the extension of black slavery would signify the fundamental reversal of priorities not only for blacks but for all political relations.[29] This was the underlying meaning of the famous passage in his 1858 "House Divided" speech:

> I believe this government cannot endure, permanently half slave and half free. I do not expect the Union to be dissolved—I do not expect the House to fall—but I do expect it to cease to be divided. It will become all one thing or all the other. Either the

> opponents of slavery will arrest the further spread of it, and place it where the public mind shall rest in the belief that it is in the course of ultimate extinction; or its advocates will push it forward, till it shall become alike lawful in all the States, old as well as new, North as well as South.[30]

This assertion that the entire Union must eventually "become all one thing or all the other" alluded to the expansive, and ultimately universal, significance of slavery as a style of political authority that could not be confined to blacks alone. Lincoln brought this allusion into full light in December 1862, at the end of his message to Congress explaining the underlying goal of the Emancipation Proclamation he was about to issue: "In giving freedom to the slave, we assure freedom to the free."[31]

In his "House Divided" speech Lincoln did not intend to endorse action to abolish slavery throughout the Union, any more than he advocated its general extension. He wanted only to maintain the clear commitment that he saw in the Declaration of Independence to the equality principle—not only thereby to proclaim the injustice of black slavery and incline public "belief . . . in the course of [its] ultimate extinction" but more immediately to signal that slavery was a disfavored exception in American political relations and thereby to reinforce the proposition that equality was the universal ideal.

Many Southerners misread Lincoln's purposes, however, and construed this speech, and the Republican party platform generally, as the harbinger of an aggressive attack on slavery in the South. Lincoln's assurance in his first inaugural address that he did not intend to interfere with the existing slavery institution was "pathetic"; but contrary to Hofstadter's reading, the pathos was in the Southerners' incapacity to understand the principled basis of that assurance and to reconsider the course of secession that made civil war inevitable. Lincoln offered this assurance to demonstrate that he honored the southern whites' claims to equality just as he expected them to respect his claims. And this commitment to mutuality dictated that he would take no unilateral subjugative act against them so long as they would desist from aggression against him, as represented by the unconsented extension of slavery into the territories. The southern secessionists would not accept Lincoln's assurance, however; and they resolved to withdraw from the Union because he had refused to acquiesce in their demands for the extension and acknowledged legitimation of slavery.

Southern secession was, accordingly, an escalated act of aggression. Many Northerners construed secession as an attack against the Union as such; but Lincoln did not see it in this abstractly reified mode. From his perspective, secession was an assault against the political relationship of equality and mutuality that the Union comprehended. Secession, that is, was as much a breach of the prior commitments to mutual respect for equal status embodied in the Union as was the initial southern demand for the territorial expansion of slavery. Secession was an illegitimate weapon in political conflict among equals, as much as coerced impositions.

These propositions were at the core of Lincoln's admonition in his inaugural address that if one party to a political dispute "will secede rather than acquiesce, they make a precedent which in turn will divide and ruin them." This precedent would, moreover, not only divide and ruin the southern Confederacy; it would also ruin the remaining Union by destroying the integrity of the institutional processes that had previously constrained political conflict within the framework of a commitment to equality and mutuality. This is the reason why Lincoln concluded that the South's demand for extension and legitimation of slavery, coupled with their threat to secede, imposed an unacceptable alternative on the North of bowing "to anarchy or to despotism." This was the reason why, as Lincoln saw it, he was obliged to defend the integrity of the Union against this aggressive act.

In order to constrain coercion within the democratic ethos, it is not enough, however, for a warrior to insist or to believe that his adversaries are the aggressors and he is merely defending himself. Even if sincerely believed, this defensive claim is as readily invoked on both sides as the conviction that each adversary in a polarized dispute seeks oppressive enslavement of one another. The hallmark of the democratic use of coercion is not simply in its invocation as a defensive response to aggressive provocation; once invoked, the coercion must also remain rigorously confined to defensive goals. The democratic defendant, that is, must avoid any effort to destroy his adversaries; he must aim only at achieving effective stalemate, a mutual acknowledgment that neither they nor he is entitled to coercive impositions.

This was Lincoln's aim throughout the War—not to subjugate the South but to restore the Union as a political relationship among equals. Thus, he stated in his annual message to Congress in December 1861, "I have been anxious and careful [that the war] shall not degenerate into a violent and remorseless revolutionary struggle."[32] And in August 1862 he wrote an open letter, responding to Horace Greeley's editorial urging immediate emancipation, "If I could save the Union without freeing *any* slave I would do it, and if I could save it by freeing *all* the slaves I would do it; and if I could save it by freeing some and leaving others alone, I would also do that."[33]

There was undoubtedly some narrow political calculation in Lincoln's ostentatious hesitancy regarding emancipation; unionism was much more popular than abolitionism in the North. As the war persisted, abolitionism became more acceptable when many Northerners redefined its purpose as a measure not to help blacks but to punish white Southerners; but Lincoln still held back. In March 1862, he asked Congress to offer "pecuniary aid [to] any state which may adopt gradual abolishment of slavery," still hoping to induce consensual emancipation. In May 1862, the commander of Union forces occupying islands off the South Carolina and Georgia coasts issued a sweeping declaration of martial law abolishing slavery in those states; Lincoln immediately revoked the order and repeated his offer to slaveholders. Compensated, gradual emancipation, he said, "would come gently as the dews of heaven, not rending or wrecking anything. Will you not embrace it?" He then added this ominous warning, "You can not if you would, be blind to the signs of the times"; he had already pointed to these signs in his March message to Congress, that unless slaveholders agreed to his offer, "it is impossible to foresee all the incidents which may attend and all the ruin which may follow."[34]

In all of these messages, Lincoln was speaking to and attempting to appease many audiences: abolitionists and their increasingly adamant allies among Republican officeholders; Northern public opinion, generally wary of abolitionism, and increasingly weary of and vengefully retaliatory for war sacrifices; and Southerners who might be wavering between unionist and secessionist sentiment. Lincoln's hesitancy and the ambiguity of his statements about emancipation can be readily characterized as the calculations of a cautious self-serving politician. But even if Lincoln were completely comprehended by this characterization, his effort to harness others' self-interest in his own service would still represent something of a triumph for Madison's original goal: that the structure of our political institutions should rely on aggregated selfish ambition as the building-blocks for public virtue. Lincoln was certainly ambitious; he was, however, not only ambitious on his own account but also in the service of the democratic ideal that all men, sinners as well as saints, should be treated as equals. His Emancipation Proclamation, freeing some slaves and leaving others alone as he had anticipated in his letter to Greeley, was much more than a bill of lading. In this document, Lincoln was still appealing to the possibility of voluntary reconciliation; he was still struggling to constrain "all the incidents which may attend and all the ruin which may follow" from the escalating impulses toward retaliatory vengeance on both sides; he was still trying to demonstrate—as he said on the Gettysburg battlefield nine months later—that a nation "dedicated to the proposition that *all* men are created equal . . . can long endure." There surely is moral grandeur in this endeavor.

Even at the very moment that the war began, Lincoln displayed his aversion to coercion and his insistent pursuit of mutuality. When the secessionist government of South Carolina blockaded and demanded the evacuation of Fort Sumter, Lincoln resolved to resupply the fort only with food, and publicly promised that he would make "no effort to throw in men, arms, or ammunition." This decision was in one sense a brilliant tactical maneuver, as James McPherson has observed, in forcing the secessionists either to take the first aggressive act by firing on "unarmed boats carrying 'food for hungry men'" or to acquiesce in the permanent presence of a Union fort in the Charleston harbor, thus awarding an "important symbolic victory" to the North.[35] More fundamentally, however, Lincoln's decision was part of his effort to avert war, not to provoke it or to claim "victory" in the opening salvos.[36] Lincoln was not prepared to accept defeat; thus he refused to surrender the fort. If he had resolved to arm the fort or to send warships to reinforce it, this would have signaled his intention to apply force against the secessionist government and, even in some limited sense, to impose his will on it. Lincoln's decision to send only unarmed boats carrying food indicated instead that he sought stalemate and invited a reciprocal renunciation of force. His only demand was for acknowledged equality, not for surrender.

Throughout the war, Lincoln never lost sight of his initial understanding that nothing more than stalemate could or should be achieved. As he said in his first inaugural, "When, after much loss on both sides, and no gain on either, you cease fighting, the identical old questions as to terms of intercourse are again upon you." Stalemate meant, however, that Lincoln would not surrender to the secessionist imposition of "anarchy or depotism"; and because the secessionists defined their war aims in terms that permitted no reconciliation, the war continuously escalated in destructive intensity.

The Emancipation Proclamation, when it was issued in January 1863, did not in itself signal a transformation in Lincoln's own war goals. Lincoln himself privately acknowledged that the Proclamation would change "the character of the war" to become "one of subjugation" by which the "South is to be destroyed and replaced by new propositions and ideas."[37] He continued to insist, however, that this was not his goal, that he freed slaves only to "weaken the rebels by drawing off their laborers" and to forestall European assistance to the South.[38] Lincoln told his Cabinet that emancipation was "a military necessity, absolutely essential to the preservation of the Union. [Because the slaves are] undeniably an element of strength to those who had their service . . . we must free the slaves or be ourselves subdued."[39] The liberality of his offer of amnesty, announced in the fall of 1863, marked the persistence of Lincoln's intention to restore relations between northern and southern whites on the basis of mutually acknowledged equality.[40]

Lincoln's issuance of the Emancipation Proclamation did not indicate that he was prepared to subjugate some in order to vindicate equality for others. The Proclamation, like the mounting savagery on the battlefields, did indeed have its own internal impetus that moved both sides relentlessly away from any possibility of ending their conflict as acknowledged equals rather than as victor and vanquished. But Lincoln did not embrace this impetus; he resisted it.

By the end of the war, however, the abolition of slavery had been transformed in Lincoln's own mind from an incidental means for preserving the Union into an independent war goal. The central question for fully understanding Lincoln's political thought, and his concept of equality specifically, is to identify why this transformation occurred for him. Lincoln revealed this reason in August 1864, in two letters he never mailed and in a private conversation with Republican political leaders. Both the draft letters and the private conversation suggest, moreover, that Lincoln only then was resolving his ambivalence about imposing emancipation for its own sake.

August 1864 was a dark time for Lincoln. Union forces had suffered a series of sharp setbacks, the war seemed endlessly bogged down, and Lincoln himself thought that George McClellan, the Democratic "peace candidate," would almost certainly defeat him in the November presidential election and would immediately acquiesce in the southern secession. At this desperate juncture for Lincoln's hopes to restore the Union, and for his personal political ambitions, intermediaries suggested that the Confederacy might be led back into the Union if emancipation were withdrawn as a condition for peace negotiations. Lincoln drafted two letters indicating his willingness to consider this proposal. In one, to a northern Democrat, he stated, "If Jefferson Davis wishes . . . to know what I would do if he were to offer peace and re-union, saying nothing about slavery, let him try me."[41] In the other, he drafted instructions for a special envoy to go to Richmond with a proposal "that upon the restoration of the Union and the national authority, the war shall cease at once, all remaining questions to be left for adjustment by peaceful modes."[42] But Lincoln never sent either letter—a decision clearly signifying, and perhaps even marking the moment of, Lincoln's final conclusion that emancipation had become an independent war goal for him.

Lincoln's basic motive in reaching this conclusion was revealed even in the text of the draft he wrote to the northern Democrat. Before setting out his challenge to Jefferson Davis, Lincoln appeared to contradict the offer, as if he were still struggling with his ambivalence. After noting that more than 100,000 black soldiers had joined the Union forces following his issuance of the Emancipation Proclamation, Lincoln stated that these soldiers would withdraw if they thought the Union intended "to betray them. . . . If they stake their lives for us they must be prompted by the strongest motive . . . the promise of freedom. And the promise being made, must be kept." Two days after he wrote this draft letter, Lincoln met with two Republican party leaders who conveyed concerns about the unpopularity of the war generally and emancipation specifically. Lincoln responded first by insisting that the "sole purpose" of the war was to restore the Union and that the "Emancipation lever" had been necessary only to "subdue this rebellion." But then he went further: "There have been men who proposed to me to return to slavery the black warriors"; but, he said, "I should be damned in time and in eternity for so doing. The world shall know that I will keep my faith to friends and enemies, come what will."[43] Several days later, Lincoln stated to several Cabinet officers that he was ready to lose the presidency and thus even the possibility of restoring the Union rather than abandon emancipation.[44]

"The promise being made, must be kept." This, I believe, was the core source of Lincoln's commitment to defend the equality of blacks against their enslavement by southern whites: not an abstract allegiance to the equality principle as such nor a revulsion to the institution of slavery. Lincoln did believe in the equality principle, and he did abhor slavery. But these moral attitudes did not make him an abolitionist; they were not sufficient for him to override his obligation to respect the equality of southern whites. As Lincoln saw it, this was an obligation entered in the framing of the Union and sealed in the mutual burdens borne by North and South to defend that political relationship against foreign adversaries and to sustain it among themselves. Before the war, and even when he signed the Emancipation Proclamation, Lincoln did not have the same sense of obligation toward black slaves.

The limits of Lincoln's commitment to slaves was starkly revealed in an address he made to a deputation of free blacks whom he called to the White House in August 1862, just four months before issuing his Proclamation. At that meeting, Lincoln urged these blacks to leave this country and to lead newly freed slaves into foreign colonization. "Your race suffer very greatly," Lincoln stated, "by living among us, while ours suffer from your presence. . . . If this is admitted, it affords a reason, at least, why we should be separated."[45] As Frederick Douglass angrily observed at the time, Lincoln showed "no sincere wish to improve the condition of the oppressed . . . [He] expresses merely the desire to get rid of them, and reminds one of the politeness with which a man might try to bow out of his house some troublesome creditor or the witness of some old guilt."[46] Lincoln encircled his exhortation with an acknowledgment that slavery was "the greatest wrong inflicted on any people" and that unjust but insuperable practical obstacles confronted any free black from "being placed on an equality" with any white. But Douglass was surely correct that Lincoln's "tone of frankness and benevolence [was] too thin a mask not to be seen through."

It is not clear, however, that behind this mask was racial animosity toward blacks; Douglass himself subsequently met Lincoln and quickly acquitted him of this charge.[47] Lincoln's espousal of, and his genuine support for, black colonization may have been morally obtuse; his position was as insensitive as—and I would say, no different from—the common attitude that we owe more vivid obligations and must bear greater sacrifices for our own family than for strangers and for our own fellow-citizens than for inhabitants of distant lands. Black colonization made moral sense for Lincoln because he saw blacks as foreigners, or more precisely as resident aliens in the Union. The Emancipation Proclamation did not in itself change Lincoln's view of blacks; they were passive recipients of his benevolence or, in even more limited terms, merely instruments for his goal of ending the southern white rebellion rather than deserving claimants in their own right.

The change in Lincoln's vision came, and the transformation of emancipation from a subsidiary to an independent war goal followed, from one consequence of the Emancipation Proclamation: that the freed blacks joined Lincoln to fight and die for the Union. This fact did not mean that Lincoln no longer was obliged to regard white Southerners as his equals and could readily subjugate them without regard to their wishes. But now that Lincoln was engaged in an independent, mutual relationship with blacks, their claims for his respect had fully equal status with the claims of whites in the South or North. Lincoln's conception of equality demanded that he try to honor all of these conflicting claims, by assiduously seeking some middle ground on which all could agree.

Even at the very end of the War, when the northern military victory appeared imminent and he had been re-elected, Lincoln still tried to find some basis for compromise between the claims of southern whites and blacks. In February 1865, Lincoln held a ship-board meeting with Confederate leaders, including Vice President Alexander Stephens, in an unsuccessful attempt to explore the possibility of ending the War. According to Stephens's later account of this meeting, Lincoln insisted that all blacks freed by the Emancipation Proclamation must remain free and that the institution of slavery itself was "doomed"; but he showed some flexibility on two counts about the prospect of complete abolition. First, Lincoln noted that the Thirteenth Amendment, which had just been proposed by Congress, might be ratified by the southern states "prospectively, so as to take effect—say in five years." Second, he offered compensation for emancipation, stating that "the people of the North were as responsible for slavery as the people of the South."[48] When he returned to Washington, he drafted a message to Congress asking for an appropriation of $400 million, about fifteen percent of the slaves' 1860 market value, half to be paid after the Confederate states "abandoned resistance to the national government" and the remainder after the Thirteenth Amendment was ratified.[49] The Cabinet unanimously recommended against this proposal, however, and Lincoln never sent the message.

When it became clear that common consent between the white North and South could not be found, Lincoln no longer saw himself morally authorized to ignore the black claims to equality that he previously had subordinated to his commitments to white Southerners. By the end of the war Lincoln clearly viewed the black soldiers in the same way that he had always viewed white Southerners. This was, moreover, the same way that Lincoln demanded white Southerners see him—as a participant in a voluntarily entered relationship that could not subsequently be abandoned for unilaterally determined self-interest. This was the bedrock axiom for which Lincoln fought the Civil War—not equality as an abstract principle but equality that had come to life in active association, where burdens and benefits had been shared and accordingly must be equally accounted for.

There is a fundamental underlying connection between Lincoln's relational conception of equality and Madison's political thought. Madison's conception of the proper design for federal political institutions directly parallels Lincoln's practical understanding of the source of both the binding obligation between him (and by extension the white North) and black soldiers and the obligations owed to the Union by the white South. The vivid respect for black equality that arose for Lincoln only in his direct experience of a common enterprise with blacks is, in effect, a practical validation of Madison's insight regarding the interactive implications of the institutional structure of the Constitution. By drawing out the connection between Madison's thinking and Lincoln's conception of the binding force of his political relationship with both black slaves and white Southerners, we can ultimately see the reasons why both Lincoln and Madison rejected the idea of judicial supremacy in constitutional interpretation.

Madison saw institutional interaction as the means for transforming political disputes from self-absorbed factionalism into mutual pursuit of a unifying vision of public virtue. By his conception, respect for mutual equality did not precede political relations but grew from the interactive process by which alienated and potentially hostile rivals come to see one another as reciprocally connected fellow-citizens. Madison's goal was not to override or disregard the subjective passions of factional disputants but instead to transform the disputants' own perspectives by bringing their conflicts into national forums. The elected representatives in those forums would not impose their own wishes on their disputatious constituents; they would represent their constituents' claims. But because each representative's constituency comprised such diverse claimants (unlike the more narrowly circumscribed units of local government), each national spokesman would himself be drawn toward engaging in a complex calculus of accommodating conflicting claims, simply as a necessary prelude toward making representations on behalf of his constituents to other national officeholders. In this enlarged compass for political disputes, Madison imagined, a mindset would naturally emerge that was disposed toward mutually respectful accommodation—the necessary condition for honoring the equality principle. But Madison did not intend to displace the clash of competing self-interests by creating some institutional structure—as he put it, "some power altogether independent of the people"[50]—that would stand impartially outside this conflict. Madison meant instead to create political institutions where the clash of self-interest might be reflected but diffused so as to promote harmonization.

Lincoln's emphatic rejection of the legitimacy of secession rested on a similar commitment to the national institutional framework as a necessary instrument for realizing the equality principle— though Lincoln did not rely on Madison's refined speculations about the comparative advantages of national over state or local forums because he confronted a cruder challenge than Madison had faced. Lincoln's problem was that, by the act of secession, one of the disputants refused to engage in any political interaction with its adversary. And this refusal, as Lincoln properly saw it, was more obviously destructive of the equality principle than a self-interested legislative majority's unilateral subjugation of an equally self-interested opposing minority—which was Madison's subtle, though equivalent, concern.

For Madison, as for Lincoln, the rejection of any external locus of social control fundamentally distinguishes their egalitarianism from modern versions that posit some fixed conception of equality that can be authoritatively applied by an "enlightened" or "objective" calculator. In the modern versions, whether the egalitarian principle is formulated in some pre-social contract (such as John Rawls essayed) or through some utilitarian calculus (such as Jeremy Bentham bequeathed to modern econometricians), the formulation depends on the existence of an observer who can stand outside social relations and impartially calibrate equal portions of disputed social resources. Madison clearly saw, however, that no such observer can exist, among humans at least, "as long as the reason of man continues fallible [because] the connection subsists between his reason and his self-love."[51]

Madison's egalitarianism, in common with Lincoln's more generalized commitment, did not rely on objective observation but rested wholly on the subjective evaluations of the social disputants themselves. From their perspective, if one person regarded himself as oppressed by others, no one could conclusively refute that belief; but, at the same time, no one was obliged to accede to this belief at the cost of his own sense of equal treatment. For Madison and Lincoln, one person's claim of wrongful inequality should be a prelude to political conversation with the purported wrongdoer. In this conversation, each would be obliged to regard the other as an equal and accordingly to persuade the other that his contrary understanding of their relationship was inaccurate. Neither party properly could resolve this dispute by unilateral assertions (just as no third party could resolve the dispute from a stance outside the relationship). The question whether equal treatment existed in the relationship could only be legitimately resolved if and when the disputants themselves mutually arrived at a common characterization. This shared understanding might never come, of course; and one or both of the disputants might choose to break away from the effort to persuade and instead seek to impose his definition of the relationship on the other. As Madison and Lincoln saw it, however, this coercive move would be an axiomatic breach of the equality principle.

For Lincoln specifically in the Civil War crisis, the conflicting conceptions of equality in northern and southern white claims regarding the Union's dissolubility or in southern white and black claims regarding property rights in slaves could not be unilaterally adjudicated. If the conflicts proved intractable—as in fact they did—then Lincoln saw a terrible dilemma, not a clear-cut call for action to subordinate one claimant to the other. This generalization follows: that in any regime committed to this understanding of the equality principle, there can be no proper role for an authoritative resolution of disputes that overrides the subjective evaluation of any of the contesting parties. Both Lincoln and Madison accordingly came to the conclusion that in the American governance scheme, judicial supremacy in constitutional interpretation cannot be justified.

Recall Lincoln's conception of the judicial role in this passage from his first inaugural address: "If the policy of the Government upon vital questions, affecting the whole people, is to be irrevocably fixed by decisions of the Supreme Court, the instant they are made, . . . the people will have ceased to be their own rulers, having to that extent practically resigned their government into the hands of that eminent tribunal."[52] Lincoln had given no systematic thought to the practice of judicial review until the Supreme Court overturned the Missouri Compromise in its 1857 *Dred Scott* decision.[53] The conception he sketched in his inaugural address was a distillation of his position in the Illinois senatorial campaign debates with Douglas, where he had criticized *Dred Scott* in these terms:

> If this important decision had been made by the unanimous concurrence of the judges, and without any apparent partisan bias, and in accordance with legal public expectation, and with the steady practice of the departments throughout our history, and had been in no part, based on assumed historical facts which are not really true; or, if wanting in some of these, it had been before the court more than once, and had there been affirmed and re-affirmed through a course of years, it then might be, perhaps would be, factious, nay, even revolutionary, to not acquiesce in it as a precedent. But when, as it is true, we find it wanting in all these claims to the public confidence, it is not resistance, it is not factious, it is not even disrespectful, to treat it as not having yet quite established to a settled doctrine for the country.[54]

This critique directly parallels Madison's conception that constitutional interpretation does not belong to the Supreme Court alone but must take place over a prolonged time involving many different institutional participants and that no important interpretive issue would be finally settled until, in Lincoln's paraphrase, the resolution had "been affirmed and re-affirmed through a course of years." Neither Madison nor Lincoln ever systematically outlined the ways in which the judiciary should interact with other institutions in order to accomplish this gradual accretion of constitutional doctrine. The challenges that Lincoln confronted, first in the territorial slavery controversy and then in waging the Civil War, did provide, however, a model for judicial conduct in addressing the polarized conflicts that are recurrently reflected in constitutional litigation. By the example of his conduct, Lincoln taught that the principle of equality was the foundational premise of American democracy; that this principle cannot be vindicated by any coercive imposition (whether by majority rule, by judicial fiat, or by armed force); that an aggressive imposition by one disputant must be met with defensive force by (or on behalf of) the other; that this defense must aim only at producing stalemate rather than victory for the erstwhile victim; and that this stalemate will signal to both antagonists that they must resolve their dispute somehow by mutual agreement.

During the course of the nineteenth century, as we will see in the following chapters, the Supreme Court embraced a conception of judicial supremacy, with increasingly extensive scope following the Civil War, that was antithetical to the egalitarian conception of political relations that Lincoln represented and the corresponding structure of institutional relations that Madison had conceived. This nineteenth-century version of judicial authority came under criticism during the twentieth century, especially during the 1930s when the Court attacked FDR's New Deal and again in the 1970s and 1980s, as a reaction to the Warren Court's ambitions. This modern critique has not been grounded, however, in the egalitarian ideals of Lincoln and Madison. Its central premise has been rather a reversion to a conception of majority rule that was enunciated not by Lincoln but by his adversary, Stephen Douglas.

For Lincoln, majority rule was an expedient but imperfect approximation—and ultimately an insufficient expression—of the fundamental egalitarian principle that "no man is good enough to govern another man, without that other's consent." By contrast, Douglas's position that majority rule was the only proper means for resolving the territorial slavery dispute finds direct linear expression among those modern critics who identify the "root difficulty" of judicial authority in its "counter-majoritarian force." Alexander Bickel formulated his criticism in these terms;[55] but even more than in Bickel's work, the rejection of Lincolnian egalitarianism in favor of majority rule, independently valued as such, is at the center of the most prominent modern critic of judicial authority, Judge Robert Bork.

Bork comes to his majoritarianism from the premise that "there seems to be no rational way of securing moral agreement in our culture."[56] Regarding such issues as abortion and capital punishment, Bork concludes, "our public moral debates . . . have been interminable and inconclusive because we start from different premises and have no way of convincing each other as to which are the proper premises . . . That is why, where the real Constitution is mute, we should vote about these matters rather than litigate them." Bork's deference to the "real Constitution"—that is, the document as understood from an originalist perspective—itself rests exclusively on his commitment to majority rule: "Those who ratified the Constitution may have lacked a shared systematic moral philosophy . . . They were [however] elected legislators and under no obligation to justify moral and political choices by a philosophy to which all must consent."[57]

Bork thus ostentatiously turns away from what Lincoln called the "sheet anchor of American republicanism"—the principle that mutual consent is the only basis for political relations among equals. Of course this consent is difficult, and may even be impossible, to achieve in practice; Lincoln preeminently understood this in his lifetime. But Lincoln also understood—as Madison had grasped in more hopeful times—that if we abandon the effort to persuade one another, then we will have embraced the tyranny of some over others. Such tyranny may be inescapable in disputes where, as Bork suggests, "we start from different premises and have no way of convincing each other." To conclude, however, as he does, that this state of mutual hostility is an acceptable basis for constructing a political philosophy is to jettison from the start any possibility of vindicating the principle of equality in political relations.

We may conclude that egalitarianism itself is a disputable principle of political philosophy. But this principle, as Lincoln observed, was at the core of the founders' conception of relations among themselves, and in the Fourteenth Amendment this principle was explicitly acknowledged and generalized in application to "all persons." Accordingly, even if we accept Bork's premise that the constitutional framers were "under no obligation to justify [their] moral and political choices," we cannot remain faithful to their injunctions if we embrace a conception of majoritarianism that is inconsistent with the framers' commitment to equality in political relations, even in the limited compass that they applied the equality principle in the original document itself.

Unfortunately, however, judicial authority—as it has come to be conventionally conceived—does not vindicate the equality principle any better than majority rule; both Lincoln and Madison clearly saw this in their critiques of judicial supremacy in constitutional interpretation. When Bork's critics embrace judicial supremacy as preferable to majority tyranny, they fall into the trap that Lincoln and Madison identified: thus the sterility of the contemporary debate between proponents and opponents of "judicial activism," that these adversaries offer only an equally unsatisfactory choice between majoritarian autocracy and judicial autocracy.

There is a better alternative. But we cannot fully grasp this alternative—nor see why, notwithstanding all its difficulties, it is preferable to the currently proferred choice between majority and judicial rule—unless we first understand when and why the conventional conception of judicial supremacy took hold in our constitutional scheme. By tracing the historical narrative of the development of this idea and its connections with the political events that overwhelmed the egalitarian ideal, we will see both the obstacles to and the possibilities for rekindling this Lincolnian ideal and its Madisonian institutional embodiments in our own time.

II

JUDICIAL SUPREMACY IN PRACTICE

4

The Marshall Court
Conflicts

THE CONVENTIONAL VIEW today is that judicial supremacy in constitutional interpretation was fixed virtually at the outset of our enterprise—if not by the specific intent of the founders, then by John Marshall's early endorsement of Hamilton's position in the famous lawsuit against Madison brought in 1801 by William Marbury, Hamilton's Federalist Party proxy. Thus in 1958 a unanimous Supreme Court averred that *Marbury v. Madison* "declared the basic principle that the federal judiciary is supreme in the exposition of the law of the Constitution, and that principle has ever since been respected by this Court and the Country as a permanent and indispensable feature of our constitutional system."[1]

This view is wrong, however, on at least two grounds. *Marbury* did not clearly declare this principle but was at most ambiguous about it and in spirit was closer to Madison than Hamilton. And though Marshall's Court did more clearly endorse the Hamiltonian conception of its role sixteen years later, in *McCulloch v. Maryland*, "the Country" did not promptly give homage to this view but engaged in intense conflict about it until after the Civil War. In Part II, I will set out the narrative of these events; but though this story is not widely remembered today and is thus worth telling for its own sake, that is not my principal purpose. I will trace how the choice was made between the competing conceptions of judicial authority over the course of the nineteenth century in order to show that the experiences and the reasoning on which this choice was based do not necessarily have the same force for us today.

We, however, are gripped by force of habit and in this sense are less free than our predecessors. They vividly saw alternatives that are hidden from us as a result of the choices they made. My reconstruction of their choosing is an attempt to liberate our imagination, to recapture their sense of open possibilities, so that we can re-examine for ourselves the strength of their reasons and the relevance of their experience for us.

The central issue in choosing among the competing conceptions of judicial authority was, for them as for us, the role of courts in addressing polarized social conflict. This issue cannot be adequately approached through philosophic abstraction alone. The problem of polarized conflict is embedded in concrete circumstance that, for each generation, gives the underlying philosophic questions specific shape and weight, as *Brown v. Board of Education* does for my generation. To find the wellspring for the founding generation's choice among competing conceptions of judicial authority, we must consult not only their writings but their lives— not only what they thought about the political conflicts that entangled them but the personal experience and social identity that structured their perception of those conflicts.

Hamilton, Marshall, Madison

Approaching Hamilton and Madison in this way suggests sources for their philosophic differences. Madison's biography is the easiest to sketch. He was (like his closest friend and political ally, Jefferson) the eldest son of a wealthy, socially prominent family who was expected to follow his father, and did so, in both deserving and obtaining the willing deference of social inferiors.

Hamilton's biography was very much different—an instantiation of Tolstoy's observation that while all happy families resemble each other, each unhappy family is unhappy in its own way. Hamilton's mother left her husband and infant son and, after serving a prison term for "whoring" (on a complaint initiated by her husband), lived in the West Indies with James Hamilton, a ne'er-do-well son of a prominent Scottish family. Alexander was the youngest of two sons born during this cohabitation. Some five years after Alexander's birth, James Hamilton abandoned the family and never saw them again. Eight years later, Hamilton's mother died, leaving almost no resources; and even this pittance was taken away in a vindictive lawsuit brought by the former husband to declare their legitimate son the sole heir to his mother's estate.

But Alexander Hamilton was resourceful, ambitious, and highly intelligent. He found a patron who supported his education and subsequent emigration in 1772, when he was about eighteen years old, from the West Indies to New York. Hamilton enrolled in Kings College (now Columbia University) and quickly became engaged in patriot pamphleteering. Soon after the Revolutionary War began, he attracted George Washington's attention and became a trusted and increasingly important aide. In 1780 Hamilton married the daughter of a wealthy, socially established and politically active New Yorker—a "stroke," as one historian has observed, by which Hamilton the "parvenu . . . completed the process of gentrification."[2]

Hamilton was thus a self-made man in an era when this social paradigm was not yet much celebrated: "the bastard brat of a Scot's pedlar," as John Adams uncharitably described him.[3] It is therefore not surprising that Hamilton would have a special sensitivity regarding the legitimacy of social authority, that he would not easily tolerate ambiguities in such matters that Madison could more comfortably contemplate. But Hamilton's sensitivity also gave him clearer access to his contemporaries' concerns than they may have articulated for themselves.[4]

Even if the gentry status of his associates was more deeply rooted than Hamilton's, none of them could avoid some sense of the insecurity that Hamilton conveyed in his attitudes and in his person. The social authority of the gentry was generally under challenge at the time of the Revolution—most clearly in the scrambling mercantile atmosphere of the North, where Hamilton prospered as an attorney, but also in the South, where customary deference to gentry had been noticeably strained by the Great Awakening of the 1740s and 50s. This eruption of religious fervor has been convincingly portrayed by Rhys Isaac as an implicit revolt by socially inferior whites (tentatively joined in holy patrimony by black slaves) against gentry authority. This revolt was thus both a precursor of and an impetus toward the domestic alliance forged between gentry and commoner against the foreign domination of

British colonial rule.[5] In this sense, the American Revolutionary War for "home rule" was a temporary lull in the domestic struggle over "who should rule at home."[6] It is, moreover, revealing that the itinerant preachers who appeared in the Great Awakening as rivals to the locally dominant gentry should hold out an image of divine sovereign authority that required submission more absolute and unquestioning than any member of the gentry dared to demand, except from his slaves.[7] This paradoxical rejection and simultaneous embrace of harsh, even enslaving, authority was mirrored in Alexander Hamilton's personal experience, his political philosophy generally, and his conception of judicial authority specifically.

Hamilton was unusual among his generation, however, only in the acuteness with which he felt and the acuity with which he addressed the problem of constructing legitimate social authority. As Wiebe observed,

> By operating a step removed from the involvements of his contemporaries, [Hamilton] saw what they missed, and hence he could maneuver with a remarkable precision. Yet by escaping their turmoils, Hamilton missed what they saw, and hence he could lose contact with the wellsprings of American political life. In 1790 his singular vision led him to the pinnacle of power; by 1800 his singular blindness had toppled him.[8]

Two issues were central in Hamilton's rise and fall. The first, on the ascendant arc, was his program for national economic development capped by the federal government's assumption of debts the states had incurred during the Revolution. This issue was the fulcrum for the open split between Hamilton and Jefferson. In 1790 the Virginia legislature resolved that the debt program was "dangerous to the rights and subversive of the interest of the people [and] repugnant to the Constitution of the United States."[9] Hamilton immediately responded that the Virginia resolution was "the first symptom of a spirit which must either be killed or will kill the constitution" and should be met by "the collective weight" of the national government.[10]

The second issue, on the descendant arc, was the passage of the Alien and Sedition Acts in 1798. These measures were the culmination of the decades' escalating, increasingly polarized conflict about the proper national response to the outbreak of the French Revolution, to the war between France and Britain, to Pennsylvania farmers' refusal to pay the federal excise tax on liquor (the "Whiskey Rebellion" suppressed in 1794 by Hamilton's dispatch of federal troops), and to John Jay's negotiated treaty with Great Britain. In particular, the continuing Republican criticism of the Jay Treaty after its Senate ratification in 1795 was viewed by the Federalists as an especially egregious violation of the gentry norm that dispute was legitimate only before but not after the adoption of governmental measures.[11]

In this overheated atmosphere, the Federalists who controlled the national government concluded by 1798 that the opposition on these various matters led by Jefferson and Madison was undermining the very foundation of legitimate authority. From this conclusion came enactment of the Alien and Sedition Acts, the former increasing executive authority to deport aliens (thus protecting the country from the foreign intrigues of French agents) and the latter prohibiting "false, scandalous, and malicious" criticism that might bring "contempt or disrepute" to the government (thus protecting against internal subversion). The partisan purpose of the Sedition Act in particular was revealed by the pointed omission of the vice-presidency (then held by Thomas Jefferson) from the list of governmental offices specifically protected from defamatory criticism.

Enforcement of the Sedition Act was immediately aimed at Republican newspaper editors in principal cities. Most of the cases were brought to trial in the election year of 1800.[12] The defendants found no protection from the federal judiciary for their rights to political dissent; the constitutionality of the Act was explicitly upheld in several of these cases, including at least two where Supreme Court Justices presided in their capacity as circuit-riding judges.[13] In one of these cases, Justice Samuel Chase delivered a stinging jury charge that identified the heart of the criminal offense as the exercise of political dissent; the defendant intended, he said, "to mislead the ignorant, and inflame their minds against the President, and to influence their votes on the next election." The defendant was convicted and sentenced by Chase to six months in federal prison and a stiff fine.[14]

The Republican opposition took their efforts against the Alien and Sedition Acts to state legislatures not only because they expected a hostile reception from the federal judiciary but because throughout the preceding decade Jefferson and Madison had cultivated a network of the state-based gentry leadership as the focus of their campaign against the centralizing measures of the Hamiltonian Federalists.[15] This campaign had forged a practical alliance with the leaders of the initial, anti-Federalist opposition to the ratification of the Constitution. When the Virginia and Kentucky legislatures passed their resolutions against the Acts, Hamilton saw this larger political alliance at work and disregarded the fine lawyerly distinctions that separated Madison's version of "interposing state authority" from Jefferson's proclamation of "nullification."[16] By Hamilton's lights, both states were engaged in treason; he urged George Washington to return from retirement to command a federal army that would "put Virginia to the Test of resistance" and ultimately break it into several small states.

Other Federalists were equally aroused. President Adams thundered that Virginia must answer "whether this country has in it a Faction to be crushed, a faction to be humbled in dust and ashes."[17] Justice James Iredall wrote his wife that the state resolutions were "steps which directly lead to civil war" and that the national government was ready "to oppose force to force."[18] The Congress passed an explicit enactment authorizing the army to "suppress insurrection."[19]

The actual outbreak of civil war was never imminent. The federal army at the time numbered only about 3,500 men, mostly stationed at frontier garrisons as precautions against the Indians; and Virginia alone could readily have mustered a much larger militia if directly challenged.[20] Indeed, in retrospect, it seems most likely that this decade-long dispute that had driven Jefferson and Madison to forge their alliance with the state-based gentry did more to preserve than endanger the Union.[21] The prospect that the Republican opposition would be driven to violent resistance by the harsh Federalist suppressions was, moreover, almost immediately mooted by their victory in the election of 1800.

In electoral terms, however, the Republican victory was hardly overwhelming. Outside the South, they won just Pennsylvania and New York, defeating the Federalists by only eight electoral votes (and if the southern states had not had the representational bonus awarded by the Constitution for their slave population, the Republicans would have lost).[22] As Jefferson himself foresaw, immediately before the election, "should the whole body of New England continue in opposition to [Republican] principles of government . . . our government will be a very uneasy one."[23] The Republican victory thus did not solve the problem of polarized conflict for the new republic. It seemed to do nothing more, at least as many of the disputants saw it, than to turn the tables between oppressor and oppressed.

But two fortuitous events intervened. The first was the *opera buffa* error of the Republican party strategists in the electoral college voting. Article II, section 3, of the Constitution provided that "the Electors shall meet in their respective States, and vote by Ballot for two Persons" with the winner as President and the second-place finisher as Vice-President. In this provision, the founders expected free-ranging deliberation rather than factionally organized contests in the electoral college; and the Republican organizers did not anticipate the significance of the college voting procedure when they constructed their lists of electors committed to the party slate of Jefferson and Burr. As a result, every Republican elector faithfully voted for both men, and each man received the same number of votes. Article II provided that the House of Representatives, voting by states, should resolve electoral college ties; in 1800, a majority of states in the lame-duck House were controlled by the defeated Federalist party. Thus came the irony that the first seriously contested presidential election in our history would be decided by the losing party.

For the defeated Federalists, the temptation was enormous to choose Burr over Jefferson, a temptation that the ambitious and less-than-principled Burr secretly fed. Such manipulations were not alien to Federalist thinking. Earlier, when the composition of the newly elected New York state legislature clearly foretold Jefferson's victory, Hamilton had proposed an equally questionable course; he urged Governor John Jay to reconvene the lame-duck legislature in order to call a new election under terms more favorable to Federalist prospects. "The scruples of delicacy and propriety," Hamilton said,

> ought to yield to the extraordinary nature of the crisis. They ought not to hinder the taking of a legal and constitutional step to prevent an atheist in religion, and a fanatic in politics, from

getting possession of the helm of state. . . . The reasonable part of the world . . . will see it as a proceeding out of the common course, but warranted by the particular nature of the crisis and the great cause of social order.[24]

Jay rejected Hamilton's proposal; but the tie vote in the electoral college gave Hamilton a renewed opportunity to take "a legal and constitutional step to prevent" Jefferson's accession.

This time, however, Hamilton resisted the temptation and was instrumental in persuading a sufficient number of Federalists to abstain in the House vote so that Jefferson would be elected. Hamilton was partly moved by his greater distaste for Burr's character than even his harsh view of Jefferson's. But there were two elements beyond this. The first was that, at Hamilton's urging, a Federalist envoy approached a friend of Jefferson to solicit assurances on several matters: the maintenance of public credit and of naval strength, neutrality in the war between France and Britain, and "the preservation in office of our friends except in the great departments in respect to which and in future appointments he ought to be at liberty to promote his friends."[25] Though Jefferson made no explicit promises on these matters, the intermediaries appeared to reach a delicately stated understanding of one another's needs.[26]

Second, and more important, with the reality of electoral defeat clearly upon them, the Federalists were led to consider, as Richard Hofstadter observed, "whether there was enough left of the spirit of concord or patriotism after the rancor of the preceding years to warrant thinking that they could endure Jefferson's possession of power."[27] The happenstance that the Federalists were required to choose the instrument of their defeat meant that, in psychological terms, they offered more than impotent surrender to the victor; the Federalists directly participated and thereby acquiesced in their defeat, even though without enthusiasm.

In his inaugural address, Jefferson responded with magnanimity:

Let us restore to social intercourse that harmony and affection without which liberty and even life itself are but dreary things. . . . Every difference of opinion is not a difference of principle.

We have called by different names brethren of the same principle. We are all Republicans, we are all Federalists.[28]

These conciliatory sentiments did not mark the end of partisan struggle in Jefferson's tenure. But the constitutional structure within which the conflict thus far was waged had brought the competing parties into a process of "consultation and accommodation"—not by the carefully wrought mechanisms that Madison had envisaged toward this end but by the Rube Goldberg contraption of the electoral college: yet the structure had worked in Madisonian terms.*

The electoral imbroglio was one fortuitous event that tended to temper the hard edges of polarized conflict following the Federalist defeat. A second fortuity had even a longer-range significance. This was the resignation ostensibly for health reasons of Chief Justice Oliver Ellsworth in December 1800. President Adams quickly nominated the former Chief Justice John Jay who, though quickly confirmed, also declined, partly on health grounds and partly because he viewed the Court as unable to "obtain the energy, weight, and dignity" necessary to "support . . . the national government."[29] On January 20, 1801, Adams nominated his Secretary of State, John Marshall, who was confirmed a week later by the lame-duck Federalist Senate.[30]

This last-minute accession was not an auspicious beginning to Marshall's judicial career, particularly because it occurred in conjunction with the feverish efforts generally of the defeated Federalists to fill the judicial branch with their own partisans. Though Marshall's nomination was not, strictly speaking, one of the "midnight appointments" to the federal courts that the Adams' administration pressed until the last possible moment before Jefferson's inauguration, the new Chief Justice carried to his office an unmistakable odor of partisan scrambling. Indeed, although Marshall himself accepted his commission and first presided as Chief Justice on February 4, he continued to serve as Secretary of State

---

*The Republicans quickly voted, however, to jettison this particular structural mechanism; by the time the 1804 election was held, the Twelfth Amendment had been ratified to provide separate balloting in the electoral college for President and Vice President. See Hofstadter at 139 n.17.

at Adams' request until Jefferson's inauguration.[31] Thus, it was John Marshall as Secretary of State who remained in his office into the early morning hours of March 4, 1801, completing the formalities for last-minute judicial commissions and handing them to his brother James for delivery. It was John Marshall who was the direct instrumentality of the "midnight appointments" that appeared, at least to the Republican victors waiting to take their hard-won command of the national government, as an illegitimate grasping for power.

This aura of illegitimacy was not lifted from Marshall's head until 1805. Immediately on taking office, the new Republican Congress began a systematic effort to unravel the partisan advantage that the Adams' administration had obtained in packing the federal judiciary. Its first action was to repeal the Judiciary Act of 1801 which had created a new intermediate appellate tribunal with sixteen judgeships, all filled in February 1801 with Federalist appointees. Indeed, the immediate spur for Jefferson's support of the repeal effort was Marshall's brief opinion for the Court in December 1801, granting the motion of William Marbury that cause be shown why Madison, the new Secretary of State, should not be ordered to deliver the judicial commission appointing Marbury justice of the peace for the District of Columbia—a commission that had been signed by the old Secretary, John Marshall, but too late for his brother to effect delivery. Jefferson responded to Marshall's show-cause order that the Federalists "have retired into the Judiciary as a stronghold . . . and from that battery all the works of Republicanism are to be beaten down and erased."[32] Thus, the federal judiciary, at least, was removed from Jefferson's list of ecumenical party identification.

After repealing the 1801 Act, thus effectively removing the sixteen appellate judges from office, the Republican Congress turned its attention to other Federalist judges. The House first impeached a Federalist district judge in New Hampshire; and, after his removal by the Senate in 1804, impeachment was aimed at Justice Samuel Chase, Marshall's colleague on the Supreme Court, who was notorious for his aggressive enforcement of the Sedition Act. Chase was ultimately acquitted by the Senate in March 1805; but until then a palpable threat hung over Marshall that he would be the next candidate for removal.[33]

This swirl of partisan controversy around the federal courts generally and the Supreme Court specifically in the immediate aftermath of the Republican victory of 1800 had a paradoxical consequence. The controversy neither created nor exacerbated polarized conflict between the defeated Federalists and the victorious Republicans. This conflict was already there. Jefferson's conciliatory inaugural address was scant reassurance to many Federalist leaders who described his election as plunging them into a "deep abyss of a frightful despotism" and rendering them "*slaves,* [and] to no very desirable masters."[34] If the Republicans had been able to take command of the federal judiciary in quick succession after securing the executive and legislative branches, the Federalist opposition would only have been further confirmed in their bitter sense of subjugation.

The signal advantage of Marshall's accession to the Court was not, however, that the Federalists were comforted in their defeat.* The greater significance was the intense motivation of the Federalist judges, and of John Marshall in particular, to give explicit attention to the role of the courts in addressing polarized conflict. If the Republicans had taken quick control of the Supreme Court, the new Justices would not have searched as Marshall did for creative uses of judicial authority in such conflict; they would most likely have viewed their accession to the Court as Jefferson viewed his election as President: an indicator that the problem of polarized conflict was about to solve itself, since men of virtue were now in command.

This view of "civic virtue" as a solution to the problem of social conflict was the conventional gentry wisdom of the day: that the

---

*Many Federalists were not reassured; they regrouped in the New England state legislatures, where they retained electoral dominance, and some sought to use these redoubts as increasingly active centers of resistance to national authority. Thus in 1803 and 1804 there was active plotting for secession in New England, though no serious steps were actually taken, see Hofstadter at 161–62; and in 1809, borrowing a leaf from the strategy of the Republican opposition in 1798, the Federalist-dominated Rhode Island legislature resolved to "interpose" its sovereign authority to resist Jefferson's embargo measures, though in 1799 this legislature had condemned as unconstitutional the Virginia resolution's identical stance. See H. Jefferson Powell, "The Original Understanding of Original Intent," 98 *Harv. L. Rev.* 885, 934–35 (1985).

"evils of faction" would disappear in response to the moral teachings and self-evident authority of disinterested statesmen, presided over by a "patriot king" exemplar.[35] Hamilton stood apart from this conventional view in his hard Hobbesian vision of the stubbornness of self-interested motivation and the consequent need for stronger executive leadership for suppressing social conflict.[36] Madison also held unconventional views that arose from his rigorous application of the conventional premises that "men were [not] angels"[37] and that "enlightened statesmen will not always be at the helm."[38] Though Madison did suggest that virtuously disinterested leaders would be more likely to emerge in enlarged republics than in smaller jurisdictions,[39] and though he guided his own conduct as President by the "patriot king" model,[40] he did not rely on these ideals. He was much more intent on structuring governmental institutions so that their interlocking mechanics would produce virtuous interactions rather than simply providing a forum for the interaction of virtuous men.[41]

John Marshall also stood apart from the conventional gentry faith that leadership by virtuous men would transcend polarized conflict; but his separate stance differed from both Hamilton and Madison. In his intellectual temperament, he was not as single-minded as Hamilton, nor as ready to substitute force for persuasion; and he was neither as subtle nor serenely balanced as Madison. In personal terms, Marshall's differences from these two men were even more pronounced; he stood in an intermediate social position between Hamilton the parvenu and Madison the gentryman. Marshall's biography has none of the Dickensian dark drama of Hamilton's; but there is more of the self-made man, more of Horatio Alger, in it than in Madison's.

Marshall was the eldest of twelve children in a respectable but not prosperous Virginia farming family. Unlike the plantation-based gentry, Marshall's family had no fixed homestead but moved continuously westward with the advance of the frontier settlements, and they raised crops for their own subsistence rather than for the market. Marshall's father worked to provide a formal education for his eldest son that neither he nor his other children obtained. Marshall was thus exceptional in his social surroundings, unlike Madison in his; and Marshall successfully strove to surpass his father, whereas Madison needed only to match his.

A recent biographer observed that Marshall could not "be content as the farmer or the frontiersman his father had been [and they were thus] typical of the families coming to the New World: the son taking a step beyond the limits reached by the father."[42] But the restless striving that this filial ambition represents was not yet the dominant social narrative in Marshall's time. Classical patrician ideals were still powerful in the founding era; and, as Gordon Wood has noted, "the southern planter gentry whose leisure was based on the labor of their slaves . . . came closest in America to fitting the classical ideal . . . of disinterested gentlemenly leadership."[43] The emerging basis for social conflict in the founding era was competition between these two social types, the established patrician and the self-made man. Even though few of the most vocal competitors for political dominance at that time cleanly fit either of these typologies—since the "patricians" were engaged in commercial pursuits, and many of the "self-made men" still tried to cover themselves in the trappings of leisured culture—adversarial lines were nonetheless discernable along these axes, with increasing sharpness in the decades after ratification of the Constitution.

Whatever the motivating source for Marshall, almost immediately after ratification he became increasingly isolated in Virginia politics as he clearly identified himself with the Federalist party and its nationalist policies. The life-long mutual antipathy between him and Jefferson was one reflection of Marshall's political estrangement from the gentry-based Republican establishment in Virginia.[44] This estrangement nourished an attitude in Marshall that he revealed in a notable letter to Charles Pinckney, the Federalist presidential candidate opposing Madison in 1808: "The federalists of Virginia constitute, you know, a small [and] oppressed minority of our state. . . . We found ourselves abused, insulted, and maltreated by all, [and] perceived no assurance on which we could confidently rely that the political system which had been adopted would [not] be changed by any of them."[45]

Thus, when Marshall accepted his commission as Chief Justice, he was—unlike Hamilton or the leading New England Federalists—already well-practiced in seeing himself as an "abused, insulted, and maltreated" minority representative. His sense of political, and perhaps even personal, vulnerability was reinforced by the active threat of impeachment that hung over him until Justice Chase's acquittal. But even after 1805 when this threat had been dispelled, even in the 1830s when he had attained great public prestige as the last officeholder of the founding generation, Marshall never shed a sense of embattlement. His private correspondence was almost continuously studded with laments about the vulnerability of his Court and the fragility of the nation's commitment to the Constitution.[46] His public pronouncements in judicial opinions always resounded with highflown assurance; but beneath this confident surface, artfully wrought defensive stratagems were always at work.[47]

Marshall's personal predilections, his political identification, and his institutional status made him superbly situated to address, in a more systematic fashion than Hamilton or Madison had done, the role of judicial authority in addressing polarized conflict. He was more cautious than Hamilton in relying on forced resolution of conflict, because he saw greater vulnerabilities in his institution and his protective mission. He was more rigorous than Madison in thinking about the judiciary not only because of his institutional affiliation but because unanticipated political events made the judiciary a more important instrument for Madison's conflict-diffusing purposes than Madison himself had understood. In particular, in his *Federalist* essays, Madison had not foreseen that party organization would tend to unite the executive and legislative branches, thereby limiting the competition on which he relied to diffuse and ameliorate partisan conflict. The judicial branch thus assumed greater structural significance for Madison's basic purpose than he had foreseen; and Marshall seized the possibilities.

Marshall was not, however, single-minded in his approach. At different times, he took elements from Madison's and from Hamilton's thinking and elaborated them in independent, and sometimes contradictory, directions. Marshall's legacy is thus somewhat ambiguous; he did not clearly choose between the competing conceptions of judicial authority (though by the end of his tenure he had strongly inclined toward the Hamiltonian), as much as he extended and illuminated the possibilities inherent in both conceptions. The Hamiltonian dominance came after Marshall's time, accompanied by the social triumph of the mythic self-made man, the archetype that Hamilton so starkly represented. In his middling position between Hamilton and Madison, the embodiment of gentry command, Marshall stands as a transitional figure in the evolution of the conception of American political authority.

The Madisonian Marshall

John Marshall's opinion in *Marbury v. Madison* is widely viewed as the cornerstone establishing the judiciary as the authoritative interpreter of the Constitution. As I stated at the outset of this chapter, this view is erroneous. *Marbury* was at most ambiguous for this claim and fits most comfortably into Madison's schema in *Federalist* 51 of equal interpretive authority among coordinate branches of the federal government. It is true that *Marbury* refused to enforce a congressional act on the ground that it violated the Constitution. But this refusal did not need to rest on a claim of judicial supremacy in constitutional interpretation; judicial equality would have been sufficient. According to Marshall, the congressional act gave jurisdiction to the Supreme Court that was explicitly forbidden by Article III. If the Court were subordinate to the Congress, then it would have been obliged to accept the designated jurisdiction; if, however, the Court and Congress were equally authorized to interpret the Constitution, then the Court was not only entitled but obliged to ensure that its actions corresponded to its own interpretation of the Constitution. Marshall's justification in *Marbury* for judicial authority to invalidate the jurisdictional statute was confined to this conception of institutional equality and carefully avoided any claim for judicial supremacy.

Marshall's invocation of judicial equality rather than supremacy was implicit in the three hypothetical examples he cited to clinch his case for the Court's authority to overturn congressional acts. In all three examples, Congress would not simply have violated the explicit commands of the Constitution but would have directed the courts actively to participate in their violations.* After setting

---

*The examples were an export duty imposed by Congress, notwithstanding the explicit prohibition in the Constitution, "and a suit instituted [by a customs official] to recover it"; a bill of attainder or ex post facto law passed by Congress, notwithstanding the explicit constitutional prohibition, and a "person [is] prosecuted under it"; and a congressional law defying the explicit constitutional con-

out these examples, Marshall proceeded to argue that judicial review authority arises from the fact that the Constitution "direct[s] the judges to take an oath to support it." As many subsequent commentators have said, this oath argument does not support judicial supremacy since members of Congress and the President take the same oath. But in the context of the specific examples Marshall had set out, his oath argument was not intended to establish judicial supremacy: "This oath," Marshall said, "certainly applies, in an especial manner, to [the judges'] conduct in their official character. How immoral to impose it on them, if they were to be used as the instruments, and the knowing instruments, for violating what they swear to support!"[48]

The relative modesty in Marshall's justification for judicial review may have been merely tactical. Subsequent commentators have viewed *Marbury* generally as a brilliant maneuver to aggrandize judicial authority—by lecturing Jefferson and Madison on the illegality of their action in withholding Marbury's commission, by insisting that a judicial remedy must be available to redress Marbury's injury, and by invalidating a congressional act—while at the same time giving his opponents no opportunity to contradict any of these claims because Marshall declined to exercise jurisdiction in the specific case. Marshall's opinion was a dazzling performance; and he may indeed have intended his equality-based justification for judicial review to be merely a waystation toward subsequent claims for judicial supremacy in constitutional interpretation. But viewing *Marbury* in this light obscures its most interesting lesson.

On February 24, 1803, when Marshall delivered his opinion in *Marbury,* it is unlikely that a long-range goal of establishing judicial hegemony over the other branches was in the forefront of his attention. He had a more urgent concern arising from the immediate, aggressive threats by the legislative and executive branches wholly to subjugate the judiciary.* The establishment of

---

ditions for treason convictions by reducing the required number of witnesses from two to one or by admitting confessions made "out of court."

*Even the date of Marshall's opinion implied the imminence of judicial subjugation. In April 1802, immediately after repealing the 1801 Judiciary Act, the Republican Congress abolished one of the two Supreme Court Terms that prejudicial equality was not only a sufficient basis for explaining the formal holding of *Marbury;* equality was a sufficient, and exceedingly ambitious, goal for judicial self-defense.

Viewed in this context, *Marbury* does not teach the conventionally drawn lesson of the virtues of judicial supremacy in constitutional adjudication. As a claim for institutional equality and nothing more, *Marbury* is a model for judicial efforts to address the inherent contradiction in democratic theory that I identified in the first chapter: *Marbury* is, like *Brown v. Board of Education,* a paradigm of the polarized conflict between adversaries that exposes the contradiction between majority rule and equality.

The conflict in *Marbury* was waged between governmental institutions—executive and legislative branches, which sought to subjugate the judiciary (and by implication the Federalists who saw the judiciary as their practical and symbolized representative). In *Brown,* the conflict was between subjugating whites, who dominated state and national government, and blacks, who appealed to the judiciary for practical and symbolic representation. In *Marbury,* moreover, the executive and legislative branches asserted that their campaign to subordinate the judiciary was a justifiable response to claims of judicial supremacy,[49] just as southern whites, after the Civil War, justified their subjugation of blacks by claiming that blacks were attempting to dominate them. In both cases, *Marbury* and *Brown,* the vulnerable party (the judiciary and blacks) identified equality as the core principle at stake; and the central task for judicial intervention was to vindicate this principle in a conflict where the stronger party insisted that equality was irrelevant and that the real issue was who would subjugate whom. The central judicial task in both cases, that is, was to find some means to transform a polarized conflict into a relationship of mutually

---

viously had been authorized by statute, thus in effect forcing the Court to remain in adjournment for fourteen months (from December 1801, when it had granted the show cause order in *Marbury,* until February 1803). The clear purpose of this action was to postpone the possibility that the Court would rule on the constitutionality of the Judiciary Act repeal. In the House debate, a Federalist congressman asked whether this postponement was precedent for "the virtual abolition" of the Court: "If the functions of the Court can be extended by law for fourteen months, what time will arrest us before we arrive at ten or twenty years." 1 Warren at 222–23.

acknowledged equality. This transformation would signify that each of the adversaries could adequately defend itself; and this mutually acknowledged equal defensive capacity would establish the foundation for an ultimate negotiated, and therefore mutually satisfactory, resolution.

This was not Marshall's vocabulary in *Marbury*. But this vocabulary is consistent with his actions and with the contemporary meanings ascribable to his actions. Marshall conveyed the basic purpose of transforming a polarized conflict into a relationship of mutually acknowledged equality by repeatedly appealing to the ideal of the rule of law. After first finding that the formal completion of Marbury's commission had created a "vested legal right," Marshall invoked this ideal:

> The very essence of civil liberty certainly consists in the right of every individual to claim the protection of the laws, whenever he receives an injury. One of the first duties of government is to afford that protection. . . . The government of the United States has been emphatically termed a government of laws, and not of men. It will certainly cease to deserve this high appellation, if the laws furnish no remedy for the violation of a vested legal right.[50]

In this view of "laws" as the protector of individual rights, there was common ground between Marshall and his adversary, Jefferson. Here is Jefferson's version in his 1801 inaugural address:

> During the contest of opinion through which we have passed the animation of discussions and of exertions has sometimes worn an aspect which might impose on strangers unused to think freely and to speak and to write what they think; but this being now decided by the voice of the nation, announced according to the rules of the Constitution, all will, of course, arrange themselves under the will of the law, and unite in common efforts for the common good. All, too, will bear in mind this sacred principle, that though the will of the majority is in all cases to prevail, that will to be rightful must be reasonable; that the minority possess their equal rights, which equal law must protect, and to violate would be oppression. Let us, then, fellow-citizens, unite with one heart and one mind.[51]

Jefferson was thus explicit both in identifying the potential conflict between the majority will and the "equal rights" of the minority and in asserting that "equal law must protect" the minority against "oppression." It was a short step from this premise for Marshall to claim that judges were an appropriate instrumentality for this protective, conflict-transcending, and therefore unifying purpose for the law. This was the point of Marshall's assertion that Marbury's claim to his commission should be characterized as an "individual right" rather than as a "political" claim subject to defeasance by the discretionary action of executive officials chosen by majority rule. This characterization of Marbury's claim was, of course, debatable; "politics" in the ordinary understanding of that word surely engulfed the circumstances of Marbury's appointment. But Marshall was in effect asking Jefferson to transcend the divisive politics of "the contest of opinion through which we have passed" and to give content to the unifying terms of his inaugural address, that the defeated "minority possess their equal rights, which equal law must protect."

From a technical perspective, Marshall's depiction of Marbury's "individual right" to office-holding status was not the only debatable conclusion in his opinion. Every legal characterization was at least questionable—from Marshall's initial judgment that actual delivery of the commission was not necessary in order to "vest" the office (or a "right" to the office) in Marbury, to his forced reading of the statute supposedly granting original jurisdiction to the Supreme Court, to his truncated quotation from the Constitution supposedly establishing that Congress could not give this jurisdiction to the Court.[52] None of these characterizations was demonstrably wrong; each was, however, sufficiently debatable that Marshall could responsibly have endorsed its opposite. An impartial reading of "the law" did not, and could not, resolve these open choices for him.

This kind of impartiality was not, however, Marshall's basic claim for the rule of law. He meant to invoke the law in the spirit of Jefferson's inaugural, as an impartial instrument for transcending political conflict and protecting defeated minorities. Marshall bent his technical readings of the legal materials before him toward the accomplishment of this purpose. But Marshall's impartiality as a judge was itself suspect. Indeed, from the perspective of our current norms of judicial conduct, it is almost incredible that Marshall failed to excuse himself from this specific case; and almost comic that he solemnly presided over the preliminary proceedings where witnesses, including his brother James, testified about whether the then-Secretary of State had properly completed all of the formalities in Marbury's commission.

Our modern conventions about judicial withdrawal are, however, derived from the conventional jurisprudential conception that a judge must be unimpeachably impartial before he or she can adjudicate the case. Marshall's stance in *Marbury* was wholly different. At the outset of the case, he appeared to be an obvious partisan; his implicit goal was to demonstrate that he could transcend his partiality and to appeal for others to follow his example. Marshall's chosen instrument for accomplishing this goal was the persuasive force of the reasoning he set out in his opinion.

The invocation of reasoned discourse as the only proper modality for resolving the dispute in *Marbury* was a self-conscious and ostentatious choice by Marshall. There was another course open to him, on at least two technically sufficient grounds. The first was that Madison, the defendant in the case, never responded to the Court's initial order to show cause why Marbury's commission should not be awarded to him; as Marshall plainly stated at the outset of his opinion, "no cause has been shown." Marshall might have ended his opinion abruptly there, awarding a default judgment to the plaintiff. There were substantial reasons for declining this course, however;[53] at its base, a default judgment would have been nothing more than a disrespectful rejoinder to Madison's apparent disdain for the Court and would have been inconsistent with Marshall's basic purpose in searching for means to transcend this kind of pitched conflict.

The second possibility technically available for bypassing persuasive discourse in the case would have been for Marshall to apply a traditional equitable remedy after finding that Marbury had a right to the commission which had vested prior to its actual delivery. The remedy could follow from the time-honored formulation that a court of equity regards what should be done as done: thus the Supreme Court might have ruled that because Marbury's commission should have been delivered, he was entitled to serve as a justice of the peace as if the commission had been delivered.* This would not have ended all controversy; executive officials could still have refused to honor Marbury's subsequent official actions or to pay his salary. But this equitable remedy would have conclusively settled the legitimacy of Marbury's status, at least from the perspective of the federal judiciary; and Marshall was not prepared to reach such a conclusive resolution.

This was the heart of Marshall's strategy: to avoid reaching a conclusive resolution of the dispute. But if this had been the whole of his strategy, he could have accomplished it more swiftly than by the serpentine route he chose. Marshall avoided a conclusive resolution only at the very end of his opinion by ruling that the Supreme Court had no jurisdiction to entertain Marbury's suit; but as a technical matter he could have addressed the jurisdictional question at the outset (and by modern conventions at least, this should have been his initial inquiry, in order to establish the unquestionable legitimacy of his authority to "speak the law"—his "juris/diction").

Marshall chose, however, a different order of inquiry: first, whether Marbury had a vested right to the commission; second, whether courts of law might properly provide a remedy for this right; and only third, whether the proper tribunal for such remedy was the Supreme Court where Marbury had filed suit. As many commentators on the case have observed, this order of inquiry permitted Marshall to lecture Jefferson about Marbury's rights without fear of contradiction, since he did not actually command the executive branch to do anything. This was clearly one aspect of the brilliance of Marshall's *tour de force*. The basic reality is, however, that Marshall and his Court lived in fear of imminent contradiction. To be sure, Marshall did not want to give needlessly provocative impetus to this already-churning Republican effort, and his refusal to exercise jurisdiction was consistent with this goal. But if he had been single-mindedly intent on avoid-

---

*Marshall belittled the physical significance of the commission in another context in his opinion. Arguing that judicial consideration of Marbury's right to the commission did not intrude on executive prerogatives or "the secrets of the cabinet," Marshall observed that the controversy "respects a paper, which, according to law, is upon record, and to a copy of which the law gives a right, on the payment of ten cents." 5 U.S. (1 Cranch) at 170.

ing provocation, the more modest, cautious course would have been to decline jurisdiction at the outset without lecturing Jefferson or holding out the prospect for Marbury that he might file suit in District Court and readily prevail on the basis of Marshall's disputation in the first two-thirds of the opinion.*

Marshall was not avoiding provocation. He was appealing to reason and avoiding the invocation of force. He thus held out a model for resolving the controversy not only between Marbury and Madison but between the Court and its adversaries in the executive and legislative branches, between the electorally defeated Federalists and the victorious Republicans. This was Marshall's ideal of the rule of law: not rule by judges but rule by reason.[54] The question of judicial supremacy—whether judges were the privileged embodiment of reason—was not central to Marshall's concern at the time. The crucial issue was whether reason would prevail over force in partisan conflict and, to this end, whether the other branches would give equal respect to the judiciary's claim to reason. Jefferson had identified this issue in his inaugural address: "that though the will of the majority is in all cases to prevail, that will to be rightful must be reasonable; that the minority possess their equal rights, which equal law must protect." This was the basis for Marshall's appeal to Jefferson.

But Marshall did not renounce the possibility of force. In technical terms, he held only that Marbury had filed suit in the wrong court; he strongly suggested, on the basis of the legal principles set out in his preliminary lecture to Jefferson, that Marbury could ultimately obtain a judicial order enforcing his right to the commission in another court. Marbury, in fact, did file suit in federal district court immediately after Marshall's decision. On the face of it, therefore, Marshall did nothing more than postpone the use of judicial force; coercion still hovered in the background.

In this apparent postponement without renunciation of force, Marshall instinctively identified the unique advantage of the ju-

---

*Jefferson was in fact angered by Marshall's lecture, which he viewed as extrajudicial obiter dicta, though he was not at all aroused by Marshall's claim for judicial authority to invalidate congressional acts, which was the basis for declining jurisdiction. See 1 Warren at 244 (Jefferson's "indignation over Marshall's opinion continued hot up to the day of his death.")

diciary in implementing the Madisonian conception of governance by consultation and accommodation. The central problem for this conception is its vulnerability to coercive disruption. Every imaginable rule for collective decision-making is open to manipulative self-dealing. But decisional rules that appear to require the renunciation of force are especially vulnerable because they open the possibility for first-strike advantage. Thus the cooperative mindset, which is necessary for the successful implementation and long-range stability of the Madisonian conception, appears easily displaced and ultimately overwhelmed by narrowly competitive self-aggrandizement.[55]

John Marshall did not solve this problem in *Marbury v. Madison;* but he did visibly, and even ostentatiously, call it into attention. Marshall, that is, appealed for the transcendence of aggrandizing partisan conflict; but he promised that if cooperation were not forthcoming, the conflict would not only persist but escalate in intensity. This promise was embedded in masterfully ambiguous doubletalk. Marshall of course did not say that, unless Jefferson cooperated, a federal district court would wage partisan battle for its fellow-Federalist Marbury; he did say, however, that the judiciary would do battle for Marbury as a partisan on behalf of the "rights of individuals." And Marshall of course did not say that the judiciary would defeat Jefferson in this battle; he could not promise this since, as Hamilton had observed in *Federalist* 78, the judiciary was clearly "the least dangerous branch." But as Marshall's lecture pointedly reminded him, Jefferson must know that if he chose to ignore a definitive judicial order on Marbury's behalf, more than Marbury's interests or even John Marshall's personal and institutional interests would be at stake. Jefferson might successfully withhold Marbury's commission in the teeth of a direct judicial order; but then he must reckon with the possibility that Marbury's extra-judicial partisans would see themselves as generally threatened by his conduct and accordingly mistrustful of their capacity to protect their interests by peaceful recourse to judicial or electoral processes.[56]

The specific effect of Marshall's ruling in *Marbury* was thus to bring a pause in the battle—a calculated appeal for reconsideration by the erstwhile victors, a plea to the strong from the weak (Marbury, his defeated political allies, and his vulnerable judicial protectors) for accommodation and reconciliation, and an implicit threat that the weak might otherwise be driven to desperate and socially destructive measures of self-protection. A direct judicial order in Marbury's favor would have had these same implications; but the strategic brilliance of Marshall's solution, declining jurisdiction and thus not resolving the controversy, conveyed these implications in bold relief and at the same time gave considerable room on all sides for recourse to negotiated settlement. Thus, Marshall not only followed the intended inclination of Madison's structural scheme toward consultation and accommodation among all of the governance institutions; he seized and instinctively elaborated on the special strengths of the judiciary in facilitating this goal in intensely polarized disputes where, as Madison himself had understood, consultative processes are least likely to be invoked or to succeed.

It is of course ironic that Marshall should act to vindicate this Madisonian conception of governance in a dispute where Madison was a principal antagonist; but Madison had implicitly anticipated this ironic possibility in his earlier writings. He did not trust his own capacity to transcend self-interest any more than he trusted others. This general incapacity was, as Madison saw it in *Federalist* 10, the basic problem in governance:

> No man is allowed to be a judge in his own cause, because his interest would certainly bias his judgment, and, not improbably, corrupt his integrity. With equal, nay with greater reason, a body of men are unfit to be both judges and parties at the same time; yet what are many of the most important acts of legislation but so many judicial determinations, not indeed concerning the rights of single persons, but concerning the rights of large bodies of citizens? . . . Justice ought to hold the balance between them. Yet the parties are, *and must be,* themselves the judges.[57]

In this passage, Madison did not intend to exempt specific judicial determinations of individual rights from the inevitable taint of self-interest; for everyone, he held, a "connection subsists between his reason and his self-love [so that] his opinions and his passions will have a reciprocal influence on each other."[58] This was the basis for Madison's adamant opposition to judicial supremacy in constitutional interpretation; and whatever conception of the judicial role was established by *Marbury v. Madison,* John Marshall's opinion and his role in this great foundational case surely shows the force of judges' self-interest in constitutional adjudication.

From a Madisonian perspective, however, Marshall's blatant self-interest does not necessarily impeach the integrity of his decision. As much as any other element in the case, Marshall's personal interest made starkly visible the underlying problem of partisan conflict that Madison's conception of governance attempted to resolve. As Madison saw it, partisan conflict could be appropriately resolved, and the legitimacy of the social order established, only by a mutual renunciation of self-aggrandizement and coercion on all sides, only by a visibly sustained commitment to processes of consultation and accommodation rather than to force. From a Madisonian perspective, this renunciation can as a practical matter occur only interactively and continuously. Since self-aggrandizing motives are so powerful and social trust is consequently so tentative and fragile, this renunciation will not reliably occur unilaterally or by means of a general social contract that preemptively binds all possible antagonists. It thus follows from the Madisonian perspective that the adjudicative process, like all institutional processes, cannot as a practical matter—and therefore need not as a principled matter—begin with a binding renunciation of self-aggrandizing coercion and commitment to reasoned discourse. The very purpose of the adjudicative process, as in all institutional interactions, is to bring all of the adversarial participants, necessarily including the judges, to the conclusion that they should affirm this difficult and always fragile commitment. *Marbury v. Madison* embodies this interactive, Madisonian conception of the governance process.

Direct parallels can also be seen between Marshall's defense of Marbury's claim against the aggressively victorious Jeffersonian Republicans and Lincoln's later defense of the Union position at Fort Sumter—parallels which illuminate the uses of judicial authority in vindicating the equality principle. Both Marshall and Lincoln withheld application of coercive force and yet they refused to surrender their own claims to equal institutional status, or to abandon their institutional espousal of the equality principle on behalf of the threatened disputants whose cause they represented. Both Marshall and Lincoln thereby visibly attempted to redefine the terms of a polarized political conflict, to persuade the initial aggressor to abandon his pursuit of unilaterally imposed victory and instead to embrace the principle of equality as the basis for a continuing political relationship with his apparently vulnerable adversary. Both Marshall and Lincoln carefully limited themselves to demanding equality rather than subjugative supremacy (and both were misread by their antagonists). Both men invoked loyalty to the Constitution and its "rule of law" as the basis for resolving conflict; in both cases they identified specific substantive provisions for this resolution in the constitutional text, but more fundamentally they pointed to the institutional framework established by the Constitution, premised on mutually acknowledged equality, as the only possible instrument for peaceful transcendence of polar conflict.

There is, finally, an instructive parallel between *Marbury* and *Brown v. Board of Education.* Though Madisonian and Lincolnian premises can be discerned in both *Marbury* and *Brown,* the Court was not led in either case to embrace these premises by a self-conscious understanding or endorsement of them. In both cases, the Court was led much more by the force of circumstances—by the immediate threat to social order arising from the fierce partisan conflict in both *Marbury* and *Brown,* coupled with the Justices' own recent experience of the hopeful possibilities of social collaboration (in establishing a new government in the two decades before *Marbury* and successfully waging war against the Great Depression and international fascism in the two decades before *Brown*). But whether or not the Justices were self-conscious about it, the central similarity between *Marbury* and *Brown* which links them to Madison and Lincoln is in the distinction both cases draw between the proclamation and the enforcement of rights. Marshall's principled lecture to Jefferson joined with his denial of jurisdiction to give immediate effect to those principles was precisely paralleled in the principles proclaimed in *Brown I* immediately followed by the enforcement delay announced in *Brown II.* In both cases, the Court clearly meant to appeal for voluntary acquiescence to the principles it endorsed. By withholding immediate enforcement, the Court at least implicitly acknowledged what the fierce partisan conflict in the cases clearly connoted: that the legitimacy of the principles adduced by the Court to resolve the conflict would not be adequately established unless all parties ultimately agreed to their application. In both cases, contrary to the current teachings of conventional constitutional theory, the Court did not withhold its intervention until it had established its unimpeachable authority to resolve the controversy. In both cases, the Court invoked its authority in order to precipitate a process of collaboration and accommodation by which it might earn legitimacy both for itself and for the principles it invoked to transcend the partisan conflict.

In the specific aftermath of *Marbury*, the Court essentially accomplished this goal. William Marbury himself never received his commission; after he filed suit in federal district court, a series of procedural delays carried the case beyond the expiration of the five-year statutory term to which his commission applied and the suit was ultimately dismissed as moot.[59] But Jefferson's adamance regarding Marbury's commission did not carry him toward further attacks on the Federalist-dominated judiciary. Though the Republican leader in the Senate, John Randolph, worked assiduously throughout 1804 to impeach Justice Chase, Jefferson never endorsed the enterprise. Marshall's homiletic in *Marbury* almost certainly played no direct role in motivating Jefferson's silence. Two weeks after deciding *Marbury*, however, the Court unanimously upheld the constitutionality of the Republican repeal of the Judiciary Act of 1801, which had been the centerpiece of Jefferson's attack on the Federalist domination of the judiciary.[60] Moreover, the Senate vote on Chase's impeachment did not take place until March 1805, when Jefferson was about to be inaugurated for a second term—this time having won the electoral votes of every state but Connecticut and Delaware. Against this background of greater national unity, evident restraint by the Federalist-appointed Justices, and Jefferson's "decisive" silence,[61] six Republican Senators voted with nine Federalists to acquit Chase and the impeachment failed to obtain the necessary two-thirds (though it was supported by a simple majority of nineteen Republican Senators).

By this close margin, the basic principle for which Marshall had contended in *Marbury*—the independent, coordinate status of the federal judiciary—was vindicated. William Marbury obtained no personal benefit from the lawsuit he initiated; like the schoolchildren who were the named plaintiffs in *Brown v. Board of Education,* Marbury's satisfaction would come only from the ultimate acceptance of the principle advocated on his behalf. From the comfortable distance of almost two centuries, the principle in *Marbury* seems self-evidently correct—an easy decision, even if the politics of the case were difficult. But, like *Brown* in 1954, the principle and the politics of *Marbury* could not be disentangled except by a deliberative process that was carefully cultivated and sustained by the Supreme Court.

The Hamiltonian Marshall

This is the opening of John Marshall's 1819 opinion in *McCulloch v. Maryland:*

> In the case now to be determined, the defendant, a sovereign State, denies the obligation of a law enacted by the legislature of the Union, and the plaintiff, on his part, contests the validity of an act which has been passed by the legislature of that State. The constitution of our country, in its most interesting and vital parts, is to be considered; the conflicting powers of the government of the Union and of its members, as marked in that constitution, are to be discussed; and an opinion given, which may essentially influence the great operations of the government. No tribunal can approach such a question without a deep sense of its importance, and of the awful responsibility involved in its decision. But it must be decided peacefully, or remain a source of hostile legislation, perhaps of hostility of a still more serious nature; and if it is to be so decided, by this tribunal alone can the decision be made. On the Supreme Court of the United States has the constitution of our country devolved this important duty.[62]

This magisterial paragraph marks the distance that Marshall's Court had traveled since the vulnerable days of Jefferson's first term. By 1819 five of the seven Justices had been appointed by Republican Presidents; only Marshall and Bushrod Washington held commissions signed by John Adams. *McCulloch* was nonetheless a unanimous decision upholding the congressional act that established the second Bank of the United States and invalidating a state law that taxed the operation of the Bank—a decision that Alexander Hamilton would have applauded both for its endorsement of the national government's role in financial policy and its conception of the Supreme Court's constitutional role in federal–state relations. *McCulloch* was not, moreover, a unique decision in its apparent embrace of Federalist tenets; during the preceding decade, a unanimous Court (with a majority of Republican appointees) had acted to protect federal laws from state interference and had upheld its own authority to overturn state-court decisions in such matters.[63]

Not only the Court but the Union itself was more firmly established in 1819 than in the divided days of *Marbury*. When Madison left the presidency two years before, John Adams wrote Jefferson in an unusual (though characteristically tempered) burst of euphoria that, "notwithstanding a thousand Faults and blunders, [Madison's] Administration has acquired more glory and established more Union, than all his three Predecessors, Washington, Adams and Jefferson, put together."[64] The long-sought grail of national unity seemed to be within grasp. James Monroe had been elected president in 1816 with 183 of 217 electoral votes. Throughout his two terms there was no significant organized opposition party, and he would be reelected in 1820 by only one vote short of a unanimous electoral vote. In his first inaugural, Monroe declared that "discord does not belong to our system" and that "the American people . . . constitute one great family with a common interest."[65]

This national harmony was not complete; personal rancor was still common in political debate generally. In 1820, during congressional deliberation on Missouri statehood, intense controversy suddenly erupted about the future of slavery in the territories generally; and, though the Bank of the United States had been rechartered in 1816 in a flush of nationalist enthusiasm after the successful second war against the British, a financial panic in 1818 had led many states, including Maryland, to take retaliatory action against the Bank.

This was the immediate context of Marshall's decision in *McCulloch:* a conflict between state and federal governments against an apparent background of widespread national unity. Thus Marshall's prefatory observation that the controversy "must be decided peacefully [by the Supreme Court], or remain a source of hostile legislation, perhaps of hostility of a still more serious nature," might have been simply a rhetorical flourish. But it was clearly more than that for Marshall. The depth of his concerns about "still more serious" hostility are apparent in a letter he published under the apt sobriquet "Friend of the Court" in 1819, responding to critics of his opinion in *McCulloch*:

> The zealous and perservering hostility with which the constitution was originally opposed, cannot be forgotten. The deep rooted and vindictive hate, which grew out of unfounded jealousies, and was aggravated by defeat, though suspended for a time, seems never to have been appeased. . . . The leaders of this plan, like skilful engineers, batter the weakest part of the citadel. . . . The judicial department, being without power, without patronage, without the legitimate means of ingratiating itself with the people, forms this weakest part; and is, at the same time, necessary to the very existence of the government.[66]

Marshall thus remained gripped by the spectre of polarized conflict. Unlike in *Marbury*, Marshall's opinion in *McCulloch* was a response more to his pervasive underlying concern than to the immediate dispute at hand. Unlike in *Marbury*, moreover, Marshall was less concerned with appeasing the immediate adversaries than with averting future hostilities. If Marshall had been more concerned with resolving the immediate dispute, his opinion could have reached the same results—both upholding the congressional act and invalidating the state tax on the Bank—by a more direct and at the same time more conciliatory route than he actually pursued.

The central constitutional issue in validating the congressional act was whether the Bank's creation was "necessary and proper" for carrying out the specific enumerated powers granted to Congress by Article I.* The Bank's opponents argued, as Madison

---

*Article I, section 8, provides that "Congress shall have power . . . to make all laws which shall be necessary and proper for carrying into execution the foregoing powers, and all other powers vested by this Constitution in the government of the United States."

had done in 1791 opposing Hamilton's plan for establishing the first Bank, that a stringent standard of "necessity" must be met under this clause in order to keep congressional authority from intruding on state preserves. But in signing the charter for the second Bank in 1816, Madison himself acknowledged that the historical experience of the first Bank and contemporary financial needs satisfied an appropriately constrained construction of the "necessary and proper" clause. Marshall could have assumed the most stringent imaginable standard of "necessity" and even so, on the basis of this specific history, the Bank bill would still have passed muster. Indeed, at the outset of his opinion, Marshall in fact made this argument but only in passing, on the way to his more fundamental inquiry as if, he said, "the question [were] entirely new"[67]—as if, that is, the dispute were as novel and raw as it had been in 1791 when Hamilton's proposed Bank bill opened the rift between Federalists and Republicans.

Marshall then ruled not simply that the Court would eschew a stringent standard of "necessity" in favor of a more relaxed one in judging the validity of the congressional act but that the Court would apply no standard at all. The "necessary and proper" clause, he held, gave no warrant to the judiciary to review the "necessity" of any particular means that Congress might choose in carrying out "ends [that were] legitimate . . . within the scope of the constitution."[68] To the immediate critics who were concerned with protecting state prerogatives against federal incursions, Marshall's opinion appeared to give virtually limitless scope to congressional authority, on the ground that almost any measure could be construed as a "means" to some constitutionally approved "end."[69] In his anonymous newspaper defense of his opinion, Marshall insisted that the criticism was misplaced, citing the statement in the Court's opinion that "should Congress, under the pretext of executing its powers, pass laws for the accomplishment of objects not entrusted to the government," those laws would be invalidated.[70] Marshall's critics, then and afterward, were not mollified but continued to believe that Marshall intended to implement Hamilton's original conception of boundless and supreme national authority.

This criticism, like the common view of Marshall's supposed farsighted strategy in *Marbury* to lay the groundwork for an ultimate claim of judicial supremacy, misses the heart of Marshall's immediate anxiety. In *McCulloch,* Marshall was less concerned with expanding the scope of congressional authority than with identifying the proper role of the Supreme Court in suppressing conflict between national and state governments. He was unwilling to use the "necessary and proper" clause as an instrument for controlling congressional authority—not because he wanted to vest unlimited authority in Congress but because he did not consider the clause to be an effective instrument for judicial resolution of conflict.

"The word 'necessary,'" he said, "has not a fixed character peculiar to itself. It admits of all degrees of comparison. . . . A thing may be necessary, very necessary, absolutely or indispensably necessary. To no mind would the same idea be conveyed by these several phrases."[71] The pre-litigative history of the dispute regarding the Bank—from 1791 when Madison argued that it was not "necessary" within the meaning of Article I, section 8, to 1816 when Madison agreed that it was "necessary"—not only illustrated Marshall's proposition but demonstrated, for Marshall, why the necessity standard would not serve his basic purpose: to give the judiciary tools for authoritatively and conclusively ending factional conflict. This is the vision of judicial authority that lay beneath Marshall's conclusion in *McCulloch* that "to inquire into the degree of [a law's] necessity would be to pass the line which circumscribes the judicial department, and to tread on legislative ground."[72]

This same concern with identifying judicial regulatory techniques for conclusively ending conflict was even more clearly apparent in Marshall's consideration of the second issue in *McCulloch,* the validity of the state tax on the Bank's operations. Marshall held that all state taxes on the operation of federal instrumentalities were inherently void. A more limited rule was available for resolution of the immediate dispute; the Maryland tax was aimed only at the federal Bank and exempted state-chartered institutions. Marshall was not content, however, with a nondiscrimination principle. "That the power of taxing [a federal instrumentality] may be exercised so as to destroy it, is too obvious to be denied," Marshall asserted. To an untutored eye, it might also seem obvious that a court might rebuff a "destructive" tax while permitting "nondestructive" state measures. Moreover, absolute prohibition of state taxation meant, in the context of the bank dispute, that states would effectively be disabled from levying taxes on state-chartered banks unless they were prepared to confer competitive advantages on the judicially immunized, untaxable federal bank. This was surely a legitimate rationale for a nondestructive state tax; and an accompanying nondiscrimination principle would powerfully inhibit any destructive impulses since state-imposed ruin would fall equally on state and federal facilities.

But Marshall refused to consider, as he put it, "the perplexing inquiry, so unfit for the judicial department, what degree of taxation is the legitimate use, and what degree may amount to the abuse of the power."[73] This is virtually identical to Marshall's reason for refusing to assess the validity of a congressional act based on the "degree of its necessity." Like necessity, "to no mind would the same idea be conveyed" in evaluating degrees of destructiveness in taxation. Marshall claimed, however, that a flat rule forbidding all state taxation provided

> an intelligible standard, applicable to every case to which the power may be applied. . . . We have a principle which is safe for the States, and safe for the Union. We are relieved, as we ought to be, from clashing sovereignty; from interfering powers; from a repugnancy between a right in one government to pull down what there is an acknowledged right in another to build up; from the incompatibility of a right in one government to destroy what there is a right in another to preserve.[74]

This heated portrayal of the issue at stake—"clashing sovereignty," "interfering powers," "repugnancy [and] incompatibility" of rights to "destroy [and] preserve"—was only the beginning of Marshall's fervor. He immediately attacked the question from a different angle, in this illuminating extended passage:

> That the power to tax involves the power to destroy . . . [is a] proposition not to be denied. But all inconsistencies are to be reconciled by the magic of the word CONFIDENCE. Taxation, it is said, does not necessarily and unavoidably destroy. To carry it to the excess of destruction would be an abuse, to presume which, would banish that confidence which is essential to all governments.
>
> But is this a case of confidence? Would the people of any one State trust those of another with a power to control the most

insignificant operations of their State government? We know they would not. Why, then, should we suppose that the people of any one State should be willing to trust those of another with a power to control the operations of a government to which they have confided their most important and most valuable interests. In the legislature of the Union alone, all are represented. The legislature of the Union alone, therefore, can be trusted by the people with the power of controlling measures which concern all, in the confidence that it will not be abused. This, then, is not a case of confidence, and we must consider it as it really is.

If we apply the principle for which the State of Maryland contends, to the constitution generally, we shall find it capable of changing totally the character of that instrument. We shall find it capable of arresting all the measures of the government, and of prostrating it at the foot of the States.[75]

Here is the embattled passion which Marshall more fully vented when he was cloaked as an anonymous newspaper correspondent: the "zealous and perservering hostility with which the constitution was originally opposed . . . the deep rooted and vindictive hate" directed against "the very existence of the government." This was not, Marshall openly proclaimed, "a case of confidence, and we must consider it as it really is." It really was WAR.

As Marshall saw it: but he also distorted what he saw. When Marshall insisted "we know" that the people of one State would not trust those of another to control their affairs, he ignored the structural foundation of the federal government. He spoke as if federal and state governments were wholly separate entities though in fact each state was directly represented both formally and practically in the Senate, and at least practically in the presidency since in 1819 most state legislatures still directly chose presidential electors. The people of each state as such accordingly exercised mutual control of their common affairs. Marshall imagined separate and inherently antagonistic sovereigns but, as Madison had clearly seen, the structural intertwining of the federal and state governments indivisibly blurred sovereignty; and though antagonisms might arise among states and between some states and the federal government, the regular interactions among states within the structural framework of the federal government might, as Madison hoped, engender transcendent mutual trust. But Marshall was not confident of this possibility; and lacking confidence, he set out a structure in *McCulloch* for the relations of federal and state governments that, if followed, would reduce rather than enhance the opportunities for developing trust. Just as Marshall imagined implacable hostility in *McCulloch* where a calmer observer would see reconcilable conflict, Marshall responded in *McCulloch* in ways that increased rather than allayed antagonism.

The ways in *McCulloch* that Marshall rejected opportunities for interactive conciliation and thereby unwittingly worked to heighten mistrust can be concretely illustrated in a hypothetical example he used early in his opinion. In arguing for interpretive latitude in construing the constitutional grants of congressional authority, Marshall said:

> Take, for example, the power "to establish post offices and post roads." This power is executed by the single act of making the establishment. But, from this has been inferred the power and duty of carrying the mail along the post road, from one post office to another. And, from this implied power, has again been inferred the right to punish those who steal letters from the post office, or rob the mail. It may be said, with some plausibility, that the right to carry the mail, and to punish those who rob it, is not indispensably necessary to the establishment of a post office and post road. This right is indeed essential to the beneficial exercise of the power, but not indispensably necessary to its existence.[76]

By his artful juxtaposition of the two implied powers—carrying the mail and criminally punishing mail theft—Marshall obscured an important distinction. If the federal government established post offices but hired no one to carry the mails, it is unlikely that they would find a bureaucratic organization already in place within state governments to do the job, particularly for interstate deliveries. Protecting against mail theft is, however, not much different from the ordinary police function of protecting everyone within state borders against theft while at home or on the road; and an individual state's capacity to address interstate flight by criminals is similarly not much different whether the problem is theft of mail or other movable property.

Accordingly, when Congress established the postal service and also provided federal criminal penalties for mail theft, someone might have asked why the latter measure was truly necessary.* The sponsors of the new law might have responded that state police forces were demonstrably inadequate for the special tasks involved, or even that state authorities had been consulted and declined their services; or the sponsors might have responded that they assumed without any direct experience or evidence on the matter that states were generally hostile to the national government and would accordingly encourage theft of federal mail; or the sponsors might have said that they simply hadn't thought about the possibility of relying on state police assistance.

These three different responses express dramatically different visions of the character of relations between the federal and state governments. If the overall success of our constitutional scheme depends on fostering mutual confidence between these two sets of institutional actors, then only the first response is satisfactory. If it is proper for the judiciary to construe the Constitution so as to contribute to the overall success of the enterprise, then the judges might rule that only the first response would satisfy the command of Article I, section 8, that congressional exercise of a nonenumerated power such as enacting criminal laws against mail theft must be "necessary and proper."

If, of course, a court were to invalidate a federal criminal provision on this ground, this ruling would not be fixed and immutable for all time. Experience might prove the need for such laws based on the subsequently demonstrated inadequacy of state enforcement efforts (whether because of inefficiency, inattention, or active bias). Congress might then re-enact the law and ask the Court to reconsider on the ground that what was not constitutionally "necessary" yesterday has become so today (just as Mad-

---

*Madison in effect raised this question in 1791 when he opposed the creation of the first Bank of the United States. He noted that during the Revolutionary War, the Continental Congress had established a bank of North America notwithstanding the absence of explicit authority in the Articles of Confederation. The bank, he said, "was however the child of [wartime] necessity . . . [But] did the United States pass laws to punish the counterfeiting of the notes of that Bank? They did not, being convinced of the invalidity of any such law—the bank therefore took shelter under the authority of the State." Remarks on the Bank Bill, U.S. House of Representatives, February 8, 1791, 13 *Papers of Madison* 386.

ison had changed his view of the Bank's constitutionality based on the actual experience of its necessity). On the face of it, these multiple interactions might seem to breed rather than reduce conflict: the Court actively oversees the original congressional deliberations to assure adequate respect for state police prerogatives, thus forcing the federal government into at least initial, and most likely grudging, dependence on state capabilities; and if federal needs are not met then, perhaps after angry recriminations, Congress returns for yet another round of argument in court. As Marshall concluded in another context in *McCulloch,* how much simpler to have a clear-cut rule that would settle these conflicts at the outset regarding the existence of authority to pass the law (whether to establish a bank, to tax the bank or to punish mail theft). With such a rule, he said, "we are relieved, as we ought to be, from clashing sovereignty; from interfering powers."

But Marshall did not acknowledge the possible cost of avoiding such clashes. What if, in the hypothetical example of mail theft, the federal government, at first forced reluctantly to depend on state police power, learns that the states are in fact reliable protectors of the federal interest. Has the federal government not also learned that the states may be more trustworthy generally than it originally suspected? And what might each state learn about the strength of its general commitment to the federal enterprise in the very process of being enlisted as an active participant? It is possible, that is, that the happy resolution of the initial conflict regarding the mail theft laws would teach that similarly satisfactory accommodations might be reached in other, apparently unrelated federal–state conflicts. Marshall's instinct in *McCulloch* to suppress conflict at the outset might purchase peace in the short run but thereby deprive all parties of repeated opportunities to experience and accommodate conflict. And so small suspicions would grow unchecked by interactive experience into deeper mistrust and more rigorous estrangement. And with this insult not appeased and that rebuff not atoned, we may finally arrive at secession and civil war.

Was Marshall then clearly correct when he claimed in *McCulloch* that "an intelligible standard, applicable to every case . . . [yields] a principle which is safe for the States, and safe for the Union . . . [by avoiding] clashing sovereignty [and] interfering powers"?

Marshall was led to this conviction because he saw implacable hostility and deep-rooted hatred in all social conflict, because—as he said outright in *McCulloch*—he saw only the possibility of "magic" and not a reliably invoked human capacity in "the word CONFIDENCE." *McCulloch* did not cause the American Civil War, but its underlying attitude did.

The fundamental component of that attitude was Hamilton's view of unitary sovereignty. In *McCulloch,* Marshall both embraced and elaborated on Hamilton's view. First, he explicitly rejected the competing conception of unitary sovereignty that Jefferson had set out in the Kentucky Resolution, that the Constitution had been adopted "as the act of sovereign and independent States." It would follow from this view, Marshall said, that the "powers of the general government . . . are delegated by the States, who alone are truly sovereign; and must be exercised in subordination to the States, who alone possess supreme dominion."[77]

Marshall responded that the people, not the states, had adopted the Constitution. "It is true," he said, "they assembled in their several States—and where else should they have assembled?" To this comic *non sequitur* he added this false assertion: "No political dreamer was ever wild enough to think of breaking down the lines which separate the States, and of compounding the American people into one common mass"[78]—thus ignoring, or perhaps more likely in ignorance of, Hamilton's wild dream of national consolidation which he reported to the Philadelphia Convention in his extended free association on June 18, 1787. But Marshall did not intend to implement Hamilton's original wish for national supremacy, even if he had known of it. Marshall was instead intent on implementing, and elaborating the implications of, Hamilton's subsequent vision in *Federalist* 78 of judicial supremacy.

Marshall did not speak directly of judicial supremacy in *McCulloch;* he spoke only of the competing claims for supremacy between the federal and state governments. Indeed, in specifically rejecting state authority to tax federal instrumentalities, Marshall seemed to envision a virtual Hobbesian sovereignty in the national government; the state tax was invalid, Marshall held, because "it is of the very essence of supremacy to remove all obstacles to its action within its own sphere, and so to modify every power vested in subordinate governments, as to exempt its own operations from their own influence."[79] But this observation had a careful qualification embedded in it: the national government was supreme only "within its own sphere"; and it was the role of the Supreme Court to delineate that sphere. This was the meaning of Marshall's prefatory statement that "this tribunal alone" had "the important duty" of "peacefully" adjudicating "the conflicting powers of the general and state governments . . . and the supremacy of their respective laws, when they are in opposition."

Marshall thus drew out the underlying implication of Hamilton's view of the judicial role: as the supreme overseer of the constitutional scheme, not so much imperial as umpireal. In carrying out this role, Marshall chose techniques that would reduce the occasions for conflict between the federal and state governments and would accordingly minimize the need for repeated judicial interventions to resolve these conflicts. This was his basic underlying rationale for refusing to adjudicate differing degrees of necessity, thus disclaiming any judicial use for the "necessary and proper" clause, and for adopting a blanket rule against any state taxation rather than calibrating differing degrees of legitimacy and abuse in successive cases (or even endorsing an antidiscrimination rule which might invite continued federal–state conflict). Marshall thus laid the groundwork for the theory of "dual sovereignty" among the federal and state governments, which emerged more explicitly in later Supreme Court jurisprudence— a theory that gave central importance to the judicial role in delineating and patrolling the boundaries between the two sovereigns.[80]

Marshall and Andrew Jackson

A decade later, the dispute that Marshall had claimed to resolve in *McCulloch*—whether the people or the states had adopted the Constitution—re-emerged as the central political conflict of the day. In the Nullification Crisis of 1828–1832, however, the Court played no role—notwithstanding its self-definition as the constitutionally designated umpire to decide federal–state conflicts "peacefully" or the greater likelihood in this conflict than in *McCulloch* of "hostility of a still more serious nature." In a series of actions between 1828 and 1832, South Carolina challenged the authority not only of the federal courts but of any federal agency to review state action. The terms of battle were directly reminiscent of the struggle over the Alien and Sedition Acts in 1798; the South Carolina legislature copied Jefferson's language in the Kentucky resolution, to declare "utterly null and void" the 1828 and 1832 tariff acts increasing impositions on manufactured goods.[81] In a further ironic parallel, the second-ranking federal executive officials, Vice Presidents Thomas Jefferson and John Calhoun, were the draftsmen and principal strategists for the challenge to federal authority mounted respectively by Kentucky in 1798 and South Carolina in 1828.[82]

In 1798, however, the federal judiciary did play a more active role upholding national authority in the prosecution of the Sedition Act than in 1828–1832. In its nullification measures, moreover, South Carolina directly attacked federal judicial authority, specifically prohibiting any appeals to the Supreme Court regarding its actions.[83] But notwithstanding the Marshall Court's rulings on behalf of its own authority against such state measures and its clear stance in *McCulloch* favoring the national government against state sovereignty claims, the Jackson administration did not actively seek to invoke judicial support in this conflict.

Jackson was in fact no friend of federal judicial authority. Though he fiercely opposed the constitutional position of the nullifiers, viewing their claims as acts at "the brink of insurrection and treason,"[84] Jackson was at the same time intent on disputing judicial claims for supremacy in constitutional interpretation. In 1832, as the prolonged nullification crisis was reaching its climax, two events occurred that signaled Jackson's resistance to judicial authority. The first, in March 1832, was the Supreme Court's decision in *Worcester v. Georgia*,[85] overturning state assertion of jurisdiction over the Cherokee tribe as inconsistent with superceding federal treaties and thereby challenging one of the key planks in Jackson's policy toward Indians. Though Jackson did not actually say what was popularly ascribed to him—"John Marshall has made his decision, now let him enforce it"—he was not prepared to give active support to the decision.[86] Indeed, on December 4, 1832—just one week before Jackson sent a blistering condemnation of the South Carolina nullifiers to the Congress— Jackson informed Congress that it was "impracticable as yet to make a satisfactory adjustment" of the Cherokees' dispute with

Georgia,[87] thus patently ignoring the "adjustment" of the controversy previously announced by the Supreme Court.

A second, even clearer indication of Jackson's attitude came in July 1832, when he vetoed the congressional act renewing the charter of the Bank of the United States. Jackson explicitly maintained that the Bank was unconstitutional notwithstanding the contrary ruling in *McCulloch*. The Court's constitutional interpretations, Jackson said, "ought not to control the coordinate" branches and the "opinion of the judges has no more authority over Congress than the opinion of Congress has over the judges, and on that point the President is independent of both."[88]

It is thus not surprising that Jackson would ignore Marshall's implicit offer in *McCulloch* of judicial assistance to vindicate national authority in the Nullification Crisis; he did not want to strengthen the Court generally or the *McCulloch* decision specifically. In his Nullification Proclamation of December 10, 1832, Jackson railed against South Carolina and its compact theory of state sovereignty but did not cite the Supreme Court's decision even as indirect support for his position.[89] He did criticize as unconstitutional South Carolina's prohibition of appeals to the Court but only in passing, as one illustration of the state's general assault on the Constitution.[90] One month later, Jackson sent his so-called Force Bill Message to the Congress, where he revealed his deeper disregard for the significance of federal judicial authority in this dispute. As a result of South Carolina's actions, he said, "the execution of the laws is rendered impracticable even through the ordinary judicial tribunals of the United States";[91] though Jackson urged the Congress to expedite removal of suits from state to federal court to protect customs officials against state harassment, his central proposal in the Force Bill Message was that Congress should acknowledge executive power to act alone by authorizing the President to deploy military force against state resistance "without the ceremony of a [congressional war] proclamation."[92]

Jackson thus virtually ignored federal judicial authority in the Nullification Crisis and was openly opposed to it in other contemporaneous disputes; and among the advocates for states' rights, the South Carolina nullifiers were not alone but only the most outspoken in contesting federal judicial authority as part of their resistance to federal authority generally.[93] Vice President Martin Van Buren, for example, prepared a report in 1833 for adoption by the New York legislature that, while rejecting the nullifiers' claim for each state "solely" to decide the constitutionality of federal acts, also denied that the Supreme Court was the "exclusive expositor of the Constitution" and instead argued that ultimate interpretative authority rested in the states acting together.[94] In this report, Van Buren—like Calhoun in his original draft of the state nullification measure—invoked the precedent of the Virginia and Kentucky Resolutions. Though the two men disagreed in their reading of this precedent, they agreed that the Resolutions were fundamental constitutional documents that had, in effect, been ratified by the election of 1800 and that *McCulloch* was accordingly an atavistic Federalist heresy.[95] This enshrinement of the "Spirit of 1798" was a widely shared orthodoxy in American political life both before and after the *McCulloch* decision.[96] Though there were different versions of the orthodoxy among its adherents, all agreed that the principal tenet of the faith was inconsistent with any federal judicial claim for final interpretive authority regarding the Constitution. The Nullification Crisis as such did not damage the Court's authority and even helped it indirectly, by focusing Jackson's fury on the nullifiers' challenge to his authority and diverting his attention from the Court's challenge in *Worcester v. Georgia*. But the Crisis also implicitly revealed that, even at the end of his tenure, Marshall's claim for judicial supremacy in constitutional interpretation reigned supreme only in his own Court.

The Nullification Crisis ended inconclusively. After Jackson's Force Bill Message, both sides backed away from open confrontation, but neither the federal nor state antagonists admitted practical or ideological defeat.[97] The dispute between the Court and state authority in *Worcester v. Georgia* ended with a similarly inconclusive accommodation.[98] Each of these institutional combatants— the President, the Court, and the states—was thus able to defend itself against the others' claim for submission and none was able to prevail over the others. The elaborately interwoven network of competing institutional actors and powers thus worked by Madisonian means to a Madisonian result: stalemate leading to negotiated accommodation.

But no one in authority at the time drew Madison's theoretical lesson from these encounters. This is the critical constitutional significance of the Nullification Crisis: that it marked the virtual eclipse in constitutional discourse of Madison's theory, set out in *Federalist* 51, of the virtues of infinitely divided, equally and endlessly competitive claims for sovereign authority.

John Calhoun identified the underlying logic of his nullification doctrine and its opposition to Madison's conception of sovereignty in his *Discourse on the Constitution* published almost two decades later:

> There is no difficulty in understanding how powers, appertaining to sovereignty, may be divided; and the exercise of one portion delegated to one set of agents, and another portion to another: or how sovereignty may be vested in one man, or in a few, or in many. But how sovereignty itself—the supreme power—can be divided—how the people of the several States can be partly sovereign, and partly not sovereign—partly supreme, and partly not supreme, it is impossible to conceive. Sovereignty is an entire thing;—to divide, is—to destroy it.[99]

John Marshall never endorsed this purist theoretical perspective; he was quite willing to use the language of divided sovereignty in describing federal–state relations.[100] Nonetheless, he shared a basic underlying presupposition with Calhoun that drove him also to embrace a unitary conception of sovereignty; as Calhoun put it in his *Discourse,* in a passage directly critical of Madison's *Federalist* 39:

> How . . . is it possible for institutions, admitted to be so utterly repugnant in their nature as to be directly destructive of each other, to be so blended as to form a government partly federal and partly national? What can be more contradictious? This, of itself, is sufficient to destroy the authority of the [*Federalist Papers*] on this point,—as celebrated as it is.[101]

Marshall also viewed the federal and state governments as "utterly repugnant in their nature"; this was the basis for his conclusion in *McCulloch* that it was not simply unwise or dangerous but theoretically incoherent for states to have taxing authority over federal instrumentalities.[102] Though Marshall would not have used this terminology, the repugnancy and implacable hostility that he saw between federal and state governments led him to conceive the judiciary as the ultimate guardian and repository of unitary national sovereignty.

Joseph Story, Marshall's younger colleague on the Court, gave more systematic exposition to this conception in his *Commentaries on the Constitution* published in 1833 as a direct response to the Nullification Crisis. Story was more rigorous than Marshall in insisting that "sovereignty" had never attached to the states after the Revolution and had always rested in the national government, first under the Articles of Confederation and then in the Constitution.[103] But Story's underlying aim was the same as Marshall's, to deduce from this unitary conception of national sovereignty "that there is a final and common arbiter provided by the constitution itself, to whose decisions all others are subordinate; and that arbiter is the supreme judicial authority of the courts of the Union."[104] Story's argument was the mirror image of Calhoun's: identify the locus of unitary sovereignty and there was the ultimate arbiter of the meaning of the Constitution.

The arguments set out on both sides of the nullification controversy were an anathema to Madison. Lodged in iconic isolation at his Virginia plantation, Madison wrote a rebuttal to one of the nullification proponents that was equally a rebuke to the opponents:

> This idea of an absolute separation [and] independence between the Government of the United States and the States Governments as if they belonged to different nations alien to each other has too often tainted the reasoning applied to Constitutional questions. Another idea not less unsound and sometimes presenting itself is, that a cession of any part of the rights of sovereignty is inconsistent with the nature of sovereignty, or at least a degradation of it. This would certainly be the case if the cession was not both mutual [and] equal, but when there is both mutuality [and] equality there is no real sacrifice on either side, each gaining as much as it grants.[105]

Though Madison's endorsement and reflected prestige was assiduously sought by each of the antagonists in the nullification controversy, his specific views were ignored by almost everyone. Madison was by now an honored but redundant relic.

The clearest indication of Madison's nullification was his invocation of "mutuality and equality" as the underlying basis of the constitutional arrangement. From Madison's perspective, the negotiated settlement of the conflict between Jackson and South Carolina regarding nullification and among Jackson, Georgia, and the Supreme Court in *Worcester* could have been characterized as an application of the basic constitutional premise of mutuality and equality among the competing institutional actors. By these same lights, from Lincoln's subsequent perspective, this negotiated settlement would have corresponded to the stalemate he sought in the Civil War. In the Nullification Crisis itself, however, none of the actors viewed their settlement as Madison or Lincoln would have seen it. For each of the combatants, negotiated settlement was a momentary truce in unrelenting hostility. Their terms of battle were emphatically not Madison's or Lincoln's, not simply to defend one's equal status against the other's depredation. The common goal among all disputants was to establish the unquestioned dominance of one over the others.

The Nullification Crisis was thus a pivotal moment in the development of American constitutional law. The terms of constitutional discourse had moved decisively away from the conception of institutional equality that Madison had formulated for relations both between the state and national governments and within the branches of the national government. The Hamiltonian conception of hierarchic relations now reigned virtually unchallenged. The locus of ultimate constitutional supremacy was hotly disputed between claimants for state and national authority and, within the national government, between Andrew Jackson's Presidency and John Marshall's Court. Within a generation, these disputes would erupt into Civil War—precipitated not only by the conflicting claims for state and national supremacy but also by the related conflict between Roger Taney's Court and Abraham Lincoln's Presidency regarding the *Dred Scott* decision and the constitutional status of territorial slavery. The firestorms generated by these conflicting claims for institutional supremacy obscured, however, the fundamental agreement among the rival claimants regarding the terms of battle: that one among them should reign supreme.

What might explain the emergence of this fundamental shift in constitutional discourse around the Nullification Crisis? One part of the explanation can be found in a subtle difference in Andrew Jackson's claim as compared with the claims of the other antagonists at that time. For Marshall and for the state nullifiers, the dominance each sought was essentially institutional in its character: a victory for the Court or for state government as the locus of supreme interpretive authority. Jackson's stance was different: his theoretical positions were inconsistent, sometimes favoring state authority (as in his opposition to the Court in *Worcester*), sometimes favoring national authority (as in his opposition to the nullifiers). As Tocqueville observed at the time, Jackson was intent on aggrandizing personal and not institutional authority.[106] Madison was himself troubled by Jackson's personalized vision of presidential authority, and his friends among the first families of Virginia were even more alarmed at "King Andrew's" pretensions.[107] These gentlemen implicitly understood that Jackson rejected their ideal of social authority; and they feared the possibility that this rejection was now widespread in American society. In fact, the irrelevance of Madison's conception of sovereignty in the Nullification Crisis debate reflects the eclipse of this gentry ideal.

In the gentry world, gradations of social authority were clear and social deference was observed; but explicit claims of authority and demands for deference were inconsistent with the etiquette of the regime. The basic ethos of the ideal was that authority came "naturally" and deference would be offered "willingly"; to demand social deference would virtually disqualify one's claim for it. The approved form of openly waged social conflict was not between superior and inferior but within the same social rank; and the aim of such conflict was not to establish dominance but to reassert claims of equality within rank. The bitter personal rancor that almost invariably accompanied this intra-gentry conflict arose because personal disagreement seemed to imply inequality: if one disputant were right, then the other must be wrong. Conflicts thus quickly became personalized; and these personalized disputes could be successfully resolved only when both parties agreed that neither claimed superiority over the other.

The gentry code of dueling epitomized this social understanding. Duels were fought to remedy personal affronts and consequent derogation of equal status, not to kill or even to humiliate an opponent but to restore mutually acknowledged equality between the disputants.[108] In walking through the intricacies of this etiquette, dueling deaths did sometimes occur; but this was not the socially prescribed goal, nor the likely outcome, of duels.[109]

Andrew Jackson was an outlander in this gentry world. He was notoriously quick to take affront and equally quick to issue dueling challenges—too quick for genteel taste but nonetheless not outside all bounds of accepted practice. But Jackson did not know how to redress affronts within gentry practice. In his duels, Jackson shot to kill. This widely reported attribute was one source for the gentry's disdain toward Jackson.[110] As the gentry saw it, Jackson's disputes remained personal quests for self-assertive dominance in violation of the gentry ideal that personal conflicts must be resolved so as to reaffirm the self-effacing, depersonalized norm of mutually acknowledged equality.

Jackson craved gentry acceptance, and he aped the forms of the gentry ideal in his pursuit of wealth and slaves and in the grandeur of his plantation estate. But he was really a frontiersman; he lived by the Indian-fighter code of kill or be killed. For the resolution of disputes between social superiors and inferiors, this code's palpable demand for submission destroyed the gentry sense of legitimacy. For the resolution of disputes within the superior rank, this code destroyed the unifying framework of egalitarianism within gentry relations.

Jackson's accession to the presidency ended the dominance of the gentry ethos in American political life. In personal terms, he was the first President without established gentry credentials; his predecessors had all been scions of the Virginia plantation-owning elite, except for the two Adamses (who, as George Washington's chosen heir and the son of that heir, qualified within the terms of the dynastic succession). In broader terms, the social basis for gentry dominance had been undermined during the preceding decades, as Robert Wiebe observed, by "a dramatic expansion of territory and a perpetual migration of people [that] snapped [the gentry] networks of personal authority, stretched its base beyond tolerable limits, and finally toppled the entire structure."[111] Beginning around 1830, moreover, a "vast, altogether unprecedented" number of new immigrants began flooding into America, even further attenuating the shared sense of common bonds that had underwritten gentry rule.[112]

These social developments powerfully confirmed the premise on which John Marshall had built his opinion in *McCulloch v. Maryland*: that mutual trust, "the magic of the word CONFIDENCE," was a chimera in governmental affairs. However much Marshall may have been seen by the end of his life in 1836 as the last gentry officeholder in the American republic, he was an early exemplar of the frontiersman, the self-made man, in his basic attitude toward social authority. Tocqueville saw this attitude in 1831, which he characterized with the newly coined word, "individualism":

> Aristocracy links everybody, from peasant to king, in one long chain. Democracy breaks the chain and frees each link.
>
> As social equality spreads there are more and more people who, though neither rich nor powerful enough to have much hold over others, have gained or kept enough wealth and enough understanding to look after their own needs. Such folks owe no man anything and hardly expect anything from anybody. They form the habit of thinking of themselves in isolation and imagine that their whole destiny is in their own hands.
>
> Thus, not only does democracy make men forget their ancestors, but also clouds their view of their descendants and isolates them from their contemporaries. Each man is forever thrown back on himself alone, and there is danger that he may be shut up in the solitude of his own heart.[113]

Andrew Jackson himself appeared to confirm Tocqueville's analysis, in naming his Tennessee estate "The Hermitage."

The gentry ethos, and its mythic ideal of naturally harmonious social relations, was in its own time subject to considerable strain. The revolutionary break with Great Britain both expressed this strain and appeased it by providing a patriotic bond of fellow-feeling among the newly freed colonists. The Jacksonian era offered a new formulation for political relations that similarly both expressed and appeased the social disorder implied by its individualist, competitive ethos. The new formulation was to put party competition at the center of politics. Even as James Monroe, in the flush of his near-unanimous re-election to the presidency in

1820, proclaimed the ultimate triumph of the gentry ideal in the disappearance of the evils of party factionalism, this new idea—that party competition was a virtue—found expression among the younger generation in the newly professionalized calling of politician. Jackson's election in 1828 was an organizational triumph of this new breed; and with it, the old idea of the evils of factionalism yielded to the new idealization of party competition.[114]

In one sense, this new ideal appeared to abandon the old pursuit of national unity because it posited that there would and should always be an organized political opposition striving to wrest command of government from the reigning incumbents. In practical terms, however, the new ideal was touted as a more reliable instrument for overcoming the threats to national unity that competition among self-interested factions always present. With the shrewd eyes of practicing professionals, the new breed of political leaders tinkered with the structural details of the electoral system—in such matters as providing that state electoral votes be awarded on a winner-take-all rather than proportional basis in presidential elections and that members of Congress be elected from districts rather than at-large within states—so as to underwrite the two-party system and militate against multiparty fractionation.[115] The new political leaders thus pursued the Madisonian goal by Madisonian means: fostering processes of consultation and accommodation and disfavoring impregnably narrow factionalism by the self-conscious design of institutional structures.

This new ideal of party competition could thus ameliorate but it could not transcend the problem of intense polarized conflict any more than could the predecessor gentry ideal of national unity. Indeed, the existence of this problem nagged even more insistently at the edges of the newly dominant conception. The old ideal tended to suppress expression and therefore awareness of polar conflict, treating it as a kind of shameful secret that afflicts even the best of families; the new ideal was a stylized expression of polar conflict. Political debate took on an inflammatory, almost revolutionary, tenor—as in Jackson's Bank veto message, that forces of wealth and privilege were conspiring to enslave "the humble members of society" and that, in self-defense, the common man must rise and crush these oligarchies.[116] Though the politics actually practiced and the governmental policies actually adopted in this new era of acknowledged party competition were in fact minimally disruptive of existing social entitlements, the rhetoric of competition always underscored the apparent fragility of any consensus thus achieved.[117] Unlike the gentry, no one among the practitioners of the new politics avowed that from these immediate conflicts an overarching and unifying public good would ultimately emerge. There was only the Manichaean vision that evil always threatened to overwhelm good, and that politics was an endless and endlessly divisive struggle.

Led by these premises, America marched toward war. And from that experience, the conception of judicial authority that Hamilton had glimpsed and that Marshall had elaborated would emerge triumphant.

5

The Black Race within Our Bosom, the Red on Our Borders

THE DISPLACEMENT of the gentry ideal of political authority was not the only source of the fundamental shift in constitutional discourse marked by the Nullification Crisis. Substantial portions of the American population—most notably, blacks and Indians—had always stood beyond the reach of this ideal.[1] For white relations with these people, the competitive premise of rule or be ruled had always been prominent. As this premise took hold for relations among whites in the Jacksonian era, it became even more openly and harshly avowed for relations between the races; and, in dialectic fashion, this premise increasingly dominated all political discourse.

The conventional, self-congratulatory accounts of constitutional history maintain that the initial assumption of political equality among white males was extended by the Civil War amendments to men of all races. But it is equally correct to say that the Civil War experience extended white subjugation of Indians and blacks to relations among whites themselves. By reconstructing this dark aspect of American constitutional development, we will see the ways in which these subjugative assumptions shaped not only the political relations but the specific understanding of judicial authority that emerged from the War.

The core premise of these subjugative assumptions was the inevitability of irreconcilable hostility. In the early colonial era, relentless hostility had been acknowledged in relations first between whites and Indians and then between whites and black slaves.[2] By the time of the founding generation this stark polarization had been softened or disguised, however, regarding both Indians and blacks by white protestations of beneficence and vague hopes of peaceable reconciliation. These protestations were less robust than the founders' constant refrain that political conflict among whites would be peaceably transcended in the harmonizing glow of republican virtue; but they served the same soothing purpose.

Jefferson was typical of his generation in these matters. After predicting in his *Notes on Virginia* in 1781 that white prejudice and black grievance would "probably never end but in the extermination of one or the other race," Jefferson immediately drew back to a more comforting conclusion: "I think a change already perceptible, since the origin of the present revolution. The spirit of the master is abating, that of the slave rising from the dust, his condition mollifying, the way I hope preparing . . . for a total emancipation . . . with the consent of the masters."[3] Similarly, regarding white–Indian relations, Jefferson wrote in 1803 that although "our strength and their weakness is now so visible that they must see we have only to shut our hand to crush them," nonetheless he would restrain this violence "from motives of pure humanity only,"[4] and he envisioned "the ultimate point of rest and happiness for [Indians, which] is to let our settlements and theirs meet and blend together, to intermix, and become one people."[5] Jefferson echoed his earlier attitude toward black–white relations with this observation about Indians: "After the injuries we have done them, they cannot love us, which leaves no alternative but that of fear to keep them from attacking us, but justice is what we must never lose sight of and in time may recover their esteem."[6]

Like most of his generation, Jefferson took only a few, halting steps to promote the likelihood of black emancipation or Indian assimilation and even then quickly drew back.[7] Virtually all of his actions were thus ultimately consistent with the premise of unrelenting hostility; and yet, like most of his generation, Jefferson never endorsed this premise but remained troubled and confused. As Madison wrote in 1826, "Next to the case of the black race within our bosom, that of the red on our borders is the problem most baffling to the policy of our country."[8]

Red and White

The Jacksonians were much more successful in resolving the founders' confusion toward Indians. Though ritualized protestations of beneficence persisted, annihilating subjugation of Indians became more openly and predominantly embraced in both word and deed. Even the language of beneficence shifted in a revealing way. Jefferson's ambivalence was reflected in the change from the beginning of his presidency, when he regularly addressed Indians as "brother," to the end, when he called them his "children."[9] Jackson, in this as in most matters, did not vacillate; as President he always identified himself as the Indians' "great father."[10]

Jackson's certitude was even more evident in his actions. Jefferson and his generation were not prepared to accept any Indian interference with the steady expansion of white settlement; but they were torn between two inconsistent means toward this expansionist goal, either encouraging Indian assimilation to white agricultural and social practice or pressing them to pack their savage mores intact and move westward beyond white settlements. The Jeffersonians tried to accommodate these inconsistent policies by invoking the ideology of "free choice" for the Indians. They asserted that white military force would be used only defensively against Indian aggressions, and they offered Indian tribes apparently liberal grants of goods and new territory in exchange for agreements to leave their traditional lands. Though there was considerable hypocrisy in the implementation of this policy, the premise of Indian self-determination did serve to slow the pace and to constrain the baldest acts of white depredations.

Jackson's national reputation was based in considerable degree on his service as the field expeditor of this apparently voluntarist and gradualist approach toward the removal of Indians from white-coveted territory. The grateful citizens of Mississippi named their state capital for him, not because of his military triumph against the British at New Orleans in 1814 but because of his skill in combining threats of annihilation with overtly sweet words of reassurance that produced the 1820 treaty removing the Choctaws from the rich delta lands of their state.[11] During the preceding seven years, Jackson had negotiated treaties that were sufficiently dressed in voluntarism to appease the ratifying conscience of the Senate and that effectively forced southern Indian tribes to abandon extensive areas of the South.[12]

As President, Jackson suppressed the exterminatory rhetoric that had marked his earlier career, and thus in his public statements he sounded like his gentry predecessors.[13] Nonetheless, he swept away the hesitancy and assiduous attention to the forms of voluntarism that had previously characterized national policy. During his administration, all of the remaining southern Indian tribes were expelled through treaties obtained either by deceptive inducements or direct coercion. The entire United States east of the Mississippi River was virtually emptied of Indian inhabitants.[14] This expulsion was, moreover, carried out with devastating brutality. Most Cherokees, for example, refused to acknowledge the validity of the ratified treaties but were corralled by federal troops into prison camps and then sent west along the "Trail of Tears." Of the 18,000 Cherokees in this forced march, some 4,000 died.[15] (One overall measure of the devastation inflicted by the Indian removal policy is the generally agreed estimate that, between 1800 and 1850, the total Indian population in the area now comprising the United States declined from 600,000 to 250,000.)[16]

Jackson's effectiveness in removal of the Indians was, for the most part, based more on the single-minded ruthlessness of his commitment to this goal than on any significant ideological difference with the Jeffersonians. Jackson did, however, make one important doctrinal shift. Unlike his predecessors, he claimed that state governments had criminal and civil jurisdiction over the Indian tribes within their borders. Immediately after his election in 1828, Georgia, Alabama, and Mississippi acted on this premise. State laws abolished the tribal unit, making it illegal for tribes to punish lawbreakers or regulate the behavior of their members. They forbade public tribal assemblies, stripped the chiefs of their power, divided up Indian territory for auction in state land lotteries, and denied Indians the right to vote, to bring suits, or to testify in court.[17]

Jackson in turn seized on these state actions as the linchpin in his argument for swift and complete removal of the Indian tribes. In his first message to Congress, Jackson requested authority to offer Indian tribes an exchange of land west of the Mississippi and federal appropriations for the costs of transport. The measure, approved by close vote in 1830, was bitterly attacked as a barely disguised betrayal of previous treaty arrangements but was defended by Jacksonians on the ground that, as a result of the state jurisdictional claims, the federal government could best protect the tribes by expediting their removal.[18] Jackson himself told the Indian tribes that westward migration was in their self-interest, as their only possible defense against the destructive implications of state jurisdiction. Thus in 1830 he addressed a Chickasaw delegation from Mississippi:

> You have long dwelt upon the soil you occupy. . . . Now your white brothers are around you. States have been created within your ancient limits, which claim a right to govern and control your people as they do their own citizens, and to make them answerable to their civil and criminal codes. *Your great father has not the authority to prevent this state of things.* . . .

> To these laws, where you are, you must submit;—there is no preventive—no other alternative. Your great father cannot, nor can congress, prevent it. The states only can. What then? Do you believe that you can live under these laws? That you can surrender all your ancient habits, and the forms by which you have been so long controlled? If so, your great father has nothing to say or to advise. . . . His earnest desire, is, that you may be perpetuated and preserved as a nation; and this he believes can only be done and secured by your consent to remove to a country beyond the Mississippi.[19]

Jackson's predecessors in office had a markedly different conception of the relationship of states and Indian tribes; this conception was the basis for John Marshall's ruling in *Worcester v. Georgia* that states had no authority to extend their jurisdiction over the Indian tribes and that such measures were inconsistent with federal treaties. Jackson's avowal that he "has not the authority to prevent" state exercise of territorial jurisdiction was thus apparently disingenuous. Prior presidents believed that they lacked practical capacity effectively to protect Indian tribal integrity against state-sponsored incursions and overlooked the possibility that a determined invocation of federal armed force might have helped to vindicate federal treaty obligations. But Jackson's objection was not made on pragmatic grounds; as his Force Bill Message of 1832 clearly indicated, he was not reluctant to use federal armies to enforce federal prerogatives against state resistance. Rather, Jackson rejected *Worcester* on the basis of principle, not pragmatism. As his Bank veto message of 1832 indicated, he did not consider himself bound by any constitutional interpretations rendered by the Supreme Court. Jackson was thus, by his own lights, quite sincere in his disavowal of authority to override state claims for jurisdiction over Indian tribes within their territorial boundaries.

The heart of Jackson's conception of state authority over Indian tribes was the Hamiltonian conception of unitary sovereignty. Jackson revealed this premise, and spelled out the resulting syllogism, in an 1831 letter to his secretary of war: "Who are the people of the union? . . . All those subject to the jurisdiction of the sovereign states, none else." It then followed for Jackson that Indians were subject "to the sovereign power of the state within whose sovereign limits they reside. . . . Absolute independence of the Indian tribes from state authority can never bear an intelligent investigation, and a quasi independence of state authority when located within its Territorial limits is *absurd.*"[20] Jackson also deduced from this premise that the federal government need not, and should not, negotiate treaties with Indian tribes as if they were sovereign nations. As military commander, he repeatedly advocated unilateral seizure of Indian lands; as President, he bowed to the conventions of past practice by signing dozens of treaties, but he nonetheless repeatedly denied any formal recognition of tribal sovereignty.[21] Jackson thus disclaimed the logical absurdity (as he saw it) of an *imperium in imperio.*

On this issue, Jackson and John Marshall were in complete agreement; both men embraced a conception of unitary sovereignty that was inconsistent with any claims for Indian tribal sovereignty. Both Jackson and Marshall thus conclusively resolved an issue that the framers of the Constitution had left confused.[22] The two men differed on the question whether this unitary sovereign authority over Indians was lodged in the state or national governments; Jackson favored the former, Marshall the latter. But in their common denial of Indian sovereignty, they revealed a shared underlying premise that was driving the American polity generally away from the Madisonian conception of divided sovereignty in political relations among whites.

Marshall identified this premise with considerable clarity in his 1823 opinion for the Court in *Johnson v. McIntosh*.[23] The question in the case was whether private individuals could purchase land from Indian tribes; the Court held that the tribes had no property rights to convey but merely a "right of occupancy" which could be "extinguish[ed] . . . either by purchase or by conquest"[24] only by the United States government as the successor to the British crown's "exclusive right [as] the discoverer to appropriate the lands occupied by the Indians."[25] Marshall acknowledged that "this restriction may be opposed to natural right, and to the usages of civilized nations, yet, if it be indispensable to that system under which the country has been settled, and be adapted to the actual condition of the two people, it may, perhaps, be supported by reason, and certainly cannot be rejected by Courts of justice."[26]

What then was the "actual condition" that overrode considerations of "natural right" and "civilized" usages? "The tribes of Indians inhabiting this country," Marshall said, "were fierce savages, whose occupation was war, and whose subsistence was drawn chiefly from the forest. To leave them in possession of their country, was to leave the country a wilderness; to govern them as a distinct people, was impossible, because they were as brave and as high spirited as they were fierce, and were ready to repel by arms every attempt on their independence."[27]

Ordinary warfare with these "fierce [though brave] savages" was not possible, as Marshall saw it; for ordinary warfare has an end when the "law which regulates, and ought to regulate in general, the relations between the conqueror and conquered" comes into effect.[28] By this law, hostility is supplanted by mutual disengagement, and perhaps even a grudging accommodation, by which each party acknowledges the other's rights, including property rights (with the proviso that the conquered party has fewer rights and less property than before). But this status was not possible with Indians because warfare with them could never end; the white settlers "were under the necessity of abandoning the country . . . or of remaining in their neighborhood, and exposing themselves and their families to the perpetual hazard of being massacred." Accordingly, a new principle for political relations must be found, as Marshall put it, "adapted to the condition of a people with whom it was impossible to mix, and who could not be governed as a distinct society."[29]

In *Johnson v. McIntosh,* Marshall devised one new principle, that the Indian tribes had no marketable property rights except in transactions ("by purchase or by conquest") with the United States. The underlying premise of this principle was that the Indians could have no independent relations with anyone; they were perpetually subjugated to—or, in economic terms, permanently locked in a monopsonist relationship with—the federal government. Eight years later, in *Cherokee Nation v. Georgia,*[30] Marshall drew from this prior ruling a generalization to describe the novel political relationship he saw between white and native Americans:

> Those tribes which reside within the acknowledged boundaries of the United States can[not], with strict accuracy, be denominated foreign nations. They may, more correctly, perhaps, be denominated domestic dependent nations. They occupy a territory to which we assert a title independent of their will. . . . [T]hey are in a state of pupilage. Their relation to the United States resembles that of a ward to his guardian.[31]

The immediate context of this case was a challenge brought by the Cherokee tribe against Georgia's laws extending state jurisdiction over them. The Cherokees alleged that, as a "foreign state" within the meaning of Article III, they were entitled to bring an original action in the Supreme Court, but Marshall, writing for a divided Court, dismissed the claim. In one sense, Marshall's ruling resembled his strategic maneuver in *Marbury,* where he had also refused to accept original jurisdiction, thus avoiding a clash with the Executive branch while at the same time inviting the possibility of future litigation.[32] Unlike *Marbury,* however, the Cherokees not only pursued this possibility but reappeared in the Supreme Court just one year later, and Marshall did then directly challenge the President's policy. But more fundamentally, while Marshall's jurisdictional finding appears strained in *Marbury,* his conclusion that the Cherokees were not a "foreign state" but were instead the "wards" of the federal government appears to follow more from principle than from strategy for Marshall. Indeed, his immediately subsequent ruling in *Worcester v. Georgia* rested on the same principle, that the states could not apply their laws to the tribes because the Indians had an exclusive, dependent relationship with the federal government.[33]

For all their apparent differences, Marshall and Jackson had the same view of political relations between whites and Indians: that perpetual warfare existed between them and from this brute fact it followed that the whites must either eliminate the Indians (whether by physical removal or annihilation) or impose a single source of subjugating authority over them. Marshall seemed more regretful in his articulation of this view and more sincere in his protestation of beneficence than Jackson;[34] but Marshall was more imbued with gentry ideals than Jackson. Marshall's opinions on white–Indian relations between 1823 and 1832 marked him as a transitional figure from the soft gentry view that conflict might someday be supplanted by peaceful assimilation to Jackson's unambivalent embrace of endless war.

Black and White

The same transition from a softheaded gentry conception to a hardhearted Jacksonian conception occurred, during the same span of time, regarding political relations between whites and blacks. Neither Marshall nor Jackson took significant public positions in this matter;[35] and no single event like the wholesale removal of Indians from the southern states epitomized the hardening of white Jacksonian attitudes toward black slavery. A hardening did, however, occur. By the 1830s, relations between blacks and whites were conceived—both in the South and the North— as perpetual warfare. As with Indians, the founding generation had muted their conflict-ridden actuality with vague but persistent avowals that peaceful, mutually satisfactory relations between whites and blacks might someday be found through the gradual emancipation of slaves. The founders were, however, only half-hearted in this belief; and as with Indians, the succeeding generation more resolutely concluded that blacks and whites could never live peacefully together as equals.

Virginia manumission laws illustrate this evolution. In 1782 the Virginia legislature, pressed by Quaker lobbyists, essentially removed all legal obstacles to voluntary liberation of slaves by individual masters.[36] By 1790 the number of free blacks in the state had increased from 3,000 to 12,000, constituting some four percent of the black population and the largest absolute number of free blacks in any state. In 1793 the legislature forbade free blacks from entering the state, but the internal population continued to rise. By 1810, more than 30,000 free blacks lived in the state, representing some seven percent of the total black population. By then, however, Virginia had turned away from its prior hospitality toward liberated slaves; free blacks were pressed to leave the state, and those who remained were subjected to increasingly stringent controls regarding travel, employment, education, and weapons possession.[37]

This progression of official attitudes in Virginia, from tentatively endorsing at least the principle of equal status for some blacks toward rejecting any practical acknowledgment of this status, proceeded into the Jacksonian era with increasing adamancy in slaveholding states generally. The terms of public discourse about blacks also changed significantly during this time. Before 1830, the dominant view had been that blacks were intellectually and morally inferior but that this status arose from their degraded social situation;[38] by 1850 this environmentalism had been virtually superseded by the new "science of ethnology," which claimed innate and hierarchically arrayed differences among races.[39]

This changed attitude did not mean that all or even most white Southerners in the Jacksonian era rejected the founders' pious hopes for emancipation and instead became committed to the perpetuation of slavery as an institution. As William Freehling has recently demonstrated, this hardened view was clearly dominant only in South Carolina. In all of the other slaveholding states, and particularly in the "upper South," popular sentiment favoring the gradual abolition of slavery remained a potent political force. By 1830, however, virtually no white Southerner saw any possibility that there might ever be equal political relations with blacks; those who envisaged abolition of slavery also insisted as a necessary corollary that blacks would be expelled.[40]

There was considerable disagreement among Southerners about both the means and the destinations for this expulsion.

Some advocated establishment of African colonies and provision of public funds to induce both emancipation by white slaveowners and migration by the freed slaves; this was the platform of the American Colonization Society founded in 1817.[41] Others invoked the earlier example of the northern states, whose gradual emancipation statutes gave slaveowners ample opportunity and motive to sell their slaves southward; these Southerners maintained that slaves should all be transported into the "deep South" or the newly settled western territories. By this route, blacks themselves would not be freed, but at least the "upper South" would be free of them.[42]

Whatever differences existed among Jacksonian-era Southerners regarding the perpetuation or beneficence of slavery, there was virtual unanimity that, as with Indians, whites and blacks were locked in perpetual combat. From this perspective, Northerners who advocated banning slavery from the territories were as frightening for white Southerners as the abolitionists who demanded instant elimination of slavery everywhere; from the first until the last congressional debates on territorial slavery, Southerners regularly invoked the nightmare that unless slavery could be expanded to the territories, whites would be "pent in and walled around on exhausted soil—in the midst of a [black] people strong in idleness [and prone] to revolt and murder."[43] Any continuing political relationship between whites and blacks, according to this view, must be predicated on their relentless mutual hostility. The founding generation understood but at the same time recoiled from this predicate; by the Jacksonian era, whites at least throughout the South accepted it. From this predicate, equal political relations between whites and blacks were inconceivable.

The master–slave relationship had been, of course, sharply unequal throughout the eighteenth century. Its stark hierarchy was evident in a Virginia law, enacted in 1669, that "if any slave resist[s] his master . . . [and] by the extremity of the correction [administered by the master] should chance to die," the master's actions would not be a punishable felony; but the evident harshness of this law was explicitly hedged by the benevolent-seeming rationalization that murder of one's slave could never be intentional or "malicious," as required for felonious convictions generally, because no "man [would] destroy his own estate."[44] Even so, for the Virginia gentry of the founding generation, this rationalization was not enough to soften the brutal reality that the law ratified; the law was repealed in 1788.[45]

By the beginning of the Jacksonian era, however, the public etiquette that demanded soft words to mask cruel practice had significantly receded. In 1828 Judge Thomas Ruffin wrote an opinion for the North Carolina Supreme Court in *State v. Mann*[46] that stands as the most severe depiction in American jurisprudence of the social imperative for the master's absolute subjugation of his slave. According to Ruffin's account of the case, the slave "committed some small offense" and fled as her master "undertook to chastise her"; the master then "shot at and wounded her." The master was convicted of assault on the ground that his conduct was "cruel and unwarrantable, and disproportionate to the offense committed by the slave." In reversing the conviction, Ruffin rejected any analogy between parent–child and master–slave relations.

> The difference is that which exists between freedom and slavery—and a greater cannot be imagined. In the one, the end in view is the happiness of the youth, born to equal rights with that governor, on whom the duty devolves of training the young to usefulness in a station which he is afterwards to assume among freemen. . . . With slavery it is far otherwise. The end is the profit of the master, his security and public safety; the subject, one doomed in his own person and his posterity, to live without knowledge and without the capacity to make anything his own, and to toil that another may reap the fruits. What moral considerations shall be addressed to such a being to convince him . . . that he is thus to labor upon a principle of natural duty, or for the sake of his own personal happiness? Such services can only be expected from one who has no will of his own; who surrenders his will in implicit obedience to that of another. Such obedience is the consequence only of uncontrolled authority over the body. There is nothing else which can operate to produce the effect. The power of the master must be absolute to render the submission of the slave perfect.[47]

On its face, this portrayal of master–slave relations is more harsh than John Marshall's depiction of white–Indian relations in his trilogy of cases between 1823 and 1832, where he invoked the familial metaphors of "pupilage" and "wardship." But there is a deeper similarity. Both Ruffin and Marshall begin with the premise of unending conflicts of interest, of perpetual warfare, between the parties; both men deduce from this premise that the resulting relationship must necessarily be the total and exclusive subordination of one by the other. For Marshall, absolute sovereignty over Indians rested with the federal government; for Ruffin, absolute sovereignty was in the master over his slave.

Indeed, Marshall's use of familial metaphors had no operative significance for him as a judge. The imagery served only as a piously expressed hope that the federal government, in whom Marshall the judge vested absolute sovereignty, would use its exclusive authority in a beneficently paternal way. Ruffin framed his stark portrait in the same mode: "I most freely confess my sense of the harshness of this proposition [that the master's power must be absolute]; I feel it as deeply as any man can; and as a principle of moral right every person in his retirement must repudiate it."[48] Ruffin's fundamental claim was thus not that masters must keep their slaves in a permanent state of terror to extract obedience from them, any more than Marshall claimed that the federal government must always hold an unsheathed sword over Indian heads. For both men, morality and good sense dictated that authority over slaves and Indians be exercised with paternal compassion and restraint. For both men, the jurisprudential import of the principle of undivided sovereignty was a grant of power to the master or the federal government; but even more than this, it was a constraint on judicial interventions in the relations between whites and blacks or Indians.[49]

Ruffin's opinion in *State v. Mann* thus has more obvious affinity with Marshall's opinion in *McCulloch* than with his Indian trilogy. The connection with *McCulloch* is most apparent in Ruffin's explanation of the reasons why courts cannot adequately distinguish between abusive and acceptable applications of force by masters:

That there may be particular instances of cruelty and deliberate barbarity where, in conscience, the law might properly interfere, is most probable. The difficulty is to determine where a Court may properly begin. . . . The danger would be great, indeed, if the tribunals of justice should be called on to graduate the punishment appropriate to every temper and every dereliction of menial duty. No man can anticipate the many and aggravated provocations of the master which the slave would be constantly stimulated by his own passions or the instigation of others to give; or the consequent wrath of the master, prompting him to bloody vengeance upon the turbulent traitor—a vengeance generally practiced with impunity by reason of its privacy. The Court, therefore, disclaims the power of changing the relation in which these parts of our people stand to each other.

This is the same rationale that led Marshall to disclaim any judicial authority to regulate relations between the federal and state governments by deciding whether congressional laws were "necessary" or state taxation of federal instrumentalities was "excessive." As Marshall concluded regarding judicial construction of the "necessary and proper" clause, so Ruffin said about gradations of punishment: "The difficulty is to determine where a Court may properly begin." And as Marshall opined about the inherent destructiveness of any state taxing power, so Ruffin claimed regarding master–slave relations, that "the many and aggravated provocations" by the slave would inevitably be followed by the master's "bloody vengeance . . . practiced [in] privacy."

In *McCulloch,* that is, Marshall dismissed the possibility that the Court should play any active mediating role in federal–state relations for the same underlying reason that Ruffin disclaimed this role for master–slave: because the relationships were too deeply and inherently antagonistic for any prospect of mediation. Marshall accordingly embraced bright-line rules that would dampen disputes and discourage recourse to courts—an absolute ban against state taxation, a blanket refusal to adjudicate the necessity of congressional acts—just as Ruffin adopted his bright-line stance because "we cannot allow the right of the master to be brought into discussion in the courts of justice," and every slave "must be made sensible that there is no appeal from his master."

The apparent practical consequence of both rulings was to vest absolute, unreviewable power in one of the warring parties, the federal government and the master. This was the basis for the fierce attacks on *McCulloch* by southern states' rights advocates and on *Mann* by northern abolitionists.[50] Both Marshall and Ruffin subsequently defended against this charge. Marshall in his pseudonymous newspaper letters pointed to the passage in his opinion that promised judicial intervention "should Congress, under the pretext of executing its powers, pass laws for the accomplishment of objects not entrusted to the government." There was no comparable hedge in Ruffin's opinion, but he supplied it eleven years later in an opinion affirming the conviction of a master for killing his slave. In *State v. Hoover*[51] the master had inflicted "the most brutal and barbarous whippings, scourgings and privations" on the slave while she was pregnant and immediately after childbirth, though her supposed infractions were small and in any event dubious. Ruffin cited his prior opinion in *Mann* for the proposition that the "master may lawfully punish his slave; and the degree must, in general, be left to his own judgment and humanity, and can not be judicially questioned." Nonetheless, Ruffin continued, "the master's authority is not altogether unlimited. He must not kill." The master's acts in this case, moreover,

> do not belong to a state of civilization. They are barbarities which could only be prompted by a heart in which every humane feeling had long been stifled; and indeed there can scarcely be a savage of the wilderness so ferocious as not to shudder at the recital of them. Such acts cannot be fairly attributed to an intention to correct or to chastise. They can not, therefore, have allowance, as being the exercise of an authority, conferred by the law for the purposes of the correction of the slave, or of keeping the slave in due subjection.[52]

Both Marshall and Ruffin thus endorsed exceptions to their general rule of judicial nonintervention. The exceptions, moreover, relied on the same technique—that the judge would examine the motive of Congress or the master to ensure that the challenged action was not based on a "pretext" for the accomplishment of forbidden purposes. Marshall apparently believed that this basis for judicial review was more solidly self-defining than assessing degrees of "necessity" or "excessiveness" in state taxation; Ruffin apparently claimed judges could easily differentiate the murderous brutality of the master in *Hoover* from less extreme inflictions. In both instances, however, the exceptions were at odds with the dominant animating spirit that had led both men to eschew judicial involvement in the broad category of disputes, federal versus state, master versus slave. Neither Marshall nor Ruffin could hold firm to their initial resolve because their shared underlying premise—that the disputing parties were relentlessly at war—led them somewhat hesitantly and others more emphatically to the conclusion that these disputes pervasively threatened the social order and that some superseding authority, some ultimate absolute sovereign, must be found to impose an end to this endless conflict.

In slave relations, the southern state governments increasingly claimed this ultimate sovereign role during the Jacksonian era, effectively overriding the autonomy of individual masters and the shibboleths regarding their private property rights in slaves. The clearest instance of this supersession was in the increasingly stringent restrictions on manumissions, thus limiting masters' authority to dispose of their slave property as they saw fit.[53] Other legislative enactments attempted to force masters to assume more responsibility in policing their slaves. Thus, for example, a North Carolina law specified that "no slave shall go at large as a free man, exercising his own discretion in the employment of his time," and that slaveowners who "consent to [such conduct] or connive thereat [shall be] deemed guilty of a misdemeanor" and fined.[54] An Alabama law required that all male slaveowners were required (in person or by substitute) "to perform patrol duty . . . visit[ing] all negro quarters [and] all places suspected of entertaining unlawful assemblies of slaves."[55] Another Alabama provision prohibited slaves "from keeping dogs" and fined "the master or owner, who shall permit his slaves to keep dogs contrary to this law."[56] State codes directly imposed tight controls on slaves generally[57] and provided compensation for part or all of the slaves' market value as an inducement to masters against shielding slaves from the state penal law.[58]

State laws also overrode masters' authority in ways that were seemingly beneficial to slaves. Notwithstanding Ruffin's aversion to any suggestions of judicial oversight in master–slave conflicts, many southern state laws not only proscribed the murder of slaves but also prohibited especially brutal punishments such as dismemberment[59] (and some even required masters to provide "proper" clothing and food to their slaves).[60] These protective state laws were more than window-dressing to appease northern antislavery sentiment. Though the prohibition of black testimony against whites severely inhibited effective enforcement, and though public authorities were more lax toward "gentlemen of standing" than toward overseers or small slaveholders, nonetheless these protective laws were noticeably if not invariably enforced.[61]

The Jacksonian-era state slave laws thus overrode masters' autonomy in two directions: they required the generous master to impose more stringent controls on his slaves than he might prefer, and they required the brutal master to inhibit his depredations. This conjunctive state policy had a single underlying rationale: as Willie Lee Rose has put it, to "domesticate" slavery by institutionalizing "a more regular and systematic labor system."[62] The possibility of some future, equal political relationship between whites and blacks, however dimly imagined during the founding generation, was conclusively expunged from southern society. In one sense this newly hardened social conviction acknowledged the ineradicable existence of the polar conflict between masters and slaves that Judge Ruffin had so starkly portrayed in *Mann;* and this understanding was embodied in the increasingly stringent state controls over slaves. But in another sense, the acknowledged permanence of this conflict demanded some soothing salve, even if only for cosmetic purposes, to calm both slaves and masters in their daily interactions and to divert attention from the hostile polarity of their ultimate interests.

For some Southerners, as William Freehling has suggested, the belief that all blacks could be expelled (to foreign colonies, or from the "upper" into the "deep" South, or into unpopulated territories) served this soothing purpose. For others, imagining slavery as a beneficent "positive good" could accomplish this goal; thus John Calhoun proclaimed in an 1838 Senate speech condemning the rise of abolitionist proselytizing in the North:

> This agitation has produced one happy effect at least; it has compelled us at the South to look into the nature and character of this great institution, and to correct many false impressions that even we had entertained in relation to it. Many in the South once believed that [slavery] was a moral and political evil; that folly and delusion are gone; we see it now in its true light, and regard it as the most safe and stable basis for free institutions in the world.[63]

Whatever route southern whites chose to eradicate the founding generation's ambivalence regarding slavery, they did not succeed as they had done with Indians. The Indians themselves had been removed, beyond the borders, along with the founders' prior ambivalence toward them; but the blacks remained, as Madison had said, "within our bosom" in the South. Notwithstanding Calhoun's confident proclamation, nagging doubts remained about whether slavery was indeed "safe and stable." As Tocqueville wrote in 1831:

> Danger of a conflict between the blacks and whites of the South of the Union is a nightmare constantly haunting the American imagination. The northerners make it a common topic of conversation, though they have nothing directly to fear from it. They seek in vain for some means of obviating the misfortunes they foresee.
>
> In the southern states there is silence; one does not speak of the future before strangers; one avoids discussing it with one's friends; each man, so to say, hides it from himself. There is something more frightening about the silence of the South than about the North's noisy fears.[64]

The heart of Judge Ruffin's judicial strategy in *State v. Mann* was to maintain this silence by virtually eliminating the occasions for public scrutiny of master–slave relations. But as Tocqueville's observation implied, white fears could not so readily be appeased. The increasingly extensive network of state regulation reflected a new strategy for confronting the incessant underlying warfare between master and slave: the state would now take active charge of all contentious aspects in the relationship and impose a single-minded order.

White and White

The antebellum South achieved remarkable success in suppressing virtually all open expression of conflict between its blacks and whites. This conflict was, however, vocalized with increasing volume and stridency after 1830 by northern whites. Two events were emblematic of this new era of sectional strife: in 1831 William Lloyd Garrison founded the *Liberator,* the organ of his campaign for the immediate, total abolition of slavery; and eight months later, Nat Turner led a slave revolt in Virginia, the most extensive and bloodiest uprising in the antebellum South. Abolitionist literature was found among Turner's band, and southern whites seized the occasion for the time-honored practice of blaming "outside agitators" for internal troubles.[65]

White Southerners soon moved to impose the same silence on national forums that they sought at home. In 1835, responding to the receipt at the Charleston post office of thousands of abolitionist tracts addressed to prominent local citizens, a southern mob seized and burnt the mailings; and southern congressmen proposed a federal law forbidding postal delivery of any mail containing material proscribed by local law. President Jackson responded by endorsing legislation to prohibit "the circulation in the Southern States, through the mail, of incendiary publications intended to instigate the slaves to insurrection."[66] In the same year, an abolitionist petition was submitted in the House of Representatives advocating legislation to ban the interstate slave trade and eliminate slavery in the District of Columbia. After a "long and nasty debate that lasted six weeks and drove members to come to the chamber armed with knives," the House adopted the so-called Gag Rule specifying that all petitions regarding slavery or its abolition be automatically "laid upon the table [without] either being printed or referred [to any committee] and that no further action whatever shall be had thereon."[67] Even so, southern congressmen were not satisfied but repeatedly urged that such petitions be turned away, in effect, at the House door rather than being accepted even to lay permanently "upon the table."[68]

At this same time, antislavery advocates turned to the courts. Previous litigation efforts on behalf of slaves had focused almost exclusively in the northern states on the detailed provisions of the gradual emancipation statutes that had been enacted there during the founding generation, and in the southern states on the details of the various manumission statutes. This litigation was designed to help particular slaves toward freedom rather than to undermine the institution of slavery. In the mid-1830s, a new breed of antislavery litigation appeared in state and federal courts—litigation intended to assault slavery as such by challenging the processes for recapturing fugitive slaves.[69]

In the sense that such litigation sought to protect the freedom of individual blacks, it resembled the earlier efforts. But unlike them, the new fugitive slave advocacy directly incited conflicts between the policies, the citizens, and often the officials of free and slave states. The patent visibility of this conflict was the reason why, as Robert Cover put it, the fugitive rendition process was the single leading courtroom crucible for abolitionists after 1835.[70] And this very visibility was the reason why in 1842 the Supreme Court, ruling in the first case involving fugitive slaves that had ever reached its docket, tried to close off all routes for abolitionist legal challenge, thus imposing a gag-rule of its own design.

The case was *Prigg v. Pennsylvania*.[71] Justice Story wrote the principal opinion which, though styled "the opinion of the Court" in the official report, did not receive majority support for all of its elements. Seven of the nine Justices wrote separate opinions, and none neatly identified the cumulative result of their individually stated views. Even in this detail, there is evidence of the distance that separates the founding generation from the Jacksonian era; John Marshall had died seven years earlier and, at least in *Prigg*, nothing remained of his almost invariable practice of achieving unanimity and speaking with a single institutional voice—nothing, that is, except the misleading designation that Justice Story delivered "the opinion of the Court." The Court's fractionation in *Prigg*, starkly visible though denied, mirrored its times.

In its own terms, Story's opinion is an extraordinarily revealing document. Other Justices on the Court may have been moved to shut off abolitionist-sponsored litigation because of their support for slavery; but Story had been an outspoken opponent of the institution in extrajudicial statements and had revealed this aversion in earlier cases.[72] Story had different concerns in *Prigg*, which he revealed at the outset of his opinion:

> Before proceeding to discuss the very important and interesting questions involved in this record, it is fit to say, that the cause has been conducted in the Court below, and has been brought here by the cooperation and sanction, both of the state of Maryland, and the state of Pennsylvania, in the most friendly and courteous spirit, with a view to have those questions finally dis-

posed of by the adjudication of this Court; so that the agitations on this subject in both states, which have had a tendency to interrupt the harmony between them, may subside, and the conflict of opinion be put at rest.[73]

Story acted on this concern not simply by resolving the specific controversy in the case but by answering, so as to "finally dispose" of, virtually all imaginable questions involved in interstate claims for the return of fugitive slaves. Story's answers, moreover, followed the pattern that Marshall had set in *McCulloch* for walling off controversy between the state and federal governments, just as his prologue echoed Marshall's preface in *McCulloch* that the Supreme Court alone had the constitutional "duty" of resolving "source[s] of hostile legislation, [and] perhaps of hostility of a still more serious nature."

The specific controversy in *Prigg* arose under a Pennsylvania statute in 1826 prohibiting the removal and enslavement of any "negro or mulatto" from the state "by force, fraud or false pretense." In 1837 Prigg obtained an arrest warrant from a Pennsylvania magistrate for Margaret Morgan and her children, alleging that she had escaped five years earlier from Prigg's employer, a Maryland slaveowner. When the state constable delivered Morgan to the magistrate, however, he "refused to take further cognisance of the case; and thereupon [Prigg] did remove, take, and carry away" Morgan and her children into Maryland. Prigg was subsequently convicted of violating the Pennsylvania statute.[74]

Two provisions of federal law were relevant. The fugitive slave clause of the Constitution, Article IV, section 2, provided that "no person held to service or labor in one state, under the laws thereof, escaping into another, shall, in consequence of any law or regulation therein, be discharged from such service or labor, but shall be delivered up on claim of the party to whom such service or labor may be due." In 1793 Congress enacted that "the person to whom such labor or service may be due . . . is hereby empowered to seize or arrest such fugitive from labor, and to take him or her before any [federal] judge . . . within the state, or before any [state] magistrate . . . and upon proof to the satisfaction of such judge or magistrate, either by oral testimony or affidavit" that the person seized is in fact a fugitive slave, "it shall be the duty of such judge or magistrate to give a certificate thereof to such claimant."[75] (This federal statute had been enacted in response to a controversy that arose in 1791 after a black man was forcibly taken from Pennsylvania to Virginia, the abductors were indicted under a Pennsylvania antikidnapping law, and the Virginia governor refused extradition.)[76]

Justice Story concluded that the Pennsylvania statute under which Prigg was convicted violated both the 1793 federal law and the fugitive slave clause of the Constitution. The federal law, Story reasoned, excluded any state regulation because the inherent "nature" of the slave rendition process required "that it should be controlled by one and the same will, and act uniformly by the same system of regulations throughout the Union." Without such uniformity, Story said,

> each state is at liberty to prescribe just such regulations as suit its own policy, local convenience, and local feelings. . . . The time, and mode, and limitation of the remedy; the proofs of the title . . . may be prescribed in one state, which are rejected or disclaimed in another. One state may require the owner to sue in one mode, another in a different mode. One state may make a statute of limitations as to the remedy, in its own tribunals, short and summary; another may prolong the period, and yet restrict the proofs; nay, some states may utterly refuse to act upon the subject at all. . . . The right, therefore, would never, in a practical sense be the same in all the states. . . . The duty might be enforced in some states; retarded, or limited in others; and denied, as compulsory in many, if not in all.[77]

From this recitation of possible interstate regulatory differences, Story concluded that it was "scarcely conceivable that the slaveholding states would have been satisfied" when the 1793 statute was enacted "with leaving to the legislation of the nonslaveholding states, a power of regulation which would or might practically amount to a power to destroy the rights of the owner."[78]

On the specific facts of *Prigg*, the Pennsylvania statute did not appear to prescribe different standards or procedures from the 1793 act for fugitive slave claims; on its face, the state statute appeared to complement the federal act by, in effect, requiring regularized recourse to a state magistrate or federal judge rather than removal of an alleged fugitive by force, fraud, or false pretense.[79] In other cases, however, abolitionist lawyers had argued that states could exercise choice regarding their participation in fugitive slave rendition, for example, by permitting jury trial, requiring adversarial confrontation, and regulating the burden of proof regarding slave status. Story's condemnation of interstate variation was clearly aimed past the facts of *Prigg* at the overall litigation agenda of the antislavery bar.

Story could have reached a very different conclusion on these general matters, however. He might have construed the spare directive of the 1793 law, that certification of fugitive slave status should follow "upon proof to the satisfaction of such [federal] judge or [state] magistrate," to permit state-prescribed variations in order to protect state prerogatives regarding "its own policy, local convenience, and local feelings"; he might have concluded that the option provided in the 1793 statute between recourse to a state or federal officer meant that Congress intended to respect differing state sensitivities while providing an alternative, federally administered remedy for those who chose to use it; or he might have found that this alternative availability meant that the federal judge would oversee the state rendition processes to ensure that the state regulatory power would not be used as a pretext "to destroy the rights of the owner." But just as Marshall in *McCulloch* viewed the possibility that state taxing power might be used "to destroy" a federal instrumentality as the ground for invalidating this power altogether, so Story concluded that states could not be trusted to exercise any judgment whatever about fugitive slave rendition. "Construe the right of legislation as exclusive in Congress," Story said, "and every evil, and every danger vanishes."[80]

Marshall's concern about the explosive implications of federal–state conflict led him to negate any state taxing power; Story drew a similarly rigid conclusion from the same premise, that the states should be wholly excluded from any involvement in fugitive slave issues. Thus he suggested, though the question was not directly at issue in *Prigg*, that Congress had no authority to require state participation in fugitive slave rendition and that the reliance on state magistrates by the 1793 act was unconstitutional. The most Story would concede was that "state magistrates may, if they choose, exercise that authority, unless prohibited by state legislation."[81] That is, the only route Story offered to a state concerned about the seizure of alleged fugitive slaves within its territory was to remove itself from any participation in the transactions.

This same premise led Story to find a specific constitutional flaw in the Pennsylvania statute at issue in *Prigg*. Though, as I noted, that statute could have been construed as complementing the intention of the 1793 federal act to require recourse to the judicial process before removing an alleged fugitive slave from state territory, this construction would not pass muster for Story. He read the fugitive slave clause in the Constitution to provide that "the owner of a slave is clothed with entire authority, in every state in the Union, to seize and recapture his slave" without any public process. The only qualification Story acknowledged to this private right of "recaption or reprisal" was that the owner must not engage in "any breach of the peace, or any illegal violence."[82] Story excluded the possibility that the 1793 statute might have required recourse to a federal judge or state magistrate; the federal act itself became simply an option that the slavecatcher might or might not choose to pursue. Story thus completely devalued the importance of some public regulation to ensure that slavecatchers would not seize free blacks; indeed, he ignored the fact that this occurred in *Prigg* itself. Though Margaret Morgan may have been an escaped slave, no one could claim that her child born in Pennsylvania was a slave under that state's law; but Prigg seized the free child along with the alleged slave mother and her other children.[83]

Prigg thus epitomized the central administrative problems in the fugitive slave rendition issue: because the Pennsylvania magistrate refused to act on the slavecatcher's petition, the Maryland owner's property rights in the escaped slave were jeopardized; and because the slavecatcher acted on his own initiative, a free black person was enslaved. On its face, by excluding any state protective processes and granting a private seizure right to slavecatchers that overrode even the federal procedures, Story's resolution appears to acknowledge only the slaveowner's property claims and to give no weight at all to the rights of free blacks.[84] It is possible, however, that Story saw himself as providing significant practical protection to blacks, notwithstanding the fearful implications of the private recaption right, by permitting states to exclude themselves from the enforcement enterprise. Some free-state whites were willing to protect escaped slaves; unless slave-catchers could enlist the active assistance of local law enforcement personnel, their private recaption rights might have little effective force; and exclusive resort under the 1793 act to the few federal judges residing in any state probably would be an empty remedy for most slavecatchers. This, at any rate, was the posthumous justification that Story's son offered for his father's apparent apostasy from the abolitionist cause in *Prigg*.[85]

Whatever the plausibility of this view of his motives, it seems likely that Story was less concerned with finding some balance between the rights of slaveowners and free blacks than with protecting the social order generally and the Union specifically from "the agitations on this subject in both [free and slave] states," as Story put it in his prologue to *Prigg*, "which have had a tendency to interrupt the harmony between them." The unmistakable thrust of Story's opinion was to close off virtually all public forums in the free states where visible conflict might be waged regarding the recapture of fugitive slaves. By this means, Story would insulate free-state officials from any morally troubling or politically unpopular involvement in the fugitive rendition process, and thus remove them from temptations to nullify their formal constitutional obligations toward the slave states; and by these same means, Story would end the abolitionist-sponsored litigation that could capitalize on the appealing contexts of specific case advocacy to mobilize northern, and inflame southern, public opinion.

The underlying premise of this conflict-suppressive endeavor was that the dispute over slavery had become so polarized between North and South, and even in the North itself, that the issue could not be peaceably debated, much less resolved. From this premise, it followed that the only chance for preserving social order was rigorously to remove the issue from public view. This was the logic of the gag-rule adopted by the House in 1835. It was Judge Ruffin's explicitly avowed logic in *Mann,* that if a court is asked "which power of the master accords with right, the answer will probably sweep away all of them [. . . and therefore] we cannot allow the right of the master to be brought into discussion in the courts of justice."[86]

As a factual description of the state of public opinion at the time, however, this premise may have been wrong. There was indeed considerable protest by northern abolitionists about the fundamental evil of slavery. But it was not at all clear that these views were widely shared in the North or that Northerners even mildly sympathetic to abolitionism were prepared directly to obstruct public enforcement efforts to return acknowledged fugitive slaves to their southern owners.[87] Nor was it clear that most Southerners were opposed to protecting free blacks from enslavement; though southern practice was increasingly inclined to treat all blacks as slaves, nonetheless the principle acknowledging the possibility of black freedom remained intact, and small groups of free blacks remained highly visible within the South throughout the antebellum era.[88] There was accordingly at least a potential basis when *Prigg* was decided in 1842 for some accommodation on the basis of mutually acceptable principles and practical applications that might transcend the apparently divisive dispute.

The existence of these unifying bases for transcending conflict could not be confirmed, however, unless public forums were available for their identification. To succeed in this enterprise, such forums must somehow facilitate sustained efforts to reach accommodation by patient and repeated unravelling of the polarizing rhetoric and the underlying suspicions with which the most vocal and aroused disputants approached the issues. Even if no resolution of the conflict between some or most of the disputants could ever be found, because the slaveowners' claims were necessarily in diametric opposition to the abolitionists' convictions about the inherent evil of slavery, nonetheless a sustained effort to find some discrete areas of common ground might soften the harsh edges of conflict and lead one side away from its insistence on the status quo and the other away from its resistance to gradual, meliorist reform.

To those who view the Civil War as an "irrepressible conflict," this may seem an empty speculation; but from contemporaries' perspectives, there were many reasons for believing otherwise. As William Freehling has recently underscored, secessionists were intensely fearful of the possibility that the upper South ultimately would find common ground with the North by opting for gradual emancipation coupled with the expulsion of blacks, a course that would increase both the concentration of blacks and the vulnerability of the slavery institution in the deep South.[89] If the incredibly destructive Civil War had been averted, and if the subsequent vicious southern white retaliation against the forceably freed blacks had not occurred, even at the cost of delayed emancipation, would the nation generally and the oppressed blacks specifically have gained more or suffered less?

There are no certain answers to this question. But this much seems clear: that the meliorative possibilities implicit in this question could only have been explored at the time by a sustained commitment to public processes, in Madison's phrase, of "consultation and accommodation" and that this commitment was not fostered—indeed, it was actively undermined—by the Supreme Court. A different road was, however, available to the Court in the fugitive slave litigation. A brief counter-historical detour to explore this road will illustrate the role that courts can play generally in easing polarized conflict and promoting Madison's institutional ideal—even if it appears that this ideal could not (or perhaps even should not) have succeeded in averting the Civil War.

Consider, first of all, the potential Madisonian uses of litigative disputes about particular procedural remedies such as the right to a jury trial, adversarial confrontation, and the allocation of burdens of proof in facilitating public deliberation generally. To debate such remedial questions appears to assume the continued legitimacy of the slavery institution; and the abolitionists were not willing to concede this proposition. But even so, if these various remedial measures were accepted, the abolitionist lawyers could hold their ground and use them as means for presenting, in the context of repeated fugitive slave cases, some glimpse at least of their fundamental moral conviction about the evils of slavery.

If the right to jury trial were granted, further specific questions would then arise: May the abolitionist lawyer directly appeal to the jury to nullify the fugitive slave law? Even if the judge refuses to permit such a direct appeal, are there any circumstances where the evidence so clearly establishes the slaveowner's claim to the fugitive that the judge should refuse to send the issue to a jury or should overturn a jury verdict or, instead, should the jury always have the final word? Such detailed questions about the specific implementation of fugitive slave rendition processes do not directly reach the underlying fundamental issue about the moral legitimacy of slavery. But this issue is pervasively implicated in each of these details, in fine-tuned adjustments of the relative advantage that the practical workings of the rendition process give to one or the other side in the underlying debate.

Judicial consideration of these details also would necessarily impinge on the work of other governmental institutions and, accordingly, would present opportunities for the judge both to promote and to shape public deliberation about the fugitive slave controversy in these other institutions. For example, when an abolitionist lawyer demands a right to jury trial in a fugitive slave rendition case, the judge must identify and rank the various possible sources for finding that right. Because the cases arise under the 1793 federal law, the constitutional guarantees of criminal and civil jury trial in the fifth and seventh amendments are available; but these guarantees would have markedly different institutional significance depending on whether the Congress had specifically considered the jury trial issue in enacting the 1793 law. If Congress had decided against juries, then a court must invalidate the act to find the right and thereby impose a virtually definitive end to any further debate on the issue; by Madisonian lights, a court should be exceedingly reluctant to take this course. If Congress had not considered the issue, however, (as in fact it had not), a court could and should be much less constrained. Finding the right in this institutional context would give some advantage to one side without definitively defeating the claims of the other. Such a ruling would instead invite further debate on this issue in another institutional setting, the Congress, and thus promote a further round of the processes of consultation, now involving more numerous and varied parties, that Madison extolled in *Federalist* 10.

Another set of institutional actors, the state legislatures, also would be highly relevant to a judge's disposition of the claimed jury trial right. The 1793 Act provided for rendition proceedings before federal judges or state magistrates; when an abolitionist lawyer demanded a jury trial in either forum within a particular state, the judge could ask whether the state legislature itself had enacted such requirement to govern the conduct of its magistrates in fugitive slave cases. If there were such a state requirement, then a judicial ruling against the right could rest on two different grounds: either that the state legislature was barred by the federal Constitution from this action—as Story effectively ruled in *Prigg*—which would definitively close off this legislative setting for debate; or that, even though the state could govern the conduct of its own officials, slave rendition proceedings brought before a federal judge were not subject to the state's provision—a ruling which would not definitively close debate about the jury trial issue but would provide alternatives within the same state. (A judge might also sensibly conclude that the state-mandated jury trial was a procedural requirement that should govern federal as well as state fugitive slave cases conducted within the state, unless Congress explicitly directed otherwise.)[90]

Assume, however, that Congress in the 1793 act had already explicitly excluded jury trials in federal or state rendition proceedings but that a state legislature had nonetheless required juries. A court could—and, by Madisonian lights, should—invalidate this federal law on the ground that it interfered with constitutionally protected state prerogatives. This constitutional ruling would vindicate the Madisonian purpose of ensuring the availability of different forums for continued deliberation on this intensely disputed factional issue; Congress could impose its no-jury rule on its own officials but not on state officials as such, and state legislatures would be free to adopt variant conclusions in this matter.[91] In the specific context of this dispute, moreover, Congress itself would be able to re-examine the relative importance of barring jury trials in all possible fugitive slave proceedings, either by amending the 1793 act to exclude state officials from the rendition process, or by choosing to retain the states in the rendition process in order to enlist their more effective administrative machinery and the added legitimacy thereby afforded to the federal goal of returning fugitive slaves. If Congress chose to retain the states for these advantages, however, the states would be entitled to insist that the price of its assistance would be respect for the right to a jury trial.

Other variations on these institutional interactions can be imagined on this issue. A judge might conclude, for example, that even though Congress had not considered the existence of a right to jury trial in the 1793 Act, the judge would not impose it unless the state legislature in the particular jurisdiction had so enacted. The advantage of this course would be to relieve the judge of his own or others' suspicion that, in imposing a jury right, he was acting on the basis of his idiosyncratic personal morality. There is, however, an alternative—and preferable—way for a judge to pursue this same self-effacing goal by ruling for a jury trial even if the state had not imposed the requirement so long as neither the state nor Congress had explicitly forbidden it. The judge need not and should not ground this ruling on the existence of a clear constitutional right to a jury trial; the judge could conclude that constitutional concerns are sufficiently implicated that the right should be denied only in response to an explicit legislative directive. By this ruling, the judge would protect himself against the error of relying on his idiosyncratic personal morality as a basis for judicial action while in effect provoking deliberation in these other institutional settings if the state legislature or Congress were sufficiently aroused by this judicial ruling.[92]

There is one signal advantage of this judicial ruling to establish the jury trial right in the face of legislative silence—that the judge thereby alters the status quo. This unsettling capacity is perhaps the most valuable aspect of the judicial role in the Madisonian design: where the issues dividing the litigants are intensely and fundamentally polarizing, and yet for whatever reason these issues have not been openly debated in legislative forums, some judicial intervention can dislodge the status quo and provide some degree of advantage, even if only marginal, to the currently disadvantaged disputant, and this intervention can serve to promote subsequent institutional processes of consultation and accommodation.[93]

From this perspective, one historical event in the context of *Prigg* had particular salience. The gag-rule adopted by the House of Representatives to block presentation of abolitionist petitions raised a considerable constitutional issue. On its face, this House action appeared to transgress the First Amendment guarantee of "the right of the people peaceably . . . to petition the Government for a redress of grievances." It may be that the authority of "each house [to] determine the rules of its proceedings" under Article I, section 5, immunized this specific House action from judicial invalidation. But there was an appropriately indirect way—a Madisonian way—for the Court to address the constitutional issue raised by the gag-rule. The dispute-suppressive intent that lay beneath this House rule was the same animus behind the 1798 enactment of the Alien and Sedition Acts to punish political protest. Madison's condemnation of these laws in the Virginia Resolution, and his invocation of state legislatures as alternative institutional forums for redressing grievances when the national forums had been wrongfully foreclosed, points to the proper judicial remedy in *Prigg*: In response to the House gag-rule, the Supreme Court should have opened other institutional forums for public deliberation on the fugitive slave question.

In *Prigg*, however, Justice Story imposed his own gag-rule. His constitutional ruling for the slaveowner's private recaption right blocked any expression of concern by a public institution for the freedom of blacks; and on this issue, Story's opinion was joined by every member of the Court but Justice McLean. Story left open only one option for public expression of this concern; by concluding that congressional authority over fugitive slaves was "exclusive," Story permitted states only to remove themselves from the rendition process altogether but to exert no other independent influence on that process. This option of removal is itself a kind of gag-rule, though self-imposed; or, to vary the physical imagery, the only response to a perceived moral evil permitted by this option is to shut one's eyes. On this issue, however, the Court majority did not clearly endorse Story's view, and Chief Justice Taney explicitly rejected it, insisting that Congress could force states to participate in the rendition process notwithstanding their general or specific procedural objections.[94]

This disagreement between Story and Taney corresponds to the difference regarding public involvement in slave discipline between Judge Ruffin's position in *Mann* and subsequent legislation and case-law mandating active state engagement. In *Mann*, Judge Ruffin treated the master's disciplinary power as unreviewable for the same reasons that Story vested an unreviewable right of recaption in the master, to permit the master's effective control of his slave without involving others or imposing moral tension on them. But other lawmakers saw an even greater threat to public order if the master refused or was unable to subjugate his slave (by discipline or by recapture), notwithstanding his private right to do so. This fear led these lawmakers (southern legislators and judges, and Taney in *Prigg*) to override anyone's moral qualms by imposing (on masters in the exercise of discipline, on free states in the fugitive rendition process) a universal, publicly enforceable duty to subjugate slaves.

This persistent fear of slave disorder, and correspondingly escalating imposition of public force not simply on slaves but on the entire society, grew from the initial premise that both Story and Ruffin shared: the premise that the master–slave relationship was perpetual warfare. This same premise spread for Story in *Prigg* to the conception of conflict between whites regarding slavery: here too, he saw only warfare and so little prospect for peaceful accommodation that the issue must be rigorously excised from public debate, in court or legislature.

To maintain such silence in the face of persistent fears requires not only continuous but ever-increasing surveillance that feeds an endless cycle of repression, actual or imagined eruptions, and intensified repression—a psychological imperative as true for individuals as for society at large. The Supreme Court cases and the surrounding congressional controversy regarding slavery offer a microcosm of this cycle. The effort undertaken in *Prigg* to suppress public debate about slavery was not successful; in response to escalating extra-judicial conflict, the Court renewed its suppressive effort with even greater force fifteen years later in *Dred Scott v. Sandford.*[95]

During this interim, dispute specifically about the fugitive slave question had been pushed back by the route that Story had marked in *Prigg*. Several northern states had accepted his invitation and enacted "personal liberty" laws that forbade their officials from participating in enforcement of the 1793 rendition act, even prohibiting the use of state jails for detaining alleged fugitives.[96] Notwithstanding Taney's position in *Prigg* that states could be compelled to assist in the recapture of fugitive slaves, Congress enacted the Fugitive Slave Act of 1850, creating an administrative cadre of federal commissioners to preside over the rendition process—thereby, as Story had urged, removing state officials from any involvement.[97] This enactment did not end public dispute about fugitive slaves; there were a few notorious cases in the 1850s when local vigilante groups interfered with the federal rendition process and, most notably in Wisconsin, when state officials effectively collaborated with these resistance efforts.[98] After *Prigg,* however, the major focus of public dispute about slavery shifted to the status of slaves in the territories; and this issue quickly became a convulsive national preoccupation.

The crystalizing event occurred in 1846. During debate in the House of Representatives on President Polk's proposal for an appropriation to purchase territory from Mexico, as part of a settlement of the Mexican War, Representative David Wilmot of Pennsylvania proposed an amendment—the Wilmot Proviso—that in any such acquisition "neither slavery nor involuntary servitude shall ever exist." The House narrowly adopted this proviso by a vote that confounded the existing Whig–Democrat party alignments and overwhelmingly followed North–South sectional lines.[99] The amended bill died in the Senate; but suddenly, like a damburst, the question of territorial slavery became not simply the central issue but virtually the only issue in national political debate. Just two years later, Senator Thomas Hart Benton compared the issue to the Biblical plague of frogs: "You could not look upon the table but there were frogs, you could not sit down at the banquet but there were frogs, you could not go the bridal couch and lift the sheets but there were frogs. [So it was with] this black question, forever on the table, on the nuptial couch, everywhere."[100]

In 1820 the question of territorial slavery had briefly flared in national politics and was quickly extinguished in the adoption of the Missouri Compromise, which restricted slavery to future territories south of the latitude $36° \ 30'$. The Wilmot Proviso ignored this demarcation and thus reopened the question; and once reopened, it could not be resolved. After four years of bitter stalemate, Congress enacted a series of measures collectively known as the Compromise of 1850. In addition to enacting the new Fugitive Slave Act, Congress organized two new territories, Utah and New Mexico, but carefully made no provision regarding the status of slavery there. Instead, Congress seemingly delegated regulatory authority to the new territorial legislatures; but, at the same time, it refused to decide what regulatory authority had been or could be delegated. By an artfully designed provision, the statute said only that the territorial legislative power "shall extend to all rightful subjects of legislation consistent with the Constitution of the United States." Then, as if to underscore the institutional significance of this verbiage, the statute authorized and expedited direct appeals regarding the status of slavery from the highest territorial courts to the Supreme Court.[101]

Congress thus turned directly and self-consciously to the Court for the resolution of the central political conflict of the day. As one Senator observed at the time, Congress had enacted a lawsuit, not a law.[102] The role that Marshall had construed for the Court in *McCulloch*—to resolve issues that would otherwise "remain a source of hostile legislation, perhaps of hostility of a still more serious nature"—was thus apparently endorsed for the first time in American political history by a majority of the disputants in a highly charged conflict. Appealing to the Court was the only common ground that the combatants could seem to find.

In 1854, with passage of the Kansas–Nebraska Act, Congress not only organized these territories but explicitly repealed the Missouri Compromise and replaced it with the evasive formula of 1850.[103] Within a year, the Kansas territory erupted into open warfare among proslavery and antislavery settlers: "Bleeding Kansas," it was called.[104] But no court case answered the invitation in these new laws; no newly organized territorial legislature took any action regarding slavery that would provide an occasion for litigation.

This was the background when *Dred Scott v. Sandford* came to the Supreme Court in 1856. In the 1830s Scott had been taken by his owner from Missouri, a slave state, to live first in Illinois, a free state, and then in the Wisconsin Territory, a free jurisdiction under the terms of the Missouri Compromise. The central question in the case was whether the Missouri courts were required to recognize Scott's free status when his owner brought him back to that state around 1840. The case thus did not arise under the new congressional enactments, and the first impulse of a majority of the Justices was to reach a decision on the relatively narrow ground that Missouri courts were free to decide for themselves whether to apply external state or federal policies within their state.[105]

Two of the northern Justices, McLean of Ohio and Curtis of Massachusetts, indicated, however, that they would dissent from this ruling and in the course of their opinions would affirm the constitutional authority of the Congress under the Missouri Compromise to have barred slavery from the Wisconsin Territory. It seems likely that the five southern Justices on the Court were already eager to rule against congressional authority over territorial slavery but were reluctant to reach this conclusion without support from at least one northern colleague. The dissenters' position gave the Southerners a basis for appeal to Justice Grier of Pennsylvania, who agreed that if McLean and Curtis intended to address the territorial slavery issue generally, then the entire Court must speak to the issue and, moreover, dispose of it at once and for all.[106]

But more was at stake, even for the southern Justices, than simply affirming the rights of slaveowners. Taney in particular appeared less concerned with protecting slavery, notwithstanding his personal status as a Maryland slaveowner, than with subduing the bitter sectional controversy about slavery.[107] This concern was most openly expressed by Justice Wayne of Georgia, in his concurring statement in the case:

> The Court neither sought nor made [this] case. . . . We have only discharged our duty . . . as the framers of the Constitution meant the judiciary to [do]. . . . The case involves private rights of value, and constitutional principles of the highest importance, about which there had become such a difference of opinion, that the peace and harmony of the country required the settlement of them by judicial decision.[108]

Wayne's sentiment echoed President James Buchanan's observation in his inaugural address, just two days before the Court decided *Dred Scott,* that the status of territorial slavery was "a judicial question which legitimately belongs to the Supreme Court of the United States, before whom it is now pending, and will, it is understood, be speedily and finally settled. To their decision, in common with all good citizens, I shall cheerfully submit, whatever this may be."[109]

These were, then, the immediate background events when Chief Justice Taney spoke for the Court on March 6, 1857, in *Dred Scott v. Sandford.* Taney rejected Scott's claim for freedom on two related grounds: that he could not bring suit in federal court because all blacks (not simply black slaves) were barred from federal citizenship, which was necessary for federal court jurisdiction; and that in any event Congress had no constitutional authority to enact the Missouri Compromise of 1820, under which Scott claimed freedom.[110] Ironically, of course, Congress had already implicitly overridden the Missouri Compromise in 1850 and had explicitly repealed it in 1854. The Court was technically foreclosed from speaking directly to the questions posed to it by these latter acts, since the claims raised in *Dred Scott* hinged on earlier events; but clearly intent on answering these broad questions, the Court found an adequate proxy in its invalidation of the Missouri Compromise.

This was the first time since *Marbury* that the Court had overturned a congressional act. Unlike *Marbury,* however, *Dred Scott* could not be justified simply as an assertion of judicial equality or institutional self-defense. The constitutional invalidation in *Dred Scott* rested on a claim of judicial supremacy over the Congress in constitutional interpretation—the first time in the Court's jurisprudence that this claim was embedded in a holding and was necessary to sustain its internal logic.

On its face, the conjunctive effect of the Court's two rulings, against black citizenship and against the validity of the Missouri Compromise, appeared similar to the strategic consequence of Justice Story's opinion in *Prigg*—comprehensively removing the prohibition of territorial slavery from any public debate, as Story had attempted in *Prigg*. Under the *Dred Scott* rulings, the exclusion of slavery from the territories could not be considered by the federal government because Congress lacked any legislative authority to address the issue; the exclusion of slavery could not be considered by any territorial legislature because Congress lacked any authority to delegate jurisdiction over this issue to such legislatures; and even federal court inquiry regarding any territorial slavery issue was, if not wholly barred, at least exceedingly difficult to obtain because all blacks, slave or free, were disqualified from claiming federal court jurisdiction.

The only locus for debate permitted by *Dred Scott* was in each state legislature after statehood had been achieved; Congress was even apparently barred, according to Taney's reasoning, from specifically excluding slavery from any territory as a condition for admission as a state.[111] As a practical matter, legislative policy toward slavery in a newly admitted state would be dictated by the views of a majority of the territorial settlers; the apparent result of the Court's ruling was therefore to delegate the ultimate legislative decision to the competing, private actions of slaveowners and free soil advocates in choosing to migrate to the territories before statehood.

This practical context very much differs from the circumstances of *Prigg.* In that case, removing debate about fugitive slaves from northern state legislatures, judges, and juries effectively insulated the combatants from direct confrontation. Under *Prigg,* the slaveowner could pursue his quarry into the North and attempt to exercise his newly granted private recaption right; but, under Story's regime in *Prigg,* the slaveowner would most likely be dissuaded from this pursuit by his inability to rely on local enforcement assistance, especially in confronting the hostility of northern abolitionists. This, of course, was the reason why Taney insisted in *Prigg* that, beyond the private recaption right, states were obliged to assist the slaveowner and that Congress had authority to enforce that obligation on the states.

In the practical context of the territorial slavery dispute, however, the most likely consequence of *Dred Scott*'s removal of exclusionary authority from the Congress and the territorial legislatures was exactly the opposite of *Prigg*'s. Rather than discouraging the combatants from seeking out direct confrontation, *Dred Scott* promoted this result. Because the ultimate decision about excluding or permitting slavery could only be made after statehood had been achieved, slaveowners and abolitionists would both have the greatest incentive to rush into newly organized territories to establish dominance before statehood. This race had occurred in the Kansas territory before *Dred Scott;* and Bleeding Kansas appeared to be the most likely model for all territories after *Dred Scott*—an ironic consequence for the Court, which had proclaimed its intention, in Justice Wayne's words, to establish "the peace and harmony of the country . . . by judicial decision" of the territorial slavery issue.

Taney appeared to address this problem, at least indirectly, in his *Dred Scott* opinion. Slaves are property, he said, and the fifth amendment forbids the federal government from depriving any person of property without due process; it then followed for him that a congressional act excluding slavery from the territories deprived the slaveowner of his property and "could hardly be dignified with the name of due process of law." A second step might also seem to follow from his reasoning: just as the federal government could not deprive a slaveowner of his property, and just as federal and state governments were obliged by the fugitive slave clause to assist slaveowners in recapturing their property, so the federal government would be obliged to take affirmative action to protect slaveowners in the territories. Taney did not take this step in his *Dred Scott* opinion; but others outside the Court took it for him.

Southern Senators, led by Jefferson Davis of Mississippi, soon proposed legislation establishing a federal slave code for the territories. Davis stated that, since neither Congress nor a territorial legislature could "impair the constitutional right of any citizen of the United States to take his slave property into the common territories . . . [it is therefore] the duty of the federal government there to afford, for that as for other species of property, the needful protection."[112] This southern demand cut to the core of the northern Democrats' effort, led by Stephen Douglas, to remove the territorial slavery issue from national political debate by insisting that the question was reserved by the principle of "popular sovereignty" to residents of the territories; but Taney had already undermined this position in *Dred Scott* by denying any exclusionary authority to the territorial legislatures as such, and the southern Democrats simply drew out the logic of Taney's ruling. Douglas remained adamant, however, against any direct congressional endorsement of territorial slavery such as Davis demanded; this dispute was the basis for the mass defection of the Southerners from the Democratic Party in 1860 and their decision to run a rival candidate on a slave-code platform. This fateful split of the national Democratic party assured the election of Abraham Lincoln—a presidential candidate whose name did not even appear on the ballot in ten of the eleven states that were to become the Confederacy.[113]

The Supreme Court's decision in *Dred Scott* thus did not bring "peace and harmony" to the country. The decision did not cause the Civil War; but it did nothing to reduce the likelihood of war and probably even hastened this result, if only by inflaming northern fears and emboldening southern leaders to escalate their demands for national legitimation of slavery.[114] The Court had already set this course in *Prigg;* by shutting off all possible meliorist interventions in the fugitive slave rendition process, either in northern state legislatures or in constitutional litigation, the Court drove the abolitionist lawyers out of public institutions into the streets. The Court gave them virtually no option but to join Garrison there, as he burned a copy of the Constitution, describing it as a "compact with the devil" and proclaiming that only destruction of the Union could abate the evils of slavery.[115]

Dred Scott continued the course. But unlike *Prigg,* which did at least reduce the occasions for direct conflict between proslavery and antislavery combatants, *Dred Scott* increased the incentives for such encounters, driving each side to more desperate or provocative claims which, in turn, increased the apparent need, if public order were to be preserved, for some single sovereign authority to exert command over the warring parties. The Congress and the President had already called more directly on the Supreme Court to accept this sovereign role, and the Court itself had already gone further toward embracing this role for itself in the *Dred Scott* case than at any earlier time in American history. But these inflated expectations, paradoxically enough, had led the Court to issue blustering commands that only provoked heightened disobedience and ignited more violence.

Red, White, and Black

This, then, is the story of the American polity that is not part of our celebratory, patriotic tradition: that our conception of political and judicial authority took shape in response to a pitched battle between whites and Indians, whites and black slaves, and among whites about the legitimacy of black slavery. During the Jacksonian era, the American political vocabulary shifted toward virtually open and incessant warfare in its depiction of political relations between master and slave, settler and Indian, and the white North and South. A common fear lay beneath this shift—a fear that Tocqueville revealed in his separate characterizations of the three races.

Tocqueville maintained that, for whites, American society had given birth to a new personality type, the individualist, by breaking the "one long chain" of aristocratic social organization and "free[ing] each link":

> Not only does [this democratic uncoupling] make men forget their ancestors, but also clouds their view of their descendants and isolates them from their contemporaries. Each man is forever thrown back on himself alone, and there is danger that he may be shut up in the solitude of his own heart.[116]

Though Tocqueville did not draw out the comparison between this portrayal of whites and his depiction of blacks and Indians, the basic similarity is unmistakable. Of blacks:

> The United States Negro has lost even the memory of his homeland; he no longer understands the language his fathers spoke; he has abjured their religion and forgotten their mores. Ceasing to belong to Africa, he has acquired no right to the blessings of Europe; he is left in suspense between two societies and isolated between two peoples, sold by one and repudiated by the other; in the whole world there is nothing but his master's hearth to provide him with some semblance of a homeland.[117]

Of Indians:

> It is impossible to imagine the terrible afflictions involved in [their] forced migrations. The Indians leaving their ancestral fields are already worn down and exhausted. . . . There is famine behind them, war in front, and misery everywhere. In the hope to escape so many enemies, they divide up. Each one of them in isolation tries furtively to find some means of subsistence, living in the immensity of the forest like some outlaw in civilized society. The long-weakened social bond then finally breaks. Their homeland has already been lost, and soon they will have no people; families hardly remain together; the common name is lost, the language forgotten, and traces of their origin vanish. The nation has ceased to exist.[118]

Tocqueville may have overstated the extent to which blacks and Indians had lost contact with their ancestral roots;[119] the real significance of his depictions is not that they were true for blacks or Indians but that they were the dominant white view of these groups. Seen through white eyes, Tocqueville's portraits of blacks and Indians appear to be nightmarish exaggerations of the characteristics that the whites saw in themselves—of isolation from their ancestral past, from contemporaries, and from a predictable future. Indeed, the migrations that the Jacksonian whites singlemindedly forced on the Indians appears from this perspective, as Michael Paul Rogin has observed, "to impose the American experience of uprooting and mobility upon the Indians."[120] Andrew Jackson explicitly made the connection in an address to Congress:

> Doubtless it will be painful [for the Indians] to leave the graves of their fathers, but what do they more than our ancestors did nor than our children are doing? To better their condition in an unknown land our forefathers left all that was dear in earthly objects. Our children by thousands yearly leave the land of their birth to seek new homes in distant regions. Does humanity weep at these painful separations from everything animate and inanimate, with which the young heart has become entwined? Far from it. It is rather a source of joy.[121]

Perhaps. But then again, perhaps not.

The whites, however, defended themselves by an act of political imagination against the fate Tocqueville saw for Indians and blacks—that whites too might lose "even the memory of [their] homeland," that they might have "no people" or even a "common name." Unfortunately—or perhaps one should say, predictably— American whites pursued two diametrically opposed defensive strategies against this fate. One strategy was to invest the Union with romantic and even mystical significance in order to provide more than "some semblance of a homeland." A second, opposed strategy was to bestow such significance on sectional loyalties based on more particularist common bonds: the southern way of life entwined around slavery; or the dedication of the northern free states to personal liberty for whites and abolition of black slavery. The competition for allegiance between these two idealizations, national and sectional, was fought with escalating intensity throughout the Jacksonian era—a competition waged not only between different adherents but even more extensively fought within the minds of individuals in both sections. The very identifications that white Americans embraced as antidotes to the fear of social disintegration thus turned in a destructive dialectic on one another.

A distinctive style of political authority emerged from this disintegrative fear—a style forged in the battles between reds, whites, and blacks during the Jacksonian era. These intensified struggles all arose from the dissolution of the gentry ideal of social authority. Though this ideal had been sharply challenged by the mid-eighteenth century, the colonial secession from Great Britain gave indigenous gentry authority an extended life; but as the founding generation died out, and the centrifugal forces released by the Revolution undermined belief in the existence of unifying bonds beneath the surface of factional disputes, the gentry ideal disappeared. The last president to claim fealty to this ideal was John Quincy Adams and even at the moment of his election in 1824, he was already an anachronism. Adams's subsequent career, following his defeat by Jackson in 1828, itself illuminates the linkage between the heightened race-based conflicts and the new style of political authority that displaced the gentry ideal.

Adams had been elected president by the House of Representatives after receiving only minority support in the popular vote and the electoral college. Nonetheless, he proclaimed in his inaugural address that the "baneful weed of party strife" had been uprooted from national politics and that "ten years of peace, at home and abroad, have assuaged the animosities of political contention and blended into harmony the most discordant elements of public opinion."[122] During his presidency he conceived and repeatedly portrayed himself as transcending partisan conflict by retaining ardent political opponents in office, even in Cabinet positions, and presenting grand plans for national economic growth while confronting the absence of popular support for his proposals with the forthright gentry admonition to Congress not to "fold up our arms and proclaim to the world that we are palsied by the will of our constituents."[123]

Like his father from whom he had imbibed the "patriot king" model of national leadership, the son showed a genius for uniting the country, but only against himself. Like his father, moreover, John Quincy Adams's electoral defeat did not shake his faith in the existence of a transcendent public good or his capacity to know that good. The son's critique of his loss took a twist, however, that the father would not have followed. John Adams had also been defeated by a southern slaveowner; but the elder Adams would not have described Jefferson's campaign platform as merely a mask for the protection of slavery or his election as a triumph for the Slavocracy, as the younger Adams saw Jackson's victory. John Quincy Adams drew a tight link, that is, between the popular rejection of the gentry ideal of disinterested public leadership implicit in his defeat and the evils of slavery.

The younger Adams's syllogism was as follows: In Jackson's partisan appeals to states' rights and free trade, he cultivated "the instincts of greed and avarice which are the essence of competition" by which "each man strives to better himself at the cost of his neighbor." This self-seeking striving "embodied the principle of public plunder," which was itself "the materialization of the principle of evil." The most egregious expression of these twin evils of public plunder and private self-aggrandizement was the subjection of one man to the "personal slavery" of another.[124] Thus, John Quincy Adams saw the threat to the gentry ideal not simply in the overall social values that Jackson espoused but specifically and principally in the institution of slavery as such.

Unlike his father, moreover, John Quincy Adams did not retreat from national public life after his defeat; in 1830 he was elected to the House of Representatives, where he served until his death in 1848. During that tenure, Adams was persistently and passionately outspoken against slavery, leading the parliamentary opposition to the gag-rule and generally assuming the mantle of the first national champion of the abolitionist cause.[125] In his own career Adams thus mapped the route by which the existence of slavery became identified as the principal threat to the gentry ideal, on the ground that slavery was the embodiment of self-aggrandizing private plunder and therefore inherently antagonistic toward the gentry-prized pursuit of public goals that transcended factional self-seeking.

Adams's condemnation of slavery, however, was itself anachronistic in a revealing way. By the end of the antebellum period, the most politically potent critics of slavery were not outright abolitionists but advocates of "free soil" in the territories. For these critics, the central abomination of slavery was its devaluation of the pursuit of private gain by freely self-aggrandizing individuals[126]—precisely what Adams saw, through the lens of his commitment to the gentry ideal, as the defining attribute of slavery itself. These critics thus extolled the virtues of free labor while channeling their fears of economic and social subjection into hostility toward southern slavery. Apologists for slavery were quick to see the internal tension in their opponents' claims, and spoke repeatedly of the evils of "wage slavery" and the superior benevolence of their plantation-style slavery.[127] As John Quincy Adams had seen, notwithstanding their apparent differences, these proponents and opponents of slavery both relied on the same underlying conception of political authority: a unitary, unlimited ruling force. For Southerners, this conception was embodied in the master's relationship to his slaves; for northern advocates of "free labor," this conception was not expressed in a social relationship but was nonetheless implicitly endorsed in their approbation of the self-aggrandizing individual uninhibited by any social constraint.

The starkness of this unitary, fundamentally embattled conception of political authority was evident throughout the Jacksonian era in the dominant white view of political relations with Indians and with blacks. This same severity did not become fully evident for relations among whites until the end of this era, when competing claims exploded in the Civil War—when, that is, northern whites claimed authority to subjugate resistant southern whites in order to preserve the Union, and Southerners claimed unlimited authority to continue their subjugation of blacks. This war between the whites was waged, moreover, with a ferocity that exceeded any previous European experience of warfare. The closest previous pattern was the warfare that American whites had waged against Indians, which, like the goals of both North and South in the Civil War, sought to destroy the essence of their political identity and ultimately escalated toward the goal of slaughtering all of them.[128]

This was the background for the growing acceptance of the idea of judicial supremacy as an instrument for governing political relations among whites. This idea of judicial supremacy was a pale version of the conception of political authority that arose from the subjugative warfare between whites and Indians, masters and slaves, or northern and southern whites; but there were common features nonetheless. In particular, the claim for absolute, unreviewable authority was the common hallmark of judicial authority and these other assertions of political supremacy. The underlying links between these various forms of authority are also suggested by the fact that the claim for judicial supremacy in constitutional interpretation was not widely or definitively accepted in American society until after the Civil War—not simply in temporal sequence but as a direct response and imagined antidote to the War. By the end of the nineteenth century, following the trail already marked by mid-century for white relations with Indians and slaves, the Supreme Court had become the virtual embodiment of absolute sovereign authority.

6

The Civil War
Rules

THE DOMINANT VIEW in the North in 1860 was that the southern states would never act on their threats to secede.[1] Immediately after secession in 1861, the dominant southern view was that the northern states would acquiesce after a "short and glorious war."[2] These expectations on both sides were shattered. But neither side quickly came to terms with the implications of the four years of civil war that followed. The War was so pervasively destructive—of life, of property, and of prior assumptions about social relations within and between the two sections—that, when it had ended, those who had lived through it could only gradually grasp its significance.

One consequence was obvious immediately: the War had destroyed the prior scheme of social governance in the South. Though it may have been less obvious, the War had destroyed the prior scheme in the North as well. The North had fought to preserve the Union; but it had not succeeded, and could not succeed, in this goal. The old Union had been voluntarily constituted; the new, post-war Union had a radically different constitution. This fundamental change in the character of American political authority, moreover, had different meanings for the generation that had presided over the Civil War and for those who had fought in its trenches. The older generation not only carried residual assumptions from the antebellum times but struggled to hold onto these assumptions as comfortably familiar landmarks in an unknown terrain. The younger generation had no direct knowledge of these old pathways; they knew only the transformative experience and the leveled landscape of the War itself.

Both generations' attitudes toward political authority generally, and judicial authority specifically, were dramatically affected by the War; but each generation reacted in distinctive ways.

Home Front: The Chase Court and Congress

On the eve of the Civil War, two challenges had been aimed at Supreme Court authority that were as profound and as politically salient as the 1798 campaign against the Alien and Sedition Acts. The two challenges were the actions of the Wisconsin Supreme Court to invalidate a federal law without regard for any subsequent federal judicial review and the position taken by Abraham Lincoln before his election (and reiterated in his inaugural address) contesting the Supreme Court's authority to bind other federal branches in the interpretation of the Constitution. Both of these challenges were directed at proslavery decisions by the Court: the Wisconsin court ruled against the constitutionality of the Fugitive Slave Act of 1850, and Lincoln inveighed against the *Dred Scott* case. Like the 1798 attacks by the Virginia and Kentucky legislatures on the Alien and Sedition Acts, the substantive principles advanced by the Wisconsin court and Lincoln were soon vindicated by political events. Unlike 1798, however, the institutional premises of the latter-day challenges almost immediately thereafter disappeared from American constitutional discourse.

The Wisconsin court's challenge to federal judicial supremacy was avowedly based on the old Jeffersonian Republican states-rights orthodoxy known as the "Spirit of 1798." In overturning the Fugitive Slave Act and ordering the release from federal custody of an abolitionist convicted of assisting a slave's escape, the state court dismissed

> the doctrine early broached, but as early repudiated, that any one department of the [federal] government is constituted the final and exclusive judge of its own delegated powers. No such tribunal has been erected by the fundamental law. The judicial department of the federal government is the creature by compact of the several States, as sovereignties, and their respective people. . . . To admit that the federal judiciary is the sole and exclusive judge of its own powers, and the extent of the authority

delegated, is virtually to admit that the same unlimited power may be exercised by every other department of the general government.[3]

In 1859, two years after its *Dred Scott* decision, the Supreme Court unanimously overturned the Wisconsin court's action, resoundingly affirming "the power of this court to decide, ultimately and finally," the constitutionality of congressional acts.[4] The Court, moreover, made clear that its authority stood above both Congress and the states in order to avert "force and violence"[5] between federal and state authorities. Without such a "calm and deliberate arbiter," the Court warned, "revolutions by force of arms" would inevitably result.[6]

There is considerable irony in this clash between the United States and Wisconsin supreme courts. Just two years later, revolutionary "force and violence" between federal and state governments did erupt in the Civil War. The principle of state sovereignty for which the antislavery Wisconsin court spoke was the avowed basis for the southern states' secession in order to preserve slavery. And in this ultimate conflict, neither the federal government nor the seceding states appealed to the "calm and deliberate" arbitration proffered for such disputes by the Supreme Court.

In *Dred Scott*, of course, the Court had tried to avert civil war by definitively resolving the most obviously divisive substantive dispute about territorial slavery. It is thus not surprising that, on taking control of the executive branch in 1861, Lincoln would not turn to the Court to "speedily and finally settle" the slavery controversy, as James Buchanan had done just four years earlier at his inauguration. Lincoln instead explicitly rejected any such institutional role for the Supreme Court. In his inaugural address, Lincoln retrospectively criticized the Court in *Dred Scott* for purporting "irrevocably" to decide the institutional status of territorial slavery. He did not directly consider whether the looming conflict over state secession should be referred for adjudication to the Court. A question of constitutional interpretation was, however, at the core of the secession conflict—a question that Lincoln unilaterally resolved in his inaugural address. "I hold," Lincoln proclaimed, "that, in contemplation of universal law and of the Constitution, the Union of these States is perpetual."[7] This was "the most important single act of American constitutional interpretation" in our history.[8] It is a striking jurisprudential fact that civil war followed directly from this legal interpretation and that, notwithstanding John Marshall's claim in *Marbury v. Madison* that "it is emphatically the province and duty of the judicial department to say what the law is," the Supreme Court said nothing at the time.

Forty-two years earlier, in *McCulloch v. Maryland,* Marshall had ruled against the compact theory of state sovereignty on which the 1861 secessionists relied. But the seceding states purported to avoid this ruling by acting not through their regularly constituted legislatures but through the same format of specially convened, popularly elected conventions that had originally ratified the Constitution.[9] The Court might have declined to resolve the secession issue, if it had been presented, on the ground that it was a "political" question committed to other branches, as Taney had ruled in the 1849 dispute regarding the legitimacy of two rival state governments in Rhode Island.[10] In that case, however, Taney found that there were no justiciable standards in the Constitution for resolving the controversy; this would not necessarily hold for judicial consideration of the existence of a constitutional right to secession. Moreover, Taney had ruled in the Rhode Island case that Congress was the appropriate institution for deciding the issue. Even if the Court were not prepared to address the secession right in 1861, it might have decided whether the President could act alone, as Lincoln did, in resolving this issue.

The Supreme Court did belatedly consider the legitimacy of Lincoln's action in an 1863 case specifically addressing his imposition of a blockade of southern ports before any congressional war declaration.[11] By a five to four vote, the Court upheld Lincoln's action; but the appearance of impartiality in this endorsement was diminished by the fact that three members of this narrow majority had been appointed by Lincoln after the outbreak of hostilities and confirmed by a Senate from which the southern states had removed themselves. The four dissenters rested their case on the proposition that Congress alone was constitutionally authorized to declare either war or a state of insurrection, and that its retroactive declaration (made after the southern states had withdrawn) was insufficient to legitimize the President's prior actions.[12] It thus seems at least plausible that in 1861, if the question had been presented, the Court would have ruled that states had no constitutional right to secede—drawing on its recent precedent against the Wisconsin state court's nullification proclamation in *Ableman v. Booth*—but that the President could act only with explicit congressional authorization to counteract state assertions of this right.

This ruling would not have satisfied the southern states. In any event, their theory of secession, drawn from Jefferson's Kentucky Resolution, deprived federal courts of any authority to decide this issue, and they, accordingly, would not have sought judicial review. From Lincoln's perspective, such a Supreme Court ruling would have had the tactical advantages of both invalidating the secessionists' legal claim and indicating to the southern states that they could protect this claim only by retaining their representation in Congress (and thus, paradoxically, remaining in the Union). By 1861, however, this kind of pragmatic reasoning was scarce in southern councils;[13] and, from Lincoln's perspective, there were enormous risks in entrusting his cherished ideal of perpetual union to a Supreme Court dominated by proslavery Southerners, notwithstanding the apparently favorable auguries of the Court's recent jurisprudence.[14] Accordingly, in this central constitutional crisis, none of the adversaries sought judicial review, and the Supreme Court stood at the sidelines of the conflict.*

The Civil War itself, however, brought the Court into the center of such conflicts for the future. The impact of the War on the Justices' attitude toward judicial authority is first of all suggested by the fact that, in its immediate aftermath, the Court invalidated congressional acts with unaccustomed frequency. By 1865 a majority of the Justices had been appointed by Lincoln; but in 1866

---

*The court did directly address the legality of secession four years after the War had ended and, not surprisingly, ratified the northern victory. Chief Justice Chase, writing for the Court, disposed of the question in a single paragraph, on the ground that the Articles of Confederation had established a "perpetual" Union, the preamble to the Constitution had declared its intention "to form a more perfect Union," and, accordingly, "what can be indissoluble if a perpetual Union, made more perfect, is not?" Texas v. White, 74 U.S. (7 Wall.) 700, 724–25 (1869).

and 1867 this reconstituted Court rendered two decisions that Republican congressional leaders viewed as virtual reiterations of the *Dred Scott* apostasy.[15] In *Ex parte Milligan,* the Court overturned the military trial of a civilian and stated that Congress had no constitutional authority for such trials where the civil courts "were open" and there were no hostile armies.[16] Though the Court had avoided decision on this question during the war itself, Chief Justice Taney had reached this same conclusion in 1861 in his capacity as Circuit Justice for Maryland.[17] *Milligan* in effect ratified Taney's decision and was widely viewed as a "staggering blow to the plans for the use of the military forces in the process of Reconstruction then being matured by Congress."[18] In 1867 the Court administered an even more direct blow at congressional reconstruction efforts by invalidating office-holding disqualifications that Congress had imposed on anyone who had "given aid" to the Confederacy. These disqualifications, the Court held, violated the constitutional bans against ex post facto laws and bills of attainder.[19]

These two decisions were not, as it turned out, opening volleys in a judicial campaign against Reconstruction. In later cases, the Court was elaborately careful to avoid any wholesale challenge and, for the most part, refused any adjudication on the merits of various Reconstruction enactments.[20] It was nonetheless plausible to compare these two decisions with *Dred Scott*—not, as outraged Republicans maintained at the time, that the Court was a political partisan on behalf of the South but that the intensely polarized civil conflict continued to push the Court toward more extensive claims for superseding authority over congressional acts.

On this score, Supreme Court invalidation, immediately following the War, of several apparently insignificant congressional acts reveals even more than the political heat generated by *Milligan* and the office-holding disqualification cases. The smaller cases suggest that judicial invalidation of congressional acts had become, at least as the Court now saw it, a routine aspect of judicial work.[21] Having waited fifty-four years between its first and second exercise of judicial review authority, from *Marbury* to *Dred Scott,* the postbellum Court seemed almost giddy in its quick repetitions of the enterprise.

As important as the War might have been for the Justices'

attitude toward judicial authority, the War had a more directly demonstrable and more important impact on congressional attitudes. In contemplating the reconstruction of the Union, the ghost of *Dred Scott* haunted the deliberations of the Republican-dominated Thirty-ninth Congress and ultimately could not be exorcised. Before the War, opposition to judicial supremacy in constitutional interpretation had been the Republican rallying-cry, epitomized both in the Wisconsin Supreme Court's antislavery invocation of the "Spirit of 1798" and in Lincoln's direct attacks on *Dred Scott* in his 1858 debates with Stephen Douglas and his first inaugural address—an opposition which rested on precedents that, though rejected by the Court itself, nonetheless remained persistent and salient in American constitutional discourse throughout the antebellum era. It is thus ironic that the Fourteenth Amendment enacted by the Republican Thirty-ninth Congress more directly endorsed Supreme Court authority as the ultimate constitutional arbiter over other federal branches than any previous provision in the Constitution. The framers of the Fourteenth Amendment embraced this exalted umpireal role because the traumatic experience of the Civil War had confirmed the grim warnings of Marshall and Taney that this was the only institutional means for averting "hostility of a still more serious nature"[22] or of repeated "revolutions by force of arms."[23]

The victorious Republicans did not immediately embrace judicial authority in the wake of the War. The Thirteenth Amendment abolishing slavery referred only to, and thus appeared to rely exclusively on, congressional enforcement of its terms.* The first draft of the Fourteenth Amendment, as reported in February 1866 by the Joint Committee on Reconstruction to the House of Representatives, explicitly gave Congress "power to . . . secure to all persons in the several States equal protection in the rights of

---

*"Congress shall have power to enforce this article by appropriate legislation." Thirteenth Amendment, section 2. The question whether this section gave exclusive interpretive authority to Congress or permitted judicial review of congressional interpretation was subsequently disputed in Congress during deliberations on the Civil Rights Act of 1866 and the enactment of the Fourteenth Amendment. See Burt, "Miranda and Title II: A Morganatic Marriage," 1969 *Sup. Ct. Rev.* 81, 86–90.

life, liberty, and property."[24] This draft provision said nothing about the judiciary; it even appeared effectively to exclude any judicial review of congressional actions.* The House did not act on this first draft, however; and the second draft of the amendment, reported by the Joint Committee in April, took a very different approach. This revised version directly proclaimed that "[no] state shall make or enforce any law [denying equal protection, et cetera]"—the present form of the Fourteenth Amendment. The underlying purpose of this revision was clearly to annoint the judiciary as the guardian both against states and Congress of the principles won on the battlefields of the Civil War.

In the interim between February and April 1866, the framers had thought more clearly about the prospect that representatives of the defeated rebel states would someday inevitably reenter Congress.[25] Because they could not trust future Congresses to protect their battlefield victory, they turned to the Court.** Nothing in the original text of the Constitution so clearly had recognized this transcendent judicial role; and though the Bill of Rights did more directly invite judicial enforcement of its terms against congressional action, this judicial authority neither excluded nor was necessarily superior to state authority. By contrast, the Fourteenth Amendment at one clear stroke elevated the judiciary above both Congress and the states. As Representative (later President) James Garfield observed in the House debate, "[We] pro-

---

*The draft provision gave Congress "power to make all laws which shall be necessary and proper to secure [the rights]," i.e., reiterating the formula in Article I, section 8, of the Constitution that, according to John Marshall's interpretation in *McCulloch,* excluded any judicial oversight of congressional action.

**Representative John Bingham was the principal draftsman of both the February and the April drafts of the amendment; in his retrospective reflection on the reasoning that led him to the April revision, Bingham stated that in the interim he had "reexamin[ed]" Chief Justice Marshall's opinion in Barron v. Baltimore, 32 U.S. 243 (1833), refusing to enforce the Fifth Amendment against state governments on the ground that, unlike the bill of attainder clause and other direct proscriptions in the Constitution against state action, the Bill of Rights did not say "no state shall . . . ." Bingham said, "I noted and apprehended as I never did before, [these] words [and a]cting upon [Marshall's] suggestion I did imitate the framers of the original Constitution," thereby enlisting the judicial enforcement that Marshall had withheld in *Barron.* Cong. Globe 42d Cong. 1st Sess. App. p. 84 (March 31, 1871).

pose to lift that great and good [principle of equality] above the reach of political strife, beyond the reach of the plot and machinations of any party, and fix it in the serene sky, in the eternal firmament of the Constitution."[26]

If Garfield truly believed that the Supreme Court dwelt in this "serene sky" beyond "political strife," he must somehow have forgotten about *Dred Scott*, decided by a presumably less ethereal body just nine years earlier. By any realistic measure, the Supreme Court's conduct in *Dred Scott* should have disqualified it from this exalted role. But by 1866, in the wake of a brutal Civil War, the wish for some oracular transcendence of political conflict was stronger than any practical appreciation of its unattainability. The Supreme Court was not a realistic candidate for this role; it was, however, the only imaginable candidate. Congressional reverie about the exaltation of the Supreme Court was a kind of temporary amnesia that took hold during the deliberations on the Fourteenth Amendment.

The framers of the Fourteenth Amendment roused themselves soon enough, however. Though they did not repudiate their prior reliance on judicial authority, they clearly revealed their intense ambivalence about it. John Bingham, the principle draftsman of the amendment, provided the most striking evidence of this conflicted attitude. Just six months after Congress had sent the amendment to the states for ratification, Bingham addressed the possibility that the Supreme Court might act contrary to the wishes of a congressional majority:

> The original jurisdiction of that court is very restricted . . . by the terms of the Constitution. Their appellate jurisdiction . . . depends exclusively upon the will of Congress. If [members of Congress] are at all apprehensive of any wrongful intervention of the Supreme Court . . . sweep away at once their appellate jurisdiction in all cases. . . . Do that, and let that court hereafter sit to try only questions affecting ambassadors, other public ministers and consuls, and questions in which a State shall be a party, as that is the beginning and end of its original jurisdiction.[27]

If this jurisdictional denial were not sufficient to discipline the Court, if, notwithstanding, "the court usurps power to decide political questions and defy a free people's will," then Bingham envisioned an even more punitive response: "It will only remain for a people thus insulted and defied to demonstrate that the servant is not above his lord by procuring a further constitutional amendment . . . which will defy judicial usurpation by annihilating the usurpers in the abolition of the tribunal itself."[28]

It is thus striking that just six months after Congress approved the most extensive grant of judicial authority anywhere in the Constitution in order to guard against future congressional action, the principal draftsman of that amendment asserted that Congress might overturn judicial rulings by the simple expedient of denying jurisdiction to the Court. The irony is further compounded by the immediate context of Bingham's threat. One month earlier, the Supreme Court had decided *Ex parte Milligan,* which not only challenged military trials of civilians but suggested more generally to Bingham and his allies that the Court might question the credentials of the reconstructed southern legislatures to participate in the ratification of the Fourteenth Amendment.[29] Thus Bingham threatened to decimate the Court's jurisdiction, and even ultimately to abolish it, unless the Court acquiesced in the ultimate ratification of an amendment granting it ostensibly transcendent authority over the actions of the national and state governments. This is surely a textbook example of ambivalence. Bingham, moreover, was not alone in this conflicted stance. Within a year an extensive series of measures were proposed in the Congress (and some were adopted) to curb judicial power.*

---

*In 1868 Congress repealed the Court's jurisdiction to hear appeals in federal habeas corpus proceedings alleging constitutional violations. See Ex parte McCardle, 74 U.S. (7 Wall.) 506 (1869). The House approved a measure requiring two-thirds vote of the Court to invalidate any congressional act. Cong. Globe, 40th Cong., 2d Sess. 489 (1868). Representative Bingham further suggested reducing the Court's membership to three, so that the two-thirds rule would necessarily follow. Id. at 483–84. Bingham's suggestion built on the precedent established by Congress in 1866, one month after its approval of the Fourteenth Amendment, reducing the Court membership from ten to seven, effectively barring any nominations from President Andrew Johnson. See 2 Warren at 421–22. Representative Garfield might presumably have justified this measure as lifting the Court "beyond the reach of the plots and machinations" of the President. It is difficult to see, however, how anyone could imagine that the subsequent congressional actions signified the Court's transcendence of "political strife." After

In one sense, this attitude toward judicial authority among the framers of the Fourteenth Amendment reiterates the ambivalence that reigned in the Constitutional Convention itself. Recall John Dickinson's observation in 1787 regarding "the power of the Judges to set aside the law[:] He thought no such power ought to exist. He was at the same time at a loss what expedient to substitute."[30] But if ambivalence is the right word to describe Dickinson's attitude, some more potent phrase must be found to characterize the self-contradiction of Bingham and his colleagues in 1866–67, to express their greater intensity and wider ambit of mood swing. Perhaps this comparison: that if the founders' ambivalence is equated with neurotic conflict, then the framers of the Fourteenth Amendment were in the grip of a manic episode.

This is of course hyperbole. But there nonetheless is a serious point beneath it. The mood of any historical period is always more difficult to examine than its recorded words. Lawyers in particular, working from their powerful professional commitment to rational, verbalized discourse are inclined to narrow their attention to these words and to discount the relevance of mood—reading the lyrics but ignoring the melody—when they scrutinize the past to identify the intentions of long-dead legislators or judges. My suggestion that the framers of the Fourteenth Amendment were in the grip of a mania is meant to lean against this narrow professional inclination.

I do not mean that the framers should have been civilly committed. I do mean that we today cannot understand their attitude toward judicial authority unless we can somehow grasp the emotions that pulled at and gave specific shape to the words they spoke. Freud used parapraxes, "slips of the tongue" when the spoken word appears to contradict the speaker's intended meaning, as one route toward demonstrating the existence and importance of this emotional substrata. For our purposes the logical contradictions in the framers' statements about judicial supremacy over or subordination to congressional authority serve the same purpose. Freud used this technique most prominently, moreover, in a work that he evocatively titled *The Psychopathology of Everyday*

Grant's inauguration, the Court was restored to nine members. Act of April 10, 1869, ch. 22, 16 Stat. 44.

Life. It is in this spirit that I mean to speak of a psychosis among the framers: it is a "normal" psychosis, in the same sense that Freud identified the extreme emotions engendered by romantic love as a normal psychosis.[31] For the framers, however, their psychotic state was grief.

". . . *this terrible war*"

Consider these raw facts:

- 620,000 soldiers died in the Civil War: 360,000 from the North, 260,000 from the South; and some 50,000 southern civilians were killed. This death toll is higher than the combined numbers of Americans killed in all other wars, from the Revolution through the Vietnam War.[32]
- Just over two percent of the American population died in the Civil War (1.6 percent of the more populated North and 2.8 percent of the South). By contrast, in World War II, 0.28 percent of the American population were killed (384,000 deaths). If the World War II ratio had equaled the northern proportion in the Civil War, some 2.5 million would have died; if the ratio had equaled southern proportions, the sum would have been almost 5 million.[33]
- The slaughter inflicted in individual battles exceeded all past experience of warfare. At Antietam on a single day, September 17, 1862, some 4,800 soldiers were killed. In the entire Revolutionary War, only about 4,000 died. When the Battle of Shiloh was fought, in April 1862, it was the bloodiest battle ever to take place in the Western Hemisphere. By the end of the war the deaths at Shiloh ranked seventh place among Civil War battles.[34]
- As the war continued, battlefield casualties climbed exponentially. In May–June 1864, 65,000 northern and 35,000 southern soldiers were killed or wounded. This amounted to three-fifths of the total number of combat casualties suffered both by the Union army and the smaller Confederate army during the entire previous three years.[35]

These were the numbers; and each number had a name, a face, a family. So Mary Chesnut testified in her diary, in July 1862 when the prospect of southern victory still seemed alive:

J[ames] C[hesnut, Jr.] met the Haynes. They went on to nurse their wounded son—found him dead. They were standing in the corridor at the Spotswood. Although he was staying at the president's, J.C. retained his room at this hotel. So he gave his room to them. Next day, when he went back to his room, he found that Mrs. Hayne had thrown herself across the foot of the bed—and never moved. No other part of the bed had been touched. She got up and went back to the cars—or was led. He says these heartbroken mothers are hard to face.

After all, suppose we do all we hoped. Suppose we start up grand and free—a proud young republic. Think of all these young lives sacrificed! If three [yankees] for one [confederate] be killed, what comfort is that? What good will that do Mrs. Hayne or Mary DeSaussure? The best and bravest of one generation swept away! Henry DeSaussure has left four sons to honor their father's memory and emulate his example. But those poor boys of between 18 and 20 years of age—Haynes, Trezevants, Taylors, Rhetts, &c&c—they are washed away, literally, in a tide of blood. There is nothing to show they ever were on earth.[36]

The most eloquent northern diarist of the era was Abraham Lincoln. Here is his accounting in March 1865, when northern victory finally seemed assured:

Neither party expected for the war the magnitude or the duration which it has already attained. . . . Each looked for an easier triumph, and a result less fundamental and astounding. Both read the same Bible and pray to the same God, and each invokes His aid against the other. It may seem strange that any men should dare to ask a just God's assistance in wringing their bread from the sweat of other men's faces, but let us judge not, that we not be judged. The prayers of both could not be answered. That of neither has been answered fully. The Almighty has His own purposes. "Woe unto the world because of offenses; for it must needs be that offenses come, but woe to that man by whom the offense cometh." If we shall suppose that American slavery is one of those offenses which, in the providence of God, must needs come, but which, having continued through His appointed time, He now wills to remove, and that He gives to both North and South this terrible war as the woe due to those by whom the offense came, shall we discern therein any departure from those divine attributes which the believers in a living God always ascribe to Him? Fondly do we hope, fervently do we pray, that this mighty scourge of war may speedily pass away. Yet, if God wills that it continue until all the wealth piled by the bondsman's two hundred and fifty years of unrequited toil shall be sunk, and until every drop of blood drawn with the lash shall be paid by another drawn with the sword, as was said three thousand years ago, so still it must be said, "The judgements of the Lord are true and righteous altogether."

This mournful recounting was not a private document. It was Lincoln's second inaugural address—almost half of all that he said on this state occasion.[37] His inaugural address in 1861 had a very different character: in common with his predecessors and successors, much longer and more impersonal, even legalistic, in tone as he appealed to the southern states to remain in the Union and warned of the consequences of secession. His 1865 address, however, is not comparable to any other public document in American history: our President envisioning that the entire nation, "both North and South," may deserve Divine condemnation for the past offense of maintaining "American [not merely southern] slavery" and may thus properly be punished so that "all the wealth" accumulated from the nation's founding "shall be sunk" in bloody retribution.

Five weeks later Lincoln himself was dead, a belated casualty of the Civil War. He was not, however, the last victim. From virtually the first moment of the War's end, the defeated southern whites turned toward blacks with increasingly vengeful savagery. In some measure, this "wave of violence that raged almost unchecked in large parts of the postwar South"[38] can be explained as scapegoating. But more than this, the explosion of white violence against blacks was an expression of the underlying basis of the slavery relationship that had been held in check by two forces now destroyed by the War. The economics of slavery had previously given whites strong motives to protect their financial investment in blacks, both inhibiting individual masters' brutality toward their slaves and prodding white legislators and judges to protect the owners' interest in their slaves against other whites' depredations. Emancipation shattered these incentives.

Slavery also rested on an intense affective relationship between whites and blacks—not affectionate in any ordinary sense but nonetheless a complicated mixture of positive and negative feelings derived from the face-to-face contact between most masters and slaves, even on the large plantations.* This close physical proximity virtually demanded that the whites suppress the hostile components of their relations with blacks—actively (and consciously) by maintaining rigorous controls but even more pervasively by masking this hostility from their own awareness in order to preserve peace of mind in their thousand daily interactions.** The War itself strained these customary self-protective psychological maneuvers in whites' attitudes toward blacks.

Mary Chesnut spoke to this unraveling in two diary entries early in the War:

> *September 21, 1861.* . . . I began to read one [letter] aloud; it was from Mary Witherspoon—and I broke down. Horror and amazement was too much for me. Poor Cousin Betsey Witherspoon was murdered! She did not die peacefully, as we supposed, in her bed. Murdered by her own people. Her negroes.

> *September 24, 1861.* . . . Hitherto I have never thought of being afraid of negroes. I had never injured any of them. Why should they want to hurt me? Two-thirds of my religion consists in trying to be good to negroes because they are so in my power, and it would be so easy to be the other thing. Somehow today I feel that the ground is cut away from under my feet. Why should

---

*Only one-quarter of southern slaves lived on plantations with more than fifty slaves; half lived on farms with fewer than twenty slaves. Eugene Genovese, *Roll, Jordan, Roll* at 7. Among the large plantations, most slaves lived with resident owners and "a large additional minority with part-time resident owners." Id. at 12. For an extensive account of the complex emotional bonds between white mistresses and their slaves, see Elizabeth Fox-Genovese, *Within the Plantation Household: Black and White Women of the Old South* (Chapel Hill: Univ. North Carolina Press, 1988.)

**Leon Litwack has noted how "insistent" antebellum slaveowners were "about their sense of security and equanimity" with their slaves; he quoted an English visitor to the South in the early months of the War who concluded, "There is something suspicious in the constant never-ending statement that 'we are not afraid of our slaves.'" *Been in the Storm So Long: The Aftermath of Slavery* 18 (New York: Vintage Books, 1979).

they treat me any better than they have done Cousin Betsey Witherspoon?

[My sister] Kate and I sat up late and talked it all over . . . Kate's maid came in—a strong-built mulatto woman. She was dragging in a mattress. "Missis, I have brought my bed to sleep in your room while Mars David is at Society Hill. You ought not to stay in a room by yourself *these times*." And then she went off for more bed gear.

"For the life of me," said Kate gravely, "I cannot make up my mind. Does she mean to take care of me—or to murder me?" . . .

That night Kate came into my room. She could not sleep. Those black hands strangling and smothering Mrs. Witherspoon's gray head under the counterpane haunted her. So we sat up and talked the long night through.[39]

This mistrust was magnified with Emancipation and the War's end. Many whites responded to their former slaves' pleasure at freedom as if they had been betrayed.[40] And indeed this new self-assertion by blacks starkly revealed the self-deception that whites had indulged by insisting to themselves that they had been engaged in a relationship of reciprocal familial affection with their slaves. With Lear-like rage, these spurned parents turned on their imagined ungrateful, serpent-toothed children.

Thus almost nothing was left of the old motives, economic or affective, that had masked or softened the hostility between southern whites and blacks. As much as the Jacksonian era had moved toward acknowledging the existence of a state of perpetual warfare between these races, the Civil War itself pushed this acknowledgement even more openly into view as the exclusive defining characteristic of the relationship. What kind of lasting political affiliation between southern whites and blacks could be built from this premise?

The Civil War also posed this question, with almost equal intensity, for the prospect of lasting relations between southern and northern whites. Lincoln had closed his first inaugural address with this appeal to southern whites: "We are not enemies, but friends. We must not be enemies. Though passion may have strained, it must not break, our bonds of affection."[41] The four years of devastation that followed this appeal had surely shattered these affectionate bonds on both sides. Though Lincoln ended his second inaugural "with malice toward none, with charity for all," this promise was difficult to sustain on either side.

If Lincoln had lived . . . If his successor had been less stubbornly committed to implementing reunion without any attention to fundamental social change in the South . . . If congressional leaders had been more willing to foster fundamental change by redistributing land and other social resources to the freed blacks . . . If the North had sustained its commitment to protecting the political rights of the freed slaves and maintained its paramilitary presence in the South for more than a decade after the War . . . Perhaps one or more of these hypothetical alternatives could have averted the bitter consequences that in fact followed from the War. Recent historical scholarship at least invites this speculation by convincingly revising the accounts that had become conventional wisdom by 1900: that vindictive, foolish Reconstruction policies were imposed on the South by a combination of radical congressional leaders, rapacious white carpetbaggers plundering the South for their own gain, and ignorant emancipated blacks without capacity either for political leadership or self-directed gainful employment.[42]

There was, however, one insoluble problem that inhibited the realistic ameliorative possibilities for any Reconstruction policy. The problem was not at its root the racial bias against blacks that is evident in the conventional distortion of Reconstruction history, though this bias did have an important role in the failure of Reconstruction. The root problem was clearly identified by the principal architect of the conventional critique, William A. Dunning. At the outset of his seminal historical account, published in 1907, Dunning observed:

> To the people of the North [southern submission in 1865] meant that their passionate demand of 1861 had been realized—the Union was preserved; to the people of the South it meant that their bitterest forebodings of that year had come true—they were subjugated by an alien power. Thus no more in the return of peace than in the inception and progress of hostilities was there

any harmony between the sections, or probability of harmony, as to the meaning of the situation. In such ineradicable divergence of opinion and feeling is to be found the key not only to the genesis of the Civil War, but also to the problems of reconstruction.[43]

Unless the implacable hostility between the white North and South—the "ineradicable divergence of opinion and feeling"—could somehow be erased, then the political bonds preserved by the War could only be sustained on the basis of permanent, even though suppressed, warfare.

This was the meaning that a majority of northern whites drew from the initial reports of persistent violence by southern whites against blacks, coupled with the swift enactment by the reconvened southern legislatures of the notorious "Black Codes" that appeared to reimpose conditions of enslavement on the newly freed blacks. However much most northern whites held derogatory views of blacks, their dominant response in the congressional elections of 1866 was that southern whites were refusing to acknowledge military defeat. As Leon Litwack observed, although "federal officials, both in the Freedmen's Bureau and the Union Army, had implemented labor policies [toward freed blacks] which were strikingly similar," nonetheless the southern white legislators "had moved precipitately, impetuously and carelessly."[44] Dunning similarly concluded that even though "a few of the enactments, such as that of Mississippi excluding the blacks from leasing agricultural land, were clearly animated by a spirit of oppression . . . after all, the greatest fault of the southern lawmakers was . . . that, when legislating as a conquered people, they failed adequately to consider and be guided by the prejudices of their conquerors."[45]

This is not to say that the Black Codes or their particular provisions more quietly ratified by federal officials were fair-minded or beneficial toward blacks, notwithstanding Dunning's contrary assertions.[46] The fundamental problem for Reconstruction policy was, however, that the dominant northern view of freed blacks was much more as pawns in the continued hostilities with southern whites than as independent actors worthy of attention in their own right. This was notable even in the adoption of the Fifteenth Amendment guaranteeing voting rights to black men. Of all the

Reconstruction measures, this amendment appeared most fully to endorse the principle of full political equality regardless of race; but even here, the principle was diminished by a motive that was clearly important in the adoption of the amendment—to effect an alliance between the newly franchised southern blacks and their white Republican benefactors against white Southerners returning to the Union counsels. Thaddeus Stevens, this most radical champion of racial equality, had himself opposed black enfranchisement until 1867, when he endorsed it to "insure the ascendancy of the Union [Republican] party."[47] As C. Vann Woodward has noted, "This ulterior motivation . . . is the incubus with which the Negro was burdened before he was ever awakened into political life."[48]

Because the northern commitment to black equality was shallow, it could readily be displaced by other concerns. Two other concerns in particular pressed forward with increasing intensity throughout the Reconstruction decade. The first was the rising tide of white guerrilla resistance under the Ku Klux Klan banner, aimed not only at blacks but at white Republican officeholders in the South. As Eric Foner described it, "In its pervasive impact and multiplicity of purposes . . . the wave of counterrevolutionary terror that swept over large parts of the South between 1868 and 1871 lacks a counterpart either in the American experience or in that of the other Western Hemisphere societies that abolished slavery in the nineteenth century."[49] The reconstructed state governments appeared unwilling to contain this terror.[50] Congress responded with the Ku Klux Klan Acts of 1870 and 1871, displacing state criminal law with federal authority and thus radically breaking with the old constitutional dogmas of state autonomy. And the Grant Administration launched an effective legal offensive, "culminating in the use of troops to root out the South Carolina Klan."[51] But the experience only underscored for the North that the Civil War had not yet truly ended and that the need for continued deployment of federal military force appeared unending.

The second northern concern was more focused on the North itself, on growing anxiety about internal social disorder that seemed to echo events in the South. The New York City draft riot of 1863 was an early harbinger of this fear. Initially provoked by the class discrimination etched on the face of the draft law's \$300 commutation clause, these riots quickly spread to attacks over four days against factories and docks, opulent homes of the commercial elite, and, above all, against blacks in "a virtual racial pogrom." This riot was "the largest civil insurrection in American history apart from the South's rebellion itself." Order was not restored until the arrival of federal troops, fresh from the Union victory at Gettysburg. As Foner observed, the riots exposed "the class and racial tensions lying just beneath the surface of the city's life [which were] exacerbated by the war experience . . . and haunted New York's elite long after its suppression, serving as a reminder of the threat posed by a 'dangerous class' whose existence could no longer be denied."[52] This "dangerous class" as the elite saw it was largely composed of recent immigrants; Irish immigrants were particularly prominent in the riots themselves, and foreign immigrants came to northern cities in increasing numbers during the War and thereafter.[53]

Northern concerns about internal class-based disorder were translated into southern Reconstruction policies. Most directly, these concerns mooted any consideration of southern land redistribution to freed slaves. Despite the self-evident justice of Thaddeus Stevens' proposal for such redistribution—the fabled "forty acres and a mule"—as partial compensation for lives spent at forced labor, few Republicans were prepared to endorse it. Northern Republican editorialists charged that this proposal was "a war on property . . . to succeed the war on Slavery" and that the precedent established by land confiscation "would not be confined to the South."[54] Northern class-based concerns about potential labor disorder was also reflected, though less directly acknowledged, in the quick adoption by the Freedmen's Bureau of policies designed to drive freed slaves away from southern cities where many had migrated immediately after the war and to force them into binding labor contracts on agricultural plantations.[55] The Freedmen's Bureau thus worked to insure against the creation of a landless, rootless class of urban menial laborers, which mirrored the increasingly fearsome prospect of northern economic developments.

These northern concerns exploded in the Depression of 1873 and, almost at a single stroke, eclipsed public debate about the persistence of the southern rebellion with almost obsessive attention to issues of economic class conflict.[56] Northern voters immediately reacted in the congressional elections of 1874. They erased the massive Congressional majority Republicans had enjoyed since the South's secession, transforming the party's 110-vote margin in the House into a Democratic majority of sixty seats.[57] This stunning change—the greatest reversal of partisan alignments in the entire nineteenth century—did not, however, presage a reign of Democratic ascendancy. In fact, this election initiated a new era of party stalemate: the Republican party did not reestablish its electoral dominance until 1896. In the twenty-year interim, the same party controlled the presidency and both Houses of Congress for only six years and, moreover, no president served a full term with a Congress of his own party.*

The presidential election of 1876 vividly foretold this stalemate. The contest between the Republican Hayes and the Democrat Tilden ended inconclusively. The outcome hinged on voting results from three southern states still under military rule; though initial returns indicated an easy victory for Tilden, these returns were quickly contradicted amid angry charges of fraud and military interference by the Republican administration. Suddenly the country was in the grip of a new constitutional crisis. There was no clear directive in the Constitution for resolving this dispute in tallying the electoral college votes. In particular, Article II, section 1, was completely ambiguous regarding the respective responsibilities of the House and Senate in counting the vote; and, not surprisingly, the Democratic House and Republican Senate now opted for diametrically opposed interpretations.

When the lameduck Congress reconvened in December 1876, a renewed outbreak of civil war appeared likely—even more so, to many observers, than the prospect of war had appeared just before Lincoln's inauguration in 1861.[58] This political stalemate and the looming likelihood of armed conflict was to a war-weary

---

*Republicans ruled both the presidency and Congress in 1881–83 and 1889–91 and the Democrats so ruled in 1893–95. By contrast, for the fifty years after the 1896 election, the same party controlled both the executive and legislative branches for all but six years (1911–13, 1919–21 and 1931–33). *Congressional Quarterly's Guide to U.S. Elections* 1116–17 (Washington, D.C., 1985, 2d ed.).

public another episode in the unending saga of Reconstruction. It clearly signified that the surrender at the Appomattox Courthouse had not ended the Civil War, that guerrilla resistance in the South had replaced the open clashes between contending armies, and that although this resistance might have been momentarily quelled in the Ku Klux Klan campaigns of 1871, it would inevitably reappear. Moreover, it now seemed that the clash between the ideologies of free and slave labor had now somehow spread to the North itself, with the words "free" and "slave" appearing in different guises. The electoral impasse between Hayes and Tilden suggested that the Civil War had only led to a stalemate between these still-ineradicably opposed antagonists.

Lincoln had warned against this outcome in his first inaugural address. After a war of appalling destructiveness, his prophecy was borne out—the "identical old questions,"[59] though in some new guises, were still unresolved. To Northerners, however, Lincoln's prediction seemed erroneous in one particular: the South, it seemed, was prepared to "fight always."

Many Northerners thus drew the conclusion that Henry Adams retrospectively described in his *Education,* that as "a young man [he had] helped to waste five or ten thousand million dollars and a million lives, more or less, to enforce unity and uniformity on people who objected to it."[60] By 1867, "in view of the late civil war, [he] had doubts of his own on the facts of moral evolution."[61] Where, then, should this disillusioned, devastated generation turn? Adams pointed the direction that he had found by 1870: "Although step by step, he had been driven, like the rest of the world, to admit that American society had outgrown most of its institutions, he still clung to the Supreme Court, much as a churchman clings to his bishops, because they are his only symbol of unity; his last rag of Right."[62]

Deus ex Machina: The Waite Court

In the immediate crisis of the Hayes–Tilden stalemate, the country turned to the Supreme Court to transcend partisan conflict and avert the renewed threat of civil war. In January 1877 Congress created a fifteen-member commission to count the disputed electoral votes. The congressional act specified that five of the members were to come from the Senate (three Republicans and two Democrats), five from the House (three Democrats and two Republicans), and the remaining five members were to be Justices of the Supreme Court. The act, moreover, specifically named four of the Justices who were to serve: two were registered Democrats and two were Republicans. These four Justices were in turn to select a fifth Justice from the Court. By this complicated mechanics, the Commission was composed of seven Democrats and seven Republicans. The four judicial members were then expected to find a fifth Justice who would stand above partisan suspicion; they chose Joseph P. Bradley.*

The Commission's deliberations turned out to be almost a caricature of partisanship. On every disputed issue, the Commission voted solidly along party lines; on every disputed issue, Justice Bradley voted with the Republicans. By a one-vote margin on the Commission, Rutherford B. Hayes prevailed. Hayes thus has a unique status in American political history: he was not simply inaugurated, he was directly elected by a Supreme Court Justice.

Justice Bradley was widely attacked, though he steadfastly insisted that he "did not allow political, that is, party, considerations to have any weight whatever in forming my conclusions."[63] Whatever the credibility of his claim[64]—and it was widely disbelieved at the time[65]—the very structure of the Commission membership, most notably including the named designation of the four other Supreme Court Justices based on their party affiliations, suggested from the outset that no one believed in the possibility of nonpartisan resolution. Nonetheless, no one could conceive any peaceable resolution to the impasse unless partisanship were somehow transcended. Thus the image of the Justices beckoned.

These events of 1876–77 vividly demonstrate the underlying impetus toward the enshrinement of judicial authority. Whatever the supposed bases for judicial supremacy in the constitutional

---

*The general assumption in Congress during the drafting of the Commission bill was that the fifth Justice would be David Davis, the only member of the Court with no prior party affiliation. Just as the bill was enacted, however, the Illinois legislature elected Davis to the United States Senate and Davis accepted, removing himself from possible membership on the Commission (and, ironically, injecting himself into politics). Justice Bradley was a registered Republican but was nonetheless widely viewed as impartial. See Woodward, *Reunion* at 153–54.

text or in antebellum judicial opinions, it could not take firm hold without a belief that the Supreme Court could stand above partisan political conflict. This belief, though improbable on its face and apparently belied in repeated practice, progressively grew in response at first to fears and then to the bitter experience of unconstrained civil warfare. Henry Adams' sacramental metaphor, that he "clung to the Supreme Court, much as a churchman clings to his bishops," suggests an adaptation of Voltaire's famous observation about the Deity: that if America had not had a Supreme Court that could promise peaceable resolution of social conflicts by appearing to transcend politics, it would have had to invent one.

The Justices' service on the Commission that elected Hayes did not complete this transcendent function; it was simply another step toward the aggrandizement of judicial authority that reached a virtual apotheosis by the end of the nineteenth century. This continued growth was itself a response to the fact that though Hayes' election marked the end of Reconstruction, it did not end the Civil War. Hayes removed all occupying military forces from the South in 1877 but this did not signify peaceful reconciliation between the North and South.[66] This withdrawal was more like a grudging ceasefire acknowledging stalemate between adversaries who had exhausted one another without resolving their antagonism.

The implicit terms of this ceasefire were that slavery was ended but that southern white supremacy would remain undisturbed. Though the end of Reconstruction signified that there was no obvious winner in the Civil War, these terms did designate one clear loser: southern blacks. Lincoln, with his unflinching tragic vision, had warned against this possibility midway through the War in an address to a delegation of freed blacks. He stated that "on this broad continent" no black is "made the equal" of any white. This, he said, "is a fact about which we all think and feel alike, I and you"; but "it is a fact with which we have to deal. I cannot alter it if I would." From this stubborn fact, Lincoln drew this conclusion:

> See our present condition—the country engaged in war—our white men cutting one another's throats—none knowing how far it will extend—and then consider what we know to be the truth.

But for your race among us there could not be war . . . Without the institution of slavery, and the colored race as a basis, the war could not have an existence. It is better for us both, therefore, to be separated.[67]

Lincoln then proposed that free blacks take the lead in establishing a foreign colony for others who might ultimately be freed by the War. In retrospect this suggestion was impractical as well as morally offensive; by the War's end Lincoln himself had retreated from it, envisioning some greater possibility for the recognition of black equality in a cautious proposal for extending voting rights to "the very intelligent [blacks], and especially those who have fought gallantly in our ranks."[68] By the end of the century, however, as race segregation practices became firmly entrenched, it appeared that the South had adopted a perverse version of Lincoln's colonization scheme: that whites and blacks would act as if they lived in separate nations, except that the black nation was utterly subjugated to the white.

This southern regime of race segregation, black electoral exclusion, a reign of vigilante terror against blacks unchecked and abetted by state authority and economic thralldom thus fulfilled Tocqueville's bitter prophecy. In 1835 he had written that if the blacks ever rose up to demand their freedom and "if the whites of North America remain united, it is difficult to believe that the Negroes will escape the destruction threatening them; the sword or misery will bring them down." He was proved correct by an ironically circuitous route in a reunited Union.*

This regime was not implemented in its full rigor or cruelty until near the end of the century.[69] In the interim, following the end of Reconstruction, the southern states were governed by the

---

*Tocqueville did foresee one alternative possibility: that the blacks of the deep South would "have a chance of salvation if the struggle between the two races comes at a time when the American confederation has been dissolved." In that event, he said, the two races would be evenly matched: the whites would have "an immense superiority in education and resources, but the blacks would have on their side numbers and the energy of despair"; and the outcome most likely would be that the whites "will in the end retreat gradually" from the deep South, "leaving the Negroes in possession of a country which Providence seems to have destined for them." Tocqueville at 358.

so-called Redeemers, who tried somehow to restore the *status quo ante bellum*. Though the principal Redeemer officeholders were not themselves drawn from the old plantation aristocracy, they nonetheless invoked a romantic image of the patrician South as the basis for social governance.* The two essential elements of this past regime, as the Redeemers saw it, were clearcut subordination of blacks and of lower-class whites. Wrapping themselves in the mantle of plantation gentry paternalism toward slaves, the Redeemers promised protection to blacks against lower-class white depredation, and large numbers of blacks, effectively abandoned by their northern Reconstruction protectors, embraced the promise. At the same time, the Redeemers promised restoration of the regime of white supremacy and stressed the need for racial solidarity among southern whites against the prospect of renewed northern aggression on behalf of blacks. Until the early 1890s, this whipsaw appeal effectively suppressed open expression both of class-based conflict among southern whites and race-based conflict between southern whites and blacks. For at least this interim period, the Redeemers thus largely achieved their goal of "invoking the past to avert the future."[70]

During this same time, the Supreme Court pursued a remarkably similar path, nostalgically invoking ideals of the antebellum past. In a series of decisions that began virtually as the northern occupying troops withdrew from the South, the Court invalidated congressional Reconstruction acts on the premise that the old constitutional tenets of state sovereignty had survived the War intact. By this reading, the War had merely refuted the secessionist claim that states were free to leave the Union, but the old ideal of "divided sovereignty" still held. As Marshall had put it in *McCulloch,* the national and state governments were "each sovereign with respect to the objects committed to it, and neither sovereign with respect to the objects committed to the other."[71] The

---

*The plantation gentry were, in large part, utterly demoralized by the social and economic wreckage of the War; because they had been disproportionately favored before the War, their losses were disproportionately high. Woodward, *Origins of the New South* at 20–22. On the psychological devastation of the gentry class, see James Roark, *Masters without Slaves: Southern Planters in the Civil War and Reconstruction* 195–209 (New York: W. W. Norton, 1977).

post-Reconstruction Court cast itself in the role that Marshall staked in *McCulloch*, as umpire of the competing claims between state and national governments—although in the altered context of the postbellum era, this judicial role might better be described as neutral patrol at the ceasefire line.

This judicial role was markedly different from the conception held by the sponsors of the Fourteenth Amendment, who had cast the judiciary as the aggressive defender against resurgent claims for state sovereignty after the rebel states had resumed their representation in Congress. The debates on the amendment both within Congress and in the ratifying state legislatures were, however, exceedingly murky regarding the extent to which it would override the old ideal of "divided sovereignty."[72] Moreover, although the Court invalidated congressional Reconstruction protections for blacks on the ground that they had been insufficiently attentive to state prerogatives, nonetheless the Court appeared intent on finding an accommodation between these two goals rather than abandoning black interests altogether.[73] Thus, in 1876 the Court invalidated congressional acts punishing interference with voting rights by state officials or private parties, but only on the ground that the federal act must specify racial motivation for the forbidden interference.[74] The Court was more sweeping in its subsequent condemnation of congressional acts forbidding racial discrimination in public accommodations such as inns, theaters, or transportation facilities. In the 1883 *Civil Rights Cases* it ruled that Congress could address only "state action" under the Fourteenth Amendment and that such racial discrimination was not a clear enough "badge or incident" of slavery to justify congressional proscription under the Thirteenth Amendment.[75] Justice Bradley, who had cast the deciding vote for Hayes in 1877, spoke not only for the Court majority in the *Civil Rights Cases* but seemingly for the war-weary white northern majority:

> When a man has emerged from slavery, and by the aid of beneficent legislation has shaken off the inseparable concomitants of that state, there must be some stage in the progress of his elevation when he takes the rank of a mere citizen, and ceases to be the special favorite of the laws, and when his rights as a . . . man, are to be protected in the ordinary modes by which other men's rights are protected.[76]

Even so, the Court majority in other cases did not disdain all special protections for blacks. It upheld congressional enactments punishing racially motivated official or private interference with voting rights;[77] and it construed the Fourteenth Amendment to invalidate state laws or official actions excluding blacks from jury service.[78]

A deeper tension in the Court's attitude toward the Civil War amendments was revealed in a case decided in 1873, just before the end of Reconstruction, that challenged the Louisiana state legislature's authority to require butchers in New Orleans to obtain slaughter-house services from only one company in the city. This was the first case in which the Supreme Court construed the newly ratified Fourteenth Amendment. It was at least ironic that this first case should involve rights claimed not by the freed slaves but by southern butchers. Nonetheless, the new amendment applied on its face to "all persons," and the resourceful lawyers for the butchers argued that the state-granted monopoly deprived them of both the "privileges or immunities of citizens" to engage in legitimate business activities and "equal protection of the laws" by inappropriately favoring one slaughter-house company over others. The Court rejected this claim, but only by a five-to-four margin.[79]

The Court majority used the occasion essentially to announce its basic strategy for the post-Reconstruction era: to narrow the reach of the Civil War amendments in order to preserve the old constitutional regime that limited federal intervention in traditional state preserves. The majority noted "the pressure of all of the excited feeling growing out of the war" that "added largely to the number of those who believe in the necessity of a strong National government." Nonetheless, the majority continued, "our statesmen have still believed that the existence of the States with powers for domestic and local government, including the regulation of civil rights—the rights of person and of property—was essential to the perfect working of our complex form of government."[80]

According to the majority, construing the Fourteenth Amendment to invalidate the state slaughter-house monopoly would have two consequences: Congress, under its enforcement authority in section five of the amendment, might pass laws either retrospectively or "in advance" overturning state laws "in their most ordinary and usual functions . . . on all . . . subjects"; and "still further, such a construction . . . would constitute this court a perpetual censor upon all legislation of the States." But when

> these consequences are so serious, so far-reaching and pervading, so great a departure from the structure and spirit of our institutions; when the effect is to fetter and degrade the State governments by subjecting them to the control of Congress, in the exercise of powers . . . of the most ordinary and fundamental character; when in fact it radically changes the whole theory of the relations of the State and Federal governments[81]

—when all of these radical consequences loom, the majority concluded, then the Court is obliged to act as it "always" has done: to hold "with a steady and even hand the balance between State and Federal power" without bowing to "whatever fluctuation may be seen in the history of public opinion."[82]

There is nobility in this conception of the Court's institutional role. The country had just passed through a cataclysmic civil war. Still in the grip of that war, constitutional amendments had been adopted that appeared on their face to effectuate drastic changes for the future. But the Justices, standing impartially above the partisan strife, offered "a steady and even hand" to remind the country of its prior traditions and identity and to calm its embattled passions. One might say that these considerations invoked by the Court majority established the premise for a ruling that the Fourteenth Amendment was itself unconstitutional—that this amendment, adopted in a rush of war fever, violated the fundamental character of the nation and the Court would accordingly ignore it. And in effect, the Court majority did just that—not by the oxymoron of explicitly invalidating a constitutional amendment but by construing it away. Using a time-honored judicial interpretive technique, the majority stated, "We are convinced that no such results were intended by the Congress which proposed these amendments, nor by the legislatures of the States which ratified them."[83]

With forced ingenuity, the majority then whittled away at the words of the amendment. It is true that the amendment guarantees equal protection of the laws to "any person"; but this must be read in conjunction with the other Civil War amendments and against the background of the War itself, whose "overshadowing and efficient cause was African slavery." Accordingly, "we doubt very much whether any action of a State not directed by way of discrimination against the negroes as a class, or on account of their race, will ever be held to come within the purview of this provision."[84] So much for the butchers' entitlement here. As for their claim that the right to engage in free trade was a protected "privilege or immunity," the majority was even more ingenious. The amendment protects "the privileges or immunities of citizens of the United States," whereas, the majority observed, the parallel clause in the text of the Constitution, Article IV, section 2, guarantees that "citizens of each State shall be entitled to all the privileges and immunities of citizens of the several States." Blithely ignoring repeated references in the congressional debates to the identity of these two formulations, the majority insisted that the Fourteenth Amendment was intended to protect only a much narrower—a "national" as opposed to a "state"—category of rights.[85] (The majority in effect took the same interpretive turn that Taney had used in *Dred Scott* when he found that free blacks might be citizens of a state but nonetheless would not qualify as "citizens" for purposes of federal diversity jurisdiction under the Constitution; not surprisingly, however, the majority did not rely on this precedent.)[86] The majority then set out a constricted list of "national" privileges or immunities that included neither the butchers' claim nor much else besides.*

At the end of their opinion, the majority Justices summarized their overriding purpose with this proclamation: "We do not see in those amendments any purpose to destroy the main features of the general system" of our government[87]—notwithstanding, they might have added, the destructiveness of the Civil War that spawned the amendments. Their strategy was the same that C. Vann Woodward identified for the southern Redeemers at the

---

*The "national privileges or immunities" acknowledged by the majority were to travel to the national capital in order to assert claims against the government, to obtain protection from the federal government on the high seas or in foreign lands, to assemble and petition for redress of grievances, to have access to federal writs of habeas corpus, and to use navigable waters throughout the United States. 83 U.S. at 79–80.

end of Reconstruction: "invoking the past to avert the future." Like the Redeemers, this strategy succeeded for only a limited time. The future belonged to a vastly enlarged conception of national authority generally and judicial authority specifically; and the voice of the future was in the dissenting opinions in the *Slaughter-House Cases.*

The principal dissenting opinion was written by Justice Stephen Field, who had been appointed to the Court by Lincoln in 1863 and served until 1897 (thus outlasting every other Justice on the *Slaughter-House* Court). Field's opinion was more straightforward than the majority effort, since the plain words of the Fourteenth Amendment more readily supported his conclusion: that the amendment applied to "all persons" not simply blacks; and it protected the "privileges or immunities of citizens" that Justice Bushrod Washington had enumerated in an 1823 opinion repeatedly cited by the framers of the Fourteenth Amendment, which included the "right [to engage in] trade, agriculture [or other] professional pursuits."[88] From this construction, Field drew the conclusion that the Louisiana law was a "grant of exclusive privilege . . . opposed to the whole theory of free government," and that it violated "the right of free labor, one of the most sacred and imprescriptible rights of man."[89]

Although Field had the easier argument from the text of the amendment, this would not alone have ensured the ultimate triumph of his reading. The words of the amendment themselves would not have overcome the considerations that had led the majority to its procrustean construction; but powerful countervailing concerns eroded this initial judicial impulse. Field himself revealed these concerns in an 1877 dissent from the Court's ruling in *Munn v. Illinois,* upholding a state law fixing maximum rates for grain storage.[90] "If this be sound law," Field complained, "all property and all business in the State are held at the mercy of a majority of its legislature."[91] By 1877 this fear of a rapacious electoral majority attacking property rights was clearly visible among conservative forces—a fear fed by the Depression of 1873 and the ensuing political upheaval, and fueled by the Great Railroad Strike that erupted in the summer of 1877, just after *Munn* was decided, and required federal troops to suppress the violence and looting.[92]

Field's dissent did not clearly acknowledge, however, that the Court majority had already come a considerable distance toward his vision in the *Slaughter-House Cases*. Though the Court upheld the state regulation, it did so on the theory that grain-storage elevators were "affected with a public interest" and the private property owner accordingly "must submit to be controlled by the public for the common good."[93] The Court did not, that is, follow the path marked in the *Slaughter-House Cases* that the Fourteenth Amendment did not apply to economic regulation.[94] The Court majority in *Munn,* and indeed throughout Chief Justice Waite's tenure until 1888, was much more hospitable to state economic regulation than the successor Court under Chief Justice Fuller, when conservative fear of predatory electoral majorities would reach fevered pitch. Even so, the groundwork was already laid in the text of the Fourteenth Amendment and its hesitant elaboration by the Waite Court for a new civil war—this time fought to preserve property, rather than to preserve the Union and destroy southern property in slaves; and this time the battle for preservation would be led by the Supreme Court.

7

Reconstructing the Constitution

IN 1877 Justice Samuel Miller complained that the Court's docket was "crowded with cases" by "every unsuccessful litigant in a State court" complaining about "the abstract . . . justice of the decision against him, and of the merits of the [state] legislation on which such a decision might be founded." These complaints, Miller asserted, "were abundant evidence that there exists some strange misconception of the scope of [the due process] provision as found in the 14th Amendment."[1] Four years earlier, Miller had written the majority opinion in the *Slaughter-House Cases* and was understandably annoyed that litigants had not acquiesced in his efforts to tame this new amendment. Miller died in 1890, just two years after Melville Fuller became Chief Justice and a year after David Brewer was appointed to the Court; and thus he was spared from witnessing the ultimate disavowal of his efforts by the Fuller Court. Miller was wrong, however, in believing that the expansive interpretation pressed by disappointed litigants in 1877 and openly embraced by the Fuller Court was based on "some strange misconception" of the amendment.

Miller's accusation was resurrected when the Justices appointed by Franklin Roosevelt embarked on their wholesale repudiation of the Fuller Court jurisprudence. Some critics, moreover, extended his indictment for this "misconception" to include a conspiracy among the framers of the Fourteenth Amendment to smuggle economic protection for corporations under cover of concern for black equality.[2] These same criticisms had been contemporaneously aimed at the Fuller Court; while James Bradley Thayer complained that the Justices misconstrued the constitutionally intended scope of judicial review, Charles Beard purported to unmask an intentional conspiracy, not among the latterday framers but among the founding fathers themselves. Beard charged that the founders merely posed as high-minded statesmen but were in fact primarily concerned with protecting their economic status against majoritarian expropriation.[3] Beard thus implicitly acquitted the Fuller Court of the Miller–Thayer charge of violating the "original intent" of the framers or founders; his accusation, however, appeared to impeach the sincerity and legitimacy of the entire constitutional enterprise—and marked the path for succeeding generations of critics among the Legal Realists of the 1930s and the Critical Legal theorists today.

All of these criticisms were, however, misguided. The framers of the Fourteenth Amendment were openly concerned with more than protecting the rights of newly freed slaves. The immediate impetus for the amendment was to allay any constitutional doubts about congressional authority in passing the 1866 Civil Rights Act which had amplified the meaning of emancipation proclaimed by the spare language of the Thirteenth Amendment.[4] But in drafting the Fourteenth Amendment, the framers went beyond this immediate concern, as indicated by the generality of its application to "all persons" and repeatedly reinforced by references to the abundant list of "privileges or immunities of citizens" that they intended to protect against state violation.

The framers were, moreover, open and self-conscious in linking their conception of the protected rights, privileges, and immunities to the founders' original concerns. Thus, regarding the first (February) draft of the amendment, which gave Congress direct authority to "secure . . . all privileges and immunities of citizens . . . and . . . equal protection in the rights of life, liberty and property," Representative Bingham explained: "Every word of the proposed amendment is to-day in the Constitution of our country, save the words conferring the express grant of power upon the Congress of the United States."[5] Regarding the final (April) draft, Bingham reiterated this claim: "This amendment takes from no State any right that ever pertained to it. No State ever had the right, under the forms of law or otherwise, to deny to any freeman the equal protection of the laws or to abridge the privileges or immunities of any citizen of the Republic, although many of them have assumed and exercised the power, and that without remedy."[6] It is not easy to understand what Bingham meant in saying that no State "ever had the right" to violate the substantive provisions of his amendment, though all aggrieved citizens were "without remedy" to enforce that right. As Alexander Bickel observed, Bingham "was a man not normally distinguished for precision of thought and statement."[7]

It is, however, possible to make sense of Bingham's statement by linking it to the founders' generalized concern about state violations of substantive rights to which they repeatedly adverted at the Constitutional Convention but only partially addressed in the final version of the Constitution. Madison was most explicit on this score, as he revealed in his concluding observation in *Federalist* 10 that the goal of the new constitution was to guard against a "rage for paper money, for an abolition of debts, for an equal division of property or for any other improper or wicked project."[8] Madison apparently considered the injustice of these redistributive schemes as self-evident. But this does not confirm Charles Beard's economic critique of the founders' motives; the self-evident injustice of these schemes, as Madison saw it, was the involuntary imposition of loss on a minority by a majority faction. This vision led Madison repeatedly to advocate one provision in particular at the Constitutional Convention: authority in the national legislature to veto state laws, not simply regarding economic redistributive measures but generally. To Madison's great disappointment, however, the Convention rejected this proposal by a narrow margin.[9]

Bingham's first draft of the Fourteenth Amendment would have effectively provided the generalized congressional veto over state laws that Madison had wanted. Though Bingham may not have had this precedent clearly in mind, this was the core sense beneath his murky understanding of the "privileges and immunities of citizens [and] equal protection in the rights of life, liberty and property" that were already acknowledged in the Constitution but "without remedy." When, however, Bingham shifted principal institutional responsibility for applying these substantive formulas from Congress to the courts, in the second draft, he radically transformed Madison's scheme.[10]

Though Madison believed that majority factions in state legislatures were enacting unjust laws, he refused to vest oversight authority (as he stated in *Federalist* 51) in "a will in the community independent of the majority—that is, of the society itself."[11] Madison would have planted his oversight authority in the national legislature because, as he summarized in *Federalist* 51, this institution "comprehend[ed] in the society so many separate descriptions of citizens as will render an unjust combination of a majority of the whole very improbable, if not impracticable."[12] Eighty years' experience under the Constitution, culminating in the bitter ordeal of the Civil War, had taught Bingham and his colleagues a different lesson: an "unjust combination of a majority of the whole" had been imposed by the southern slavocracy, and its recurrence appeared both probable and practicable whenever the rebels might be readmitted to Congress. This same experience, however, powerfully reinforced for the framers of the Fourteenth Amendment Madison's original view of the destructive implications of factional conflict—regarding not only black slavery but all forms of social subjugation by which majorities might oppress minorities.

Accordingly, when Justice Miller complained in 1877 of the "strange misconception of the scope" of the Fourteenth Amendment in litigative challenges to the "abstract . . . justice" of state legislative or judicial decisions, he was inattentive to the framers' underlying goal—a lapse that the Fuller Court confidently corrected in its generalized conception of a judicial veto over state and national legislation. Even if, however, the Fuller Court's jurisprudence was a faithful rendering of the framers' intentions, and even if the framers' revulsion at factional conflict generally was a faithful adaption of the founders' concern, neither the Fuller Court nor the framers could resolve the internal contradiction inherent in any direct attempt to surmount factional conflict. The contradiction is that there is no satisfactory principle for imposing defeat on any factional antagonist, whether the principle invoked is majority rule or any imaginable version of minority rights, that is not simultaneously translatable as the enslavement, the involuntary and oppressive subjugation, of one party by another.

Among the founders, Madison most clearly had understood the existence and implications of this contradiction and had consistently attempted to design institutional mechanisms promoting interactive processes of consultation and accommodation, in order to transform factional conflict into mutually agreed resolutions. As the last surviving founder, Madison also clearly understood that the Nullification Crisis foretold the failure of his ambition—a failure that was not generally understood until the Civil War. In *Federalist* 51, moreover, Madison had foreseen the institutional consequence of such a war:

> In a society under the forms of which the stronger faction can readily unite and oppress the weaker, anarchy may as truly be said to reign as in a state of nature, where the weaker individual is not secured against the violence of the stronger; and as, in the latter state, even the stronger individuals are prompted, by the uncertainty of their condition, to submit to a government which may protect the weak as well as themselves; so, in the former state, will the more powerful factions or parties be gradually induced, by a like motive, to wish for a government which will protect all parties, the weaker as well as the more powerful. It can be little doubted that if the State of Rhode Island was separated from the Confederacy and left to itself, the insecurity of rights under the popular form of government within such narrow limits would be displayed by such reiterated oppressions of factious majorities that some power altogether independent of the people would soon be called for by the voice of the very factions whose misrule had proved the necessity of it.[13]

By 1861 the intense polarized conflict of Madison's Rhode Island—like the warfare in Hobbes' state of nature, to which Madison alluded—had spread throughout the Union. And by 1866, "even the strong individuals [were] prompted, by the uncertainty of their condition, to submit to . . . some power altogether independent of the people." Such submission could not solve the problem of factional oppression; as Madison also foresaw, it would merely reiterate the problem.

The framers of the Fourteenth Amendment were not, however, so clear-sighted. Notwithstanding their outraged recriminatory attacks on judicial authority virtually the moment after they had surrendered to it, they did not comprehend the nature of the dilemma whose opposed horns they had firmly embraced. Though the framers understood that congressional supremacy in interpreting the amendment would undermine it, neither they nor succeeding Justices understood that judicial supremacy was also inconsistent with the equality principle itself. Madison's hopes for the faction-transcending capabilities of institutions with over-lapping, competitive authority had been overwhelmed by the fearful experience of uncontrollable conflict in the Civil War.

Occupying Force: The Fuller Court

During Melville Fuller's tenure as Chief Justice, from 1888 until 1910, American judicial authority came into its fullest flowering. Constitutional lawyers today readily recall two decisions from this era: *Plessy v. Ferguson,*[14] which upheld southern race segregation laws, and *Lochner v. New York,*[15] which overturned state regulation of maximum hours of employment. These two cases were not, however, the most important or revealing exercises of judicial authority by the Fuller Court; they were applications of substantive principles and of a conception of the judicial role that were most clearly enunciated in an 1895 decision, *In re Debs.*[16] In this case the Court unanimously affirmed an injunction issued by a federal district court against strike activities of the American Railway Union, headed by Eugene Debs, directed at the Pullman sleeping car manufacturing company. For the Justices, the Pullman Strike was in effect a reenactment of the Civil War but with a different outcome, both in process and in substantive terms.

Justice David Brewer, who wrote the Court's opinion in *Debs,* had set out his basic underlying assumptions in an address he had delivered two years earlier to the New York State Bar Association. In this comfortable setting with like-minded professional associates, Brewer spoke more openly than in his subsequent *Debs* opinion about his general view of labor conflict and the judicial role. His starting text was not the Constitution but the eighth and tenth commandments: "Thou shalt not steal." "Thou shalt not covet." Brewer made clear that his citation of this holy writ did not refer to "the foot-pad or the burglar [who were merely] vulgar and brutal criminals, in whose behalf there has as yet been organized no political party." His concern was "rather to notice that movement . . . which by the mere force of numbers seeks to diminish protection to private property." In an eloquent flight, Brewer invoked the "greatest of English orators" who, opposing legislation to permit warrantless home searches, proclaimed that the "poorest man in his cottage may bid defiance to all the forces of the crown." Brewer draped his cause in this flag:

> Here, there is no monarch threatening trespass upon the individual. The danger is from the multitudes—the majority, with whom is the power; and if the passage quoted is the grandest tribute to the liberty which existed in England, I would thus paraphrase it to describe that which should prevail under this government by the people: The property of a great railroad corporation stretches far away from the domicile of its owner, through State after State, from ocean to ocean; the rain and the snow may cover it; the winds and the storms may wreck it; but no man or multitude dare touch a car or move a rail. It stands as secure in the eye and in the custody of the law, as the purposes of Justice in the thought of God.[17]

Brewer then proceeded to identify the "two ways" in which this organized political "movement expresses itself." The first was "in the improper use of labor organizations to destroy the freedom of the laborer, and control the uses of capital."[18] The second "assumes the guise of a [legislative] regulation of the charges for the use of property subjected, or supposed to be, to a public use."[19] Against this rapacious movement, Brewer asked, "What, then, ought to be done? My reply is, strengthen the judiciary."[20] This was the skeleton of Brewer's argument; his full passion can be glimpsed in this concluding passage:

> Who does not see the wide unrest that fills the land; who does not feel that vast social changes are impending, and realize that those changes must be guided in justice to safety and peace or they will culminate in revolution? Who does not perceive that the mere fact of numbers is beginning to assert itself? . . .

> "To him that hath shall be given," is the voice of Scripture. "From him that hath shall be taken," is the watchword of a not inconsiderable, and through the influx of foreign population, a growing portion of our voters. . . . Magnifying, like the apostle of old, my office, I am firmly persuaded that the salvation of the

nation, the permanence of government of and by the people, rests upon the independence and vigor of the judiciary.[21]

At the end of his address, Brewer waved the "black flag of anarchism," the "red flag of socialism," and the "colorless" pages of the *Communist Manifesto*.[22] When the Pullman Strike erupted a year later, Brewer's colleagues on the Court answered his call to the traditional colors of American social conflict. Brewer was, moreover, the intellectual leader of the Fuller Court, and his address identified the general agenda that the Court vigorously pursued well beyond his death in 1910.

Whatever the explanation for the mesmerizing force of these concerns on the succeeding generation of judges, it is easy to understand the obsession of Brewer and his brethren. By the early 1890s, Armageddon seemed imminent; in Robert Wiebe's phrase, "men of every persuasion . . . had wrapped their minds in a catastrophic vision."[23] The earlier concerns raised by the Draft Riots of 1863 and the Great Railroad Strike of 1877 had swollen to flood tide. The pitched warfare in 1886 at the Chicago Haymarket and in 1892 between strikers and both private industrial armies and state militia at Andrew Carnegie's Homestead steel works near Pittsburgh, at the silver mines in Coeur d'Alene, Idaho, at the railroad yards in Buffalo, at coal fields in Tennessee—all of these events signified "impending anarchy."[24]

Following the 1877 railroad strike, campaigns were launched in major urban centers across the country to build militia armories. By the early 1890s, construction had proceeded in New York, Boston, Philadelphia, Chicago, St. Louis, Buffalo, and smaller cities.[25] These armories were, moreover, constructed as urban fortresses. Virtually all were built to resemble medieval castles, with towers, turrets, thick walls, and narrow windows—and some even with moats and drawbridges. These design elements were not simply echoes of an idealized past, as in the Greco-Roman structures of the early Republic, but functional features consciously constructed to withstand assault from urban working-class mobs.[26] The newspaper of the Socialist Labor Party convincingly charged in 1891:

No one who beholds the half score moated and battlemented armories which dot the streets of New York and cover every strategic vantage point; no one who knows how those [working-class men] have been weeded out of her militia who could not be relied upon to shoot down their neighbors mercilessly when ordered, until that militia has become merely an organized portion of the ruling class; no one who knows of the vast sums spent annually for enginery of repression, but refused for education; no such person can do aught but tremble for the future of New York and his country.[27]

In 1891 there was trembling on both sides of these castellated ramparts; in 1893 this fear grew toward apocalyptic intensity with the sudden onset of a major economic depression.[28] The 1894 Pullman Strike was a direct outgrowth of this depression. In response to falling profits, the company substantially cut wages but refused to reduce rents in the company town housing where most of its manufacturing employees lived. The employees struck, and the nationally organized American Railway Union voted a "sympathy strike," ordering its 150,000 members to refuse work on any train with Pullman sleeping cars until the company agreed to arbitration.

This boycott, led by Eugene Debs from the hub of the national railway system in Chicago, quickly spread throughout the country, effectively paralyzing most railroad transportation. Governor Altgeld of Illinois, recently elected with labor union support, refused either to call up state militia or to request federal military assistance against the strikers. But President Cleveland, ignoring past labor dispute precedents for national intervention only to assist state governments, resolved to dispatch federal troops. Cleveland did not, however, send troops on his own authority; he turned first to a federal district court in Chicago for an injunction against the strike and, when this was issued, deployed troops to enforce the judicial order. Debs and his associates were arrested for violating this injunction and summarily sentenced to jail by the district court. They appealed their conviction to the Supreme Court.

Whatever visions were evoked among others by these cascading events, one image was particularly salient for the Court in *Debs:* the memory of the Civil War. News accounts during the strike had quoted Debs himself as saying that "the first shot fired by the regular soldiers at the mobs here will be the signal for a civil war"[29]; and Debs' counsel in the Supreme Court argued against the propriety of judicial intervention on the ground that it could have no more effect than "read[ing] a writ of injunction to Lee's army during the late civil war."[30] But even without such direct invocations, the Pullman Strike read against the background of the recent decades' labor conflict would inevitably have recalled Civil War imagery for the men who sat on the Supreme Court in 1895.

Justice Brewer had been twenty-four in 1861. All but three of his brethren on the Fuller Court had been in their twenties and two of them had fought in the War—Harlan for the Union and White for the Confederacy.* For these young men in 1861, the Jacksonian-era assumption that social conflict was inevitable but nonetheless somehow containable was shattered by the experience of the Civil War. The wistful Redeemer spirit evident in the post-Reconstruction Court's irredentist jurisprudence was thus alien to the Fuller Court; most of the Justices sitting on the *Debs* case in 1895 had had no mature experience of antebellum America.

In his *Debs* opinion, Brewer both directly and indirectly revealed the power of Civil War memories. In order to justify the injunction, two steps were required. First, a specific national interest must be identified to justify disregarding the traditional constitutional allocation of police authority to states and specifically overriding Governor Altgeld's refusal to request federal intervention. Brewer met this difficulty first by citing the federal interest in interstate mail delivery but, more significantly, by construing the constitutional grant of congressional regulatory authority over interstate commerce to imply a general national interest in unobstructed commerce, even without direct congressional regulation.[31] This conception of a transcendent national market, protected by the collaborative actions of the federal executive and judiciary, was at least an indirect echo of Lincoln's conception of the national Union that he, as President, was independently obliged to uphold—even without a congressional war declaration and certainly without prior approval from the Supreme Court.

But even after identifying an overriding federal interest,

---

*Among the Justices who decided the *Debs* case in 1895, the median age in 1861 was 28; of the three outside their twenties in that year, White was 16, Gray was 33, and Field was 45.

Brewer had to take a second step; and here the Civil War directly figured for him. In order to justify an injunction, standard legal doctrine required Brewer to demonstrate that ordinary legal remedies would have been inadequate; and Brewer acknowledged that Congress could have provided ordinary federal criminal penalties for interferences with interstate mail and commerce. But, Brewer immediately continued, the Constitution required jury trials for federal criminal charges in the state "where the said crime shall have been committed."[32] This raised an intolerable prospect for Brewer:

> If all the inhabitants of a State, or even a great body of them, should combine to obstruct interstate commerce or the transportation of the mails, prosecutions for such offenses had in such a community would be doomed in advance to failure. . . . The whole interest of the nation . . . would be at the absolute mercy of a portion of the inhabitants of that single State.
>
> But there is no such impotency in the national government. The entire strength of the nation may be used to enforce in any part of the land the full and free exercise of all national powers . . . . The strong arm of the national government may be put forth to brush away all obstructions . . . . If the emergency arises, the army of the Nation, and all its militia, are at the service of the Nation to compel obedience to its laws.[33]

Thus did Brewer, invoking Civil War recollections when inhabitants of single states imperilled the "whole interest of the nation," dismiss the constitutional check against consolidated national authority in the jury-trial guarantee.

Brewer did more, however, than translate the struggle between railway workers and employers into a reenactment of civil war between the national government and resistant state authorities. He also wrote a different script for this war. Unlike the first Civil War, the President had sought advance authorization from the courts before sending troops; this deserved "praise," Brewer said, "that, instead of determining for itself questions of right and wrong . . . and enforcing that determination by the club of the policeman and the bayonet of the soldier, [the Executive] submitted all those questions to the peaceful determination of judicial tribunals."[34] Brewer then bestowed equal praise on the "great body" of strikers who, after "the question of right and wrong was submitted to the courts, . . . unhesitatingly yielded to their decisions."[35] This construction of the record was, however, disingenuous at best.

To support his claim for acknowledged judicial authority, Brewer cited testimony by one of the defendants:

> "It was not the soldiers that ended the strike. It was not the old brotherhoods that ended the strike. It was simply the United States courts that ended the strike. Our men were in a position that never would have been shaken, under any circumstances, if we had been permitted to remain upon the field among them. Once we were taken from the scene of action [because we were arrested under the injunction] and restrained from sending telegrams or issuing orders or answering questions, . . . our headquarters were temporarily demoralized and abandoned, and we could not answer any messages. The men went back to work, and the ranks were broken, and the strike was broken up."[36]

Brewer used this testimony to refute the Union counsel's jibe against the efficacy of injunctions. "It may be true," Brewer said,

> that in the excitement of passion a mob will pay little heed to processes issued from the courts, and it may be, as said by counsel in argument, that it would savor somewhat of the puerile and ridiculous to have read a writ of injunction to Lee's army during the late civil war. . . . But does not counsel's argument imply too much?[37]

This was not Lee's army, Brewer claimed; the defendants "were not conducting a rebellion or inaugurating a revolution," as proven "by the very testimony of the defendants," that the "great body" of strikers "unhesitatingly yielded to" the judicial injunction.[38]

This was, of course, a patent misconstruction of the defendants' testimony; by their account, the Civil War could also have been swiftly ended if Lincoln had succeeded, whether or not pursuant to a judicial order, in arresting Lee and his senior officers and removing them "from the scene of action." But Brewer misconstrued the testimony in order to prove the proposition he had proclaimed in his 1893 New York State Bar Association address, that "the wide unrest that fills the land . . . must be guided in justice to safety and peace or [it] will culminate in revolution."[39] Brewer was intent on proving in *Debs* what Chief Justice Marshall had asserted but President Jackson had ignored in *McCulloch* and what Taney had maintained but events had overwhelmed in *Dred Scott:* that the judiciary could effectively command oceanic waves of civil warfare to recede. Brewer could prove this in *Debs,* however, only by insisting that the principles he invoked commanded widespread allegiance by virtue of their moral force, and by obscuring the bald alliance forged in that case between judicial authority and overwhelming military force.

Brewer's moral commitment to private property rights and his conviction that organized labor strikes violated those rights may indeed have been widely shared in the country at large, even if not among the Pullman strikers themselves. The national election results in 1896 provided strong evidence for this concordance: William Jennings Bryan, the Democratic Party, and their new Populist allies were resoundingly defeated and a new era of Republican electoral dominance was inaugurated. But Brewer was not concerned with popular validation of his moral principles. Notwithstanding a final flourish in his *Debs* opinion that "under this government of and by the people, the means of redress of all wrongs are through the courts and at the ballot-box,"[40] Brewer fundamentally disdained all forms of popular deliberation. He revealed this indirectly in *Debs* in his assessment that juries would too likely collaborate with law-breaking strikers and that judges alone could be trusted to protect "the whole interest of the nation."[41] He proclaimed this disdain directly in his New York State Bar Association address: "The danger is from the multitudes—the majority, with whom is the power."[42]

Debs accordingly set the dominant theme for the jurisprudence of the Fuller Court: to transform all popular partisan disputes into questions for final determination by courts. This universalized claim for judicial review was embodied in the principle of "liberty" that the Fuller Court found in the Constitution. To borrow a metaphor from contemporary First Amendment jurisprudence, this liberty principle served as a wall of separation between the individual and state authority—not impregnable but presumptively so, and then only with judicial permission. Though the Fuller Court was particularly solicitous of liberty claims in economic enterprise, the principle was universally available as a judicial presumption against all state regulatory interventions; some interventions could meet this burden of persuasion and some, especially but not exclusively in economic endeavors, could not.

The Fuller Court never crisply announced that its liberty principle was a universal presumption against the constitutionality of state regulatory measures. The most prominent academic critic of the Court, however, clearly saw it as such. This was the core of James Bradley Thayer's critique in his enduringly famous *Harvard Law Review* article, "The Origin and Scope of the American Doctrine of Constitutional Law."[43] This article was originally given as a lecture in August 1893, just seven months after Justice Brewer delivered his address to the New York State Bar Association; though Thayer did not refer to Brewer's address, his article reads as if it were a rejoinder.

Thayer's central thesis was that courts should generally presume the constitutionality of legislative acts:

> [Courts] can only [overturn] the Act when those who have the right to make laws have not merely made a mistake, but have made a very clear one,—so clear that it is not open to rational question. That is the standard of duty to which the courts bring legislative Acts; that is the test which they apply,—not merely their own judgment as to constitutionality, but their conclusion as to what judgment is permissable to another department which the constitution has charged with the duty of making it. This rule recognizes that . . . much which will seem unconstitutional to one man, or body of men, may reasonably not seem so to another; that there is often a range of choice and judgment; that in such cases the constitution does not impose upon the legislature any one opinion, but leaves open this range of choice; and that whatever choice is rational is constitutional.[44]

Thayer argued for this permissive standard on both policy and precedential grounds. He joined direct issue with Brewer, in effect, only on policy: "We are much too apt," Thayer said, "to think of the judicial power of revising the acts of the other departments as our only protection against oppression and ruin."[45] "Under no system can the power of courts go far to save a people from ruin; our chief protection lies elsewhere."[46]

Brewer, of course, disagreed passionately with this judgment. As to the precedential support for the judicial role he envisioned, Brewer indirectly acknowledged that he advocated an enlargement—"magnifying, like the apostle of old, my office," as he quaintly put it, "the salvation of the nation . . . rests upon the independence and vigor of the judiciary."[47] He was apparently untroubled by the absence of direct precedent for this enlarged role because, as he saw it, the intensified social conflicts since the Civil War ("the wide unrest that fills the land [fed by] the influx of foreign population")[48] presented an unprecedented threat to individual liberty which required correspondingly increased judicial protection ("to restrain the greedy hand of the many filching from the few").[49]

Accordingly Brewer and a comfortable majority of his colleagues on the Fuller Court intervened not only to suppress the Pullman Strike but to decide for themselves the "reasonableness" of state rate regulations while giving no deference whatsoever to legislative or administrative judgments,[50] to invalidate a progressive federal income tax,[51] to decide for themselves whether states could impose maximum employment hours for miners, bakers, or women, and whether the federal government could forbid employment discrimination against union members.[52] The Court at this same time was utterly unconcerned with state and federal regulatory actions inhibiting political debate[53] or electoral participation;[54] indeed, the judicial injunction upheld in *Debs* itself forbade not only union efforts to induce sympathy strikes by "threats" or "intimidation" but also by "persuasion."[55] This sharp disjunction in judicial attitudes was not because the Fuller Court valued "economic liberty" but disdained "personal liberty"; this post-New Deal jurisprudential distinction played no role in these earlier cases.[56] The Fuller Court refused to protect political debate and electoral participation because it regarded these majoritarian processes as inherently antithetical to individual liberty, however defined; as Brewer put it in his 1893 address, "The danger is from the multitudes—the majority, with whom is the power." He noted that he was not concerned with the "burglar . . . [the] vulgar and brutal criminals, in whose behalf there has as yet been organized no political party."[57] His principle concern, that is, was with the burglars who had organized themselves in political parties.

There is some similarity between the Fuller Court's use of the liberty principle and the antebellum judicial response to polarized social conflict, in Marshall's technique in *McCulloch* for walling off contention between the national and state governments and the attempts of both Story in *Prigg* and Taney in *Dred Scott* to remove slavery from political controversy. These were all efforts to interpose judicial authority in order to suppress direct conflictual interaction among the contending parties. All of these judicial interventions, moreover, were conceived in effect as preemptive strikes to avert violent struggle in which one party would unilaterally impose his will on the other—notwithstanding the irony that, to avert this consequence, the Court itself imposed resolutions that permitted one party wholly to triumph over the other: the national government over the states in *McCulloch,* the southern slaveowners in *Prigg* and *Dred Scott,* and the propertied few in the Fuller Court decisions generally. In all of these instances, the Court not only dismissed the possibility that contending parties on their own might reach a peaceable accommodation but, more fundamentally, the Court rejected the goal of accommodation and agreed with those among the antagonists who defined their struggle as necessarily requiring the utter subjugation of their opponents.

For all the similarities between the Fuller Court decisions and these earlier judicial interventions, however, there was one striking difference. The Fuller Court's conception of its mission to eliminate political conflict was so universalized and grandiose as to dwarf the earlier judicial enterprises. Though Marshall intended to subdue direct clashes between the federal and state governments, he expected that these political conflicts would persist (but more likely remain peaceably contained) within the majoritarian institutions of the federal government itself. The Taney Court, in *Prigg* and *Dred Scott,* sought to remove only the slavery issue from political contention, on the assumption that it was severable from the vast range of other issues which would be peaceably contested within the ordinary framework of partisan competition. This was of course an erroneous judgment; the slavery issue grew in significance until it absorbed and transformed all other imaginable political issues into mere aspects of a pervasive, irreconcilable division between North and South. But the Taney Court had not set out to resolve all imaginable issues of political contention; it had tried to avert this consequence by walling off the slavery issue.

There were, however, no limits to the conflict-suppressive ambitions of the Fuller Court. Indeed, the lesson that Justice Brewer and his colleagues seemed to draw from the Civil War was that all social conflict, no matter how apparently trivial, necessarily escalates into tooth-and-claw warfare. The liberty principle in the hands of the Fuller Court was deployed to suppress all social conflict by separating each individual from any possibility of conscription into political warfare with others. Thus in *Lochner*, the Court majority was quite sincere in its claim to protect not only the bakery owner but also the bakery employee from state regulation regarding maximum hours. Each individual must decide this question for himself, the Court held; to permit its resolution by majoritarian political processes would be to destroy not simply the sanctity of private property but (as Brewer said in his 1893 address) to unleash the "whim and greed," the "foolish, selfish and cruel" impulses that always underlie the wishes of "the many [to exercise] control over the few."[58]

Profound hostility to politics thus was enshrined in the Fuller Court's liberty principle and shaped both the descriptive and normative features of that principle. Descriptively, the liberty principle rested on a static conception of social structure that portrayed individuals as essentially disengaged and that blocked any acknowledgment of interaction. This conceptual blindfold accordingly concealed how readily one man's liberty claim interactively translated into an assertion of subjugative authority over another. Normatively, this static conception carried the implication that conflict between individuals could only legitimately be resolved by severing relationships between them—by restoring or reaffirming their "natural state of liberty." The liberty principle was thus intrinsically hostile to any redistributive claim in social conflicts because such claim is premised on a continued, though restructured, relationship between the contending parties.*

---

*This intrinsic hostility to redistribution was revealed, for example, in the limited scope of disagreement between the Court majority and three of the four

The practical consequence of this rejection of redistributive claims was a rigid commitment to the preservation of the status quo. But the Fuller Court Justices could insist with perfect sincerity that this reactionary political result was not their motivating force, that this result was only the necessary consequence of the internal logic of the liberty principle. Accordingly, the Justices could base their hostility to organized strike activity in *Debs* on the premise that an aggrieved worker was only entitled to quit his employment and that he had no continued stake in the enterprise on which he could base a claim for changed terms in his employment, either as an individual or in concert with other workers. The effect of this judicial position was to forbid employees from effectively massing their strength in organized strike activities, thus underwriting employers' capacity to resist redistributional demands. But the Justices insisted that they were merely vindicating the liberty principle, which symmetrically dictated that the aggrieved employee had only the right to quit, not to seize control of the factory, which would be "coercion," just as an aggrieved employer had only the right to discharge his employee, not to change the employee's unsatisfactory work habits by chaining him to the workbench or beating him, which would be "slavery."

The Fuller Court could thus plausibly deduce their liberty principle from the underlying "free labor" ideology of the Civil War amendments. In fact, however, this liberty principle owed as least as much to the ideology of the southern slaveholding secessionists. The Fuller Court's application of the liberty principle brought into sharp relief the image that lay beneath the "free labor" ide-

---

dissenters in *Lochner*. The three dissenters acknowledged that the statute might have "had its origin" in the legislators' view that bakery employers and employees "were not upon an equal footing" but nonetheless maintained that this redistributive motive was ultimately secondary to, or perhaps even displaced by, the legislators' concern for the "health and safety" of the employees. 198 U.S. at 69, 73 (opinion of Harlan, J.). The majority contended that this ordinarily valid paternalist concern was in this case a pretext to obscure these "other motives" behind the law's enactment. Id. at 64. Only Justice Holmes in his separate dissent was prepared to validate the law even if it were not intended as a "health" measure; but this was because he alone rejected the liberty principle on the ground that it was a "particular economic theory" unsuited to serve as a general constitutional standard. Id. at 75–6.

ology—of social relations as inherently combative and subjugatory. In antebellum days, southern apologists for chattel slavery seized on this image as the basis for their charge of "wage slavery" in northern labor relations. In the postbellum world, there was an even tighter linkage between the Fuller Court's liberty principle and the underlying social imagery of slavery. Southern slaveholders, like the Fuller Court Justices, extolled a conception of liberty which barely disguised the interactive consequence of their claim for freedom to enslave others. Slaveholders, like the Fuller Court Justices, deduced from their conception of liberty that they were free to sever all political relations with adversaries and, moreover, that this secessionist claim had self-evident normative superiority over their adversaries' claim for the existence of a continuing stake in their mutual enterprise.

The southern secessionists did not go so far as the Fuller Court in generalizing for all political antagonists this right to sever relationships. But though the southern whites did not directly acknowledge this anarchic individualism at the core of their secession claim, they implicitly recognized its implication in their relations with black slaves. The slaves' grievances against their masters were, to put it mildly, at least as extensive as the southern whites' complaints against the North. The southern whites were not prepared explicitly to acknowledge the black slaves' equal rights to sever political relations; but they implicitly acknowledged the potential existence of this black claim by defining them as nonparticipants in any political association, as objects of property rather than as people in an interactive, even though subjugated, relationship.

The Fuller Court carried this same conception into its depiction of the employment relationship: the employer was the sole owner of the enterprise, the worker insofar as he was engaged in the enterprise was merely another object to be owned by the employer; there was no association in which the worker had any continuing claim. Like the southern slaveholders, moreover, the Fuller Court was not wholly blinded from the interactive consequences of this static conceptualization. The Court knew, as the slaveholders knew, that the workers were not inanimate property but that they could become excessively and dangerously animated. Thus, the Fuller Court was ready, as in *Debs*, to deploy massive force to maintain the subjugated status of workers in the employment relationship, at the same time that it denied the existence of any relationship—as the southern slaveowners had done before them.

The Fuller Court was, however, more rigorous in drawing out the logical consequence of the liberty principle that they shared with their southern forebears. The southern secessionists had insisted that their conception of liberty was not inconsistent with the maintenance of equal political relations among the seceding whites in a newly constituted Confederacy.[59] Lincoln had identified their error in his warning that the "central idea of secession is the essence of anarchy." The Fuller Court, in grounding its entire conception of social relations on the right to secession, implicitly understood this anarchic implication. The Justices had been impelled to this recognition by their experience of the Civil War. As Thomas Hobbes had been led from his direct apprehension of the English Civil War "to a view of society as so completely fragmented that he deduced the need for a self-perpetuating sovereign person or body,"[60] so the Justices of the Fuller Court conceived themselves as the necessary embodiment of the transcendent sovereign whom all would obey unquestioningly and who would itself owe obedience to no one. The Fuller Court thereby generalized the political application both of the liberty principle espoused by the defeated southern secessionists in order to preserve slavery and the conception of subjugative authority that they had understood as the only possible means for maintaining relations with their slaves.

It is therefore not surprising that the Fuller Court found *Plessy v. Ferguson* an easy case (or that its decision passed virtually unnoticed by contemporary observers).[61] By 1896, southern imposition of a rigid segregationist regime had utterly displaced the romantic racial paternalism of the post-Reconstruction Redeemers as a response to greatly intensified social antagonisms both among whites and between whites and blacks.[62] As the Fuller Court Justices saw it, this imposition was required by, and a reflection of, the same intensification of social antagonisms that had driven them to impose rigid controls on the laboring classes generally and to abandon the nostalgic jurisprudence of the post-Reconstruction Court. The format of the segregationist rules was, moreover, virtually identical to the Court's regime for quashing social conflict generally: to sever political relations between the contending parties. (Indeed, the formula of the Louisiana statute upheld in *Plessy*, mandating "equal but separate accommodations for the white, and colored races" in transportation facilities,[63] was a kind of mock-secession between these antagonists; it indirectly echoed southern secession from the North in 1861 and more directly evoked colonial secession from Great Britain in 1776, with the Declaration that it had become "necessary for one people to dissolve the political bands which have connected them with another, and to assume . . . [a] separate and equal station.")*

Racist assumptions were certainly at work in the *Plessy* decision.[64] But the Court did not need to rely on these assumptions to affirm the segregation regime. When the *Plessy* holding is viewed in the context of other Fuller Court decisions addressing polarized social conflict, it is apparent that the Justices had the same view of race relations as the founding generation: that subjugation of blacks by whites was no different in principle from any subjugation of a minority by a majority. The Justices, that is, agreed with Madison that relations between "debtors and creditors," between antagonistic religious orders, between Great Britain and her Irish or American colonies, and between whites and black slaves were based on identical premises.[65]

They disagreed with Madison, however, in judging the constitutional significance of this correspondence. Madison believed that all of these relationships were instances of unjust oppression, and that the constitutionalist's task was to design institutions to promote peaceful consultation and accommodation that might transcend the antagonism and check the impulses for oppression between these warring factions. The Justices of the Fuller Court endorsed Hamilton's competing view that this warfare was irremediable and must be ruthlessly suppressed. They embraced the

---

*The catch-phrase for the segregationist regime was not turned around in the Court's jurisprudence to "separate but equal" until McCabe v. Atchison, T. & S.F. Ry. Co., 235 U.S. 151, 160 (1914), when the Court reinterpreted *Plessy* to require that separate facilities be equal in fact. See Benno Schmidt, "Principle and Prejudice: The Supreme Court and Race in the Progressive Era" (pt. 1), 82 *Colum. L. Rev.* 444, 468–69, 485–94 (1982).

conception of political authority that Hamilton only insinuated in his public pronouncements in the *Federalist Papers,* but baldly advocated in his June 18 speech in the private deliberations at the Constitutional Convention: "compleat sovereignty,"[66] pure monarchism.

The Struggle against Judicial Supremacy

By 1905, when the Court overturned the bakers' hours law in *Lochner,* the doctrine of judicial supremacy in constitutional interpretation was firmly entrenched. The Madisonian alternative of equal interpretative authority among competing institutions was by then so completely routed that it vanished (along with the historical reputation of Madison himself) for the next half-century at least. During this time, the Court's rulings were vigorously opposed by advocates for economic regulation, rising to a bitter crescendo in Franklin Roosevelt's assault on the Nine Old Men who had presumed to invalidate the central measures of his New Deal. Constitutional law is understood today in the shadow of the practical success of Roosevelt's assault: *Lochner* is almost as much a malediction as *Dred Scott.*

But though there is apparent agreement among constitutional lawyers today that the *Lochner* sin must not be repeated, it is not clear exactly how the sin should be avoided or even what the sin was. Some critics contend that *Lochner* epitomizes the dangers of judges' using vague constitutional language, such as "due process of law," to override legislative choices and that judges accordingly should defer to majority rule except for those rare instances where the draftsmen of the Constitution indisputably commanded otherwise. Other critics allege that this position effectively endorses majority tyranny over vulnerable social or political minorities and that the *Lochner* sin was only that wealthy, conservative judges wrongfully used the Constitution to favor their own economic class's interests. By this reading, the *Lochner* sin is not committed when judges protect poor people or blacks or gays by overturning legislation enacted by a majority consisting of wealthy people or whites or heterosexuals; indeed, by this reading, when judges (who are mostly wealthy, white, and heterosexual) construe the open-textured language of the Constitution to uphold such legislation, they may be committing the *Lochner* sin of favoring their own class interests.

In my view, both of these readings of *Lochner* are wrong. *Lochner*'s error was not in choosing the wrong candidates for constitutional protection nor in its reliance on diaphanous constitutional clauses. The fault was in the judges' view of themselves, as the hierarchically supreme, definitive interpreters of the Constitution. The fault was in the Hamiltonian conception of their authority.

This same flawed view of judicial supremacy is still the core conception of those who advocate active judicial interventions in a wide range of "social" and "political" disputes but not, as they see the sin of *Lochner,* in "economic" matters. Those who read *Lochner* more broadly, as teaching that judges should virtually never overturn any majoritarian legislation, fall, however, into a different version of the same error. These critics rely on the same Hamiltonian conception of the political order that demands some identifiable, hierarchically supreme locus of ultimate authority. Hence the sterile terms of battle between the current jurisprudential combatants—judicial autocracy vs. majority autocracy—and the equally sterile, derivative doctrinal efforts to resolve this battle by drawing sharp ceasefire lines around impregnably distinct zones of judicial and legislative "sovereign authority."

The barren terms of this contemporary dispute can be traced directly to the opinions in *Lochner* itself, and specifically to the disagreement between the majority and the "great dissenter," Oliver Wendell Holmes. Though the Court majority and Holmes differed regarding the constitutionality of the bakers' hours law, they agreed at a more fundamental level; and this agreement persists in the current jurisprudential debate. By identifying these underlying elements in the jurisprudence of the *Lochner* Justices, and following them through the Roosevelt Justices' purported repudiation of *Lochner,* we can gain a deeper perspective on the current debate.

Holmes joined the Fuller Court in 1902; his *Lochner* dissent typified his position during his thirty-year tenure as he consistently dissented from his colleagues' invocation of the Fourteenth Amendment to invalidate federal and state laws. In all of these dissents, Holmes was guided by an ironic detachment that he displayed in a 1913 address:

It is a misfortune if a judge reads his conscious or unconscious sympathy with one side or the other prematurely into the law, and forgets that what seem to him to be first principles are believed by half his fellow men to be wrong. I think that we have suffered from this misfortune. . . . When twenty years ago a vague terror went over the earth and the word socialism began to be heard, I thought and still think that fear was translated into doctrines that had no proper place in the Constitution or the common law. Judges are apt to be naif, simple-minded men, and they need something of Mephistopheles.[67]

For the other Fuller Court Justices the "vague terror" of renewed civil warfare provoked by "the word socialism" brought them onto the battlefield to suppress the conflict. Like his colleagues, however, Holmes was also caught by the experience of the Civil War, though he drew different conclusions from that experience for judicial conduct. Holmes remained an uncommitted observer at the sidelines, believing that it was "premature" for the law to intervene until the war was ended: "As law embodies beliefs that have triumphed in the battle of ideas and then have translated themselves into action, while there still is doubt, while opposite convictions still keep a battle front against each other, the time for law has not come; the notion destined to prevail is not yet entitled to the field."[68] This belief led Holmes to the same conclusion that Stephen Douglas had taken in his debates with Lincoln, that popular sovereignty was entitled to prevail; but unlike Douglas, Holmes invested majority will with no special moral stature, except for the self-validating status it had won by subjugating its adversaries. Notwithstanding the apparent distance between Holmes and the Fuller Court majority, they all concurred in the same conception of social relations—as hierarchic, because subjugation of some by others was inevitable and the equality principle could therefore have no morally preferred status.[69]

During the decades between *Lochner* and the New Deal judicial decisions, a crucial shift occurred in American politics. But the Court majority and Holmes remained impervious to this shift, locked in their memories of Civil War conflict and the intensely polarized economic and political disputes of the 1890s. The New Deal marked the culmination of the change toward a more centrist politics as the dominant spokesmen in the American labor movement disavowed any agenda of radical political or economic change.[70] The national mobilization during World War I provided a harbinger of this change, as business and labor self-consciously pursued a commonly defined public goal.[71] Progressive reformers seized on this wartime experience as proof that governmental policies based on a transcendent public good, articulated by disinterested experts, could achieve harmonious economic and political relations.[72] The Court majority remained, however, firmly gripped by a conception of social relations as inherently conflictual. Although the Justices occasionally relaxed this assumption enough to validate some economic regulatory measures,[73] they nonetheless remained basically committed to the *Lochner* vision that economic regulation was, as Brewer had seen it, inevitably the expression of wrongful greed and envy by the numerous poor against the deserving rich.

The Great Depression rekindled these fears of majoritarian rapacity; and the Court again rose to the threat and struck down a series of New Deal measures.[74] Notwithstanding the provocation of the extraordinary economic hardships suffered throughout the country, however, the proletarian revolution feared by the judiciary did not erupt. Unlike 1895, moreover, when the alliance of judicial bombast and executive military force in *Debs* appeared to arrest the revolutionary tide, the deployment of judicial authority in 1935–36 was patently not responsible for this surprising calm. Roosevelt's overwhelming electoral victory in 1936 clearly signified that economically driven civil warfare was not an imminent menace. (Indeed, Roosevelt's election in 1932 had transcended even the sectional source of civil warfare, since he had received majority support in both North and South, the first President elected on this basis since 1852.)[75] If anything, the judicial assault against the New Deal recovery measures itself appeared to many observers as a provocation likely to inflame popular discontent and undermine Roosevelt's tenuous success in maintaining civil peace. Some diehard ideologues remained convinced that the New Deal was a revolutionary threat to the American social order, a Bolshevik import. After the 1936 election, however, this view was held only by an increasingly isolated minority, both in the country and on the Court.

Roosevelt was, of course, emboldened by his electoral victory to attack the Supreme Court. The threat from his court-packing plan was, however, much less influential in persuading a Court majority to reverse direction than the lesson directly taught by the 1936 election itself. That lesson was not, moreover, simply that an overwhelming electoral majority disagreed with the Court's construction of the Constitution. The lesson attended by a majority of the Justices was that, in the face of the insurrectionist provocation of the Great Depression, popular opinion had been remarkably united and any impetus toward revolutionary uprising had been surprisingly contained by Franklin Roosevelt and his New Deal. If the Court persisted in its hostility to the New Deal, more appeared at peril than its own institutional integrity.*

None of the Justices was willing, however, simply to surrender authority to the President. Those Justices most sympathetic to the animating purpose of the New Deal—Louis Brandeis, Harlan Fiske Stone, and Benjamin Cardozo—indicated that, although they opposed the *Lochner* regime of judicial dominance, they were not prepared to approve unconstrained claims for consolidated national authority or for executive dominance. This was the clear meaning of the concurring votes of these three in the Court's unanimous decision in 1935 overturning the National Industrial Recovery Act.[76] Brandeis wrote no opinion in the case, but he vividly conveyed his intentions to a presidential aide in the Justices' robing room immediately after the decision was announced. "This is the end of this business of centralization," he said, "and I want you to go back and tell the President that we're not going to let this government centralize everything. It's come to an end."[77]

Brandeis was wrong, however; "this business of centralization"

---

*There is considerable evidence that Justice Owen Roberts, whose apparent "switch" provided the fifth vote to validate New Deal measures in 1937, was not influenced by Roosevelt's court-packing proposal. According to internal Court memoranda, several weeks before Roosevelt announced his proposal, Roberts had already voted in conference with four other Justices to overrule prior cases invalidating state minimum wage laws; this was the decision, in West Coast Hotel Co. v. Parrish, 300 U.S. 379 (1937), popularly viewed as the "switch in time that saved Nine." Roberts also was the fifth vote to validate the National Labor Relations Act in NLRB v. Jones & Laughlin Steel Corp., 301 U.S. 1 (1937). See Felix Frankfurter, "Mr. Justice Roberts," 104 *U. Pa. L. Rev.* 311 (1955), and Tribe at 581 n.18.

had not ended. Within a decade, the Court had approved an array of economic regulatory measures that extensively expanded both the federal role generally and independent executive authority specifically.[78] In 1949, to no one's surprise, a unanimous Court explicitly announced that *Lochner* and its progeny had been repudiated.[79]

At first glance, the change in the Court's composition itself might suffice to explain its stunning jurisprudential shift. Since 1937, the Court membership had been completely transformed; indeed, though Roosevelt's first appointment did not come until immediately after the "switch in time" in 1937, he had appointed seven Justices to the Court by 1941. The Roosevelt Court did more, however, than renounce its immediate predecessor; it disregarded the prior historic precedents for the conduct of Justices appointed by Presidents hostile to then-current constitutional doctrine. Between 1804 and 1811, for example, Jefferson and Madison together appointed five Justices to the seven-member Court; but their "Spirit of 1798" was never written into law. Between 1862 and 1864, Lincoln appointed five Justices, but the Court nonetheless withheld carte blanche approval of his wartime actions or subsequent congressional reconstruction policies. Throughout its history, the Court generally has been notoriously resistant to quick change even through new appointments at the hands of Presidents committed to change. More, then, was at work on the Roosevelt Court than the ideological or personal commitment of new Justices to the President who appointed them.

The crucial difference was that, unlike the relationships among virtually all prior succeeding Justices, the Roosevelt Justices and their immediate predecessors had radically different visions of conflict in American society. The Justices who served from the Marshall Court through the Fuller Court to 1910, and most who served thereafter until 1937, all shared the same basic view, though with varying (and chronologically mounting) degrees of intensity: That America was divided by deep, intractable, and dangerous social conflicts. This view was occasionally challenged by other officeholders in Congress or the Presidency, most notably during the early years of the republic; but conflictual imagery regularly loomed large for those who looked at the world from the bench of the Supreme Court.

The Roosevelt Justices, however, had a fundamentally different perspective. They discarded *Lochner* and effectively repudiated judicial oversight of economic regulatory legislation because they believed that commercial disputes in American society occurred in a context of mutually acknowledged equality among the disputants and that *Lochner*-ist judicial interventions had given an unnecessary and socially disruptive advantage to one side.

Felix Frankfurter had been a particularly outspoken proponent of this view. As a law professor, he had advocated withdrawal of the judiciary from *Debs*-like interventions in labor disputes on the premise that unionization of employees "equaliz[ed] the factors that determine bargaining power," and that, notwithstanding the apparent costs of freely waged conflict between employers and unions, these "hardships and even cruelties . . . can only be diminished by bringing industry more and more within the area of collaborative enterprise." (Frankfurter cited Herbert Hoover's inaugural address as his authority: "Progress is born of cooperation in community—not from governmental restraints.")[80]

Robert Jackson had invoked the same premise, that American social conflicts generally were amenable to peaceful compromise, in his critique of the Nine Old Men, just before his appointment to the Court. Jackson had written,

> I have little fear of legislative or political clashes between the forces of liberalism and those of conservatism in the present state of our American society. Each is subject to moderating influences from a constituency which has not often in substantial numbers approved real radicalism or extreme reactionism. . . .

> But, after this political and legislative process has taken place . . . after the forces of conservatism and liberalism, of radicalism and reaction, of emotion and of self-interest are all caught up in the legislative process and averaged and come to rest in some compromise measure such as the Missouri Compromise, the N.R.A., the A.A.A., a minimum-wage law, or some other legislative policy, a [judicial] decision striking it down closes an area of compromise in which conflicts have actually, if only temporarily, been composed. Each such decision takes away from our democratic federalism another of its defenses against domestic disorder and violence. The vice of judicial supremacy, as exerted

for ninety years in the field of policy, has been its progressive closing of the avenues to peaceful and democratic conciliation of our social and economic conflicts.[81]

The belief that American society was fundamentally harmonious, notwithstanding the surface roiling of political and economic controversy, had been reinforced for the Roosevelt Justices by one central fact about the Great Depression: the fact that an American proletarian revolution did not arise from it. The Depression of 1893 had had a similar non-outcome; the consolidation of Republican dominance that followed immediately from the 1896 elections did not convince the *Lochner* Justices, however, that their fears of revolution or their polarized conception of American society were mistaken. But the Roosevelt Justices, unlike their predecessors, had been schooled in the ideology of Progressive reform. For all its variants, this ideology had a uniform underlying perspective that social conflict was "manageable," was amenable to peaceful resolution by self-consciously directed governmental interventions.[82] The heated disagreements among Progressive reformers both before and during the New Deal were disputes about which policies would succeed, not about the inherent possibility of success. As it happened, none of the varying policies pursued in the "first" or the "second" New Deal succeeded in producing economic recovery; but these recurrent failures in themselves did not call into question the basic assumption regarding the manageable, fundamentally peaceable character of American social conflict. Indeed, the failures of specific policies reinforced this basic assumption: economic conditions remained dismal and yet social strife still was contained.

The Roosevelt Justices diverged from their immediate predecessors, moreover, in an even more fundamental way than this difference in their ideological commitments to Progressivism. The old and new Justices were men of different generations. Of the seven Justices whom Roosevelt replaced between 1937 and 1941, two had been born in the 1850s (Brandeis, 1856; Van Devanter, 1859), four in the 1860s (Hughes, McReynolds, and Sutherland, 1862; Butler, 1866), and one, Cardozo, in 1870. Their replacements were born either in the 1880s (Frankfurter, 1882; Reed, 1884; Black, 1886) or 1890s (Jackson, 1892; Murphy, 1893; Douglas, 1898). The eldest Roosevelt appointee was James Byrnes, born in 1879; but he resigned in 1942, after only one year's service, and was replaced by Wiley Rutledge, who had been born in 1894. On average, the old and new Justices were separated from one another by twenty-seven years. This overall age variance was, moreover, a particularly important determinant for their differing attitudes toward social conflict: for the new Justices, the Civil War was not an almost-lived memory but a much more remote historical event.

Even though by 1937 a majority of the old Court was apparently prepared to approve New Deal legislation, this validation had a very different meaning for them than for their immediate successors. The old Court's "switch in time," reflected specifically in their approval of the National Labor Relations Act,[83] had the hallmarks of a tactical retreat in face of the threat to social order from economic chaos and Roosevelt's evident success in appeasing this threat. This is the most plausible characterization for Hughes and Roberts, who joined the majority in the NLRA case. From the perspective of the Justices who joined the Court after 1937, however, the enactment of the NLRA itself was not a tactical event but was one harbinger of a fundamental change in American life; the NLRA was one signification that civil war between labor and capital had ended, that these two great adversaries now approached one another determined (that is, legally required but also essentially willing) to "bargain in good faith."[84] The Roosevelt Justices were firmly convinced that Justice Brewer and the *Lochner* Court had been wrong in believing that irreconcilable warfare was an accurate conception of American political life. This was the basis for the Roosevelt Justices' conclusion that their predecessors had misread the Constitution.

There is an apparent oddity in this conclusion, that somehow the Roosevelt Justices thought the founding fathers had intended to launch an activist welfare state or that, notwithstanding the agrarian character of eighteenth-century America, the founders had been more alert to the governmental structure required by a highly integrated industrial economy than the later generations of judges who had directly witnessed and presided over the transformation to High Capitalism. Bruce Ackerman has drawn from this apparent anomaly the proposition that the new Justices basically concluded that Roosevelt had successfully amended the Constitution, securing effective ratification for the activist welfare state from his overwhelming electoral victory in 1936 and the hospitable congressional reception to his court-packing plan.[85] The new Justices, however, were reluctant to call this an amendment, Ackerman has maintained, because it did not fit the formalities of Article V; but their new constitutional interpretations nonetheless reflected an underlying, though unacknowledged, institutional understanding that Article V formalities were neither the only nor even the most important means for amending the Constitution.*

Ackerman's argument is ingenious; but it leads him away both from seeing the authentic links between the Roosevelt Justices and the founders, which succeeding generations had indeed lost, and

---

*In his recently published book, *We the People: Foundations* (Cambridge: Harvard University Press, 1991), Ackerman sets this account of the New Deal amendments in a richly elaborated rendering of the founders' conception of "dualist democracy," distinguishing between "normal politics" and "higher lawmaking," when the People rouse themselves from private concerns to address public principle in a sustained, decisive way. In addition to the New Deal, Ackerman identifies the adoption of the Civil War amendments and the Founding itself as the three successful moments of higher lawmaking in our history; and the Supreme Court, he claims, has no innovative role in this lawmaking but is entirely "backward-looking," both protecting the higher law during normal times when the People are occupied in narrow, factional pursuits and synthesizing the successive enactments of higher law principle.

Ackerman does not, however, adequately confront the significance of the intense polarized conflicts that produced the popular mobilization he extols. The founders may have anticipated and approved the possibility of episodic eruptions of higher lawmaking, as Ackerman suggests; but the actual events—a calamitous Civil War and its century-long grim consequences, and the near-disaster of the Great Depression, with its fearsome prospect of implacable class warfare—cast a darker complexion over this higher lawmaking process than Ackerman's somewhat romanticized narrative admits. Ackerman's account explains and justifies, as he refreshingly acknowledges, the Supreme Court's "backward-looking" response to these events in *Dred Scott* and in *Lochner*-ist resistance to ameliorative regulatory efforts (at 64–65, 99–103). But if we credit the dangers of polarized conflict, and understand the destructive implications of such conflict for the egalitarian principle at the core of our constitutional scheme, then a different role appears for the Court—a role that "looks forward" toward the possibility of promoting mutually agreed resolution of polarized conflict. Or, at the very least, the Court should not exacerbate such conflicts by its interventions, as in *Dred Scott* and *Lochner*, notwithstanding Ackerman's prescriptions to the contrary.

from understanding the deeper source for their reinterpretive enterprise. It was plausible for the Roosevelt Justices to conclude that their predecessors had misread the Constitution because they started from the more basic premise that these elders had misunderstood the world to which the Constitution applied. To adapt von Clausewitz's dictum: In a world of irreconcilable factional hostility, majority rule is obviously nothing more than warfare by other means. This was the *Lochner* world, and in it majority rule understandably had no special moral sanction. In a world, however, where factional hostility could be transcended, majoritarian institutions had an important, unique, and ultimately most salutary role. This was the founders' world—or, more precisely, this was the world as Madison, most notably and self-consciously among the founders, saw it—a world that, as Madison also saw, had virtually faded away by the time of the Nullification Crisis. Madison's world did not fully reappear—it simply did not seem plausible—until the New Deal had displaced McKinley Republicanism as the dominant defining force in American political life; and this was the rediscovered world to which the Roosevelt Justices appealed for their re-reading of the Constitution.

The Roosevelt Justices did not, however, fully understand the jurisprudential significance of their rediscovery of the Madisonian world. They did not, that is, explicitly acknowledge that by displacing the Hamiltonian presupposition that social relations were inherently, irreconcilably combative, they also called into question his theoretical commitment to the necessity for unitary, hierarchically superior sovereign authority. In their own case-law—most notably, as we will see in the next chapter, in *Brown v. Board of Education*—the Roosevelt Justices eschewed the Hamiltonian conception of judicial supremacy and embraced a Madisonian conception of shared, almost indistinguishably overlapping, authority among the Court and majoritarian institutions. But the Hamiltonian theory of judicial supremacy was so deeply embedded in the Justices' minds that they could not find a jurisprudential language suitable to describe the enterprise they had undertaken. They accordingly invoked Hamilton's description even while they were applying Madison's conception, thus misleading their successors and possibly even themselves about their endeavor.*

---

*Among the immediate predecessors of the Roosevelt Justices, only Louis

There was, moreover, an important difference among the Roosevelt Justices themselves. Though they all agreed that economic conflict was not based on irreconcilable antagonisms, that the civil war between labor and capital had ended, they disagreed about the extensiveness of this characterization regarding conflict in American society generally. Felix Frankfurter and Hugo Black were the great antagonists on this issue among the Roosevelt Justices. Frankfurter was inclined to believe that this society was fundamentally united on virtually all matters and that majoritarian institutions were therefore almost always both safe and preferable forums for dispute resolution.[86] Black had a darker vision of American society, perhaps because, for him as for all Southerners, the memory of the Civil War was more alive than for other Americans; among white Southerners in particular, this memory had been passed as a sacred bond from generation to generation, as a blood feud that still had not been adequately avenged.

Black did not believe, however, that the persistent polarized conflict between North and South or between black and white Southerners was the same, either in intensity or in principle, as economic and social conflicts in American life generally. Frank-

---

Brandeis provided even a rudimentary model for rethinking the Hamiltonian premises of judicial supremacy. Though he and Holmes had consistently voted against the Court majority, to uphold majoritarian economic regulations, Brandeis did not share Holmes's moral agnosticism or his dog-eat-dog view of social relations. Brandeis was accordingly not willing to give virtually automatic deference to majoritarian enactments. Brandeis believed that factional combat could be transcended by commitment to a "common good," if appropriate institutional mechanisms were devised to bring the combatants to this shared vision through "patient, careful argument, willingness to listen and to consider." This was Brandeis's credo in his successful career as a mediator in labor conflicts, and he carried this conviction into his work on the Court. In most of the disputes that came to the Court, however, Brandeis thought his brethren were insufficiently appreciative of the "reasonableness" of the legislative enactments. Brandeis was accordingly never pressed to articulate his differences with Holmes or to crisply identify what I would call the Madisonian cast of his jurisprudence. It is thus misleadingly easy to lump him with Holmes as a single-minded advocate of judicial restraint and majority rule. For an exploration of notable instances of disagreements between Brandeis and Holmes, and the Madisonian implications of Brandeis's position, see Robert A. Burt, *Two Jewish Justices: Outcasts in the Promised Land* 18–34 (Berkeley: Univ. California Press, 1988).

furter did not believe that the sectional conflict, and racial antagonisms within the South, were as readily reconcilable as other conflicts in American life. This was shared ground enough for these two men and their colleagues ultimately to agree that majoritarian institutions did not warrant deference regarding the conflict between southern blacks and whites, that the Court must address and attempt to overturn the subjugative premises at the core of this conflict.

Throughout the 1940s, as cases challenging various aspects of the southern segregationist regime came to the Court, the Justices struggled among themselves to devise an adequate conception of their institutional role and specifically to avoid the judicial interventionist sins of *Lochner* that they had so recently identified as such. One decision in particular epitomized their intellectual difficulty. In 1938 the Court decided *United States v. Carolene Products,* a case that marked the transition from the Nine Old Men to the Roosevelt Court. In this decision, the Court upheld congressional authority to prohibit interstate shipment of skimmed milk filled with nonmilk fats, a measure that would have been skeptically received and most likely overturned by the Court that decided *Lochner.* The Court's opinion was written by Harlan Fiske Stone, and joined only by Chief Justice Hughes, Brandeis, and Roberts. Hugo Black and Stanley Reed had just joined the Court, the first of the Roosevelt appointees; but Reed did not participate in the decision, most likely because he had been Solicitor General when the case was filed, and Black concurred only in the result. McReynolds and Butler remained unrepentant adherents to *Lochner*ism (and Cardozo was too ill to participate). The *Carolene Products* opinion was thus, in effect, a testament by the "born-again" members of the old Court of their new constitutional faith.

In the text of the opinion, Stone announced that "regulatory legislation affecting ordinary commercial transactions" would be presumed constitutional unless "it is of such a character as to preclude the assumption that it rests upon some rational basis."[87] (Thus the 1893 debate between Justice Brewer and Professor Thayer belatedly was resolved in Thayer's favor.) The opinion did not, however, give blanket endorsement to Holmes's *Lochner* dissent or his reflexive and virtually automatic deference to majority rule. In footnote four, perhaps the most frequently cited footnote in the United States Reports, the *Carolene Products* Court stated, "There may be narrower scope for operation of the presumption of constitutionality" in three categories of cases: legislation that violates a "specific prohibition of the Constitution"; legislation that "restricts . . . political processes" such as "the right to vote," to "disseminate information," to organize politically or to "peaceabl[y] assemble"; and legislation "directed at particular religious, or national, or racial minorities." The footnote concluded with the pregnant observation that "prejudice against discrete and insular minorities may be a special condition, which tends seriously to curtail the operation of those political processes ordinarily to be relied upon to protect minorities, and which may call for a correspondingly more searching judicial inquiry."[88]

There was, however, a striking omission in this footnote that points to the problem posed for the Court in its interventions. The Court's hostility toward legislation restricting political processes or aimed at racial, religious, or other "discrete and insular minorities" implicitly seemed to rest on the premise that the dispute between the winning majority and losing minority had not been effectively constrained by their mutually acknowledged equality. Footnote four said nothing, however, about the relationship between this underlying premise and the remedial implications of the judicial interventions. When the Court encountered such legislation, would it not simply overturn the hostile act but also undertake to redress the vulnerability of the minority so that the antagonists were in fact likely to approach one another with mutual respect in this and future disputes? But how might the Court accomplish this, especially in light of the deeply disrespectful antagonism between parties reflected by the enactment of the hostile legislation itself? Alternatively, should the Court devise a resolution not only for this specific dispute but for others between these same unequal parties that, in the Court's view, would have been the likely outcome if the antagonists had regarded one another as equals? But even if the Court could find its way to this equilibrium through the bitter mutual recriminations of the opposed parties, could the Court thereby work toward the democratic goal that ultimately neither disputant "should feel that he stands in the power—at the mercy—of the other"?* Or should

---

*The phrase is Brandeis's, from an address he delivered in 1904 to a group

the Court use its power on behalf of the otherwise vulnerable disputant without considering the impact of its intervention as advancing or impeding the mutual empowerment of both disputants?

The *Lochner* Court had ignored these questions because it did not pursue the goal of mutual empowerment among social adversaries; and the *Carolene Products* Court, fresh from its disavowal of *Lochner,* had not yet seen these consequential concerns. In *Brown v. Board of Education,* however, the Court directly confronted these questions and answered them—though without explicit acknowledgment—according to the vision of equality that Lincoln had expressed and the corresponding egalitarian conception of the institutional framework that Madison had espoused.

---

of employers who had just concluded a bitter labor strike. Implicitly invoking the Madisonian conception of the role of institutional structure in achieving harmonious social relations, Brandeis stated, "Some way must be worked out by which employers and employees, each recognizing the proper sphere of the other, will each be free to work for their own and for the common good. . . . To attain that end, it is essential that neither should feel that he stands in the power—at the mercy—of the other." Rpt. in Louis Brandeis, *Business—A Profession* 24–25 (Boston: Small, Maynard & Co, 1914).

III

EQUAL AUTHORITY IN PRINCIPLE AND PRACTICE

8

An Egalitarian Response: Brown v. Board of Education

IN DECEMBER 1938, seven months after deciding *Carolene Products*, the Supreme Court overturned a southern school segregation law. In an opinion by Chief Justice Hughes, the Court ruled that Missouri was required to provide equal access to separate education within the state, rather than sending a black law school applicant to another state while maintaining a white law school in Missouri; in this case, as in *Carolene Products*, only Justices McReynolds and Butler dissented.[1] Though occasional Court decisions since *Plessy* had challenged various aspects of southern race laws,[2] none had questioned school segregation practices. Indeed, John Marshall Harlan, who had dissented in *Plessy*, wrote the opinion for a unanimous Court that first upheld school segregation laws.[3] Like *Carolene Products*, the Missouri law school case was not only a sharp break with past judicial attitudes but also a herald of the future: an initial indication that, contrary to the views of the Justices who had decided *Lochner, Plessy*, and *Debs*, the subjugative assumptions at the core of the race segregation regime now appeared anomalous.

Although the Roosevelt Justices intensively elaborated the initial impulses expressed in these two cases, toward a diminished judicial role in commercial controversies and increased interventions in race conflict, they based their actions on different assumptions about the underlying character of the disputes. Unlike commercial controversies, where they withheld virtually all judicial intervention because they saw fundamental harmony beneath the apparently combative surface of the disputes, the Roosevelt Justices were deeply ambivalent in their characterization of race conflict.

If the Roosevelt Justices had viewed race conflict in the same unambiguous format as the *Lochner* Court had viewed economic conflict—as nothing more than subjugative warfare—they would have seen no justification for withholding swift, aggressive intervention on behalf of the vulnerable minority.*

Questions

However benign economic conflicts may have appeared to the Roosevelt Justices, they could not overlook the brutality of southern race conflict and the persistent advantage maintained by whites over their black antagonists. Nonetheless even in these intense hostilities, the Roosevelt Justices—or, more precisely, some more emphatically than others on this Court—saw a recognizable kinship with economic disputes, that southern whites and blacks fundamentally shared the same vision of a just society notwithstanding the visible surface of their discord. This optimistic understanding was memorialized in 1944 by Gunnar Myrdal, a Swedish social scientist invited by the Carnegie Corporation to study American race relations for the twentieth century as Tocqueville had done for the nineteenth. Myrdal's book, *An American Dilemma,* was widely praised; if it was not instrumental in shaping the views of the Roosevelt Justices, it was influential for some at least as a confirmation of what they already believed and wanted to believe.

Myrdal's central thesis was that "a strong unity" and "a basic homogeneity and stability" existed in this country: "Americans of all national origins, classes, regions, creeds, and colors, have something in common: a social *ethos,* a political creed. . . . This 'American Creed' is the cement in the structure of this great and disparate nation."[4] This Creed rested on "ideals of the essential

---

*There is a further possible distinction between the two groups: that *Lochner* Justices unambivalently sympathized with the vulnerable wealthy minority while the Roosevelt Justices identified in some substantial measure with the white victimizers. For the moment, I want to set this plausible speculation aside in order to focus on the justifications for withholding judicial intervention that the Roosevelt Justices were prepared consciously to acknowledge to themselves and to their public.

dignity of the individual human being, the fundamental equality of all men, and of certain inalienable rights to freedom, justice, and a fair opportunity."[5] As Myrdal saw it, however, there was a dilemma:

> The "American Dilemma" . . . is the ever-raging conflict between, on the one hand, the valuations preserved on the general plane which we shall call the "American Creed," where the American thinks, talks, and acts under the influence of high national and Christian precepts, and, on the other hand, the valuations on specific planes of individual living, where personal and local interests; economic, social, and sexual jealousies; considerations of community prestige and conformity; group prejudice against particular persons or types of people; and all sorts of miscellaneous wants, impulses, and habits dominate his outlook.[6]

Notwithstanding Myrdal's depiction, this was not a true dilemma because, according to his analysis, it was potentially reconcilable in its own terms:

> In America as everywhere else people agree, as an abstract proposition that the moral general valuations—those which refer to man as such and not to any particular group or temporary situation—are morally higher. These valuations . . . are incorporated into the American Creed. The other valuations . . . are commonly referred to as "irrational" or "prejudiced," sometimes even by people who express and stress them. They are defended in terms of tradition, expediency or utility.[7]

Myrdal's underlying conviction that the "American dilemma" was ultimately resolvable led him—after a thousand pages elaborating the expressions of race conflict in social, economic, and political contexts—to an avowal of Progressive faith in "disinterested" expert intervention:

> We are entering an era where fact-finding and scientific theories of causal relations will be seen as instrumental in planning controlled social change. . . . The American social scientist, because of the New Deal and the War, is already acquiring familiarity with planning and practical action. He will never again be

given the opportunity to build up so "disinterested" a social science. . . .

Social study is concerned with explaining why . . . potentially and intentionally good people so often make life a hell for themselves and each other when they live together, whether in a family, a community, a nation or a world. The fault is certainly not with becoming organized *per se*. In their formal organizations . . . people invest their highest ideals. These institutions regularly direct the individual toward more cooperation and justice than he would be inclined to observe as an isolated private person. The fault is, rather, that our structures of organizations are too imperfect, each by itself, and badly integrated into a social whole.[8]

In his final paragraph, Myrdal issued this call to arms: "To find the practical formulas for this never-ending reconstruction of society is the supreme task of social science. . . . We have today in social science a greater trust in the improvability of man and society than we ever had since the Enlightenment."[9]

From our vantage today, this faith in social science appears touchingly naive and a touch arrogant. This was, however, the abiding credo of one member of the Roosevelt Court; and even beyond Frankfurter, this avowal was at least plausible to the others. The Court's unanimous opinion in *Brown* cited Myrdal and other social scientists for the proposition that psychological knowledge had changed since *Plessy*, and that the "modern authority" of social science had now demonstrated that segregated education "generates a feeling of inferiority as to [black children's] status in the community that may affect their hearts and minds in a way unlikely ever to be undone."[10] Indeed, many people read *Brown* as relying solely on the authority of social science to support its result, since there were no prior judicial precedents and since the Court explicitly stated that the historical materials regarding the meaning of the Fourteenth Amendment were "not enough to resolve the problem with which we are faced [but] at best they are inconclusive."[11]

This is, however, a misreading of the *Brown* opinion. The Court did not rely on the authority of social science. It did—or at least some Justices did—rely on the same source of authority that Myrdal had invoked for his social science claims: the authority of disinterested reason. Frankfurter was most explicit on this score; reason was for him the source of all legitimate social authority, whether in science or law. Insofar as Myrdal's study satisfied scientific norms of disinterested inquiry, it could be cited as both an authority for and an exemplar of judicial action.

To Frankfurter and like-minded Justices on the *Brown* Court, however, it was clear—as it was clear to Gunnar Myrdal—that reason had not yet prevailed in American race relations. As Myrdal had put it, the dominant perspective, especially among white Southerners, was based on "personal and local interests; economic, social, and sexual jealousies . . . [attitudes] commonly referred to as 'irrational' or 'prejudiced,' sometimes even by people who express and stress them." For Frankfurter and like-minded Justices, as for Myrdal, the American creed was the embodiment of the requirements of reason—not necessarily because the ideals of individual dignity, equality, and inalienable rights were timeless, absolute truths but because these ideals were the "social ethos, the political creed" held in fact, as Myrdal also put it, by "Americans of all national origins, classes, regions, creeds and colors." The problem in race relations was accordingly that Americans generally, and southern whites in particular, had not yet understood and acknowledged what they already believed. From this perspective, the American race problem could be solved if Americans generally, and southern whites in particular, would engage in reasoned inquiry regarding their own beliefs.

A large if. Myrdal did not discount the difficulty of initiating or sustaining this inquiry; but he was optimistic nonetheless, and even saw the likelihood of violent race clashes as ultimately serving the goal of rationality.[12] None of the *Brown* Justices contemplated the possibility of violence with the same composure. Indeed, like their predecessors from *McCulloch* to *Debs,* the prospect of civil violence pushed the Justices toward active intervention. Unlike their predecessors, however, the *Brown* Justices did not try to impose an immediate, definitive resolution on the disputants: this was the significance of the Court's decision in *Brown II* to withhold immediate enforcement of the principles enunciated in *Brown I.*

A clear rationale for this course follows from the premises that Myrdal set out and that Frankfurter in particular shared. If the race conflict—like all American social conflict—was potentially resolvable by reasoned inquiry, then some institutional means must be found to promote and sustain such inquiry with and among the antagonists. Majoritarian institutions had achieved this goal for labor conflict, though *Lochner*-like judicial interventions had persistently obstructed and almost defeated the enterprise. But majoritarian institutions could not accomplish this for race conflict, not only because blacks were currently excluded from participation but because, as a consequence of this long-standing systematic exclusion both before and after slavery, southern racial antagonists never had engaged even in the rudimentary practices of reasoned argumentation (unlike labor antagonists, long before the New Deal had legitimized and regularized the institutional format for this reasoning process in the NLRA).

Accordingly, the Court's task was to devise some institutional means for inducing the racial antagonists to engage in reasoned inquiry. By this means they could be brought to acknowledge their common values and interests and, based on this understanding, reach accommodation on the issues that had previously loomed so large and divisive between them. If majoritarian institutions were not available or suitable for this purpose, judicial institutions beckoned invitingly—not simply nor primarily the imposing center in Washington but, more importantly, the individual federal district courts where respected local notables would preside over and ensure calm deliberative exchanges among the antagonists. In these institutional settings, the antagonists would be regarded, and would therefore approach one another, as equals—which in itself would constitute a radical break with the subjugative assumptions on which the racial conflict had been waged.[13]

This view of the potentiality for reasoned, mutually agreed resolution of southern race conflict was not, however, uniformly shared on the *Brown* Court. There was another view, clearly held by Robert Jackson and most likely also by Hugo Black at least: the view that subjugative assumptions remained deeply rooted and that there was no common ground, no shared commitment to a single American creed, readily accessible in the persistent conflict between southern blacks and whites. Jackson set out this view in a draft for a possible concurring opinion that he never published.[14]

Near the end of his draft Jackson concluded that "present-day conditions require us to strike from our books the doctrine of separate-but-equal facilities and to hold invalid state [laws] which classify persons for separate treatment in matter[s] of education based solely on possession of colored blood." Among the requisite "present-day conditions," Jackson cited the "spectacular progress" of blacks since Emancipation, which refuted nineteenth-century "presumptions" about the heritable intellectual or social inferiority of blacks, and the changed status of public education in our culture generally, from a "privilege" to a "right of a citizen." The Court's unanimous opinion in *Brown* reiterated these views in virtually the same terms;[15] but Jackson began his draft with added observations that did not appear in the Court's opinion.

Jackson wrote that race segregation "is deeply imbedded in social custom . . . [and] persists because of fears, prides and prejudices which this Court cannot eradicate." Blacks, he said, "suffer from . . . antagonisms that are an aftermath of the great American white conflict. The white South harbors in historical memory, with deep resentment, the program of reconstruction and the deep humiliation of carpetbag government imposed by conquest. . . . I am convinced that the race problem in the South involves more than mere racial prejudice. It is complicated emotionally with a white war and white politics." This conception of the roots of the racial conflict led Jackson to a general conclusion:

> However sympathetic we may be with the resentments of those who are coerced into segregation, we cannot, in considering a recasting of society by judicial fiat, ignore the claims of those who are to be coerced out of it. We cannot deny the sincerity and passion with which many feel that their blood, lineage and culture are worthy of protection by enforced separatism of races and feel that they have built their segregated institutions for many years on an almost universal understanding that segregation is not constitutionally forbidden.

Here, unlike Gunnar Myrdal's version, was a true American dilemma: blacks claiming, and entitled to, equal educational opportunity that could only be achieved by invalidation of race segregation laws; whites claiming, and equally entitled to, respect for the "protection" of "their blood, lineage and culture" built upon segregation laws. Jackson saw no common ground available in this conflict, at least for the foreseeable future. From accounts of internal Court deliberations, it also appears that Justice Black had a similarly stark vision of the depth and intensity of southern racial conflict.*

How should a judge respond to this intractable dilemma? Not, according to Jackson in his draft opinion, by definitive adjudication of the conflicting constitutional claims advanced by either antagonist. Not by asserting that one claimant had a constitutional right that was hierarchically superior to the other's claim. And not by ruling that, because there was no superior constitutional claim, the status quo must prevail: this was unacceptable since it would necessarily rest on acknowledging the constitutional authority of the southern white majority to adopt race segregation laws. How then could the Court signify that the whites had no legitimate constitutional authority for segregation without holding that the blacks had a superior constitutional right that had been violated?

Jackson's solution was, in effect, to refuse any judicial award of superior legitimacy to either claimant. This meant, first of all, that the white majority's segregation laws must be deprived of the legitimacy that *Plessy* had conferred. The Court had already obliquely attacked *Plessy* by more strenuously insisting on "equality" between racially "separate" facilities.[16] But this indirect pressure could not clearly delegitimize the subjugative premise of the extant regime of southern race relations—the premise embedded in the "separate but equal" formula. In order to deprive southern whites of their claim to hierarchically superior status, the Court

---

*Philip Elman, while serving as an Assistant Solicitor General, was kept informed of the Court's deliberations on *Brown* by Justice Frankfurter, for whom he had previously clerked. According to Elman, Frankfurter said: "Hugo Black . . . was scared to death—and he scared everybody else on the Court—of the political turmoil in the South that would follow from a decision ending racial segregation in public schools. . . . Black was frightening the other Justices the most. He was saying to them, 'Now look, I have to vote to overrule *Plessy,* but this would mean the end of political liberalism in the South. . . . The Klan is going to be riding again. It will be the end of liberalism in the South.'" Elman, "The Solicitor General's Office, Justice Frankfurter, and Civil Rights Litigation, 1946–1960: An Oral History," 100 *Harvard L. Rev.* 817, 825, 828 (1987).

was obliged—as Jackson clearly saw—to overrule *Plessy*. As Jackson also saw, however, in order to refuse any superior status to southern blacks, in order to treat them as equal but no more than equal to southern whites, the Court must do nothing more than overrule *Plessy*.

In Jackson's own terms, this was an uncomfortable and even baffling position. Jackson was, moreover, clearly puzzled about the consequences that might follow from a judicial proclamation invalidating segregated education. Near the end of his draft, Jackson stated, "I have no doubt of the power of a court of equity to condition its remedies to do justice to both parties and I believe that the circumstances under which a large part of the country has grown into the existing system are such that only consideration of that [i.e., justice to both parties] in framing the decree would be just." Jackson offered, however, no hint of how this squared circle might be drawn. He provided only one next step for this artistic process:

> I favor, at the moment, going no farther than to enter a decree that the state constitutions and statutes relied upon as requiring or authorizing segregation merely on account of race or color, are unconstitutional. I would order a reargument on the contents of our decree and request the Government and each of the parties to submit detailed proposed decrees applicable to each case.

When he wrote this draft, Jackson was clearly opposed to the disposition that the Court ultimately adopted after reargument, in *Brown II*.* Jackson never formulated his own alternative, however; he died during the summer after *Brown I* was decided.

Even if Jackson would have persisted in his opposition to its open-ended remand order, the Court's opinion in *Brown II* ap-

---

*In his draft opinion, Jackson criticized the United States government's suggestion—which ultimately was endorsed in *Brown II*—"that the courts assume this [enforcement] task and that we remand these cases to the District Courts under instructions to proceed with enforcement as rapidly as conditions make it appear practicable." Jackson declared, "I will not be a party to thus casting upon the lower courts a burden of continued litigation under circumstances which subject district judges to local pressures and provide them with no standards to justify their decisions to their neighbors, whose opinions they must resist."

pears to express his basic criterion: that an equitable remedy must "do justice to both parties." Thus the Court's opaque, and even avowedly self-contradictory, instructions:

> In fashioning and effectuating the decrees, the [lower] courts will be guided by equitable principles. Traditionally, equity has been characterized by a practical flexibility in shaping its remedies and by a facility for adjusting and reconciling public and private needs. . . . At stake is the personal interest of the plaintiffs in admission to the public schools as soon as practicable on a nondiscriminatory basis. To effectuate this interest may call for elimination of a variety of obstacles in making the transition. . . . Courts of equity may properly take into account the public interest in the elimination of such obstacles in a systematic and effective manner. But it should go without saying that the vitality of these constitutional principles cannot be allowed to yield simply because of disagreement with them.[17]

Where, in this paragraph, does the Court mean to rank the plaintiffs' "personal interest" in nondiscriminatory schooling when "adjusting and reconciling public and private needs"? Are "public" needs preferable to merely (?) "private" ones? Is a "personal interest" a public or private need? How do "public needs" differ, if at all, from "the public interest" which an equity court "may properly take into account" in a "systematic and effective" elimination of obstacles? If "it should go without saying" that constitutional principles cannot yield to "disagreement with them," why say it? From this confusing welter of instructions, it is apparent that the Court in *Brown II* did almost nothing more than it had done in *Brown I*—nothing more than Jackson had originally proposed for that occasion: "going no further than to enter a decree" declaring the state laws unconstitutional, and leaving the consequences of that decree for renewed argument, though at indeterminate and multiply repeated intervals.

This is on its face a confusing result. Jackson clearly had been troubled by its indeterminacy; in his draft, he had insisted, as noted, that he "will not be a party" to such unguided remand to district judges. It is, however, difficult to see what other disposition might have followed from the premises that Jackson himself set out in his draft. Perhaps Jackson never published this opinion because he was dissatisfied with the conclusion to which his reasoning led;* perhaps by the time *Brown I* was decided, Jackson was too ill to complete this draft to his own satisfaction; or perhaps Jackson decided to submerge his own complex and provocative views in the somewhat bland, conclusory formulations of Chief Justice Warren's opinion for the Court.**

Whatever his reasons for withholding publication, the reasoning in Jackson's draft opinion illuminates a path to the indeterminate result that the Court reached in *Brown II*, a path that the Court itself left murky in its cryptic opinion. Jackson's path significantly differs from the Myrdal/Frankfurter justification, but it leads to the same conclusion. Jackson did not rely on the Myrdal/Frankfurter premise that beneath the surface of the southern race conflict, the combatants truly believed in the same "American creed," so that reasoned, disinterested inquiry by a judge or by the combatants themselves would lead to fundamental agreement. And Jackson's portrayal of the virtually ineradicable sources of that conflict put him closer to the inherently combative world of the *Lochner* Justices. But Jackson relied on one central proposition in his draft opinion that markedly separates him from the *Lochner* perspective: he consistently asserted that reliance on force in social relations was wrong, no matter who invoked this force or how avowedly "self-righteous" that invocation might be.

Recall Jackson's statement in the opening section of his draft, "However sympathetic we may be with the resentments of those who are coerced into segregation, we cannot, in considering a recasting of society by judicial fiat, ignore the claims of those who are to be coerced out of it." Jackson cast this principle in a pragmatic calculus. "I am satisfied," he said, "that it would retard

---

*Frankfurter subsequently wrote that Jackson "tried his hand at a justification for leaving the matter" to congressional enforcement under section 5 of the Fourteenth Amendment "and he finally gave up." Letter to Learned Hand, February 13, 1968, quoted in Schwartz at 254. If Frankfurter was referring to the draft opinion discussed in the text, he misunderstood its import.

**Philip Elman, apparently basing his opinion on Frankfurter's confidences to him, stated, "Jackson's view was that whatever the Court did, it should do as a united Court; and what he wanted to do was erase *Plessy v. Ferguson,* simply erase it. Neither say it's wrong nor say it's right." 100 *Harvard L. Rev.* at 824.

acceptance of this decision [to end school segregation] if the Northern majority of this Court should make a Pharisaic and self-righteous approach to this issue or were inconsiderate of the conditions which have brought about and continued this custom or should permit a needlessly ruthless decree to be promulgated." At the end of his draft, Jackson again adverted to this practical concern: "In the long run, I think only a reasonably considerate decree would be an expedient one for the persons it has sought to benefit thereby." Jackson expected, moreover, that a protracted course of litigation and controversy would follow even from the most "considerate" judicial decree—though here too he saw himself offering a practical prediction rather than a desired prescription: "A Court decision striking down state [segregation laws] will not produce a social transition. . . . It is apparent that our decision does not end but begins the struggle over segregation."

Notwithstanding the pragmatic cast of all these statements, a normative premise for them can be identified: the premise that coercion, even "self-righteous" legalistic invocations of coercion, should be disavowed in social relations. This is the premise that separates Jackson's skepticism about the uses of judicial authority and his distaste for Pharisaic moralizing from Holmes's attitudes. Unlike Holmes, Jackson was not prepared to accede to majoritarian force in race segregation (or other matters); but unlike the other Justices who decided *Lochner,* Jackson was not prepared to embrace judicial coercion as an instrument to subjugate majority will. Jackson was willing to invoke a limited form of judicial coercion in *Brown,* but only to serve in effect as a precise counterweight to the coercion imposed on blacks by the white majority. Jackson was not willing to resolve the conflict in favor of blacks, as the *Lochner* Justices had done for one side in economic conflicts, but only to re-open the dispute, to force the parties back to a position of irresolution.

This was the prescriptive implication of Jackson's practical observation about the consequences of judicial intervention: "our decision does not end but begins the struggle over segregation." The judicial intervention that Jackson envisaged—"going no further than to enter a decree" declaring, but not enforcing, the invalidation of segregation laws—was a coercive act; but it was at the same time more a request than a demand, more a question than an answer. This limited intervention, disavowing coercion even more than invoking it, visibly invited a reciprocal disavowal from the white majority of the coercion they had imposed on blacks.

Jackson was uncomfortable with this invocation of judicial authority, as he was uneasy generally about any judicial involvement in the race segregation dispute. In the internal Court deliberations, he insisted that it was "a question of politics" and that "our problem is to make a judicial decision out of a political conclusion."[18] But this categorical assertion did not lead Jackson, as it would lead other constitutional theorists before and after, to insist that because the dispute was a "political question," the judiciary had no proper say in the matter. The conventional vocabulary available to Jackson distorts our understanding of his thought: he did not mean to distinguish "law" from "politics" but rather to identify that point of transition, that epiphany, where "politics" can become transformed into "law."[19] Jackson implicitly understood that the instrument for this transformation is the disavowal of coercive force in social relations.

By this disavowal, the Court in *Brown* illuminated the lawfulness of ordinary political disputes in this society—that they are conducted against a background of mutually acknowledged equal status and their resolutions depend on persuasion, notwithstanding the apparent electoral format that majority will is imposed on a dissenting minority. "Politics" thus becomes "law"—the resolution of political disputes becomes legitimate—when the disputants mutually disavow coercion. By this criterion, segregation laws were blatantly illegitimate. But by this criterion, no coercive imposition—by blacks against whites or by a judiciary on behalf of blacks—could in itself achieve legitimacy. Judicial coercion invalidating the illegitimate laws properly signified that no lawful resolution of the political dispute between blacks and whites had yet been reached; but judicial coercion, to remain lawful in itself, must do no more than this.

At this same intersection of politics and law, Lincoln had stood to confront the secessionists in 1861. His statements and his actions provide an instructive parallel with the Supreme Court's conduct in *Brown*. Lincoln's first inaugural address conveyed the same underlying message to southern whites as *Brown I*: that their denial of the equal status of their adversaries (northern whites in 1861, southern blacks in 1954) was unacceptable in principle and that the political dispute between these adversaries could be resolved peacefully only on the basis of mutually acknowledged equality. The rhetorical strategy of the two documents was also the same: nonaccusatorial and conciliatory in tone but clear and insistent in identifying the fundamental principle at stake.

Brown II and the Emancipation Proclamation were even closer in their strategic content and rhetoric: not only that both directly addressed the status of southern blacks but more fundamentally that both documents ostentatiously withheld the direct invocation of coercion to change blacks' status. Richard Hofstadter's characterization of the Proclamation could equally apply to *Brown II*: that both declined to free any blacks where the federal government might have had actual power to do so and in their tangled legalisms had the moral grandeur of a bill of lading. The *Brown* Court was also vulnerable to Hofstadter's indictment of the author of the Emancipation Proclamation: that the Justices, like other white men of their day, were morally insensitive toward blacks. The same defense is also available, however: that this sympathetic identification with whites, even if it was excessively preferential, led both Lincoln and the *Brown* Justices to withhold self-righteous denunciation of southern whites and to constrain impulses toward subjugatory aggression that were inconsistent with the principle of equality on which the blacks' claims properly rested.

Brown II was a self-conscious attempt to avoid the mutually destructive warfare and the bitter retaliatory aftermath that Lincoln unsuccessfully attempted to avert. *Brown II* conveyed the same appeal to southern whites that Lincoln expressed in 1862, in proposing voluntary, compensated emancipation a few months before issuing his Proclamation: "This proposal makes common cause for a common object, casting no reproaches upon any. It acts not the Pharisee. The change it contemplates would come gently as the dews of heaven, not rending or wrecking anything. Will you not embrace it?"[20] The strategy of *Brown II* for vindicating the equal rights of blacks was identical to Lincoln's tactic in upholding the rightful claims of the Union at Fort Sumter: to send food in unarmed ships to hungry men.

In both instances the strategy failed, as white southerners responded with massive force. Here too Lincoln and the *Brown* Court pursued similar paths. Both answered force with force; both strove to keep their coercive reactions strictly limited to defensive goals while constantly inviting voluntary reconciliation among adversaries; and both had difficulty in containing their use of coercive force within these limits. The Supreme Court's decision in *Cooper v. Aaron*[21] epitomizes all of this; it was for the enforcement of *Brown* what Lincoln's Gettysburg Address was for the Civil War, a public meditation on the meaning of the conflict whose eloquence was heightened because it was uttered on a recent battlefield while the war still raged elsewhere.

Answers

Cooper v. Aaron was decided in 1958, a year after Orval Faubus, the governor of Arkansas, had sent state militia to bar the entry of nine black students into Central High School in Little Rock. Faubus's action was in direct defiance of a federal district court decree to which the Little Rock school board had previously agreed; the board, the mayor, and the police chief in Little Rock all opposed Faubus's action, but he nonetheless asserted that violence would inevitably accompany this first small step toward integration and that the violence could be controlled not by protecting the black students but only by prohibiting their entry into the school. After fruitless attempts to negotiate with Faubus, President Eisenhower nationalized the state militia, thereby removing it from the governor's control, and sent regular army troops to occupy Little Rock and escort the black students into Central High School. Near the end of the school year, the Little Rock school board petitioned the district court and was granted permission to rescind its integration effort on the ground that the armed enforcement, while necessary to protect the black students, was utterly disruptive of the educational enterprise for everyone. The Court of Appeals reversed the district court, and the Supreme Court quickly took the case and unanimously affirmed the appellate court order.

Immediately following *Brown*, there were some movements toward voluntary compliance in the southern border states (as reflected in the Little Rock school board's acquiescence) but only adamant hostility from all of the states that had seceded in the Civil War. Faubus's actions were the most dramatic, overt expression of this hostility; but the Supreme Court took no action at the time to defend the integrity of its pronouncement in *Brown*. In practical terms, the Court was unable to take any action; aside from a handful of United States marshalls who were formally obliged to act at the specific direction of judicial officers, the Court had no armed force directly at its command to oppose the state militia that Governor Faubus had deployed around Central High School. President Eisenhower, as commander in chief, had such force; but it was clear as a formal proposition of constitutional law that the Court had no authority to direct the President to enforce its orders against resistant litigants,[22] and it was informally clear that Eisenhower was personally unsympathetic at least, and perhaps even opposed, to public school integration.[23] When Eisenhower decided to send troops against Faubus, he publicly justified his action as required to enforce judicial orders regardless of his personal views about the correctness of those orders.[24] But the Justices knew that Eisenhower could have chosen to leave them and *Brown* undefended.

The challenges presented by Faubus's action did not reach the Court until almost a year after Eisenhower had sent troops. As at Gettysburg, hostile state authority had aggressively assaulted federal territory. The battle had ended with a narrowly won federal victory, but the ultimate outcome of the overall war (and the extended commitment of federal troops themselves to the enterprise) remained very much in doubt. As Lincoln had done at Gettysburg, the Court in *Cooper v. Aaron* portrayed the conflict in its most far-reaching significance with rhetorical appeals that reached beyond the manifest uncertainties of the day. More obviously than Lincoln had done, however, the Court attempted to mask these uncertainties by insisting on its authority to command unquestioning obedience, thus directly echoing Justice Brewer and the *Lochner* Court:

> Article VI of the Constitution makes the Constitution the "supreme Law of the Land." In 1803, Chief Justice Marshall, speaking for a unanimous Court, referring to the Constitution as "the fundamental and paramount law of the nation," declared in the

notable case of *Marbury v. Madison,* 1 Cranch 137, 177, that "It is emphatically the province and duty of the judicial department to say what the law is." This decision declared the basic principle that the federal judiciary is supreme in the exposition of the law of the Constitution, and that principle has ever since been respected by this Court and the Country as a permanent and indispensable feature of our constitutional system. It follows that the interpretation of the Fourteenth Amendment enunciated by this Court in the *Brown* case is the supreme law of the land, and Art. VI of the Constitution makes it of binding effect on the States "any Thing in the Constitution or Laws of any State to the Contrary notwithstanding." Every state legislator and executive and judicial officer is solemnly committed by oath taken pursuant to Art. VI, cl. 3, "to support this Constitution." Chief Justice Taney, speaking for a unanimous Court in 1859, said that this requirement reflected the framers' "anxiety to preserve it [the Constitution] in full force, in all its powers, and to guard against resistance to or evasion of its authority, on the part of a State. . . ." *Ableman v. Booth,* 21 How. 506, 524.

No state legislator or executive or judicial officer can war against the Constitution without violating his undertaking to support it. Chief Justice Marshall spoke for a unanimous Court in saying that: "If the legislatures of the several states may, at will, annul the judgments of the courts of the United States, and destroy the rights acquired under those judgments, the constitution itself becomes a solemn mockery. . . ." *United States v. Peters,* 5 Cranch 115, 136. A Governor who asserts a power to nullify a federal court order is similarly restrained. If he had such power, said Chief Justice Hughes, in 1932, also for a unanimous Court, "it is manifest that the fiat of a state Governor, and not the Constitution of the United States, would be the supreme law of the land; that the restrictions of the Federal Constitution upon the exercise of state power would be but impotent phrases." *Sterling v. Constantin,* 287 U.S. 378, 397–98.[25]

In this extended passage, the Court pulled out all its stops: the supremacy clause, *Marbury,* John Marshall twice, four different unanimous Courts, and perhaps most revealingly, citations to Chief Justice Hughes in 1932, just before his Court struck at the New Deal, and to Chief Justice Taney in 1859 defending *Dred Scott* against an abolitionist state court. As these latter citations in particular implied, the Court in *Cooper v. Aaron* appeared to insist on unquestioning obedience from "every state legislator and executive and judicial officer" even for decisions whose moral warrant might be repudiated by future generations.

In making this claim, the Court appeared to suppress even its own doubts about its authority. One aspect of this effort occurred in successive drafts of the Court's opinion. An early draft prepared by Justice Brennan had cited *Marbury,* in the same terms as in the final opinion, for "the basic principle that the federal judiciary is supreme in the exposition of the law of the Constitution"—but immediately added that "this decision was not without its critics, then and even now, but it has never been deviated from in this Court. The country has long since accepted it as a sound, correct and permanent interpretation."[26] Other Justices objected, however, to this mildly tolerant reference to Court critics, and the final version was revised to read, as already quoted, that after *Marbury* "that principle [of judicial supremacy] has ever since been respected by this Court and the Country as a permanent and indispensable feature of our constitutional system."

Later in the same Term, however, Justice Black returned to this question in an opinion that was unlikely to attract the same immediate attention as *Cooper v. Aaron.* In a case considering the jurisdiction of state courts over commercial transactions on Indian reservations, Black discussed John Marshall's confrontation with Andrew Jackson's Indian policy and conveyed a different understanding of the relationship between popular criticism and judicial authority:

> Around 1830 the Georgia Legislature extended its laws to the Cherokee Reservation despite federal treaties with the Indians which set aside this land for them. . . . The constitutionality of these laws was tested in *Worcester v. Georgia,* 6 Pet. 515. . . . Rendering one of his most courageous and eloquent opinions, Chief Justice Marshall held that Georgia's assertion of power was invalid. . . .

> Despite bitter criticism and the defiance of Georgia which refused to obey this Court's mandate in *Worcester* the broad principles of that decision came to be accepted as law. Over the

years this Court has modified these principles . . . but the basic policy of *Worcester* has remained.[27]

Thus Justice Black acknowledged, though only from the comfortable distance of a century's hindsight, that even some Supreme Court judgments only gradually come "to be accepted as law."*

In *Cooper v. Aaron,* however, the Court was not prepared to admit this proposition, nor to acknowledge that it lay beneath the strategy of *Brown II*. Nonetheless, in their embattled opinion, the Court unintentionally testified to the uncertain status of *Brown*. This testimony appeared, following the confident trumpeting of judicial authority to command universal obedience, in the final paragraph of the Court's unanimous opinion:

> The basic decision in *Brown* was unanimously reached by this Court only after the case had been briefed and twice argued and the issues had been given the most serious consideration. Since the first *Brown* opinion three new Justices have come to the Court. They are at one with the Justices still on the Court who participated in that basic decision as to its correctness, and that decision is now unanimously reaffirmed. The principles announced in that decision and the obedience of the States to them, according to the command of the Constitution, are indispensable for the protection of the freedoms guaranteed by our fundamental charter for all of us. Our constitutional ideal of equal justice under law is thus made a living truth.[28]

There is an unacknowledged oddity in this passage. If, as the Court proclaimed earlier in its opinion, "the interpretation of the Fourteenth Amendment enunciated by this Court in the *Brown* case is the supreme law of the land," why was it necessary at the end of the opinion to reaffirm that decision? Why are the "three new Justices who have come to the Court" not bound by the prior

---

*According to Dean Guido Calabresi, who served as Black's law clerk during this Term, Justice Frankfurter returned his copy of the draft opinion in the Indian case with the notation, "I agree with *every* word, including the essay on *Brown v. Board of Education.*" By contrast, during the internal Court deliberations on *Cooper v. Aaron,* Black in particular had urged " 'more punch and vigor' in that portion of the opinion dealing with the supremacy clause issue." Hutchinson, 68 *Georgetown L. J.* at 79 n. 671.

acts of this supreme authoritative tribunal? If they are entitled to disobey, who else is equally authorized: the President who, after all, appointed these new Justices? the Senators who confirmed them? the Congress generally, which controls the size of the tribunal and sets its jurisdiction? Are these other institutional actors limited, in dissenting from *Brown,* only to selecting new Justices who might dissent on their behalf, or does their clear authority to select such Justices imply that these other actors are entitled to dissent in other ways as well?

The Court clearly did not intend to raise doubts about its own authority in *Cooper v. Aaron;* and it might have passed over in silence the potentially unsettling implications of the change in its personnel. But the context of the case made the Justices acutely aware of their institutional vulnerabilities, and it was thus not surprising that they should inadvertently underscore doubts in the very gesture that they offered to allay them.* The basic institutional lesson of *Cooper v. Aaron,* like other instances of moral posturing that betray underlying discomfort, is not what the Justices said but what they did. The lesson that the Justices actually applied was different from their adamant insistence on their unchallengeable claim to command obedience; the lesson was that they could establish their authority only by continuously soliciting the widest possible agreement to their enterprise—including, but not limited to, the new Justices Harlan, Brennan, and Whittaker, who by 1958 had replaced Jackson, Minton, and Reed and who had not previously concurred in *Brown.*

Cooper v. Aaron was in this sense a continuation of the Justices' effort in the race segregation cases even before *Brown* to act only on the basis of unanimous agreement among themselves. McReynold's splenetic dissent in the 1938 Missouri law school case, maintaining that integrated education would "damnify both

---

*In addition to their unusual reaffirmation of a prior ruling, the Justices took another wholly unprecedented step in *Cooper v. Aaron* by naming each Justice individually as a joint author of the Court's opinion rather than identifying one Justice to deliver the opinion of the Court or by issuing the opinion with the spare designation *per curiam.* Justice Frankfurter urged this extraordinary collective attribution specifically in order to emphasize that the newly appointed Justices supported *Brown;* see Warren, *Memoirs* at 298. Justice Harlan, one of the new members, subsequently suggested that the Court also explicitly reaffirm *Brown.* Hutchinson, 68 *Georgetown L. J.* at 85.

races,"[29] was the last public expression of differing views within the Court toward white supremacist practices. As the Roosevelt Justices began their deliberate march toward *Brown* throughout the race cases of the 1940s, there was no unanimity that their ultimate destination was to overrule *Plessy.* But as they addressed race segregation in a variety of contexts—in southern election practices, interstate transportation facilities, employment relations, and enforcement of residential restrictive covenants, as well as in graduate educational institutions[30]—the Justices self-consciously sought to avoid open disagreements among themselves that might both mirror and exacerbate the racial conflict reflected in the cases themselves. Throughout this decade, the Court accordingly appeared virtually united both in its hospitality to the litigative campaign against southern segregation practices mounted by the NAACP Legal Defense Fund and in its cautious hostility to those practices. This united front was, however, the product of painstaking internal Court negotiations.[31]

When *Brown* first came to the Court in 1952, challenging the validity of public school segregation generally, none of the Justices saw how their carefully wrought unanimity could persist. But by 1954, this devoutly wished consummation had been achieved. Three days after this event, Frankfurter wrote a congratulatory letter to Reed, who had been the last and presumably the most reluctant to join the *Brown* opinion:

> History does not record dangers averted. I have no doubt that if the Segregation cases had reached decision last term there would have been four dissenters—Vinson, Reed, Jackson, and Clark—and certainly several opinions for the majority view. That would have been catastrophic. And if we had not had unanimity now inevitably there would have been more than one opinion for the majority. That would have been disastrous.[32]

By Frankfurter's accounting, if *Plessy* had been overturned in 1952, three of the four Southerners on the Court (Vinson and Reed from Kentucky and Clark from Texas) would have dissented (with only Black from Alabama concurring)—a repetition of the divisive signification of the Court's sectional voting in *Dred Scott.* *

---

*In *Dred Scott,* five Southerners and one Pennsylvanian (Grier) constituted the majority; of the remaining Northerners, two dissented (McLean of Ohio and

Whatever led the Court from this initial division to its ultimate unanimity in *Brown*—Vinson's death, Earl Warren's diplomatic skills, the persistent efforts of other Justices—it was clear that all the Justices viewed this unanimity as a critically important achievement that should be sustained in their subsequent responses to the segregation cases.[33] The Justices' pursuit of unanimity explains why *Brown II*, in particular, is so difficult to decipher: because it was an amalgam of conflicting views among the Justices themselves, held together only by their mutual commitment to reach accommodation among themselves.

This mutual commitment had not taken firm hold within the Court when *Brown* first appeared on its docket in 1952. Though it is difficult to determine the precise voting alignments at that time, available conference notes and other sources suggest that in 1952 the Justices were stalemated—two (Black and Douglas) openly ready to overrule *Plessy,* three set to reaffirm *Plessy* in public schools (Vinson, Clark, and Reed), two others (Frankfurter and Jackson) unwilling to reaffirm *Plessy* but prepared to overturn it only with a united Court, and the remaining two (Burton and Minton) probably similarly inclined.[34] If this accounting is accurate, then the Court in 1952 could not muster a majority for any action, either to overturn or reaffirm *Plessy;* it decided to order reargument in effect to buy time for further deliberation within the Court. The Court's subsequent unanimous decision in *Brown I* did not, moreover, necessarily connote that the stalemate had been conclusively resolved. In one sense, the Court's decision that school segregation should be ended but only at some indeterminate distant time was a mutually agreed expression of the stalemate within the Court, that *Plessy* could neither be overturned nor reaffirmed. Even if read in this narrow spirit, *Brown I* was necessarily a stunning blow to the constitutional status of school segregation, since a unanimous Court now announced that the question apparently settled by *Plessy* must be reopened.

Curtis of Massachusetts) and one (Nelson of New York) refused to reach the substantive issues. Subsequent accounts of the internal argument within this Court strongly suggests that the five Southerners would have been unwilling to overturn the Missouri Compromise if they had not secured support from at least one northern Justice. See McPherson at 172–73.

This narrow reading might seem to discount the significance of the Court's statement in *Brown I* that "separate educational facilities are inherently unequal."[35] This statement did authoritatively remove the constitutional legitimacy that *Plessy* had bestowed on school segregation laws; but the Court carefully refused to draw from this statement the conclusion that would follow from conventional assumptions about judicial supremacy. As Lincoln had done in his conduct of the Civil War, the Court in *Brown* tried rigorously to distinguish between defensive and offensive use of its authority, between protective affirmation of the equality principle and subjugative assault waged against those who violated that principle. It is more accurate to say that in *Brown* the Court acted to impose a stalemate on the warring parties, thereby reopening the previously coerced conclusion of this warfare embodied in the race segregation regime and requiring that some new settlement be reached that would adequately honor the equal status of both parties.

Though the Justices did not formulate *Brown II* in these explicit terms, they intuitively understood that their own deliberations in *Brown I* had already exemplified the only way that the equality principle could be vindicated in polarized disputes—if the equal adversaries acknowledged stalemate, disclaimed reliance on any form of coercion (including majority rule), and painstakingly worked toward mutually agreed accommodation. The inevitable and desirable hallmarks of this principled accommodation, in which no adversary either could claim victory or lament defeat, would be temporizing irresolution and apparent incoherence: it would be, that is, *Brown II*.

From this perspective, *Cooper v. Aaron* was a defensive invocation of judicial authority, notwithstanding its atavistic rhetorical demand for absolute submission. Governor Faubus's deployment of the state militia to bar nine black students from the Little Rock high school did violate the Court's injunction to reopen the terms of the existing subjugative relationship between southern blacks and whites. Faubus refused to acknowledge, that is, the existence of the stalemated, equal relationship ordered by the Court—a relationship which did not permit coerced resolution of conflict but, once acknowledged as such, might ultimately lead to negotiated mutual accommodation.

The Court's subsequent conduct made clear, moreover, that it had commanded nothing more than this; for after *Cooper v. Aaron,* the Court fell silent. It did not speak again about the permissible terms for settling the school segregation conflict until five years later, when it struck down a patently hypocritical "voluntary attendance" scheme that permitted white parents to perpetuate race segregation by transferring their children away from any schools with blacks.[36] In the following year, the Court overruled a local board's decision to close its public schools altogether rather than accept any contact between blacks and whites.[37] These two decisions in effect reiterated nothing more than the command of *Brown I*, that the existing subjugative relationship between blacks and whites embedded in the segregation regime must be recast. Like *Brown I*, these two decisions said nothing about the specific terms of the new relationship that might satisfy the equality principle—nothing more than the delphic injunction of *Brown II*, that a new but unspecified relationship must be achieved at some indeterminate future time and that the parties should proceed toward this uncertain goal "with all deliberate speed."

In 1968 the future finally arrived, so far as the Court was concerned. *Brown II* was set aside: "The burden on a school board today," the Court stated, "is to come forward with a plan that promises realistically to work, and promises realistically to work *now.*"[38] Two large events had occurred during the fourteen year span following *Brown I* that led the Court to this conclusion in 1968: the massive indigenous uprising among southern blacks challenging the segregation regime and the recognition of the validity of this challenge by an overwhelming majority of the Congress in enacting the Civil Rights Acts of 1964, 1965, and 1968.

Before *Brown I*, the campaign against southern segregation practices had been waged almost exclusively in litigation brought by the NAACP Legal Defense Fund, a northern-based interracial organization. It was not clear (nor was it formally required) that in these lawsuits, the NAACP spoke for anyone but the few specific complainants whom they represented.[39] Southern whites persistently maintained that the vast majority of southern blacks—"their blacks"—were content with the existing regime. As implausible as this claim might seem, there was no way conclusively to rebut it because southern blacks were so effectively silenced by their formal exclusion from electoral politics and by their vulnerability to the pervasive threats of violence and economic ruin for any breach of the subjugative racial etiquette.

The Court's decision in *Brown I* emboldened southern blacks to speak for themselves. The first proclamation came in 1955 when Rosa Parks' refusal to relinquish her seat in a Montgomery, Alabama, bus precipitated an economic boycott by virtually the entire black population of the city. The Montgomery bus boycott marked the beginning of the modern black civil rights movement. The role of *Brown* in inspiring this event was made clear by Martin Luther King, Jr., as he assumed formal leadership of the boycott. Speaking in a Montgomery church, in his first civil rights testament, King stated, "If we are wrong, the Supreme Court of the United States is wrong. If we are wrong, the United States Constitution is wrong. If we are wrong, God Almighty is wrong."[40]

The Court had not anticipated that its decision in *Brown* would precipitate the massive acts of self-assertion among southern blacks that spread from the Montgomery bus boycotts to lunch-counter sit-ins, voting registration campaigns, freedom marches, and the entire panoply of civil rights activism of the succeeding decades. The Justices did, however, hope that other institutional actors would respond affirmatively to *Brown;* indeed, the Justices acknowledged among themselves that, in pragmatic terms at least, nothing would follow from the *Brown* decision unless support voluntarily came from the President and Congress.

This was the reason why the Justices formally invited the new Republican administration to participate in the 1953 reargument in *Brown.* Though the Court had not invited executive-branch participation when the case was first argued, the Truman administration had submitted an amicus brief, consistent with its past litigative positions, urging the reversal of *Plessy;* but the Eisenhower administration's position was not clear. As Justice Frankfurter noted in a letter to Chief Justice Vinson, after *Brown* had been set for reargument, "The reason for having the Government appear was not a matter of tactics or 'public-relations' [but because] the new Administration, unlike the old, may have the responsibility of carrying out a decision full of perplexities; it should therefore be asked to face that responsibility as part of our process of adjudication."[41]

The Justices also looked—longingly, one might say—toward the

Congress. But here they knew that the prospects for any support were exceedingly remote. As Justice Jackson observed during the *Brown* reargument, "I suppose that realistically the reason this case is here is that action couldn't be obtained from Congress."[42] Section five of the Fourteenth Amendment explicitly gave Congress "power to enforce, by appropriate legislation, [its] provisions." The Southerners' hold on Congress was so strong, however—from the combined effect of the seniority-based committee chairmanships in both Houses, where the repressive politics of the South gave extraordinary longevity to its congressional representatives, and the Senate filibuster rule requiring two-thirds vote to end debate on any bill—that no civil rights measure had been enacted since 1875, the year before federal troops were withdrawn from the South. Though this southern white dominance in Congress was not as directly based on threats of violence as in their home precincts, it had the same implication in all racial matters: that if there were any opposition to the subjugated status of blacks, it could not find expression, and accordingly the strength and even the existence of such opposition was in doubt.

When the Court set *Brown* for reargument in 1953, it alluded to the possibility that Congress might resolve this doubt for itself. The Court specifically asked the litigants to consider whether, even if the framers of the Fourteenth Amendment did not intend directly to abolish school segregation, section five gave authority for such action to "future Congresses."[43] In its *Brown* opinion, the Court did not address this question; but though unanswered, it hovered just out of sight then and for some years thereafter. Justice Jackson had written about the existence and importance of congressional authority, but he chose not to publish his draft.[44] In his original draft of the Court's opinion in *Cooper v. Aaron*, Justice Brennan lightly mentioned the possibility that "the problem of securing the constitutional rights of the school children by individual law suits against each school board may be such as to warrant the attention of the Congress in formulating laws pursuant to section 5 of the Fourteenth Amendment." But Justice Clark objected, admonishing Brennan to omit any reference to Congress and instead add "hoopla" about the supremacy of judicial authority.[45]

These suppressed references to congressional authority were

remote speculations in 1954 and 1958; by 1963, however, the prospect that Congress might take independent action against race segregation seemed less implausible. The Kennedy Administration had been notably more supportive of black civil rights than its predecessor.[46] Immediately following Kennedy's assassination in November 1963, Lyndon Johnson—the first Southerner to occupy the presidency since before the Civil War—proclaimed his commitment to the cause, and particularly emphasized his support for a law against public accommodations discrimination which Kennedy had proposed in June and the House of Representatives had passed in August 1963.

The civil rights movement by then had made access to public accommodations its most publicly visible demand by conducting "sit-in" demonstrations throughout the South in segregated restaurants and entertainment facilities. The Court was drawn into this issue in litigative challenges to state trespass convictions; the demonstrators' principal constitutional argument was that state enforcement of trespass laws to uphold a property owner's discriminatory motive was prohibited state action, like judicial enforcement of racially restrictive residential covenants proscribed by the Supreme Court in 1948. The first sit-in case raising this argument came to the Court in 1962; but the Court postponed decision[47] and the case was reargued in October 1963, with similar cases from other southern states.

Notwithstanding the House's prior approval of the public accommodations law, the prospect for congressional action in October 1963 seemed unlikely. While the Court deliberated its disposition of these cases, southern Senators conducted a filibuster—their perennially successful parliamentary tactic against civil rights legislation.* Though the Senate was thus restrained from deciding the substantive question by majority vote, the Court was not barred from considering the public accommodations issue on constitutional grounds.

Three of the Justices—Douglas, Goldberg, and Warren—were

---

*Since the two-thirds rule for ending filibusters had been adopted by the Senate in 1917, cloture had been attempted thirteen times on behalf of civil rights measures and had never succeeded. Lewis Froman, *The Congressional Process: Strategies, Rules, and Procedures* 119–120 (Boston: Little, Brown & Co., 1967).

prepared to resolve the issue by prohibiting state enforcement of trespass laws for public accommodations discrimination. Justice Douglas was explicit in rejecting the proposition that the Court should wait for Congress to act:

> The whole Nation has to face the issue; Congress is conscientiously considering it; some municipalities have had to make it their first order of concern; law enforcement officials are deeply implicated, North as well as South; the question is at the root of demonstrations, unrest, riots and violence in various areas. The issue in other words consumes the public attention. . . .
>
> We have in this case a question that is basic to our way of life and fundamental in our constitutional scheme. No question preoccupies the country more than this one; it is plainly justiciable; it presses for a decision one way or another; we should resolve it. The people should know that when filibusters occupy other forums, when oppressions are great, when the clash of authority between the individual and the State is severe, they can still get justice in the courts.[48]

Three other Justices—Black, Harlan, and White—were also prepared to resolve the constitutional issue. But because they concluded that enforcement of the state trespass laws was not necessarily an endorsement of the property owners' discriminatory motives and was therefore constitutionally permissible, their disposition would not have impinged directly on congressional deliberations. Indeed, Justice Black explicitly "express[ed] no views as to the power of Congress, acting under one or another provision of the Constitution, to prevent racial discrimination in the operation of privately owned businesses."[49]

The three remaining Justices—Brennan, Clark, and Stewart—did not mention the possibility of congressional action. But their balletic agility at avoiding any consideration of the constitutional status of public accommodations discrimination clearly indicated that they had moved with an eye toward Congress.* The narrow

---

*In Griffen v. Maryland, 378 U.S. 130 (1964), these three (joined by Chief Justice Warren) voted to overturn the trespass convictions on the ground that a

disposition of these three meant that there was no majority on the Court to resolve the basic constitutional issue, even though all the trespass convictions were overturned. Justice Douglas was pointedly disparaging of this equivocal result:

> We stand mute, avoiding decision of the basic issue by an obvious pretense. . . . The clash between Negro customers and white restaurant owners is clear; each group claims protection by the Constitution and tenders the Fourteenth Amendment as justification for its action. Yet we leave resolution of the conflict to others, when, if our voice were heard, the issues for the Congress and for the public would become clear and precise. The Court was created to sit in troubled times as well as in peaceful days. . . . When we default, as we do today, the prestige of law in the life of the Nation is weakened.[50]

The deferential intentions of Brennan, Clark, and Stewart toward the possibility of congressional action was apparent not only in the substance of their position but in its timing as well. Though the cases were argued in October 1963, they were not decided until the last day of the Court's term, on June 22, 1964. Justice Douglas also criticized this delay:

> On this the last day of the Term, we studiously avoid decision of the basic issue of the right of public accommodation. . . . This case was argued . . . over eight months ago. The record of the case is simple, the constitutional guidelines well marked, the precedents marshalled. Though the Court is divided, the prep-

---

deputy sheriff, rather than a park employee, initially had ordered the demonstrators to leave, thereby constituting direct state action. In Bouie v. City of Columbia, 378 U.S. 347 (1964), they found that the trespass statute as construed by the state supreme court retroactively and therefore unconstitutionally enlarged its scope. In Bell v. Maryland, 378 U.S. 226 (1964), they concluded that a state antidiscrimination law enacted after the trespass arrests might require retroactive exculpatory application and remanded the convictions to the state supreme court. In Robinson v. Florida, 378 U.S. 153 (1964), eight Justices invalidated the convictions on the ground that state law required segregated toilet facilities in restaurants and state action thus was significantly involved in the restauranteur's refusal to serve blacks. By the same vote, in Barr v. City of Columbia, 378 U.S. 146 (1964), the Court ruled that there was insufficient evidence to support a "breach of the peace" conviction against the demonstrators.

aration of opinions laying bare the differences does not require even two months, let alone eight. Moreover, a majority reach the merits of the issue. Why then should a minority prevent a resolution of the differing views?[51]

None of the Justices mentioned, however, another implication of the timing of their decision. Twelve days earlier, on June 10, the Senate had voted cloture; and on June 19, three days before the Court's decision, the Senate had approved the bill, thus virtually assuring passage of the Civil Rights Act of 1964.* These concurrent, but judicially unmentioned, events vividly suggested that for some Justices constitutional adjudication was a hermetically sealed enterprise—for Douglas, Goldberg, and Warren, at least, who announced on June 22 that they would have invalidated state laws supporting public accommodations segregation without reference to the pending congressional action.

If two other Justices had joined Douglas, Goldberg, and Warren on June 22, it is likely that the Civil Rights Act of 1964 would still have been enacted. But if this Court majority had come together and had spoken earlier, enactment of this law would have been virtually inconceivable. The constitutional ruling apparently would have solved the problem of public accommodations discrimination—enough so that the other Senators would have abandoned the arduous enterprise of defying and risking general legislative retaliation from the powerfully situated Southerners, whose seniority gave them control over the major Senate committees. Because the public accommodations issue was the most visible controversy addressed by the 1964 Act, moreover, the constitutional ruling would also have blunted popular demand for it.

There were, however, other provisions in the Civil Rights Act of 1964 that would have disappeared along with the public accommodations provision: most notably, title VI prohibiting use of federal funds in racially segregated schools and other public facilities and title VII forbidding race or gender discrimination in

---

*The cloture vote was 71–29 and the Senate vote on the merits was 73–27, 110 *Congressional Record* 13327, 14511 (1964). On July 2 the House reaffirmed its prior position, approving the Senate amendments by the overwhelming margin of 264–92, and President Johnson signed the bill that same day. Id. at 17783.

private employment. Perhaps these other provisions would have been included the following year in the Voting Rights Act of 1965. Enactment of this measure also required overriding a southern Senate filibuster; but perhaps this would have occurred without the momentum generated by the 1964 cloture vote. Perhaps President Johnson would have persisted in his public commitment to civil rights, as he did in the November 1964 election to differentiate himself from Senator Goldwater, the Republican candidate, who had voted against cloture.* Perhaps, even without already knowing that the southern filibuster was no longer invincible, Administration strategists would have responded to the March 1965 clashes in Selma, Alabama, by pressing for immediate passage of the Voting Rights Act.[52] Perhaps civil rights leaders themselves did not need the emboldening political message conveyed by the 1964 cloture vote to convince them to escalate their voter registration drives that led to the Selma confrontation.

All this might have happened even without the precedential force engendered by passage of the 1964 Civil Rights Act. But if none of this had occurred, the equality principle would have been sadly impoverished. And the Court's authority itself would have been diminished—ironically enough, by its own authoritative act ostensibly to vindicate the equality principle by invalidating the racially discriminatory application of state trespass laws.

The Court would have lost authority if the Civil Rights Act of 1964 had not been passed because that Act ratified the correctness of the Court's ruling in *Brown I*. The Congress thereby answered the question that the Court had posed in *Brown II* and bestowed a legitimacy on the Justices' enterprise that they had not and could not have obtained as a response to a coercive judicial order. The 1964 Act legitimized *Brown* precisely because the Court did not and could not command Congress to enact the 1964 Act, or more particularly, order seventy-one Senators to impose cloture against their previously invincible southern colleagues.

The fact of legitimation was apparent in the response of south-

---

*Goldwater was joined in voting against cloture only by six other nonsouthern Senators: Hayden, his colleague from Arizona, Young of North Dakota, Bible of Nevada, Mechem of New Mexico, Byrd of West Virginia, and Simpson of Wyoming. 110 *Congressional Record* 13327 (1964).

ern whites generally to enactment of the 1964 Act. Unlike their reaction to the Court's ruling in *Brown*, there was no "massive resistance" to the congressional proscription of public accommodations segregation; there was immediate compliance throughout most of the South, especially in metropolitan areas and in stores that were part of national chains.[53] Even more strikingly, the stonewalled defiance to any school integration by southern white officials quickly dissolved as a direct result of the 1964 Act. In the 1964–65 school year, only two percent of southern blacks attended schools with any white students; in 1965–66, this attendance figure rose to six percent, a year later to sixteen percent,[54] two years later to forty percent. In another two years—by the 1970–71 school year—eighty-four percent of black students in the South attended school with whites.[55]

The 1964 Act added substantial enforcement weapons to the armamentarium previously available to the courts—especially by providing executive branch personnel to monitor school district desegregation compliance and by penalizing resistant districts with loss of federal educational funding. But truly adamant white Southerners could have decided to forfeit federal funding and impoverish their schools, just as one Virginia county previously had chosen to close its public schools rather than accept any integration[56]—just as the secessionists in 1861–1865 had chosen to bring economic ruin and social devastation on themselves rather than yield any portion of their racial supremacist principles.

The 1964 Act did more, however, than throw greater firepower at resistant white Southerners; it demonstrated a full measure of their separation from and moral disgrace in the eyes of other Americans. In itself, this demonstration need not have undermined the Southerners' will to resist; they might indeed have seen themselves as beleaguered in their isolation and resolved accordingly to fight on with passionate desperation. This had been the emotional tenor of both southern secessionism in response to Lincoln's election in 1860 and the "massive resistance" after 1954 to the Court's decision in *Brown*. But the 1964 Civil Rights Act engendered a different response.

The difference, I would speculate, rested on two related factors. First, unlike the 1860s when white Southerners first withdrew from the national legislature and then were forced to beg for re-entry, in the 1960s white Southerners remained in Congress and were still visibly powerful and respected, even though no longer invincible on civil rights matters. Second, the 1964 Act was a less complete defeat for white Southerners than the *Brown* decision precisely because their Senators and Representatives remained entrenched within the Congress where, unlike their appearance before the Court, they were clearly capable of bargaining rather than begging for advantage.

Whether or not these factors explain the psychology of acquiescence among southern whites after the 1964 Civil Rights Act, they indicate why that legislation was legitimately based on democratic principle: Not because majority rule is inherently self-justified but because all participants could readily understand the legislative defeat of the white Southerners as an episode rather than an irreparable breach in a relationship, as a potentially recoupable loss in a continuous series of transactions rather than a permanent victory or crushing defeat for anyone.

The condemnation of race segregation in the 1964 Civil Rights Act thus bestowed legitimacy on the Supreme Court's ruling in *Brown v. Board of Education* in a way that the Court could never have accomplished on the basis of its authority alone. But this does not mean that the Court should have waited for congressional action rather than invalidating segregation laws on its own authority in *Brown*. The Court properly ruled in *Brown* that because race segregation laws imposed subjugation, they violated the democratic equality principle and were therefore illegitimate. The Court could do nothing more, however, in principle or in practice than delegitimize the state laws; it could not authoritatively impose a legitimate, reciprocal relationship of acknowledged equality. Such a relationship would have to be worked out, among other places, in the give-and-take of congressional debate. The Court's restraint—coupled with its implicit, continuous solicitation of a congressional response during the decade preceding the passage of the 1964 Civil Rights Act—demonstrated the answer to the question I posed at the outset: How can the Supreme Court properly adjudicate constitutional disputes, notwithstanding its questionable legitimacy to do so?

One episode in Congress's enactment of the 1968 Civil Rights Act epitomized this lesson in *Brown v. Board of Education*. The central provision of the 1968 Act was its prohibition of race discrimination in the sale or rental of housing. But unlike the 1964 and 1965 Civil Rights Acts, this measure was more aimed at northern than southern race relations, since, for the most part, residential segregation was much more characteristic of northern than southern communities.[57] By 1968, moreover, a discernible "white backlash" had appeared in American politics as a response to increasingly vocal black militants and the eruptions of riots by blacks outside the South. Riots had begun in August 1965 in the Watts area of Los Angeles and had spread during the following two summers to Chicago, Cleveland, Newark, and Detroit.[58] Although members of Congress representing northern electorates had been willing to condemn whites in the South for excluding blacks from public accommodations and from political participation, it seemed unlikely in 1968 that these officials would now act to prohibit racially discriminatory practices in their own constituencies. Southern Senators again engaged in a filibuster, requiring two-thirds of the Senate to unite against them.

On March 4, 1968, a vote was taken to impose cloture and end the filibuster. I was then legislative assistant to Senator Joseph Tydings of Maryland and watched from the Senate gallery as the votes were tallied. The outcome was not at all assured. The House had passed the bill in August 1967; the Senate floor debate had begun in January, and cloture had been unsuccessfully attempted three times, supported first by a small majority and then by sixty Senators but not by the required two-thirds vote. March 4 was the last chance.

A few days earlier, I had attended a strategy session among Senators and staff where a conversation was reported between Vice President Hubert Humphrey and a Democratic Senator from Alaska, E. L. (Bob) Bartlett, who had thus far voted against cloture. Racially segregated housing was not a politically significant concern in Alaska, but Bartlett told Humphrey that he was unwilling to change his vote because Richard Russell of Georgia, the chairman of the Senate Appropriations Committee, had promised that, in exchange for Bartlett's support, the Committee and the Congress would approve funds to build a highway link between Alaska and the "lower forty-eight" states. Large numbers of Alaskans passionately wanted construction of this highway for practical and symbolic reasons. Russell had also promised that he would come to Alaska to campaign for Bartlett at his next election in order to underscore Bartlett's role in bringing this highway to his constituents. After Bartlett reported these promises, Humphrey asked that on March 4 he at least refrain from voting until the end of the tally, so that he might reconsider his position if his vote were crucial. Bartlett agreed but nonetheless emphasized the advantages for him in persisting in his opposition to cloture, especially if his was the deciding negative vote.

On March 4 Humphrey presided over the Senate and called the roll on cloture. George Aiken, Republican of Vermont, who had previously opposed cloture, now voted for it; Norris Cotton, Republican of New Hampshire, also now voted for cloture. Humphrey completed the alphabetical roll and then began calling on Senators who, having first passed, now sought recognition. Margaret Chase Smith, Republican of Maine, had previously opposed cloture; she now voted from her seat at the front row of the chamber but spoke so quietly that no one except the Senate clerk and Humphrey heard her. Several other Senators voted, but in the rising din of voices on the floor their votes also were not generally heard.

The cloakroom door at the back of the Senate swung open and Bartlett came through; he had stayed away as he had promised and now he started down toward the well of the chamber. But Vice President Humphrey abruptly called out, "Mister Bartlett." Bartlett had not asked for recognition, and he seemed startled. He shook his head, as if to say "no," and took another step toward the well. Humphrey again called out, "Mister Bartlett." This time Bartlett swung his arms in a sweeping negative gesture and walked more quickly, almost running down the remaining steps, clearly intent on reaching the Senate clerk to obtain a precise count of the ongoing vote. But Humphrey stopped him a third time: "Mister Bartlett."

For a long moment, Bartlett stood still. Then in a strained, almost inaudible voice, he said, "Yes."

Humphrey lifted his gavel and struck it on the podium desk. "The motion for cloture," he said, "is approved."

The next morning I called Senator Bartlett's legislative assistant and asked what Bartlett had understood from Humphrey's actions. The Senator, he told me, had been puzzled; Bartlett had expected that he would not be asked to vote until he had learned the exact tally directly from Humphrey or the Senate clerk, and Humphrey had confused him by seeming to demand that he vote without knowing the count. But in that moment of confusion, he subsequently told his assistant, Bartlett decided that he didn't really need to know the vote count, that justice was too important to be exchanged for a highway, that he would not deserve re-election to the Senate if he had not been a Senator. So he voted yes.

Vice President Humphrey had addressed Senator Bartlett as the Supreme Court had spoken to the Congress in *Brown*. Humphrey could not control Bartlett's vote; but, as presiding officer of the Senate, he could force Bartlett publicly to declare himself. In this forced public declaration, Bartlett—like the other members of Congress, like the white and black Southerners represented in *Brown*—could not avoid acknowledging that he had some responsibility for the perpetuation of the grievances that the Supreme Court identified in *Brown*, and that he must decide for himself whether he was morally obliged to remedy those grievances. Bartlett—like all members of Congress, like all Americans of every race—had always carried some measure of responsibility for the subjugated status of blacks; but until Bartlett had been required to make this public declaration, he could deny this implication even to himself.

Humphrey did no more than force this publicly visible accountability on Bartlett; he did not dictate—he was not authorized to dictate—Bartlett's response. Bartlett could thus respond as an equal to his equals—to Humphrey, to the southern Senators, to the Justices of the Court, to black Americans claiming redress from him, to Alaskans insisting that he secure a highway for them regardless of its costs. This public dialogue among equals is different from an order imposed by ruler on ruled: it is the difference between a regime of moral authority and authoritarianism.

In the immediate aftermath of Congress's passage of the Civil Rights Acts of 1964 and 1965, the Supreme Court recognized this difference. Its most explicit acknowledgment came in *Katzenbach v. Morgan* in 1966. The issue in this case was the constitutionality of a provision of the Voting Rights Act that overrode state laws imposing English literacy qualifications on Spanish-speaking voters who had been educated in Puerto Rico.[59] The Court ruled that if the judiciary by itself were to interpret the Fourteenth Amendment, state literacy qualifications would not violate equal protection. Nonetheless, the Court held that, under section five of the amendment, Congress had independent authority to interpret the equal protection guarantee and could therefore independently invalidate the state literacy requirements. In identifying this independent authority, the Court was more expansive in characterizing congressional power than was necessary to uphold the challenged provision;[60] the Court was clearly intent on emphasizing the equal status of Congress in construing the Fourteenth Amendment.

The Court did not give, however, a precise account of the contours of this independent congressional authority in *Katzenbach v. Morgan*. It was apparently uneasy, and even self-contradictory, in its portrayal of the measure of congressional independence it envisioned.[61] This hesitance is understandable; unstinting recognition of independent congressional authority to interpret the Constitution would stand in considerable tension with the conventional conception of judicial supremacy—the *Debs–Lochner* grandiosity, the "hoopla" as Justice Clark privately described it in 1958—that the Court had invoked in *Cooper v. Aaron* to bolster its own embattled authority. With the enactment of the 1964 and 1965 Civil Rights Acts, it appeared that the Court's battle against segregation laws had been won—but only because the Congress had independently joined forces with the judiciary.[62] And thus, whatever its hesitancies, the Court answered the Congress in *Katzenbach v. Morgan* with a vote of thanks and of confidence for its independent action.*

---

*Judicial eagerness to enlist the Congress in a common enterprise was directly testified to by the Fifth Circuit Court of Appeals, which had been vested by *Brown II* with principal oversight responsibility for the implementation of school desegregation: "A national effort, bringing together Congress, the executive, and the judiciary may be able to make meaningful the right of Negro children to equal educational opportunities. *The courts acting alone have failed.*" United States v. Jefferson County Board of Education, 372 F.2d 836, 847 (5th Cir. 1966) (emphasis in original).

The Court's cultivation of Congress did not last long, however. An indicator of the Court's quick reassessment appeared in a decision that was not a direct assault on congressional prerogatives but, perhaps even more telling, an almost casual disrespect. On June 17, 1968—just two months after President Johnson signed the Civil Rights Act that prohibited discrimination in the sale or rental of housing—the Court decided in *Jones v. Alfred H. Mayer Co.* that an 1866 congressional act had already prohibited all racial discrimination, private or public, in the sale or rental of property.[63] The text of the 1866 law was ambiguous, and the Court's construction was at least plausible.[64] What was implausible, however, was to imagine that the 1968 Act did not supercede the older act, given that there were differences between them.* And, more importantly, it was almost impossible to understand why the Court saw fit to base its ruling on a novel construction of a century-old act just months after Congress had concluded an arduous political struggle to reach this essentially identical result. The Court observed that "it would be a serious mistake to suppose that [its reading of the 1866 act] in any way diminishes the significance of the law recently enacted by Congress."[65] But the Court surely diminished the significance of the energy spent and political jeopardy accepted by the proponents of the 1968 Act. Why would the Senate preoccupy itself with nothing but this measure during the two-months filibuster, why would the northern members of Congress risk electoral retaliation from their constituents, why would Senator Bartlett of Alaska sacrifice his own highway to enact this measure—why would all of these elected officials bear these costs if an 1866 act already accomplished the basic purpose of the 1968 prohibition on housing discrimination?

In one sense, *Jones v. Mayer* appears simply to be an impolitic decision; Justice Harlan maintained this in his dissenting position—that, in light of the later passage of the 1968 Act, the Court should have dismissed certiorari "as improvidently granted," thus

---

*The most notable difference was the exemption in the 1968 Act for owner-occupied rental property with no more than four apartments, 42 U.S.C. sec. 3603; if Congress had understood that racial discrimination would remain prohibited in such property by the 1866 act, it is difficult to understand why this exemption was provided.

leaving untouched the lower court's limitation of the 1866 Act to state-sponsored discrimination.[66] But something more than politics, more than consideration for congressional sensibilities, was at stake in this case. In *Jones v. Mayer,* the Court revealed that it had misunderstood its own prolonged enterprise in *Brown* and the significance of Congress's response to it in the contemporary Civil Rights Acts. If the Court had acknowledged, even to itself, that the legitimacy of its enterprise to invalidate segregation had been in doubt until Congress had ratified it in these acts, the Court could not have approached the 1968 Act in its posture of impartial adjudicator between the 1866 and 1968 Reconstruction Congresses. The Court's error in *Jones v. Mayer* was not so much in what it said or did as in its mood and its apparent self-conception. It viewed itself as the disengaged fount of reason whose legitimacy could be assumed or commanded, rather than as an institution at once equal to and interdependent with the other branches, continuously engaged in soliciting and earning its moral authority while it assesses the moral authority of others. In *Jones v. Mayer* itself, this error was without great consequence. But this error was only the beginning, a harbinger of the Court's attitude toward itself and its enterprise during the next two decades at least.

As the Court thus turned away from the jurisprudence of *Brown,* it squandered opportunities for promoting relations based on mutual respect for equality among social adversaries. Outside the Court, moreover, the lesson of *Brown* has been, if not lost, at least obscured by the prevalent view that its reticent implementation was a crassly unprincipled political act. This common view is wrong. The Court's cautiously deliberative pace challenged others to respond; as in Senator Bartlett's answer to the Vice President's question, there was no other way to realize the principle of equality on which *Brown* rested. Whether Bartlett's immediate constituents approved his representation on their behalf was, unfortunately, never known; he died nine months after casting the decisive vote for the 1968 Civil Rights Act. But Bartlett's willingness to transcend self-aggrandizing impulses, as with the Congress's ultimate response to the Court's charge in *Brown,* vindicated the hope that James Madison had invested in representative institutions and, in this sense, should be judged favorably. Beneath the bombast of *Cooper v. Aaron,* the Court itself acknowledged the significance of such freely chosen acts. Immediately after announcing that the three new Justices had agreed to join with the surviving members and their departed predecessors to affirm *Brown,* the Court unanimously proclaimed: "Our constitutional ideal of equal justice under law is thus made a living truth."[67]

9

Atavistic Reaction: The Nixon Tapes, the Death Penalty, and Abortion

BY THE MID-1960s, the liberal majority on the Warren Court had staked an entire jurisprudence on the vision of fundamental harmony in social relations that had provided the framework for its effort in *Brown*. The Court intervened against legislative impositions not only on blacks but on other groups who appeared similarly devalued by the majority: accused and convicted criminals, Communists, atheists, poor people, illegitimate children.[1] The Court did not see itself, however, as taking sides in a subjugative struggle between implacable adversaries; it was convinced that its interventions on behalf of these minorities would not lead to widespread social disruption but would instead be accepted by and acceptable to the majority.

This assumption was based in part on the Court's confidence not only in the fundamental harmony of American society but in its capacity to discern the values on which that harmony was based. This assumption also partly rested on the relatively limited scope of the Court's interventions in the overall structure of the relationship between the majority and minorities. Unlike *Brown*, however, these limitations were not self-consciously constructed by the Court but followed from the narrow practical context of the cases themselves. Without calculation and perhaps even against its inclination, the Warren Court did no more on behalf of these disadvantaged minorities generally than the Court had done in *Brown*: to challenge the legitimacy of the existing subjugative relationship imposed by the majority and thereby demand that the majority reconsider the terms of that relationship. As in *Brown*, these judicial interventions promoted open expression of previously suppressed social conflict but did not dictate the conclusive resolution of that conflict.*

By the late 1960s, however, tolerance for unresolved or prolonged social conflict was generally diminishing in American society. In race relations, the public eruption of the black civil rights movement, beginning with the 1955 Montgomery bus boycott, undermined and ultimately destroyed the effort by whites to deny the pervasive existence of subjugative racial politics in both the South and the North. In 1964 Martin Luther King, Jr., identified the strategy of the civil rights sit-in demonstrations and freedom marches: "Instead of submitting to surreptitious cruelty in thousands of dark jail cells and on countless shadowed street corners, he [the Southern black] would force his oppressor to commit his brutality openly—in the light of day—with the rest of the world looking on."2

This strategic provocation had stunning success in precipitating congressional action in the 1964 and 1967 Civil Rights Acts. It also had a deeper consequence. By unmasking the violence beneath the apparently peaceable etiquette governing southern race relations, the civil rights demonstrators thereby provoked unsettling questions about the governance generally of American society, not only in racial but in all matters. When inner-city rioting among blacks spread North, beginning with Watts in 1965 and sweeping like an epidemic in succeeding summers, white Northerners were suddenly forced to confront a disjunction between

---

*The reapportionment decisions of the Warren Court are an apparent exception to this generalization. In a sweeping repudiation of past practice, the Court ordered all state legislatures reconstituted to conform to the egalitarian command of "one man/one vote." Baker v. Carr, 369 U.S. 186 (1962), Reynolds v. Sims, 377 U.S. 533 (1964). But no direct substantive consequences followed from this intervention; and, although the balance of legislative advantage would be shifted away from rural toward urban or suburban voters, these groups as such did not clearly correspond to the participants in any contemporaneously waged polar hostilities (except obliquely in the South, where urban whites appeared more amenable than rural whites to repudiating race segregation practices; see Black and Black at 34–49). Thus, although the reapportionment decisions unsettled existing majoritarian practices, it was not at all clear that substantial social changes would follow from this egalitarian ruling—though this was not purposefully calculated by and perhaps contrary to the hopes of the Warren Court majority in these cases.

their image of a harmonious American society above the Mason-Dixon line and the subjugative experience loudly testified by some members of this supposedly happy family.

These events were the opening moves toward a marked shift in the conception of American political life—as if roughly to recapitulate the erosion in the early nineteenth century of the founders' belief that uncoerced social unity could be attained and its replacement with a Jacksonian atomistic, inherently antagonistic, and essentially subjugative conception of social relations. After the late 1960s, evidence of this reconception appeared on both the left and the right in the spectrum of American politics: on the left, with the generalization of the civil rights paradigm to such groups as women, gays and lesbians, disabled and elderly people—all of whom now portrayed themselves, like blacks, as once silenced by but now adamantly resistant to their oppression and stigmatization; and on the right, in the approbation of a freely competitive marketplace where only the "fittest deserve survival" and in the condemnation of majoritarian regulation to redress competitive inequalities. All of this imagery of social conflict, moreover, was given impetus by the debacle of the Vietnam War—an event almost unanimously regarded after our ignominious withdrawal in 1975 as a terrible, tragic mistake, but viewed as mistaken for diametrically opposed and mutually recriminatory reasons by the left and the right.

The first clear evidence of this shift on the Supreme Court came in 1967, when a narrow majority refused to overturn a state conviction against Martin Luther King, Jr., for leading a civil rights demonstration. The central issue in the case was not the legitimacy of King's demonstration as such; it was his refusal to obey a patently illegitimate state court injunction prohibiting the demonstration. In *Walker v. City of Birmingham* the Court ruled that even if the judicial order had violated the demonstrators' constitutional rights, King and his followers were obliged to obey until it had been overturned by a higher court. Justice Potter Stewart, in an opinion joined by Justices Black, Clark, Harlan, and White, stated:

> In the fair administration of justice no man can be judge in his own case, however exalted his station, however righteous his motives, and irrespective of his race, color, politics, or religion.

This Court cannot hold that the petitioners were constitutionally free to ignore all the procedures of the law and carry their battle to the streets. One may sympathize with the petitioners' impatient commitment to their cause. But respect for judicial process is a small price to pay for the civilizing hand of law, which alone can give abiding meaning to constitutional freedom.[3]

When the state court injunction had been originally imposed in 1963, King had stated that he was not attempting "to evade or defy the law or engage in chaotic anarchy," and that he was prepared to "risk . . . the possible consequences" of imprisonment if the Supreme Court ultimately refused to agree with his judgment that the injunction was unlawful. But, King said, he would march notwithstanding the state court order: "Just as in all good conscience we cannot obey unjust laws, neither can we respect the unjust use of the courts."[4] The Supreme Court majority held, however, that King was not entitled to act on his own conception of lawfulness, even as a provisional opinion pending subsequent judicial review. Judges alone, the Court ruled, own this entitlement.

In one sense, this ruling took the rhetorical conceit in *Cooper v. Aaron* that everyone must obey the Supreme Court's constitutional interpretations and extended this privileged status to every judge, subject only to the hierarchically superior authority of other judges. But *Walker v. City of Birmingham* did even more than this; the case had none of the limiting context of the effort in *Cooper v. Aaron* to use judicial supremacy to defend the equality principle on behalf of a subjugated minority against persistent majoritarian impositions. In *Walker,* the Court invoked judicial supremacy to preserve social order without regard to the legitimacy of that order; this was the clear implication of the Court's holding that even an unconstitutional judicial order must be obeyed.

In this sense, *Walker* exalted judicial authority even beyond the ethereal heights that the Fuller Court had reached in its suppression of the 1894 Pullman Strike; in *Debs,* at least the Court concluded that the lower court had legitimate authority in enjoining the strike. There was, however, a deeper consistency between these two decisions: the underlying fears of social disorder that led the Court in *Debs* to stretch its conception of legitimate judicial authority to accommodate this suppression were also at work in the immediate background of *Walker*. This was the testimony of Justice Brennan's dissent in *Walker*, joined by Chief Justice Warren and Justices Douglas and Fortas:

> We cannot permit fears of "riots" and "civil disobedience" generated by slogans like "Black Power" to divert our attention from what is here at stake—not violence or the right of the State to control its streets and sidewalks, but the insulation from attack of . . . patently impermissible prior restraints on the exercise of First Amendment rights.[5]

The immediate consequence of *Walker* was that Martin Luther King, Jr., served a brief term in the Birmingham city jail for protesting Southern segregation practices. This result did not mean that in 1967 the Supreme Court had abandoned its substantive conclusion in *Brown* that racial segregation violated the constitutional principle of equality. *Walker* did, however, signify a retreat from the process implications of the equality principle that the Court had implicitly understood in its implementation of *Brown*: that this principle in its own terms required the Court to view its constitutional interpretive authority as equal but not superior to others.

Within a few years, this retreat became a rout. King's assassination in 1968, the eruption of urban riots that followed, Robert Kennedy's assassination, the escalation of the Vietnam War accompanied by tumultuous social protest—all of this carried the Justices to the question that the President of Columbia University asked when he re-entered his office after the occupying students had been expelled: "My God, how could human beings do a thing like this?" Even more disturbingly, these events pushed the Justices toward Erving Goffman's impious sociological version that I quoted at the beginning of Chapter 2: "How is it that human beings do this sort of thing so rarely? How come persons in authority have been so overwhelmingly successful in conning those beneath them into keeping the hell out of their offices?"[6]

The Justices, preeminent as they were among persons in authority, would not have posed the question in precisely this way. But by 1974, with the Court substantially reconstituted by Richard Nixon's four appointees, all of the Justices—including the surviving liberal remnant from the Warren Court—responded to these doubts about the security of the social order by embracing the same conception of judicial authority that had characterized the *Debs–Lochner* regime. The impetus for this embrace was the same in the 1970s as it had been in the 1890s: a conviction that American society had become riven by irreconcilable hostilities. In the 1970s as in the 1890s, the Supreme Court single-mindedly embarked on the suppression of social conflict—sometimes by aggrandizing its own authority to impose order in contentious partisan struggles (notably in the *Nixon Tapes* and abortion cases—as in *Lochner*), sometimes by underwriting the subjugative efforts of other institutions (notably in the death penalty cases—as in *Plessy v. Ferguson*). In all of these cases the Court overrode the democratic principle of equality as the measure of legitimacy both in relations among governance institutions and in interactions among all members of the American polity.

The Nixon Tapes

On July 9, 1974, the day after the Supreme Court heard oral argument in the *Nixon Tapes* case, Justice Brennan visited former Chief Justice Warren and confidentially reported that the Court had resolved to order Nixon's compliance with the district court's subpoena of tape recordings of his conversations about the burglary of the Democratic Party headquarters in the Watergate office building during the 1972 presidential campaign. According to an account of Brennan's visit, Warren responded, "Thank God, thank God, thank God! If you don't do it this way, Bill, it's the end of the country as we have known it."[7] Because of the Supreme Court's ruling, the country was relieved from witnessing a House impeachment vote and a Senate trial. This preemptive exercise of judicial authority effectively suppressed a contentious political controversy; but contrary to Chief Justice Warren's fervent affirmation of Justice Brewer's 1893 proclamation, this "independen[t] and vigor[ous]" judicial intervention was not essential nor even helpful for "the salvation of the nation [and] the permanence of government of and by the people."

On July 24, 1974, the Supreme Court unanimously ordered President Nixon to surrender the Watergate tapes, ruling that they were required as evidence in the criminal prosecution then pending in federal district court against Nixon's aides, a prosecution in which Nixon himself had been cited by the grand jury as an unindicted co-conspirator.[8] On July 27, 29, and 30, the House of Representatives Judiciary Committee adopted three articles of impeachment against Nixon—two for his role in the aftermath of the Watergate burglary and a third for refusing to surrender these same tapes and others to the Committee for its impeachment inquiry. Though Nixon remained adamant in his refusal to honor the House Committee's subpoena, he complied with the Supreme Court's order on August 5 and, at the same time, publicly disclosed the contents of the surrendered tapes. Three days later, Nixon resigned the presidency. The House of Representatives accordingly never voted on the articles of impeachment, and the Senate never tried Nixon's conduct in office.

When the Court deliberated the *Nixon Tapes* case, it was clear that any judicial action would directly affect the pending impeachment proceedings. If the Justices had overturned the district court subpoena, thereby vindicating Nixon's constitutional claim for executive privilege, this would have significantly undermined the apparent justification for the House Committee's third impeachment article regarding Nixon's resistance to its subpoena. The Committee had already resolved that it would not seek judicial enforcement of its subpoena, on the ground that its constitutionally independent impeachment authority was not properly subject to judicial review. In any event, the constitutional justification for the Committee's subpoena was both different from and more compelling than the case for the district court's demand for presidential evidence in a criminal proceeding not directly involving his continued status in office.[9] If the Court had nonetheless vindicated Nixon's claim, these lawyerly distinctions would have been swamped in the parallel impeachment proceedings.

If the Court upheld the judicial subpoena, as it did, a different, but equally direct, impact on the impeachment proceedings was clearly foreseeable. Nixon might have refused to comply with the Supreme Court's order as he had refused to obey the House Committee; in that event, the question of the appropriate sanction for this added refusal would have complicated and perhaps slowed the impeachment course. If the Court itself subsequently found that Nixon's defiance, even though unlawful, was not punishable by any direct judicial contempt sanction because of the special constitutional status of the presidency, this conclusion could itself directly influence congressional deliberations on the president's amenability to the impeachment sanction. In any event, the House Committee might have considered itself obliged to conduct further hearings to consider whether Nixon's resistance to a Supreme Court order was another impeachable offense.

Or Nixon might have complied with the Supreme Court's order, as he did; but the specific tapes subpoenaed for the criminal prosecution might not have revealed any directly damaging information about him. This result would have cast doubt on the strength of the Judiciary Committee's case for impeachment even though the Committee had demanded additional tapes and, in any event, had recommended impeachment on grounds beyond Nixon's involvement in the Watergate burglary. These additional grounds—such as misusing confidential income tax records for political harassment, directing the use of wiretaps and other surveillance against political opponents, and maintaining a secret White House unit to engage in "covert and unlawful activities"— were more wide-ranging and ominous uses of executive authority than the specific accusations of misconduct in the Watergate affair. But Watergate had so much seized popular attention that apparently exculpatory evidence on these counts—such as the judicially subpoenaed tapes might have provided—would have swamped consideration of these other matters.

Or Nixon might have complied with the Supreme Court's order and the tapes might have revealed his direct participation in the conspiracy to cover up the Watergate burglary—as did in fact occur. And if Nixon then resigned, as he did, the other accusations about his conduct in office—conduct, as each of the three impeachment articles alleged, "contrary to his trust as President and subversive of constitutional government, to the great prejudice of the cause of law and justice and to the manifest injury of the people of the United States"—would have faded from view. No accounting of this conduct would be made, no judgment rendered by which not only Nixon but future presidents might be held responsible.

When the Court heard oral argument in the *Nixon Tapes* case on July 8, as the House Judiciary Committee impeachment hearings were about to begin, it encountered all of these risks of adverse consequences from any possible decision in the case. The Court nonetheless forged ahead. If the Court had been at all concerned, however, to minimize its impact on the contemporaneous congressional impeachment deliberations, a simple expedient was available. The Court was not required to hear the case on July 8. On May 24 President Nixon had filed an appeal from the district court's subpoena in the Court of Appeals for the District of Columbia Circuit; on that same day, the special prosecutor filed a certiorari petition requesting immediate review in the Supreme Court. On May 31 the Court granted the prosecutor's petition, thus bypassing the ordinary appellate process; the Court also ordered an expedited briefing schedule, overriding its ordinarily applicable procedure which itself would have delayed argument until fall.[10]

As if the need for quick adjudication were self-evident, the Court never explained why it adopted these extraordinary procedural measures. The district court had initially scheduled the criminal trial of Nixon's associates for September 9, and this date could not be met unless the validity of the subpoena had been previously determined; but this date could surely have been extended into the fall without jeopardizing the defendants' speedy trial rights. Indeed, under ordinary procedural rules, Nixon could not have obtained appellate review of the subpoena until after the trial had been concluded; at the outset of its opinion, however, the Court waived this customary prohibition against interlocutory (or "piecemeal") appeals in criminal trials on the ground that the President deserved special respect from the courts and should not be subjected to the burdens imposed on ordinary litigants of deciding whether to comply with a subpoena without definitive appellate adjudication.[11] The Court was thus willing to defer to one co-equal branch, the presidency, by accelerating its judgment; but it did not address the question whether deference to another co-equal branch, the Congress, might have required a slower, more stately pace—or even observance of its ordinary schedule. President Nixon, moreover, had not initiated the request for expedited review bypassing the Court of Appeals; this came from the special prosecutor, a subordinate executive branch official.

The House Judiciary Committee, by previously rejecting any judicial recourse to enforce its subpoenas against Nixon, had clearly signified that it did not want any court involvement in the ongoing impeachment process. But the Supreme Court could not restrain itself on the sidelines of this battle; it galloped into the midst.[12]

The Justices might have thought that their intervention was needed in order to ensure that impartial judgment, rather than self-aggrandizing political considerations, would prevail. Nixon had been insistently proclaiming that the pending impeachment proceedings were nothing but a partisan vendetta—a charge given some credence by the fact that a Democratic majority comprised both the House and Senate. Prevailing popular opinion clearly viewed the Court as less partisan than Congress—an opinion obviously reflected in Nixon's ultimate conclusion that he could not disobey a judicial order as he had defied the congressional subpoena (even though, as a matter of legal doctrine, the congressional authority was more firmly based in the impeachment power than the constitutional authority directly available to support the judicial subpoena). Whatever the justification for this popular distinction in most matters regarding Congress and the Court, there was a clear difference in this impeachment proceeding; if most people did not see this difference, it was only because they were bedazzled by the conventional imagery of the Court's majestic authority.

One of the Justices, however, seemed to have glimpsed the vulnerability at least of his own claim to impartiality in this proceeding. Justice Rehnquist refused to participate in the *Nixon Tapes* case, though—consistent with the Court's ordinary recusal practice—he gave no explanation for his withdrawal. His absence was simply noted at the end of the Court's unanimous opinion: "Mr. Justice Rehnquist took no part in the consideration or decision of these cases."[13] Rehnquist was the only Justice who had been a member of the Nixon Administration, having served as an assistant attorney general in the Department of Justice. Perhaps Rehnquist concluded that his impartiality was compromised because, before his appointment to the Court in 1972, he had provided some advice to the President that was at least tangentially relevant to the pending case. Or perhaps he had offered some relevant advice to his immediate superior, John Mitchell, who was then

Attorney General and was now one of the defendants in the criminal prosecution. Or perhaps Rehnquist concluded that the public appearance of his impartiality would be undermined in view of these personal associations, even though he was confident of his own disinterestedness. Any one of these reasons would have been sufficient to justify Rehnquist's withdrawal from the case; but the latter reason might also have applied to other members of the Court who, on this ground, could and perhaps should also have withdrawn.

Doubts about other Justices' impartiality in the *Nixon Tapes* case emerge most clearly from this further speculation about the reasons for Rehnquist's recusal. Notwithstanding the Court's unanimous rejection of Nixon's position, his objections to the judicial subpoena had considerable plausibility. The core of Nixon's argument was that the Constitution empowered the President to execute the laws, command the armed forces, and conduct the foreign relations of the United States, that he must consult with aides to carry out these powers, that public disclosures regarding these consultations could impair his governance capacity, and that other branches were not constitutionally empowered (and as a practical matter did not have adequate access to the range of information necessary) to weigh the possible advantages and the risks involved in such disclosures. In later cases, Justice Rehnquist was notably sympathetic to claims for litigative immunity for the President and other executive branch officials based on the general constitutional separation of powers norm.[14] Perhaps, then, Rehnquist withdrew from the *Nixon Tapes* case because he had concluded that the President should have prevailed as a matter of constitutional law, but he was unwilling to express this position, particularly as a lone dissent, in view of his past direct affiliation with the Nixon Administration and the public suspicion that might arise regarding his partiality.

This speculation does not impugn Rehnquist's motives; his withdrawal in such circumstances would be an appropriate expression of the maxim that justice must not only be done but be seen done. This speculation does, however, suggest that other Justices might have been similarly constrained from reaching a conclusion favorable to President Nixon's constitutional claim. Though Rehnquist had the most direct official connection to Nixon's Administration, three others—Chief Justice Burger and Justices Blackmun and Powell—owed their judicial appointments to this President. Perhaps none of them found any merit in his constitutional claim; but none of these Justices could have supported Nixon's claim in this case without raising some public suspicion that self-serving partisan motives were involved in their decision. (President Ford's later exercise of his constitutional authority to pardon Nixon was indeed widely viewed as a reciprocated payment for Nixon's appointment of Ford as Vice President.) The fact that the three Nixon appointees in the *Nixon Tapes* case voted against the President's position does not dispel suspicions of bias; they may have been improperly biased against him in order to make a public demonstration of their distance from him.

Self-serving partisan motives may have been more obviously and more powerfully tempting for members of Congress considering Nixon's impeachment than for the Justices in the *Nixon Tapes* case. But even if impartial judgment were less likely to prevail in the congressional deliberations, this is not an adequate reason for favoring judicial intervention in the impeachment process. Paradoxically, the greater likelihood of partisan bias in the Congress was a strong, and perhaps even the strongest, reason that the Court should have postponed its disposition of the parallel case.

The core issue both in the *Tapes* case and the impeachment proceedings was whether President Nixon himself had violated constitutional limits on self-serving partisanship. In the *Tapes* case, the Court concluded that Nixon's motives for withholding the tapes were not based on any concern "to protect military, diplomatic, or sensitive national security secrets" and that he offered no justification except for a "broad, undifferentiated claim of public interest in the confidentiality of [his] conversations."[15] Though the Court did not say so directly, the context of the case overwhelmingly implied that Nixon was not motivated by any "public interest" but only by his personal interest in withholding disclosure of the tapes. But the Court did not openly acknowledge its suspicions of him;* and it did not admit—perhaps was so self-

---

*If there were no other basis for suspicion, Nixon's status as an unindicted co-conspirator in the criminal proceeding was itself enough. The Court acknowledged this status at the outset of its opinion, when it noted the President's

righteous that it did not even perceive—that there were any grounds for suspicions of self-dealing among its own membership.

In the impeachment proceedings, all of the charges against Nixon could be distilled into this one accusation: that he had violated his constitutional "trust as President" by his relentless, unconstrained pursuit of personal political advantage. His efforts to conceal his re-election committee's role in the burglary of the Democratic Party headquarters in the Watergate building during the 1972 presidential campaign, his use of confidential tax information against a political "enemies list," his authorization of a covert investigative unit in the White House which conducted electronic surveillance against political opponents and specifically carried out a burglary to obtain psychiatric records that might disparage one such opponent, and even his refusal to disclose the tape-recordings so that the Congress could determine whether he had committed impeachable offenses—all of these charges in the three impeachment articles approved by the House Committee were variations on the same theme. The theme was that Nixon subordinated all values to one overriding goal, to secure self-aggrandizing advantage by using whatever weapons he could extract from the Executive Branch arsenal, and that this ruthless pursuit violated basic constitutional norms against partisan use of official authority. In effect, Nixon was accused of waging unrestrained warfare against his political adversaries.

Nixon's basic defense was that everybody did this, that past presidents had used their authority for partisan advantage, and that the congressional impeachment proceedings against him were themselves nothing but political warfare waged by the Democratic majorities in both Houses. This charge, as already noted, had

---

argument that the grand jury exceeded its authority in this citation and then refused to address this argument on the ground that it was "unnecessary to resolution of the question" of Nixon's confidentiality claim. 418 U.S. at 687 n.2. Nixon had argued that the Congress alone, in impeachment proceedings, was authorized to determine whether a President had committed "high crimes or misdemeanors," and the grand jury's citation trespassed on this exclusive congressional preserve. If the Court had forthrightly recognized that its implicit disparagement of Nixon's motives for demanding confidentiality was akin to, even if not directly influenced by, the grand jury's suspicions, then it would also have been obliged to address its authority to impinge on congressional prerogatives.

greater public salience than any similar accusation that might be directed at the Supreme Court. Unlike the Court, however, congressional leaders were sensitive to these charges and strove to defend themselves. The initial defense was conducted by the House Judiciary Committee in its extended public sessions watched by a large national television audience. In the gravity of their deliberations, the cogency of their arguments, and, perhaps most importantly, the bipartisan composition of the majority voting for the impeachment articles, the Committee members appeared remarkably successful in acquitting themselves as statesmen rather than politicians.*

Much more was at stake in this acquittal than the personal reputation of these members of Congress. At this moment, the entire structure of national electoral government appeared stained: not only by the suspicions about President Nixon's conduct but by the revelations about his White House aides that had emerged in the hearings of the Senate Select Committee on Watergate, by the criminal trial then pending against his first attorney general, John Mitchell, and his principal assistants, H. R. Haldeman and John Ehrlichman, by the resignation and pending criminal investigation of his second attorney general, Richard Kleindiest, by the resignation of his third attorney general, Elliot Richardson, to protest Nixon's interference with the prosecutorial investigation of his aides, and by the resignation in 1973 of Vice President Spiro Agnew after he had been criminally indicted for accepting bribes and pleaded no contest to a related charge of income tax evasion. If Nixon's defense were true, if everyone used public office as he and his associates allegedly had done, then nothing was left of the old ideal that elected officials should transcend self-

---

*The first impeachment article, focusing on the conspiracy to conceal the Watergate burglary, was approved by a 27–11 Committee vote—supported by all of the Democratic and six Republican members. *New York Times*, July 28, 1974, p. 34, cols. 2–3. The second article, dealing more generally with abuse of presidential authority, was approved by 28–10—supported by all of the Democratic and seven Republican members. Id., July 30, 1974, p. 19, cols. 3–4. The third article, regarding the Committee subpoena for the tape recordings, was approved by the narrowest margin, 21–17, with only two Republicans supporting and two Democrats opposed. Id., July 31, 1974, p. 14, cols. 3–4.

aggrandizing partisanship to pursue an encompassing public interest.

The House Judiciary Committee attempted, however, to reassert this ideal. In the impeachment articles themselves, the Committee insisted that the constitutional proscription of "high crimes and misdemeanors" comprised more than criminally indictable offenses and referred instead to a conception of public trusteeship. In the conduct of its deliberations, the Committee worked assiduously to avoid the actuality or the appearance of partisan divisions. In its decision to subpoena the Nixon tapes on its own authority, without recourse to judicial enforcement proceedings, the Committee signified that it would not admit that the judiciary had become the sole institutional repository of impartial judgment.

The Committee's conduct was the first act; whether a majority of the entire House would vote to impeach the President, whether two-thirds of the Senate would vote to convict, and whether in their deliberations both Houses would visibly transcend partisanship remained to be seen. The Supreme Court's intervention in the *Nixon Tapes* case aborted this redemptive process. Its intervention did not resolve but merely suppressed doubts about the commitment of elected officials to self-aggrandizing norms and practices.

At an earlier time in our national history, elected officials had confronted this same issue and resolved it themselves. Compared to the events surrounding the Nixon impeachment, there may have been a deeper sense of crisis following the election of 1800 and the tie vote between Jefferson and Burr—a sense that the continued existence of the Union was in doubt as a result of the intense partisan divisions between the Republicans and Federalists. Imagine, however, that this electoral tie had been broken not by the votes of the opposition Federalist Party but by a judicial order requiring the election of Jefferson. The just result would have been achieved. But this achievement would not have produced the same confidence in the character of the Union, in its rectitude and its stability, that in fact was engendered among both elected officials and the electorate.

The same issue was at stake in 1974 as in 1801: whether political adversaries acknowledged any limits in their subjugative efforts for partisan advantage. This issue, moreover, was posed not only by the immediate questions in dispute (whether Nixon would be impeached for his partisan conduct, whether the Federalist lame-duck majority in the House would secure partisan advantage in resolving the electoral college tie between Jefferson and Burr) but more fundamentally by the polarized racial and social conflicts of the day. The basic definition of the American polity was in doubt— whether it was fundamentally unified by mutual acknowledg-ment of the equal status of all participants, no matter how sharply opposed in factional interests.

By its heedless intervention in the 1974 impeachment process, the Supreme Court aborted the deliberative processes that in 1801 had reaffirmed the equality principle and its protective respect for political minorities. With ironic appropriateness, moreover, the Court in the *Nixon Tapes* case unnecessarily invoked its own supremacy, though it could have justified its decision to uphold the subpoenas based solely on a claim for institutional equality. The Court refuted Nixon's claim for an absolute, judicially un-reviewable executive privilege against compelled disclosure by quoting *Marbury v. Madison*, "that 'it is emphatically the province and duty of the judicial department to say what the law is.'"[16] Elsewhere in its opinion, however, the Court relied on the regu-lations issued by the Attorney General (explicitly reciting "assur-ances given by the President to the Attorney General") specifying that the special prosecutor would have authority to obtain judicial review "to contest the invocation of executive privilege in the process of seeking evidence."[17] The Court cited these regulations to establish that the dispute between the President and the special prosecutor was justiciable, even though ordinarily the President is constitutionally authorized to resolve disputes arising wholly within the executive branch. The Court could have further con-cluded that the regulations necessarily implied not only that the dispute was judicially resolvable but that the judiciary was entitled and obliged to consult its own independent understanding of constitutional values in making this resolution.

This entitlement and obligation does not follow from a premise of judicial supremacy but from a principle of institutional equality. The President, through his Attorney General's regulations, had invoked judicial authority in establishing the special prosecutor's office; having invoked its assistance to implement his purposes, the President was obliged to defer to the judiciary's conception of its purposes. Unless the judiciary thus asserted its independence of, and equal status with, the President, it would have subordinated itself to his construction not only of his own authority but of judicial authority as well. This is the same principle of institutional equality that was available to Chief Justice Marshall to invalidate the congressional act in *Marbury:* that Congress had invoked the Court's jurisdiction and that the Court was entitled and obliged to rely on its own interpretation of the Constitution in assessing the validity of that invocation.

The Court was not content, however, merely to assert its equality with other governance institutions. By its intervention in the impeachment process, moreover, the Court aborted the possibility that the Congress might reassert the primacy of the equality principle in our governance by condemning President Nixon for his subjugative impositions against political opponents. In its rush to impose order on a fractious conflict, the Court acted on and thereby ratified the subjugative ethos; and because it did not understand this implication, the Court unwittingly abetted Nixon's conspiracy against democratic principle.

The Death Penalty

To kill an adversary is the ultimate act of subjugation. To kill in self-defense, however, transforms this act into a protection against subjugation, an assertion of equal status against an adversary who, by his murderous aggression, has violated his obligation to respect others' equality. If the equality principle is the fundamental norm of American democracy, this is the framework by which the administration of the death penalty might be justified.

Approaching the issue through this framework quickly raises two problems for the death penalty, however. First is the problem of deterrence: if the self-defense imperative is the only permissible justification, then some preventive impact from its administration must be shown. This impact might be general rather than specific: that is, the death penalty might deter others from subjugative aggressions even if its prospect had failed to deter the actual aggressor and, moreover, was not necessary to prevent him specifically from future depredations. This general deterrence would be sufficient justification because the aggressor's act not only violated his victim's right to equal status but endangered the entire social regime of equality insofar as others might be emboldened by his actions toward their own subjugative impositions; thus the aggressor, because of exemplary implications that follow from his act, may be treated as a negative example for others.

The social exemplification implicit in the death penalty points, however, to the second problem for measuring it against the equality principle. If the principle requires that adversaries treat one another as equals, then a wrongful subjugative aggression by one must be met by a constrained defensive response—a response that visibly demands nothing more than a restoration of equal status; otherwise, the responder will himself defeat rather than vindicate the equality principle as a future basis for social relations both specifically with the offender and generally with all others. This is the lesson Lincoln tried to teach in his defense of the Union— a lesson in democratic principle that endures even though the destructive violence of the Civil War defeated his pedagogic efforts at the time.

The lesson endures, moreover, in more than Lincoln's pedagogy. It is at the core of the Civil War amendments to the Constitution which sought to vindicate the equality principle with more rigor and generality than the original document had achieved, not only by abolishing slavery but by extending national protection to everyone against state deprivations of equal status. In determining the constitutional status of the death penalty, therefore, more is at stake than the Eighth Amendment prohibition against "cruel and unusual punishment"; and though the acknowledgment in the Fifth Amendment that a person may "be deprived of life" with "due process of law" may have indicated, as originalists contend, that the contemporaneous drafting of the Eighth Amendment meant to validate the death penalty, the intensified commitment to equality in the Civil War amendments raised new doubts. The framers of the Fourteenth Amendment said nothing about the death penalty; but they had said virtually nothing about racial segregation in public schools or elsewhere, and they did repeatedly say that the substantive reach of their amendment was not fixed but open to expansive future interpretations.

Identifying the central problem in the death penalty as its

sweeping subjugative implication and its consequent inconsistency with the equality principle does not, however, make the case for judicial invalidation any stronger than the case against race segregation in *Brown*. If judges want to vindicate the equality principle against its derogations in capital punishment, they cannot achieve this goal by their own subjugative imposition, any more than the principle could be legitimately accomplished in *Brown* by judicial fiat. As a practical matter, however, judicial abolition of the death penalty readily could be implemented, and it is therefore easy to ignore the constraint on judicial impositions required by the equality principle, a lesson that could not be missed in *Brown*.

Though it was battered and bloodied by 1968, the spirit of *Brown*—in its conjunction of boldly enunciated principle and cautious, indirect implemention—still survived in the Supreme Court's first confrontation with the legitimacy of the death penalty.[18] The Court previously had addressed a few, limited questions about the administration of capital punishment;[19] but its first systemic challenge came in *Witherspoon v. Illinois,* where the Court invalidated a widely used state test for selecting jurors in capital cases that excluded those with "conscientious scruples against capital punishment."[20] The Court's opinion, by Justice Stewart, read almost like an abolitionist tract; in one footnote especially, the Court quoted with apparent approval this observation by a prominent abolitionist: "The division [between supporters and opponents of capital punishment] is not between rich and poor, highbrow and lowbrow, Christians and atheists: it is between those who have charity and those who have not. . . . The test of one's humanity is whether one is able to accept this fact—not as lip service, but with the shuddering recognition of a kinship: here but for the grace of God, drop I."[21] The Court's insistence on including such charitable humanists on all capital juries was, however, tempered by its specification that states might exclude jurors who were "invariably" or "automatically" opposed to the death penalty.[22] The uncertain scope of this qualification led Justice Black, in dissent, to observe that the Court had "decided nothing of substance, but has merely indulged itself in a semantic exercise"[23]—at the same time that abolitionist lawyers read the decision as meaning "that no one would ever be executed again."[24]

Witherspoon was thus vintage Warren Court: a boldly stated normative vision coupled with a modest enforcement regime of uncertain efficacy. The Court seemed to suggest that in a humane regime the death penalty would have no place; but whether this result would follow from its ruling, whether anything of practical significance would follow, remained obscure—dependent on future implementation by juries and interpretation by the states and lower federal courts. In effect, by invalidating the jury selection process in virtually every death penalty state, *Witherspoon* unsettled long-standing practice, seized public attention, and provoked public dispute but only hinted at the Court's predilection without definitively resolving the issue.

But *Witherspoon* was not *Brown*, 1968 was not 1954, the center could not hold. One harbinger of the difference appeared in this portion of the Court's explication in *Witherspoon*: "In a nation less than half of whose people believe in the death penalty, a jury composed exclusively of such [believers] cannot speak for the community. Culled of all who harbor doubts about the wisdom of capital punishment—of all who would be reluctant to pronounce the extreme penalty—such a jury can speak only for a distinct and dwindling minority."[25] In a footnote appended to this statement the Court cited a 1966 opinion poll indicating both a close division between supporters and opponents of the death penalty—42% favoring, 47% opposed, and 11% undecided—and an erosion of support since 1960 when the tally had been 51% favoring, 36% opposed, and 13% undecided.[26] In fact these polling results in 1966 were the modern high point of American public opposition to capital punishment. Almost immediately after *Witherspoon*, national polls began to register a shift in public opinion belying the Court's observation that death penalty supporters were "a distinct and dwindling minority": from 51% support in a 1969 Gallup poll to 56% support in a 1971 National Opinion Research Center survey to 59% support in a 1973 Harris survey.[27] By 1985 a Gallup poll found that 72% of the American public supported capital punishment, the highest percentage in the history of modern polling.[28] Whatever this shift in public attitude meant regarding support for specific implementation of executions, the polling data exemplified the change from the optimistic ethos underlying *Brown* that the country was basically unified to the darker vision of subjugative politics arising from irremediably polarized conflicts.[29] Capital punishment in its symbolic signification is civil war writ small.

Witherspoon was not the beginning of a *Brown*-like process of judicial challenge to the maintenance of the death penalty; this process faltered after 1968, however, not so much because the Justices read the new polling data but more fundamentally because they absorbed and reflected the changed ethos regarding the prevalence and permissibility of social subjugation. Ordinary political changes did occur after 1968—the election of Richard Nixon, his appointment of four Justices in quick succession, the Republican lock on the presidency into the 1990s for all but Jimmy Carter's brief, luckless interregnum; and these ordinary changes did affect the Court's disposition toward the death penalty. The deeper significance of the shift in social ethos is revealed, however, not by the increasing isolation of the liberal faction on the Court but by the fact that the subjugative ethos was effectively embraced by the liberal Justices themselves, by Brennan and Marshall as the surviving remnant of the Warren Court majority, in their outspoken judicial abolitionism and their conspicuous rejection of the cautiously incremental deliberative conception of the judicial process epitomized in *Brown*. As in the consensus between the Court majority and the dissenters (including Holmes) in *Lochner*, the fundamental lesson was in the shared conviction within the Court that polarized social conflict was inevitable and that subjugation of some by others was acceptable. The dispute among the Justices regarding judicial activism versus restraint, in the death penalty cases as in *Lochner*, was merely a disagreement about whether social subjugation should be practiced by a legislative or judicial majority.

If the jurisprudence of *Brown* had guided the Court's actions regarding capital punishment, the next step after the challenge to jury selection criteria should have come in *McGautha v. California*.[30] In that case, decided in 1971, two questions were presented: whether states were obliged to specify substantive standards to regulate jury discretion in capital cases, and whether states must separate the fact-finding processes for the guilt and penalty phases of capital trials instead of permitting jury deliberation on both issues at the same time, which was the prevalent practice. Following the *Brown* model, the Court should have answered both questions affirmatively, thus requiring states extensively to reconstitute both the substantive and procedural elements of their death penalty statutes and—not incidentally—by invalidating all extant statutes, forcing state legislatures to consider whether they wished to reinstitute them on any terms. In *McGautha*, however, the Court took a different path.

Justice John Marshall Harlan wrote the Court's opinion, holding that drafting substantive standards to control jury discretion in the "infinite variety of cases and facets to each case" was a task "beyond present human ability,"[31] and that bifurcated guilt and penalty procedures would serve no constitutionally important goal.[32] Justice Brennan, joined by Marshall and Douglas, dissented and was especially critical of the majority's refusal to require substantive standards for jury deliberations; the Court, he said, thereby validated "an unguided, unbridled, unreviewable exercise of naked power."[33] Harsh as this charge might seem against the genteel patrician who had written the Court's opinion, Harlan—like Oliver Wendell Holmes—had a genteel disinclination to join battle, even defensively, and a patrician detachment from social combat that had led him to the most consistent refusal among members of the Warren Court to invoke judicial authority against popular majorities.[34] Harlan had been out of step with the liberal optimism of the post-World War II years; in 1971, however, when he spoke for the Court's refusal in *McGautha* to take the next step following *Witherspoon* to force social re-examination of the death penalty, Harlan signaled the beginning of a resurgent judicial approbation of the subjugative ethos.

Harlan left the Court a few months after *McGautha* was decided; and the following year, in *Furman v. Georgia*,[35] the Court abruptly seemed to reverse direction, not only invalidating every extant death penalty statute but apparently ruling that no imaginable statute could satisfy the Eighth Amendment stricture against "cruel and unusual punishment." This sudden reversal was surprising not only to the litigants but to the Justices themselves. Justice Brennan later recounted that he had been convinced that *McGautha* "was not just a lost skirmish, but rather the end of any hope that the Court would hold capital punishment to be unconstitutional" and that, during the summer after the Court had granted certiorari in *Furman* to address the Eighth Amendment issue, he had prepared an opinion which he "fully expected would be a lone dissent."[36] In previous conference deliberations even Justices Marshall and Douglas, who had joined Brennan's dissent in *McGautha,* had maintained that the death penalty did not irremediably violate constitutional norms; but as Brennan reported, suddenly "there were signs that I might not be alone."[37]

Ironically, however, Brennan remained alone in *Furman* even though four other members of the Court voted with him to hold that the death penalty statutes of the United States and forty states violated the Eighth Amendment. There was no opinion for the Court in *Furman,* but even more than this, there was no plurality opinion; each of the five Justices voting to invalidate the statutes spoke for himself alone, none joined another's opinion. In its entire history the Court had never been so fragmented—certainly not since John Marshall had instituted the practice of consolidating the Justices' views in a single opinion. And even before that, when the Justices regularly issued seriatim opinions, it was easier to discern common viewpoints than in the potpourri of separate opinions in *Furman.* In its sheer bulk, *Furman* testified to the unprecedented fractionation of the Court: the five "majority" opinions and the four dissents sprawled over 232 pages of the United States Reports, the longest single spread in the Court's history.[38]

To drastically shorten a very long story, Justices Brennan and Marshall each concluded that imposition of the death penalty invariably was cruel and unusual punishment; Justice Stewart found that the death penalty was imposed on "a capriciously selected random handful" as if "struck by lightning"[39]; Justice White similarly, though separately, found "no meaningful basis for distinguishing" between those "few cases" where death was imposed "from the many" other death-eligible cases[40]; and though Justice Douglas clearly voted to invalidate the statutes, his reasoning was opaque as was his careless custom. Douglas did, however, suggest that a majority opinion might have been written in *Furman*: if the three dissenters in *McGautha* (Brennan, Marshall, and Douglas) had held to their position that states must devise substantive standards "to prevent . . . random or arbitrary choice" by capital juries, their views would be consistent with the *Furman* opinions of Stewart and White. But, Douglas concluded, no majority opinion was possible in *Furman* because "we are now imprisoned in the *McGautha* holding."[41]

This is an inexplicable lament. Even though *McGautha* had been decided only a year earlier, the Court could have overruled it. Such quick reversal would have been unusual; but as Justice Brandeis once observed, in constitutional doctrine it is often less important that a rule be settled than that it be settled correctly.[42] In *Furman,* however, the majority Justices were obviously not inclined to re-examine this new precedent even to search for some common ground on which to build a coherently unified position among them.

The Justices' failure to pursue this goal may have come in part from their chaotic recent experience in the death penalty cases. Justice Brennan's subsequent account is suggestive on this score: the Court had previously considered the *McGautha* questions regarding substantive jury standards and bifurcated procedures in 1969 when Warren and Fortas still sat on the Court; but the clear majority at that time to impose these requirements suddenly vanished with Warren's retirement and Fortas's forced resignation. If the 1969 majority for this result had held, however, capital punishment would not have vanished from the Court's docket; rather, a prolonged litigative process would have been launched, with state legislatures drafting various standards and procedures and the Court deciding which, if any, met its approval. Whatever doubts may have appeared about the institutional continuity of the Court in 1969 when the *McGautha* questions were almost answered differently or even in 1971 when the three dissenters held to their original views, by the time *Furman* was decided in 1972, the sudden appearance of the four Nixon appointees and the prospect of more to come strongly suggested that the Court would not sustain the repeated, intense scrutiny of capital punishment that would be required for serious attention to the substantive and procedural questions posed in *McGautha.*

Prolonged interaction between the Court and state legislatures, evaluating the ways that substantive standards and procedures might ameliorate concerns about the rationality and fairness of the administration of the death penalty, could progressively lead to the ultimate question of the constitutional validity of any imaginable regime of capital punishment. This increasingly focused attention would occur, however, only if a Court majority was consistently and seriously engaged in the enterprise. Justice Brennan himself later acknowledged, though in a back-handed way, that it would have been "premature [to] address" in *McGautha* the ultimate "meaning of 'cruel and unusual punishments' in the context of the death penalty." According to Brennan's account, however, when the Court immediately thereafter granted certiorari in *Furman,* "we were clearly itching toward resolving" that ultimate question.[43] If "itch" is what Brennan meant to say, then he and the other members of the *Furman* majority should have scratched it and resumed the slow, deliberative scrutiny of capital punishment that *Witherspoon* and the *McGautha* dissent had promised. If Brennan meant "inch" but said "itch" regarding the Court's progression toward resolving the ultimate question in *Furman,* then this typographical parapraxis, like unconscious slips generally, ironically illuminates the Court's error in abandoning the careful pursuit of common ground, its guilt in turning away from the interactive law-generative jurisprudence of *Brown.*

Furman, in any event, was not the Court's last words on the death penalty. Legislatures in thirty-five states responded by enacting new statutes even though the hodgepodge of majority opinions in *Furman* appeared inhospitable to this course. In 1976 the Court reviewed a representative sample of these enactments and again reversed course, though again the Justices were so fragmented in their views that no clear direction emerged. Two Justices, Brennan and Marshall, voted to invalidate all the statutes on the basis of their *Furman* views that capital punishment intrinsically violated the Eighth Amendment; four Justices, three of the *Furman* dissenters and White, voted to uphold all of the new statutes; and the remaining three, Stewart, Powell (who had dissented in *Furman*), and Stevens (who had succeeded Douglas), voted to overturn the statutes that eliminated jury discretion by requiring capital punishment for specific defined offenses but to uphold those statutes that set out general standards purporting to guide jury discretion and bifurcated the fact-finding procedures for guilt and penalty phases of the capital trial.[44]

This agglomerated voting on the Court meant that the Stewart-Powell-Stevens plurality prevailed, which in effect reversed *McGautha.* Justice Stewart said as much, though he feebly attempted to distinguish that decision: "*McGautha*'s assumption that it is not possible to devise standards to guide and regularize jury sentencing in capital cases has been undermined by subsequent experience."[45] The only available subsequent experience, however, was the action of thirty-five state legislatures—action which did not prove that adequate standards could be devised but only that there was resistance to *Furman.* In this aspect of Stewart's plurality opinion, his embrace of the *McGautha* dissent seemed more cosmetic, more a face-saving gesture to cover judicial retreat from *Furman,* than a whole-hearted commitment to evaluate the fairness, predictability, and rationality of the institution of capital punishment.

Further evidence of this disingenuous motive appeared in Stewart's account of the significance of the legislative response: "Developments during the four years since *Furman* have undercut substantially the assumptions upon which [the abolitionist] argument rested. Despite the continuing debate . . . it is now evident that a large proportion of American society continues to regard [capital punishment] as an appropriate and necessary criminal sanction."[46] Stewart had cited public opinion polls in his *Witherspoon* opinion for the proposition that death penalty proponents were "a distinct and dwindling minority," but he now acknowledged error and virtually announced that it would be wrong for him, as a judge, to resist this newly vocal public attitude:

> Capital punishment is an expression of society's moral outrage at particularly offensive conduct. This function may be unappealing to many, but it is essential in an ordered society that asks its citizens to rely on legal processes rather than self-help to vindicate their wrongs. . . . When people begin to believe that organized society is unwilling or unable to impose upon criminal offenders the punishment they "deserve," then there are sown the seeds of anarchy—of self-help, vigilante justice, and lynch law.[47]

This was the same fear of anarchy and vigilantism that Stewart had seen in Martin Luther King's disregard for the judicial injunction in *Walker v. Birmingham;* as in that case, Stewart appeared to draw the conclusion that anarchy was imminent and could be avoided only if the Court gave unquestioning validation and demanded unquestioning obedience to constituted authority, whether state legislatures or judicial officers. Though Stewart was prepared to invalidate the mandatory death penalty laws in the 1976 cases, this was only because he expected that juries would be tempted by these draconian strictures to engage in the nullification versions of "self-help [and] vigilante justice," whereas acknowledged discretion would appease this anarchic impulse.[48]

In the 1976 cases, Justice Marshall also admitted that the legislative reaction to *Furman* had "a significant bearing on a realistic assessment of the moral acceptability of the death penalty to the American people."[49] But he drew a different conclusion from Stewart's regarding the proper judicial response to this public expression. For Marshall, this legislative reaction was a tragic confirmation of the fear he had expressed in *Furman*, "that the American people have been so hardened, so embittered that they want to take the life of one who performs even the basest criminal act knowing that the execution is nothing more than bloodlust." Marshall had resisted this harsh judgment in *Furman*: "This has not been my experience with my fellow citizens."[50] But, unlike Stewart's panglossian reading of the legislative reaction to *Furman*, for Marshall it was his optimistic assessment of his fellow citizens that was "undermined by [this] subsequent experience." Marshall's response was to intensify his commitment to the abolitionist conclusion he had reached in *Furman* on the ground that a judicially-construed Constitution "is our insulation from our baser selves."[51] In these different responses to the massive legislative resistance to *Furman*, Marshall in effect invoked the *Cooper v. Aaron* text of adamant judicial supremacy while Stewart relied on its subtext that without effective enforcement power, such as President Eisenhower had provided in sending federal troops to Little Rock, the Court would be helpless. Between these poles of judicial omnipotence and impotence, however, there was a middle path available—the path that the Court had taken in *Brown II* but rejected for capital punishment in *McGautha*.

For some time after the 1976 rulings, the Court's death penalty cases did seem intent on recapturing the ground that had been lost in *McGautha*. Notwithstanding the ambiguity of Stewart's 1976 plurality opinions, during the succeeding seven years the Court's decisions did appear to scrutinize intensely and cabin incrementally the application of the penalty. Of the fifteen capital cases fully argued and decided on the merits by the Court until 1982, all but one reversed or vacated the death sentence as imposed.[52] The Court rulings during this time narrowed the application of the penalty to murderers, explicitly excluding rapists,[53] and to those who intended to kill, excluding co-felons vicariously liable for murder.[54] The Court also struck down any limitations on the kinds of mitigating evidence a defendant might present to the sentencer[55] and overturned restrictions on the defendant's access to all information before the sentencer.[56] None of these decisions required radical change in the basic workings of the state capital punishment regimes; but these kinds of small-gauge rulings, if sustained over a long period, could have had considerable impact as an aspirational model for detailed federal court review of state appellate proceedings and as an indication of an intention to sustain ameliorative pressure generally in the administration of the death penalty.

It was, however, patent on the face of the Court's rulings that this incremental process would not be sustained. This was because, unlike the segregation cases for the fifteen years on either side of *Brown*, there was no unified commitment among the Justices to this course; indeed, there was not even majority agreement on the Court during this seven-year interim. The repeated challenges in these death penalty cases came, for the most part, as a result of plurality voting in a fractionated Court: two Justices (Brennan, Marshall) opposed in all circumstances, three (Stewart, Powell, Stevens) opposed only to remedy specific procedural or substantive flaws and four (Burger, White, Blackmun, Rehnquist) usually voting to affirm death sentences (though only Rehnquist always favored this result).[57] These decisions thus were not based on a coherent shared strategy but rested only on a narrow, fragile convergence of disparate views within the Court.

In 1981 two events shattered this coalition: Stewart resigned and was replaced by Sandra Day O'Connor, who joined the bloc regularly affirming death sentences, and Powell at this same time apparently lost his taste for the scrutinizing enterprise. Since that time a Court majority consistently has turned away from any examination of the administration of capital punishment and, moreover, has progressively dismantled the instruments that previously had been used for such scrutiny. In 1983 the Court restricted federal habeas corpus review by encouraging summary dismissals[58] and permitted state appellate courts to disregard even admitted flaws in death penalty cases by expansively construing the "harmless error" rule.[59] In 1984 the Court relieved state appellate courts of any responsibility for assessing, by a so-called "proportionality review," the comparability of any particular death sentence to others imposed in that state.[60] In 1985 the Court expanded the substantive criteria by which states might exclude conscientiously opposed jurors from capital cases and restricted the scope of federal habeas review of such exclusions.[61]

This newly solidified Court majority thus resolutely looked away from evidence of serious problems in the administration of the death penalty, evidence that had steadily mounted during the preceding decade as a result of the scrutiny prompted even by the erratic course of the Court's decisions. There was, first of all, the gross evidence from the sheer volume of death sentence reversals in state and lower federal courts. According to a 1982 study, from sixty to seventy-five percent of defendants sentenced to death obtained reversals at some point in their appeals; this is roughly ten times the reversal rate in federal criminal appeals and almost one hundred times the reversal rate for general felony convictions in California.[62] In the face of heavy odds against these defendants—they were all convicted murderers, resources for their appellate representation were stretched thin, and public forbearance for them as individuals and for the review process itself was frayed—this is a staggering number of reversals. In themselves, these numbers suggest the existence of substantial systemic flaws in the institution of capital punishment, as well as persistent misgivings among large numbers of judges charged with immediate oversight authority, notwithstanding their likely general conservatism.

Beyond this general, if opaque, ground for concern, the post-*Furman* scrutiny yielded two quite specific, powerfully documented flaws with pervasive systemic implications. The first reached the Court in 1986: a finding by a federal district judge, based on meticulously examined evidence and affirmed by the Eighth Circuit Court of Appeals, that state processes for culling jurors adamantly opposed to the death penalty resulted in juries in capital cases disproportionately biased toward finding defendants guilty, as compared with the proclivity of noncapital juries. Long ago in *Witherspoon,* the Court had indicated concern about the possibility of guilt bias in capital jurors but stated that the supporting data were "too tentative and fragmentary" to demonstrate this intrinsic unfairness.[63] But when the data finally had been marshaled in 1986, the Court dismissed them, airily maintaining that states were no more required to convene impartial juries than to include equal representation of "Democrats and Republicans, young persons and old persons . . . and so on."[64] This assertion blatantly ignored the real issue, which was not whether a state was obliged to find unbiased jurors but whether it was forbidden purposefully to create bias, just as it would be prohibited from intentionally excluding Democrats or old people from juries. Justice Marshall, in dissent, aptly charged the Court majority with "a glib nonchalance ill-suited to the gravity of the issue presented and the power of respondent's claims."[65]

If the Court had responded honestly to the jury-bias problem, a remedy was possible, though cumbersome, by more rigorously bifurcating capital cases with separate juries for the guilt and penalty phases. In 1987, however, the Court was presented with a second grave systemic flaw that could not so readily be remedied. In *McCleskey v. Kemp,*[66] extensive and rigorously analyzed data demonstrated, as powerfully as any such empirical demonstration could be made, that racial bias existed in the administration of the death penalty.

From its beginnings in the mid-60s, the charge of racism was often in the foreground and always in the background of the campaign to abolish the death penalty. Justice Marshall in *Furman* partly rested his case for abolition on this ground.[67] At that time, however, it was plausible to argue, as Justice Stewart did, that "racial discrimination ha[d] not been proved" by suitably rigorous statistical criteria.[68] Following *Furman,* state prosecutors had strong motives to eliminate any appearance of racism by adjusting their administrative practices to assure that black faces were not disproportionately evident in the capital docks or on death rows, and the racial composition of these places did indeed change.[69]

The possibility that racism persisted, though in less blatant form, in the administration of capital punishment was pursued, however, by sophisticated, intensive empirical investigation supported by generous foundation funding[70]—all galvanized by the apparent promise in the welter of *Furman* opinions that rigorously demonstrated racism would seal the case against capital punishment. These studies found continued racial bias in the disproportionate rate of death sentences imposed for murders where whites were victims and where blacks killed whites as compared to same-race murders or where whites killed blacks.[71]

In 1983 this new evidence was presented in a Georgia federal district court on behalf of Warren McCleskey, a black man sentenced to death for killing a white policeman. The investigators testified that, using a complex regression analysis, six percent of all death sentences imposed could only be explained by the racial characteristics of the murderers and victims.[72] Moreover, if the most clearly heinous crimes were excluded—involving, for example, torture or rape or multiple victims—so that only the so-called "mid-range" of killings were considered, then the disparity explicable only by this race difference rose to twenty percent.[73] The district judge, however, found various statistical flaws in the investigations and held that no race discrimination was even prima facie proven.[74]

In 1987 the Supreme Court, with four Justices dissenting, took a different tack to dismiss this challenge. The Court assumed the statistical validity of the study but nonetheless ruled that, even so, it "can only demonstrate a *risk* that the factor of race entered into some capital sentencing decisions."[75] The study, that is, did not and could not show that racial bias actually occurred in the imposition of any death sentence, much less in any particular death sentence. From this perspective, the only evidence that the Court was apparently prepared to credit was the traditionally garnered testimony from and about the specific participants in specific cases—that is, official actors' admissions of race bias under adversarial examination or others' direct testimony regarding the actors' individual motives. This position recalls the means by which litigative complaints about discrimination in voting registration were rendered ineffective by many federal courts in the days before the Voting Rights Act of 1965, by insisting on laborious case-by-case proof of racial bias and correspondingly refusing to give presumptive evidentiary weight to the wholesale absence of blacks from voter rolls.[76]

If the Court had given credence to the evidence of persistent racial bias in capital punishment, a practicable remedy would have been difficult to imagine. Perhaps a scheme of mandatory death sentences based solely on the character of the offense would work; this, however, had already been held unconstitutional in the 1976 cases. Alternatively, sentencing discretion might be retained with racial bias reliably expunged if the decision were vested wholly in a judge, with juries removed from any sentencing role. This, however, would invalidate the statutory regimes in all but three death penalty states.[77] Whatever the possible remedy, by acknowledging the existence of racism in the current administration of capital punishment, the Court would be obliged to launch a wholesale restructuring of the system almost as extensive as the task initiated by *Furman*.

Such an admission would, moreover, raise doubts not only about the death penalty but about the legitimacy of social relations generally in American society. The magnitude of these suspicions is suggested by one empirical finding that the Court also disregarded in the 1986 conviction-prone jury case: not only are death-qualified jurors biased against criminal defendants, but these jurors are more likely to be white (and male) and, correspondingly, blacks (and women) are more likely to oppose the death penalty and thus to be excluded from capital juries.[78] When we add this finding to the evidence gathered in *McCleskey* that capital juries impose the death penalty with disproportionate frequency on blacks who murder whites and infrequently in response to any murders of blacks, a grim portrait of the American criminal justice system emerges. This portrait shows that law enforcement in the most serious and publicly visible cases is entrusted predominantly to groups of white men who value whites' lives more than blacks', and thus they take special vengeance on blacks who murder whites and are much less concerned about the murder of blacks. Indeed, its low valuation of blacks coupled with its special arousal when blacks murder whites suggests a law enforcement regime particularly concerned with the containment of blacks, a regime that acts as if our society were gripped by fears about, and prepared to take preemptive strikes against, an explosion of race warfare.

In this aspect, the institution of capital punishment is a magnified reflection of the most visible cleavage of polarized political conflict in contemporary America. It is also an atavistic expression of the central polarized conflict in the nineteenth century, the Civil War, in this sense: that, notwithstanding the existence of death penalty statutes in thirty-seven states today, executions have occurred almost exclusively in the slave states that had seceded from the Union (of the 121 executions carried out between 1968 and 1990, 110 took place in the former Confederate states).[79] This intertwining of racial conflict specifically and civil warfare generally points to the one precedent that most closely supports the death penalty decisions of the current Supreme Court majority: *Plessy v. Ferguson.* Not only has the contemporary Court in *McCleskey* ignored the animus of state-sponsored racial oppression behind the statutory pretense of equality, as the Fuller Court had done in *Plessy;* the contemporary Court in its death penalty jurisprudence has also endorsed, as its predecessors did in *Plessy,* the savage premises of subjugative social warfare as a model for political relations generally.

It is difficult to avoid the conclusion that capital punishment, no matter what its provocation or its mode of administration, is so grossly subjugative that it violates the core values of the democratic equality principle. If this is true, then the Court is obliged to press this lesson relentlessly until other institutions have learned it well enough to abandon the enterprise. This pedagogic effort may, of course, ultimately fail; but if the effort has been sustained for a considerable time, and still the states have not met the Court's persistent demand that the death penalty must be constrained within defensive dimensions to render it consistent with the equality principle, then the time might finally come when the Court has adequately demonstrated that this enterprise cannot conceivably succeed. Then—only then—the Court on its own authority might justifiably abolish capital punishment. Even then, this independent action would be as much a failure as a triumph of constitutional principle: a failure that the Court had struggled mightily to avert and, in light of this struggle, a necessary and justifiable failure. But a failure nonetheless: as Lincoln's waging of the Civil War was a necessary and justifiable failure.

In its death penalty jurisprudence, however, the Court has not failed in this way. Its failures have been unjustifiable—from those Justices who abruptly and self-righteously embraced abolitionism to the current majority who have turned away from any effort to learn or to teach whether the death penalty can be administered in true consistency with constitutional principle.

Abortion

In 1973 the Supreme Court decided *Roe v. Wade*,[80] invalidating all abortion prohibitions then extant in forty-six states. In its sweeping invocation of judicial authority, *Roe* had much in common with *Furman v. Georgia*. The two decisions occurred at virtually the same time: *Furman*, which overturned all state death-penalty statutes, had been decided the previous year (and *Roe* had originally been argued a month before *Furman* but was then postponed for reargument). The most striking similarity between these two decisions was their suddenness: both appeared unexpectedly—to paraphrase Justice Stewart in *Furman*—like bolts of lightning. No one who had watched the progression of the Court's prior deliberations on the death penalty, neither the most ardent litigative advocates nor the Justices themselves, had predicted the abolitionist eruption in *Furman*. And immediately before *Roe*, there was no indication that the Court was even concerned about abortion, much less that it was ready to invalidate all statutory restrictions.

Roe was only the second decision involving abortion in the Court's entire history. The first had been in 1971, just two years earlier. In *United States v. Vuitch*,[81] the Court held that a District of Columbia statute prohibiting abortions except those "necessary for the preservation of the mother's life or health" was constitutionally valid, overruling a district court finding that the statute was void for vagueness. When enacting the statute in 1901, Congress had not defined "health," and the district court accordingly had found that it was unclear whether the term referred to mental as well as physical health or, even if restricted to physical health, what measure of gravity was demanded and, moreover, whether the prosecutor or the indicted physician bore the burden of demonstrating the mother's need for the abortion. Notwithstanding these multiple uncertainties on the face of this criminal statute, Justice Black stated in his opinion for the Court, "But of course statutes should be construed whenever possible so as to uphold their constitutionality";[82] and Black proceeded to find the necessary clarification in two 1970 lower court decisions construing the statute to include "mental health" and to place the burden of proof on the prosecutor.

Black's application of the hornbook aphorism was, however, misplaced: statutes should not always be construed to uphold their constitutionality. This was the Court's error in *McGautha* when it ignored the complaint that substantive standards in death penalty statutes were in effect unconstitutionally vague; and it multiply compounded this error in *Vuitch*. By dismissing this opportunity to force states to reconsider abortion statutes in light of contemporary concerns among the Justices and elsewhere, the Court left itself the stark option of either closing off its further inquiry into the fairness of those statutes or taking sweeping revisionist authority into its own hands. *Vuitch* thus set the stage for *Roe v. Wade* as *McGautha* had done for *Furman*'s abrupt, puzzling lurch toward an apparent end to the death penalty.

Vuitch and *McGautha* were similar, moreover, in an even narrower sense. The cases were decided just twelve days apart in 1971 by virtually the same constellation of Justices: Black, Harlan, White, Burger, and Blackmun in both cases dismissing the complaints against contrary positions from Douglas, Brennan, and Marshall, with Stewart alone voting to overturn the abortion statute in *Vuitch* while joining the majority in *McGautha*. Justice Blackmun, however, almost immediately thereafter appeared ready to recant his vote in *Vuitch*. In the next year, after the Court heard argument in *Roe*, Blackmun prepared a draft opinion overturning the Texas abortion statute on the ground that it was void for vagueness.[83] Justice White responded with a draft dissent aptly observing that the Texas statute, which forbade abortion except solely to preserve the mother's life, was much clearer than the statute upheld in *Vuitch*;[84] and Justice Brennan wrote Blackmun that he "would prefer a disposition of the core constitutional question," which Douglas quickly seconded.[85] Blackmun hesitated, however, and withdrew his opinion, agreeing with four others that, because the Court was composed of only seven Justices when *Roe* was argued, since Black and Harlan had resigned and Powell and Rehnquist had not yet been confirmed as their successors, *Roe* should be reargued in the following term.

Thus *Roe* came to center stage: with the litigants arguing only for wholesale abolition of abortion statutes on privacy grounds, with at least two Justices "itching" (to use Brennan's subsequent description of the Court's mood in *Furman*) toward final resolution of this constitutional issue, and with the Court apparently viewing itself as "imprisoned" (to use Douglas's word for the impact of *McGautha* on *Furman*) by its recent holding in *Vuitch* against considering less drastic grounds for invalidity. Here, however, the Court's treatment of abortion took a different turn from its death-penalty jurisprudence. Although, as in *Furman*, the Court's action was utterly unexpected in the breadth of its denunciation of state legislation, the Court was not fractionated in *Roe v. Wade;* only two Justices, White and Rehnquist, dissented, while seven joined the majority opinion written by Justice Blackmun invalidating all state abortion statutes and erecting in their place a tripartite scheme permitting states significantly to restrict abortions only in the final trimester of pregnancy.[86]

In the immediate aftermath of *Furman*, popular opinion (as measured by polls and by the conduct of elected representatives) unexpectedly united against the discordant Court majority, reversing almost overnight the previous trend toward popular disapproval and official disuse of capital punishment.[87] The unified Court in *Roe* inspired virtually the opposite (though at the time, equally unexpected) result. The country became, also almost overnight, sharply polarized regarding abortion, and for almost two decades since *Roe* the abortion question has remained the most heated single issue in our politics. Though there had been "pro-life" advocates active in prior legislative consideration of abortion reform, they had been much less numerous and less rigidly adamant in their opposition; *Roe* gave birth to the "right-to-life" movement.[88] Perhaps the most stunning indication of its inflammatory impact was the immediately subsequent decision by the American hierarchy of the Catholic Church to launch an active, publicly visible political campaign against abortion; in the legislative struggles before *Roe*, the Church hierarchy had been discreet and somewhat reticent in its public opposition, but *Roe* stripped away this restraint.[89] The Court's pronouncement of a univocal secular morality enshrined in the Constitution was perceived by Church leaders as a frontal challenge to their claim for moral authority—a challenge with stature and clarity that had not appeared in the murky processes of earlier legislative abortion reform, and accordingly, a challenge that they must actively combat.

From the perspective of the historically dominant constitutional jurisprudence—from *McCulloch* to *Dred Scott* to *Lochner* and beyond—this social disorder fomented by *Roe* is in itself an anathema and a reversal of the proper Court role. If this is a justifiable basis for criticizing the Court, however, then *Brown v. Board of Education* is equally vulnerable to condemnation. *Brown* was as much responsible for elevating black civil rights into the central issue of national political controversy for at least fifteen years thereafter, as *Roe* has been for abortion in the succeeding two decades. And from my perspective, the justification for *Brown v. Board of Education* was its provocation of openly waged public dissension about the southern segregation regime, thus breaking the silence that had been imposed on blacks and whites in the region and the nation by the oppressive practices of that regime.

But on this ground *Brown* sharply differed from *Roe*. In 1973, when *Roe* was decided, the abortion issue had not been excluded from dispute either among the general public or in majoritarian institutions specifically. By the mid-1960s the restrictive abortion statutes enacted around the end of the nineteenth century increasingly had been criticized by impeccably respectable medical and legal professional groups, and this criticism led to legislative enactments by nineteen states between 1967 and 1973 liberalizing the permissible grounds for abortion.* At this same time, moreover, a more radical critique of abortion statutes appeared from within the newly galvanized feminist movement, a claim that liberalization was an inadequate response to the oppressive impact of all abortion restrictions and that a woman's free choice alone should govern continuation or termination of pregnancy.[90] In 1970 four states—New York, Washington, Hawaii, and Alaska—

---

*These enactments essentially followed the model promulgated by the American Law Institute in 1962 permitting abortion when two physicians certified that the pregnancy would gravely impair the woman's physical or mental health, the child would be born with a serious mental or physical defect, or the pregnancy resulted from rape or incest. See Mary Ann Glendon, *Abortion and Divorce in Western Law* 48, 173 n.197 (Cambridge: Harvard Univ. Press, 1987).

responded to this critique essentially by removing all restrictions on abortions during the first trimester of pregnancy. Unlike the other "free-choice" states, moreover, the New York statute was especially notable in omitting any prior residency requirement, thus effectively undermining other states' restrictive regimes for women who could afford the trip. The free-choice statutes were controversial: the New York act, for example, was adopted by a margin of only one vote in the state assembly; and in 1972 the legislature reversed itself to reinstate substantial restrictions, but this measure was vetoed by the governor. And though Washington voters approved their legislature's action in a 1970 referendum, voters in Michigan and North Dakota defeated free-choice proposals in 1972.[91]

When the Court decided *Roe* in 1973, it was thus not clear whether the recently enacted state laws signified the beginning of a national trend toward abolishing all abortion restrictions or even whether in the so-called liberalized states, the new enactments would significantly increase access to abortion for anyone.[92] This much was apparent, however: the abortion issue was openly, avidly controverted in a substantial number of public forums, and unlike the regimen extant as recently as 1967, it was no longer clear who was winning the battle.

Unlike race segregation, no Supreme Court intervention had been required to accomplish this result. If the Court had found the abortion statutes void for vagueness in *Vuitch*, or as Blackmun originally proposed in *Roe*, the lines of conflict would have opened immediately in all of the remaining restrictive states and perhaps even been forcibly reopened in the liberalized jurisdictions; but, even so, no clear ultimate winner would have been designated. As *Roe v. Wade* was actually decided in 1973, however, the Court awarded total victory to one troop among the combatants.

On this score too, *Brown* differed from *Roe*. *Brown* not only opened a controversy that had been conclusively resolved or ignored in other institutions but also, unlike *Roe*, *Brown* imposed no alternative, definitive resolution. *Brown*, that is, removed the victor's laurels from one of the combatants but did not bestow them on another. Moreover, *Brown* did not simply leave the combatants to their own devices for waging future conflict; the Court assiduously tried to design its intervention, through the remand device in *Brown II*, to promote institutional interactions among the combatants that might lead them toward future "consultation and accommodation"—thus tracing the Madisonian constitutional template. *Roe* was utterly inattentive to this goal; and, as it turned out, hostile toward it.

Roe's disregard for the interactions, past or future, of the contending parties was evident even in the formulation of constitutional doctrine that the Court invoked to overturn the abortion laws. The "right of privacy" served for *Roe*—just as "liberty" served for *Lochner,* just as "property" served for *Dred Scott,* just as the rigid boundaries separating state and federal "sovereignties" served for John Marshall in *McCulloch*—to insulate one party from any obligation even to acknowledge the other's complaint. Buttressed by the Court's authority, the owner of the right to "privacy" or "liberty" or "property" or "sovereignty" might say to all the world, "You may believe that my conduct harms you profoundly, but I am entitled to ignore your distress." In *Roe*—as in *Lochner, Dred Scott,* and *McCulloch*—the Court fashioned a preemptive weapon that could end the possibility of dispute even before a contentious conversation might begin.

There was, however, an alternative doctrinal formulation available in *Roe,* as in *Lochner, Dred Scott,* and *McCulloch,* that more aptly expressed the competing grievances of the combatants and, at the same time, offered them the possibility of a shared vocabulary for mutually acknowledging these grievances. The doctrinal formulation was "constitutional equality." Women subject to abortion restrictions could invoke equality in many ways: that the state constrained their freedom to engage in sexual relations unequally as compared with men; that the state's compulsory conscription of their bodies to accomplish its fetal-protective purposes was more intrusive, more extensive in its impact (in numbers of women affected and in continuous repetition), and less subject to practical constraint in operation than any compulsory conscription of men for wartime service (with its socially acknowledged self-sacrificial heroism and its political inhibition to time-limited moments of national emergency); that abortion restrictions are part of a long-standing general pattern of state-imposed devaluation and oppression of women in family and political relations. These various ways of identifying the inequalities inherent in laws restricting abortion establish a sufficient predicate for their constitutional invalidation, just as the subjugative implications of race segregation laws justified their invalidation in *Brown,* notwithstanding the absence of any explicit attention to segregation as such by the framers of the Fourteenth Amendment. But the invocation of equality to invalidate these laws points with the same gesture to the underlying significance of the equality ideal in our constitutional scheme generally: that this ideal prohibits all subjugative impositions conceived as such by those who impose or by those who are subject to them. To invoke the equality guarantee is, if honestly acknowledged, to encounter this paradox at the core of our constitutional scheme: that no coercion is legitimate, even if it is sometimes unavoidable. Thus for abortion restrictions—as for race segregation in *Brown,* for economic relations in *Lochner,* for territorial slavery in *Dred Scott,* for federal–state relations in *McCulloch*—a Court may properly overturn the coercive imposition because of its inherent inequality, but only to impose an equal status of stalemate on the adversaries, not to end the conflict, not to seize victory from one and award it to the other.

From this perspective, one plausible outcome of the abortion controversy would be the result toward which the legislative reforms were inclined after 1967 but before *Roe*'s artless intervention. If some states adopted free-choice statutes, some enacted liberalized laws (some of which, like California before *Roe,* might work in practice as free-choice), and some retained the old restrictions, no one could say that the moral issue had been conclusively resolved for or against freely chosen abortions, for or against protecting fetal life; yet women residing in restrictive states but determined to obtain abortions could find access somewhere. Two specific barriers might obstruct this possibility: residency restrictions in liberalized or free-choice states and the financial costs of travel. Both of these barriers could be addressed, however, by a Court intent on facilitating accommodation and viewing the abortion issue through the doctrinal lens of constitutional equality. Residency restrictions for abortion denies equal access for nonresidents to the "privileges and immunities" that the state provides to its own; even if the Court chooses not to resuscitate the specific protective language against such discrimination in Article IV, section 2, as reiterated in section 1 of the Fourteenth Amendment, there is ample doctrinal basis for finding that such restrictions violate the constitutional "right to travel" embedded in "the concept of our Federal Union."[93] As to financial burdens, the Court could readily rule that a state which permits access to abortion and which provides welfare benefits for medical care generally cannot engage in the gender-based discrimination implicit in withholding financial assistance for abortion specifically;[94] and if the state provides such welfare benefits to its residents, then it must provide them equally to those who travel from other states.[95]

By these invocations of the equality ideal, the Court could have facilitated the rough, tacit accommodation on the abortion dispute that the pluralist workings of the federal system might have yielded. In one sense, this result would have been untidy, even incoherent: there would be no clear resolution of the moral and constitutional principles governing abortion. But in a more fundamental sense, like the apparent incoherence of the Court's unanimous opinion in *Brown II*, this result truly would have embodied the principle of equality in our constitutional scheme.[96]

Unlike *Brown* for race segregation, the Court was not required to intervene in the abortion dispute in order to vindicate the equality ideal. Unlike *Lochner* for economic regulation or *Dred Scott* for territorial slavery restrictions, the Court was not prohibited by the equality ideal from intervening in the abortion dispute. The equality ideal permitted, though it did not require, judicial intervention in the abortion dispute in 1973, when the Court decided *Roe*: but it did not justify *Roe v. Wade*.

This does not mean, however, that twenty years later the Court would be justified in simply overruling *Roe*.[97] I have tried here to imagine how our world might have looked if a different decision had been made in 1973; but the Justices are not equally free to indulge their imagination. The Court is not entitled to ignore the consequences that have followed from its past actions, even if those actions were erroneous. The Court drew the lines of polarized confrontation and cannot now walk away from this subjugative conflict that it, more than any other institution, was instrumental in defining as such.

Perhaps the Court, even at this late date in its entanglement, might work to redefine the abortion controversy away from this subjugative ethos and toward the equality ideal. Its interventions, however, have been so maladroit and the politics of the controversy are now consequently so inflamed that it is difficult to conceive how the Court might reliably undo the damage it has done. I suspect, however, that the current Court will not see the difficulty. It has not held back from endorsing subjugative politics in its death-penalty jurisprudence. In its involvement in the Nixon impeachment proceedings, the Court obstructed the possibility that the country at large would repudiate this ethos; and there is no evidence for a different inclination on the Court today. *Roe* may soon be reversed; and in its place, so far as this Court is concerned, force will rule.

10

A Constitutional Resolution

THE COURT has not succeeded in suppressing conflict over abortion or the death penalty during the past two decades, any more than it previously had achieved this goal regarding territorial slavery in *Dred Scott* or labor relations in *Lochner*. In all of these matters, the impact of the Court's interventions was provocation rather than pacification. But these inflammatory results were not intended by, and were even antithetical to the wishes of, the Justices who ruled in all of these matters. The Court did not succeed—and could not succeed—in suppressing conflict because of the Madisonian cast of our constitutional structure, because of the competitive, overlapping, and interdependent powers vested among our governance institutions. The Court's chronic conceit, that its constitutional command should be the last word on fundamentally disputed issues, thus recurrently stumbles over the order implicitly established by the Constitution itself.

In the abortion and death penalty cases, in *Dred Scott* and *Lochner*, the Justices themselves understood this institutional reality. But they saw it as a necessity, not as a virtue. They saw it as a regrettable problem to be overcome by bombastic demands for absolute obedience, not as a happy opportunity for encouraging and guiding future conflict among the contending factions involved in the litigation. In these cases, as throughout most of the Court's history, the Justices saw themselves trapped by the formal structure of Madison's scheme, but they were inattentive or even hostile toward the spirit behind it. This spirit alone, however, can give life to the contested constitutional values of equality, liberty, and justice. When the Justices grudgingly observe the forms but struggle against their implications, they destroy those values.

This destruction arises from the conventional format of litigation itself. When the Court declares that one party is right and the other is wrong, that one party has won and the other has lost, this pronouncement itself tends to eclipse the obligation of mutual respect that each party owes to the other. Armed with this definitive proclamation, the winning party is encouraged to see itself as justifiably dismissive of the losers' claims. This even occurs, paradoxically enough, when the Court has properly identified the wrongdoing in the case as one party's refusal to give equal respect to the other (as we saw in *Brown v. Board of Education*). The winning litigant will not inevitably ignore the loser's claim for equal respect; but this disrespect is likely unless the Court itself works self-consciously against it (as we also saw in *Brown v. Board of Education*).

This assiduous attention to the claims of the wrongdoer, this insistence that his oppressive disrespect should not be met by reciprocal inflictions, may seem a hard discipline to impose on the wrongfully injured party. This imposition clearly cuts against understandable retaliatory impulses—toward the vicious white supremacists in *Brown,* or toward murderers in death penalty cases, for example. And it is possible, as Justice Stewart observed in upholding the re-enacted death penalty statutes, that unless the law approves such retaliation, then anarchic forces of "self-help, vigilante justice, and lynch law" will be unleashed. It is, however, equally likely that the original wrongdoer, stung but unrepentant from his defeat, will himself resort to these lawless inflictions in order to restore the antebellum status quo. Our history more powerfully testifies to this likelihood: The American model of vigilante justice and lynch law is the Ku Klux Klan riding to avenge the humiliation of southern slaveholders defeated in the Civil War.

Whatever gratification Northerners may have taken from their subjugating triumph over the white South, the freed slaves and their descendants paid a terrifying price for this conquest. Perhaps no remedy for the evil of slavery was possible without the vast conflagration of the Civil War; and perhaps, therefore, the century-long retaliatory inflictions against the freed slaves were also an unavoidable cost of the emancipatory process. None of us today, however—whether black or white, Northerner or Southerner—is yet free from this recriminatory cycle.

This cycle still holds in the explosively bitter resentment of so many American blacks today. Their rage, I believe, is only indirectly linked to the nineteenth-century injustices of slave status; it has a more immediate source in the humiliations and terror vindictively imposed on them in this century by southern whites (tolerated and abetted by northern whites). Vengeful resentment may have faded among southern whites today because their Civil War defeat is no longer a lived recollection for any of them; and so they are prepared to jettison Jim Crow and its visible structure of retaliatory racial subjugation. But black resentment is fueled today by living memory among the elder generation who were directly subjected to the segregation regime and the younger generation who (like the children of Jewish Holocaust survivors) still see pervasive threats to their existence and, scorning or denying their elders' apparent past subservience, vow "Never again." And so, although the old retaliatory reasons have faded for white subjugation of blacks, whites now find new reasons to fear and to subjugate blacks: self-protection in response to blacks' expression of retaliatory vengeance toward whites.

This is, unless somehow interrupted, an escalating destructive spiral. Lincoln saw it in his second inaugural address: slavery as the moral offense, terrible warfare as "the woe due to those by whom the offense came," and the possibility that God has willed this misery to "continue until all the wealth piled by the bondsman's two hundred and fifty years of unrequited toil shall be sunk, and until every drop of blood drawn with the lash shall be paid by another drawn with the sword." This judgment has not yet run its course.

The dangers are not limited, moreover, to American cities or to relations between blacks and whites. The polarized hostility of race relations, ominous in its own terms, threatens to spread across the face of all political relations. Just as we saw in the Jacksonian era, when the subjugative premises of the black–white and red–white relationships came increasingly to characterize white–white interactions, so the same antagonistic trend is visible today in the stylized Manichaean politics that regards all social conflict as a confrontation between good and evil. This is the politics that sees no shades of gray but only a clash of moral absolutes in the abortion controversy. This is the politics that, on the far Right, sees the AIDS epidemic as a justified damnation for moral turpitude and, on the far Left, sees it as a genocidal policy purposefully inflicted by the Moral Majority on gays, drug users, and blacks.

The core characteristic of this Manichaean politics—whether in matters of race or morality—is unrelenting hostility among political opponents. Because these adversaries are unwilling to acknowledge even the possibility of common ground, they cannot imagine a relationship based on mutual respect. And thus, no matter who prevails in this raw conflict, the equality principle—the constitutive element of democratic life—is defeated.

Supreme Court Justices cannot themselves arrest this progression. But they, like all others responsible for the governance of this country, should see the dangers from its uninterrupted course and take whatever ameliorative action is available to them. In practical terms, the Justices have quite limited remedial capacity. As a matter of constitutional principle, however, they are obliged to act. The outcome of these hostilities cannot legitimately rest on majority rule; judicial deference to majoritarianism in the context of polarized politics is inconsistent with the original aspirations of the founders—an aspiration that contemporary originalists of Robert Bork's persuasion have ignored.

The Justices would also misconstrue the equality principle if they conceived their task in the limited way identified by John Hart Ely, the most prominent contemporary adherent of the process school. Ely does acknowledge that majoritarian political processes are insufficient when the majority views the minority with relentless hostility (through the polarized lens of a "we/they" characterization, as he puts it). Nonetheless, Ely imagines that such polarizations are exceptional in American history or contemporary political life. Consistent with this excessively narrow conception, Ely posits that judges should decide for themselves whether a losing minority is a scorned, unequal "they" in a "we/they" relationship, rather than deferring to the subjective perception of the losers themselves. Thus, for example, using seemingly objective criteria for identifying the "discrete and insular minorities" denominated by *Carolene Products* footnote four, Ely insists that women subjected to restrictive abortion laws are not oppressed enough to warrant any protective judicial intervention in this polarized dispute.[1]

Ely's cramped definitional effort to limit the proper subjects for judicial solicitude ultimately arises from his vastly overambitious view of the proper role for judges in protecting these political losers. Relying on the conventional conception of judicial supremacy, Ely believes that judges are obliged to convert these footnote-four losers into winners; and because he regards most substantive constitutional principles as lacking determinative content, he tries to guard against the prospect of judicial autocracy by restricting court interventions to procedural matters.

The interpretationists, such as Ronald Dworkin, are undeterred by the prospect of judicial autocracy because they insist that constitutional principles do have definitive content. But they fail to understand that when a judge imposes this definition—no matter how powerfully reasoned, rooted in historic precedent, or boldly proclaimed—this herculean imposition itself works against realization of the core constitutional principle of equality. This is not simply because the judge's imposition necessarily treats both the winning and losing litigants as subordinates. It is also because the judge's definitive intervention effectively transforms the relationship between the parties into a radically different association. They now effectively relate to one another through the judge; indeed, their primary relationship is with the judge rather than with one another.

The abortion controversy provides a vivid illustration of this transformation and its harmful consequences. By pronouncing its definitive resolution in *Roe v. Wade,* the Court redirected the attention of abortion reform (pro-choice) advocates away from their partly successful campaign for legislative change. Before their Court victory, pro-choice advocates had understood that their legislative lobbying would fail unless they somehow enlisted the active sympathy of men and women who had not previously seen any direct personal stake or ideological commitment for themselves in the controversy. In soliciting support among these people, the pro-choice advocates in one sense were seeking recruits for their battle against their already-sworn right-to-life adversaries. In another—and more important—sense, however, the reformers' quest for added allies changed the character of their own enterprise. In this quest, they were required to broaden the basis for their support: in particular, beyond women who were intensely committed because they had already been driven to obtain illegal abortions to others who had not confronted the possibility of this need for themselves and also to men and women without the prospect of direct personal involvement who might nonetheless see connections with their own claims for privacy and personal autonomy in other contexts.

At this same time, abortion opponents already committed by religious conviction or direct personal experience would also be forced to seek out more broadly based support for their position if they hoped to counter the pro-choice legislative lobbying and popular mobilization efforts. The very process by which the intensely committed advocates on each side sought allies would itself increasingly focus on more general social values at stake in the controversy. Each of the factional adherents, moreover, would be motivated to temper the hard edges of their original commitment in order to attract broader support. And as this tempering occurred, the opposed factions themselves might discover some common meeting ground that had not previously appeared on either side.

The directly competing efforts to enlist broad public and legislative support would thus implement Madison's prescription in *Federalist* 10 for replacing narrow factionalism with an encompassing articulation of public values in an enlarged commonwealth. This was the process that did take place, arduously and tumultuously, between the cautiously provocative, self-effacing actions of the Supreme Court in *Brown v. Board of Education* in 1954 and 1955 and congressional passage of the Civil Rights Acts of 1964, 1965, and 1968.

But *Roe v. Wade* derailed this process for the abortion controversy. The Court's intervention drastically narrowed the participants' perspectives and truncated their educative efforts. The pro-choice winners got their majority support among the Justices and saw little need to look further. The losers did turn to legislative lobbying; but for all the passionate opposition to abortion that erupted after *Roe*, many legislators who responded to these lobbying efforts had insufficient motivation to acknowledge moral or practical urgency in their actions. The public debate was more like shadow-boxing than a seriously engaged encounter because the Justices stood figuratively and literally just outside the legislative chambers ready to impose their own resolution on the debates. In a diametric reversal of the course of the social deliberation that followed *Brown,* fifteen years or so after the Court's decision in *Roe v. Wade* the crucial audience for the rival factions' appeals had been reduced to one person: Justice Sandra Day O'Connor, the swing vote regarding *Roe* on the reconstituted Reagan Court.

If the Court had refused to intervene in the abortion controversy in 1973, the opposing factions might nonetheless have failed to arrive at a mutually respectful result. If the Court had intervened more adroitly, as I have urged in the preceding chapters for all such polarized conflicts, the combatants still might not have come to resolutions that adequately honored the equality principle. But if these hostilities persisted, even over generations' time, and if the Court remained properly concerned about safeguarding democratic precepts, the Court's goal should never change: it should repeatedly intervene in these conflicts to assure that no combatant conclusively prevails over the other. As Louis Brandeis put it, speaking of labor conflicts, "Neither [adversary] should feel that he stands in the power—at the mercy—of the other."

No doctrinal formulas, no mechanistic rules, adequately capture this judicial enterprise. There are, however, a wide array of techniques for deciding cases that are available for judges in pursuing this enterprise, techniques that can be used when judges have understood this as their proper function. In *The Least Dangerous Branch,* Alexander Bickel identified some of these techniques and extolled them in the same spirit—though not with the same explicit conception of democratic principle—that I have tried to formulate here. Thus, for example, in discussing the constitutional doctrine that criminal statutes might be held "void for vagueness," Bickel commended the doctrine as serving the primary function that "when the Court finds a statute unduly vague, it withholds adjudication of the substantive decision in order to set in motion the process of legislative decision."[2] If Justice Blackmun's initial impulse to invoke the vagueness doctrine had held in *Roe v. Wade,* the Court's intervention would have had exactly this effect; neither side could have claimed conclusive victory, but the Court would have lifted the oppression experienced by one and the advantage enjoyed by the other from the existing force of nineteenth-century restrictions. The Court would thus have brought the parties to a status of equality and then withdrawn from the conflict—at least for the moment—so that the contending parties would be effectively led to engage one another rather than look to the Court for victory.

Bickel similarly identified another constitutional doctrine that could be called into service if the combatants had resolved the abortion controversy as had in fact occurred in California. A 1967 California statute on its face provided more liberal grounds for abortion than previous state law but nonetheless still forced women to request permission from a physicians' panel and specifically excluded fetal deformity as a justification for abortion. The authorized grounds—risk to the mother's "mental or physical health"—were, however, quite indistinct; and in actual practice, during the five years before *Roe* was decided, virtually every application for an abortion was granted. By 1971 the number of abortions performed had increased by some 2000 percent compared with the number performed under the prior law. One of every three pregnancies in California was ended by a legal abortion, a frequency that did not rise even after *Roe* abolished all first-trimester legal restrictions. In practical terms, therefore, the 1967 law was a stunning victory for pro-choice forces; as one scholar has concluded, "By 1971, women in California had abortions because they wanted them, not because physicians agreed that they could have them."[3] Nonetheless, because the law on its face required women to seek permission and because fetal deformity was explicitly excluded as a justification, the pro-life forces could also maintain that their claims had not been wholly overridden; indeed, the bill was signed into law by Ronald Reagan, then governor of California (and later, of course, the official leader of right-to-life opposition to *Roe*). In the 1967 California act, then, neither combatant won or lost conclusively.

Either side might, of course, have have gone to court to seek total victory through a constitutional challenge to the 1967 act. The pro-choice forces could argue, plausibly enough, that the restrictions violated a woman's privacy right, and the pro-life forces could argue, also plausibly (before *Roe* dismissed this claim), that any legal abortion transgressed the fetus's right to equal protection of the laws. If the Court viewed the 1967 California act as I see it—a victory for the equality principle, even a model that other states might follow in devising a mutually respectful accommodation between the combatants—the best response to any constitutional challenge to the act, brought by either side, would be the constitutional doctrine of "ripeness." As Bickel explained and extolled this doctrine, it holds that even when litigants can frame a constitutional claim in convincingly logical, abstract terms, nonetheless the specific factual context of the claim can render it unsuitable, "un-ripe," for adjudication.

Bickel discussed one example of the application of this ripeness doctrine that has special relevance to the 1967 California abortion statute: the Court's dismissal in 1961 of a constitutional challenge to a nineteenth-century Connecticut statute forbidding use of contraceptives. Though this statute on its face violated sexual privacy claims, it had never been enforced against any individual user and had been invoked only once in 1940 against provision of contraceptive devices by birth-control clinics. Bickel's description of the social significance of this "disused but unrepealed Connecticut statute" applies equally to the 1967 California abortion law. This was an "exquisite balance [with] deterrent effect on unusually . . . tender consciences, plus a moral posture of the statute book agreeable to a certain portion of the population, plus the unhindered practice of birth control by another and in some measure also by the same portion."[4] In the Connecticut case, the Court ruled that the question was "nonjusticiable" and thus refused to adjudicate the constitutional challenge.[5] As Bickel noted, this result "neither strikes the statute off the books nor activates it; the effect is precisely that the Court does not tinker with the equilibrium."

A more recent Supreme Court abortion case illustrates the virtues of another technique, also identified by Bickel, for leading the contending parties away from a binding judicial resolution of their dispute. In a 1991 decision, the Court upheld an administrative regulation forbidding federally funded clinics not only from providing abortion services but even from mentioning the possibility of abortion to any patient.[6] Clinic physicians maintained that this regulation imposed wrongful abortion restrictions on their patients and speech restrictions on them. The Court rejected these constitutional claims, but it should have ruled instead that the legislative act did not authorize the administrative regulation with sufficient clarity. This ruling would have withheld conclusive victory from either proponents or opponents of the rule and impelled both to reargue the issue on their own in Congress.[7] As Bickel observed generally, in cases raising "particularly sensitive and intractable issues," the Court should demand "not merely that there be a deliberate exertion of legislative authority, but that it be explicit and thus more acutely responsible than usual." Indeed, he noted, even "in the teeth of a reasonably well-determined legislative purpose" that cuts against sensitive constitutional concerns, the Court can justifiably ask the legislature to address "certain consequences of the statute once more and more explicitly." The goal of this stringent and sometimes even artificially narrow statutory construction is, he said, "to embark upon a colloquy with the legislature."[8]

In the 1991 abortion case, however, the Court was not interested in conversation with anyone. Its apparent goal was to award conclusive victory and thereby impose an end to the abortion controversy—one might say, to impose silence even beyond the relationship between doctor and patient, as the disputed regulation provided. This was judicial autocracy on the Right as surely as *Roe v. Wade* was unjustified autocracy on the Left of the political spectrum.

If the Court is interested in pursuing conversation—as it should be—rather than imposing silence on a wide range of constitutional issues, an additional, especially useful technique appeared in the Court's jurisprudence in the mid-1970s, too late for Bickel's attention. This was the invention, in the context of gender-discrimination cases, of the so-called "middle-tier" constitutional scrutiny. Conventional equal-protection doctrine had posited two levels for judicial review of legislation: "minimal scrutiny" of all acts to assure that they were not patently irrational, and "strict scrutiny" for those statutes that clearly intersect an explicit constitutional value (for example, a racial categorization or a restriction on speech). In practice, statutes receiving only minimal scrutiny were never invalidated, while those subjected to strict scrutiny were always invalidated. Accordingly, the two-tiered judicial review was never an opening conversational gambit from Court to legislature; it was always the final word from the Court, whether upholding or overturning a statute.

The notion of a "middle tier" of constitutional scrutiny arose from the Court's attempt in 1973 to address the constitutionality of a congressional act providing more generous financial benefits for married men than for married women in the armed services.[9] Four Justices were prepared to overturn this differentiation on the ground that statutes based on gender categorizations should be subjected to strict scrutiny. Three others refused to invoke strict scrutiny because the Equal Rights Amendment had just been approved by Congress in 1972 and was then pending for ratification before the state legislatures. These three maintained that if the ERA were ratified, then—and only then—would gender discrimination become (like race) subject to strict scrutiny. Nonetheless, these three inexplicably concurred in invalidating the financial differentiation in the challenged statute.

Three years later, a Court majority announced—somewhat like the discovery of Moliere's bourgeois gentleman that he had always been speaking prose—that their "previous cases establish that classifications by gender must serve important governmental objectives and must be substantially related to achievement of those objectives."[10] This obscure verbal formulation made only one thing clear, that the Court had invented something more than minimal but less than strict scrutiny: a "middle tier." If the Equal Rights Amendment had been subsequently ratified, this jurisprudential innovation would no doubt have disappeared; but the amendment failed, and the middle tier remained operative, at least in gender-discrimination cases. Using this new doctrine, the Court has invalidated some gender differentiations and approved others.[11]

Since 1976 some Justices have acted as if middle tier were merely a disguise for strict scrutiny, while others seem to treat it as nothing more than minimal. But a middle group on the Court has striven to give distinctive content to this new tier. Their basic inquiry is to ask whether a statutory gender differentiation reflects a stereotypical, traditional bias about inherent gender differences or whether the differentiation is based on a particularized legislative inquiry identifying factually demonstrable—even if debatable—sexual differences that are relevant to the accomplishment of explicitly specified legislative goals.[12] If these Justices find that the legislature's action was based on a thoughtless stereotype, they invalidate the statute. But it follows from the logic of this judicial disapproval that the legislature might reenact the statute if it can provide a more explicit, fact-based justification for its action, which the Court in turn will scrutinize to determine—as the middle-tier formula puts it—whether the reiterated gender classification clearly enough "serves important governmental objectives and [is] substantially related to achievement of those objectives."

The Court arrived at this middle-tier formula almost by accident. It has only been applied in gender-discrimination cases, and its various applications even in this one context are difficult to reconcile. Nonetheless, mid-level scrutiny is an important jurisprudential innovation that holds considerable promise in many different contexts. Its great virtue, from my perspective, is its conversational character: when the Court invalidates a statute on this basis, this action permits and even invites a legislative response. In effect, mid-level scrutiny reverses John Marshall's conclusion in *McCulloch v. Maryland* that judges must not "inquire into the degree of [a law's] necessity."[13] Mid-level scrutiny engages precisely in this inquiry, taking into account both the government's objectives and the means chosen by the legislature to accomplish those objectives.

Unlike strict scrutiny, which also purports to address these matters, the middle tier envisions the possibility that the Court will sometimes find the requisite necessity for the legislative act. And unlike strict scrutiny, when the Court invalidates a statute under the middle-tier test, the successful litigant has not won a conclusive victory. Her triumph is only tentative, subject to later reversal if her adversary returns to the legislative battlefield. The Court's action does, however, significantly alter the terms of this subsequent combat. By overturning the original enactment, the Court shifts the balance of advantage toward the winning litigant. Her claim has been given heightened public visibility and moral sanction. The losing litigant knows, moreover, that he cannot muster the same majority to do nothing more than re-enact the identical measure that the Court has overturned; he knows that the Court stands ready to strike down the measure again unless he can provide some more persuasive justification for it. This judicial demand for greater justification might be satisfied by more powerfully reasoned arguments than the losing litigant had advanced in the original court proceeding; it is more likely, however, that this demand could only be satisfied by a more narrowly drawn statute that accordingly would inflict a less extensive defeat than the original invalidated statute.

The Court's invalidation of the original statute would shift the legislative balance of advantage toward the winning litigant in another way as well. Legislation is always easier to block than to enact. New laws not only must run the gauntlet of the executive veto but also, in the national Senate at least, are vulnerable to defeat by a filibuster that might be waged by one legislator alone. The executive veto and the filibuster can be overcome by super-majorities; but this provides significant added protection to the party who stands to gain from legislative inaction—in this case, the litigant in whose favor the Court has invalidated the original law. Mid-level scrutiny thus accomplishes openly and easily what the Court was able to achieve in *Brown* only by indirection and some dissimulation: bestowing more nearly equal status on the adversaries rather than replacing defeat forced on one party by the legislature with defeat imposed on the other by judges.

These are the logical implications of the mid-level scrutiny doctrine. Even in the context of the gender-discrimination cases where the doctrine has been applied, these implications have not yet been fully understood.[14] But with this understanding, mid-level scrutiny is admirably suited in many different contexts as a technique—like those identified by Bickel—for promoting interchange between court and legislature. The question is, then, how a court should recognize the appropriate contexts for applying these techniques.

There is a short answer to this question: all disputes which are so polarized that one party regards the other's victory as destructive of equal status and therefore intolerably oppressive. This short answer could entail, however, a lengthy and ambitious agenda for judicial activity—at least in an era like ours when many disputes are waged in such polarized terms. Racial conflict is the most prominent example; but this conflict has become, since the 1960s, the paradigm for a wide range of political and social battles drawn along such lines as gender, sexual orientation, age, disability, and fetal status. Disfavored groups in each of these dimensions now define themselves (or, for fetuses and incommunicative disabled people, are defined by others) in the same way that blacks have done, as oppressed minorities deprived of equal respect.

For some, the very length of this listing is itself an argument against it as a guide for judicial interventions. In a 1985 opinion by Justice Byron White, for example, the Court refused to apply mid-level scrutiny on behalf of mentally retarded people on the ground that "it would be difficult to find a principled way to distinguish a variety of other groups . . . who can claim some degree of prejudice [such as] the aging, the disabled, the mentally ill, and the infirm. We are reluctant to set out on that course, and we decline to do so."[15] This reluctance is explicable, in part, as an appropriate modesty about the capacity of judges to understand complex issues of social policy affecting each of these groups, and a principled concern about the impropriety of judges dictating the resolution of such policy. If, however, the basis for judicial intervention—both the principled justification in democratic theory and the self-limiting techniques that follow from that justification—is properly understood, then this reluctance should be overcome.

Indeed, in the case itself where Justice White announced this hesitancy, the Court acted to protect retarded people precisely for the reasons and in the manner that the equality principle required. A city council had enacted a zoning ordinance barring homes for "insane, feeble-minded, alcoholic or drug-addicted" people from residential neighborhoods but permitting multiple occupancy for other groups, such as college dormitories, social fraternities, or nursing homes. The Court overturned the application of this ordinance to prohibit a group home for retarded people. Justice White stated that the record of the city council's proceeding "does not clarify how" the characteristics of retarded people were relevant to their presence in a residential community or significantly different from the characteristics of other groups, such as potentially noisy college students, who were welcomed there. "Mere negative attitudes, or fear," White stated, are impermissible grounds for exclusion unless this "vague, undifferentiated fear" can be "substantiated by factors which are properly cognizable in a zoning proceeding."[16]

The Court thus, in effect, overturned the loss inflicted on the retarded litigants but did not award conclusive victory to them; instead, the Court significantly shifted the balance of advantage to them in any subsequent legislative proceeding where specific substantiating factors might be advanced to justify their residential exclusion. Justice White characterized this judicial intervention as an application of traditional minimal scrutiny, perhaps in order to disguise its novelty and its potential for expansive application in other disputes involving retarded people and other groups equally subject to "vague, undifferentiated fear" by a hostile majority. Whatever he chose to call it, this was a model for judicial vindication of the equality principle: a particularistic, carefully limited intervention encircled by a boldly stated moral condemnation of majority disrespect toward a vulnerable minority.*

The availability of this model—which is how the mid-level scrutiny doctrine itself should be understood—provides an appropriate antidote for vague, undifferentiated judicial fears about the seemingly vast implications of interventions in polarized disputes generally. The rationale for the limited character of these interventions is not, however, to calm judicial fears; it is not, as Bickel wrongly suggested, to find some middle ground between principle and expediency. These limitations necessarily follow from the principled justification for judicial action to remedy inequalities without creating judicially imposed inequalities. The equality principle itself demands particularistic, contextually circumscribed, tentatively offered judicial interventions, as opposed to grand-style moral philosophizing in the interpretationist mode, or ag-

---

*The Court should have taken this same path in 1986 when it upheld a state statute that imposed criminal penalties on gay men for engaging in consensual sexual relations in their own homes. Bowers v. Hardwick, 478 U.S. 186 (1986). Justice White, again writing for the Court, cited the same concern he had expressed in the retardation zoning case about excessive expansions of judicial authority; but he offered no comparable understanding of or protection against the majority's irrational fear and hostility toward gay people. In this case, moreover, White ignored the availability of self-limiting techniques for judicial intervention. The Court need not have questioned the legitimacy of the state's goal generally in protecting public morality by criminalizing homosexual conduct; the Court should have asked, however, what substantiating link could be demonstrated between this avowed state goal and punishment of sexual conduct between consenting adults in the privacy of their own homes. Even more narrowly, the Court could have struck down the state statute in this case because it applied not only to homosexual relations but to all oral or anal intercourse, even for a heterosexual married couple, and thus did not adequately specify—as the middle tier formula requires—an "important governmental objective" or the "substantial relationship" between that objective and the state statute.

nostic surrender to majority will. And judges, after all, are not philosophers. They are lawyers, whose stock in trade is to distill complex disputes into manageable analytic terms and to think through, step by step, the means for reaching fair resolutions. This enterprise must be philosophically, as well as historically and psychologically, informed. Law must thus draw on these other disciplines; but it is a distinctive endeavor.

This distinct, relatively modest professional curriculum points to another feature of judicial interventions in polarized disputes that also carries self-limiting implications. The ideal embodied in the equality principle can only fully be attained when all disputants are satisfied with the outcome; anything less than unanimous consent falls short of respect for the equal status of everyone. This is the vision of unanimity that guided many of the founding fathers, including Madison, even if they acknowledged that such unanimity was not likely or even possible in practice and even if, in their computations of unanimity, they recognized only a narrow class of disputants who counted as equals. But when judges intervene in polar disputes to protect the equality principle, they can pursue a less demanding conception of unanimity. Though it is obviously preferable that all disputants be equally happy with the outcome and with one another, the equality principle remains viable if everyone is equally unhappy.

This equal status is the stalemate that Lincoln, most notably, sought in waging civil war: neither complete victory nor defeat for anyone, coupled with an acknowledgment of a continued, even though contentious, relationship. Another example of this equalized stalemate is the checkerboard pattern of abortion laws toward which the various states were moving when *Roe v. Wade* intervened in 1973. As I discussed in the preceding chapter, this pattern might have taken hold—with sharp restrictions in some states, easier access in some, and free access in others (without residency requirements and with financial assistance for indigent women)— so that every woman who wanted an abortion could travel to find one, and yet there would be no explicit, univocal national commitment to the philosophy that abortion is morally and legally correct. Accordingly, no disputant in the abortion controversy would have fully won or lost; each would be just about equally unhappy. This same stalemate characterized the dispute over territorial slavery between the white North and South in 1857 when the Supreme Court intruded in *Dred Scott,* and it was emerging in relations between organized labor and employers in 1905 when *Lochner* interfered. In all of these instances, controversy still churned, the disputants remained engaged though deeply displeased with one another, and a rough equality obtained among them. Judicial interventions did not advance the equality principle in any of these instances.

Throughout our history racial conflict has almost always stood outside any egalitarian matrix, whether of equal happiness or unhappiness. The issue at stake for one or both disputants has virtually always appeared to be total enslavement on one side or the other. Sometimes this issue has found expression in a clearly subjugative relationship, as with chattel slavery or Jim Crow. At other times—such as now—the inequality is expressed by unilateral severing of any political relationship. Thus the white South seceded from relations with the North in order to protect its domination of slaves; and whites today sever relations with blacks, by retreating into suburban enclaves, in order to deny black reparative claims for equal access to financial resources and social respect.

In this persistent polarized conflict, equally persistent judicial interventions are necessary. The Court's understanding of this necessity was recently tested in several cases where, notwithstanding the continued existence of racially separate schools, local school boards maintained that judicial desegregation orders should be dissolved. In one of these cases, the plaintiff was Linda Brown Smith, the same Linda Brown who had been an eight-year-old schoolgirl in Topeka, Kansas, in 1951 when her father brought suit on her behalf to end school segregation. As a technical matter, the Supreme Court's mandates in *Brown I* and *II* were still outstanding; no court had ever found that the Topeka Board of Education was in compliance with those mandates, and in 1979, Linda Brown Smith—now the mother of two schoolchildren in Topeka—moved to reopen the original case. The revised case citation read like a caption in a family album: Oliver Brown et al., Plaintiffs, and Charles Smith and Kimberly Smith, minor children, by their mother and next friend, Linda Brown Smith et al., Intervening Plaintiffs v. Board of Education of Topeka, Shawnee County, Kansas et al., Defendants. In other words: *Brown III*.

In *Brown III*, on behalf of her children, Linda Brown Smith alleged that changed residential patterns had led to sharply segregated neighborhoods in Topeka and that the public schools were still rigidly segregated, notwithstanding the mandate of *Brown I* and *II*. The school board argued that residential segregation was not its responsibility but was simply an expression of the private decisions by white and black families to live apart, and that the litigation should be conclusively ended because the board had discharged its constitutional responsibility. After a hearing in 1986, the district court agreed with the school board, but in 1989 the Court of Appeals reversed, ruling that the school board was required to prove that "the existence of racially identifiable schools . . . had no causal connection with the prior *de jure* segregation, and that the [board] has in fact carried out the maximum desegregation practicable."[17]

In April 1990 the school board sought Supreme Court review,[18] but the Court did not respond to the school board's petition. At the same time, however, the Court granted a hearing in a similar case from Oklahoma; and in January 1991, the Supreme Court responded equivocally. Though the Court insisted that judicial superintendence to enforce the mandate of *Brown I* was "not intended to operate in perpetuity," it nonetheless kept the litigation open by remanding the case to the district court for additional inquiry regarding the involvement of public agencies in promoting the residential patterns responsible for the persistent racial segregation in the city.[19]

But still the Court kept silent in *Brown III*. On June 27, 1991, the Court adjourned for the summer without announcing its disposition of the Topeka school board's petition. The Court had, however, decided to review yet another, similar case from Georgia, where a suburban Atlanta school board maintained that it was not responsible for the persistence of race segregation, and the Court of Appeals had disagreed.[20] The Supreme Court is thus circling cautiously around the issue raised by *Brown III* and, at the same time, assiduously avoiding direct confrontation with that case itself.

This equivocal posture has been characteristic of the Court's treatment generally of affirmative-action racial preferences in such contexts as public university admissions, public and private employment, and awards of public contracts. Some Justices have asserted that the equality principle demands the invalidation of all such racial preferences, that the Constitution requires "color-blindness," and that beneficial treatment for blacks imposes inequalities on whites as surely as the favorable status of whites in a segregated regime was a wrongful imposition on blacks. (Justice Scalia has been a particularly vocal proponent of this view.) Others have claimed that the equality principle at least permits—and in many circumstances requires—racial preferences for blacks and other disadvantaged minorities both as compensation for their long history of racial subjugation and as an instrument toward fully equal relations in the future. (Justices Brennan and Marshall, in particular, have consistently urged this position.) In its decided cases over the past two decades, the Court has remained poised between—neither rejecting nor wholly vindicating—these two opposed viewpoints.

The Court as an institution did not self-consciously chart this path for affirmative action. Unlike the Court's deliberate implementation of *Brown,* this similarly cautious course arose because the Justices were unable to resolve their own internal disagreements; they fell into make-shift coalitions of plurality opinions and separate concurrences, from which equivocal results emerged.[21] In 1989 the Court appeared to abandon its equivocation; for the first time, a Court majority ruled that racial preferences intended to benefit blacks must be judged by the same demanding standard as impositions of racial supremacy for whites.[22] The Court accordingly struck down a Richmond, Virginia, ordinance reserving thirty percent of city construction projects for minority-owned businesses. The Court's opinion, by Justice O'Connor, did not make clear, however, whether it was applying strict scrutiny in its traditional usage—by which virtually no racial distinction could ever pass muster—or whether, though avowedly "strict" in theory, it was actually applying a less demanding standard—more toward the opaque middle level at work in the gender-discrimination cases.[23] Equivocation reappeared moreover, in an immediately subsequent decision where the Court upheld a racial preference for the award of broadcasting licenses by the Federal Communications Commission.[24] The Court might thus mean that, even though racial preferences by states or cities would be strictly forbidden, federal programs would be judged more leniently. But the Court, in an opinion by Justice Brennan, did not say this. It is not yet clear exactly what the Court means to say about racial preferences. After all this time, the status of affirmative action programs is still open to controversy.

Is it now time for clear-cut judicial answers regarding affirmative action? This much is clear: conflict between blacks and whites has not ended, and race relations are at least as explosively polarized now as when *Brown* was decided in 1954. Conclusive resolution of this conflict is not possible today, except in terms that one group regards as subjugation by the other. Current disputes about affirmative action and school integration are refracted facets of this larger race conflict. Continued irresolution of the larger conflict is surely preferable to a forced, inflammatory conclusion; so too for equivocal results in these derivative matters. In 1986, at the beginning of the district court hearing in *Brown III*, Linda Brown Smith said, "I am reliving the experiences of my father."[25] *Brown III* and its related contemporary cases reiterate the trials of all of our fathers in the American experience. Those trials are not yet ended.

In our persisting racial conflicts, one proposition should, however, be clear: the political relationship between blacks and whites cannot be ended by unilateral secession on either side. So long as either disputant insists that commitments are owed, that past obligations must be honored, the relationship must persist until mutual satisfaction obtains. This was the fundamental proposition that Lincoln would not surrender, his bedrock understanding of the equality principle based on mutually acknowledged respect. Current affirmative action programs call this proposition into doubt, but in a complicated and confusing way. What is the relationship between blacks and whites when, forty years after *Brown*, there are no black faces in vast, privileged areas of American social life? But if blacks appear in these social enterprises only on rigidly separate tracks, what then is the relationship between blacks and whites? In addressing these complex, high-stake questions today, the judicious course—the best hope for protecting the possibility of equal relations between blacks and whites—would be to keep the controversy alive. The judicial technique best suited for this purpose would be application of mid-level scrutiny to affirmative action programs, which would require particularistic, fact-based legislative inquiry in their initial formulation and recurrently throughout their implementation.

Public school desegregation presents a much clearer opportunity for vindication of the nonsecession imperative. In 1958, the Supreme Court properly broke its apparently equivocal silence after *Brown II* to affirm this imperative in *Cooper v. Aaron,* against Governor Faubus's refusal in Little Rock to acknowledge even the possibility that blacks and whites would ever meet as equals. This secessionist impulse is equally apparent when, forty years after Linda Brown's father sued, the Topeka Board of Education denies any responsibility for the continued separation of blacks and whites. The Supreme Court should have rejected this denial more forcefully than its equivocal response in the 1991 Oklahoma case;[26] indeed, the Court should have seized the symbolism of announcing this result in *Brown III* itself.

As a general proposition, the Court should search out opportunities to identify and reject the secessionist impulse throughout our social relations.[27] This is the basic reason that would justify the Court's action to abolish the death penalty. This penalty vividly embodies the premise that the utter annihilation of an adversary and the complete breach of any future relationship is a justifiable response to social conflict. Moreover, because race is intertwined with the administration of the death penalty, it is even more important for the Court conclusively to repudiate this subjugative premise.

But even with the death penalty, the Court is obliged to approach its abolition slowly and with visible reluctance. This is not because the Court's abolition would be presumptively less legitimate than the legislature's enactment of a death penalty statute, not because of what Bickel called the "counter-majoritarian difficulty." The Court must abstain from invoking coercive authority in abolishing the death penalty, as in all matters, because the subjugative imposition is presumptively illegitimate. In a democracy, a legislative majority should be reluctant to overrule dissenters for the same reason that a court should hold back from invalidating legislation. This is the significance of Lincoln's prescription of "the leading principle—the sheet anchor of American republicanism[:] that no man is good enough to govern another man, without that other's consent." Majority rule overrides consent as much as do judicial impositions on the losing litigant.

Unanimous consent is itself, however, not a working rule that satisfies democratic principle so long as one dissenter, by withholding consent, can impose his will on others. This is the inescapable dilemma at the core of democratic principle: that unforced unanimity is the only legitimate basis for an equal relationship and that this state is almost impossible to obtain in practice. But if we aspire to democracy, then unforced unanimity must be our guiding ideal in all social relations and in all institutions. Force is sometimes an inescapable necessity in order to defend against force; but even with this apparently justifiable coercion, we risk losing sight of the ideal while aiming to defend it. Confidence in the righteousness of our cause, even when our mission is to protect democracy, breeds contempt for democratic principle.

This is why the question posed by conventional constitutional theory is so destructive. The Supreme Court must never conclude that its authority to act or to withhold action is unquestionably legitimate. For the same reason, the Court must never conclude that other institutions or individuals have unquestionably legitimate authority to coerce anyone. Unquestionable authority is at its core an antidemocratic idea—no matter who purports to exercise that authority, no matter what its imagined source.

The Supreme Court has acted to challenge, to provoke, to unsettle previously unquestioned authorities—but only for a brief time in our history, from around 1939 until 1968, from the Roosevelt Justices through the Warren Court. For most of our history, the Court has taken a diametrically opposed path, to boost existing authority and protect it from disruptive challenge. A comfortable majority on the Court today clearly has reverted to this traditional conception of the judicial role. But even though this conception has been historically dominant, we now have a legacy that holds open a different possibility. I do not believe that this heritage is beyond recall. Though it will not soon reappear on this Court, it still can sustain us in pursuing justice together.

This country first asserted its identity in challenging the claims of some to coerce others. In drafting our Constitution, some of the successful revolutionaries tried to distinguish between oppression and justice in the exercise of coercive force. We can see today how grotesquely they failed in this effort because they accepted the continued existence of chattel slavery. But we too will fail if we conclude that their only error was in imagining that enslavement of blacks was justifiable. We will fail unless we understand that coercion in any form is the enemy of democratic life. Institutions of the law can help us toward this understanding by holding out the possibility of mutual renunciation of force and shared respect in our social relations. "Our constitutional ideal of equal justice under law is thus made a living truth."

Notes

Introduction

1. This account was provided by news reporters accompanying Lincoln; see James McPherson, *Battle Cry of Freedom: The Civil War Era* 846–47 (New York: Oxford Univ. Press, 1988).

2. 2 *Collected Works of Abraham Lincoln* 532 (Roy Basler, ed.) (New Brunswick: Rutgers Univ. Press, 1953).

3. 4 *Collected Works* 268.

4. Proposed Speech on Gold Clause Cases, February 1935, 1 *F.D.R.—His Personal Letters, 1928–1945* 459–60 (E. Roosevelt, ed.) (1950). Roosevelt had prepared this speech for delivery if the Court overturned the congressional abrogation of "gold clauses" in federal obligations; the Court in fact upheld the enactment, in Perry v. United States, 294 U.S. 330 (1935).

5. "The Law of the Constitution: a Bicentennial Lecture," delivered at Tulane University, October 21, 1986, at pp. 14–15; see also Edwin Meese, "The Tulane Speech: What I Meant," *Washington Post,* November 13, 1986, at A21.

6. Brown v. Board of Education, Order for Reargument, 345 U.S. 972 (1953).

7. Quoted in Richard Kluger, *Simple Justice: The History of "Brown v. Board of Education" and Black America's Struggle for Equality* 643 (New York: Knopf, 1976).

8. 4 *Collected Works* 168.

1. The Constitutional Question

1. Brown v. Allen, 344 U.S. 443, 540 (1953) (concurring opinion).

2. See Robert Bork, *The Tempting of America: The Political Seduction of the Law* (New York: Free Press, 1990).

3. On republican virtue, see Frank Michelman, "Foreword: Traces of Self-Government," 100 *Harv. L. Rev.* 4 (1986); Michelman, "Law's Republic," 97 *Yale L. J.* 1493 (1988); Cass Sunstein, "Interest Groups in American Public

Law," 38 *Stan. L. Rev.* 29 (1985); Sunstein, "Beyond the Republican Revival," 97 *Yale L. J.* 1539 (1988). On transcendent morality, see Michael Perry, *The Constitution, the Courts, and Human Rights* (New Haven: Yale Univ. Press, 1982). On conventional morality, see Harry Wellington, "The Nature of Judicial Review," 91 *Yale L. J.* 486, 494 (1982). On truth, see Owen Fiss, "Foreword: The Forms of Justice," 93 *Harv. L. Rev.* 1, 13 (1979). On integrity, see Ronald Dworkin, *Law's Empire* (Cambridge: Harvard Univ. Press, 1986).

4. Mark Tushnet has been the most prolific Critical Legal theorist addressing constitutional law specifically; see, e.g., Mark Tushnet, *Red, White and Blue* (Cambridge: Harvard Univ. Press, 1989).

5. Brown v. Board of Education, 347 U.S. 483 (1954). Alexander Bickel, *The Least Dangerous Branch: The Supreme Court at the Bar of Politics* (Indianapolis: Bobbs-Merrill Co., 1962).

6. Bork subsequently reiterated this position in *Tempting of America* at 81–83.

7. Id. at 82. See William Nelson, *The Fourteenth Amendment: From Political Principle to Judicial Doctrine* 21, 126–27 (Cambridge: Harvard Univ. Press, 1988). Another prominent originalist, Justice Antonin Scalia, has been led by his jurisprudential commitment to an even more blatant revision of the historical record in order to justify *Brown;* "in my view," Scalia has asserted, "the Fourteenth Amendment's requirement of 'equal protection of the laws,' combined with the Thirteenth Amendment's abolition of the institution of slavery, *leaves no room for doubt* that laws treating people differently because of their race are invalid." Rutan v. Republican Party of Illinois, 110 S.Ct. 2729, 2748 n.1 (1990) (dissenting opinion) (emphasis added). See generally, Scalia, "Originalism: The Lesser Evil," 57 *Cincinnati L. Rev.* 849 (1989).

8. In the memorandum, Rehnquist had written, "I realize that it is an unpopular and unhumanitarian position, for which I have been excoriated by 'liberal' colleagues, but I think *Plessy v. Ferguson* was right and should be re-affirmed." Quoted in Bernard Schwartz, "Chief Justice Rehnquist, Justice Jackson, and the *Brown* Case," 1988 *Sup. Ct. Rev.* 245, 246. In his confirmation hearings, Rehnquist claimed that the memorandum "was intended as a rough draft of a statement of [Jackson's] views . . . rather than [mine]." Id. at 247. Regarding the implausibility of this claim, see generally id. and Kluger, *Simple Justice* at 606–09.

9. *New York Times,* October 24, 1987, at A16. On the significance of *Brown* in the transformation of southern politics, see generally Earl Black and Merle Black, *Politics and Society in the South* 11, 159, 206–12 (Cambridge: Harvard Univ. Press, 1987).

10. See Ely at 157–170.

11. See Bruce Ackerman, "Beyond Carolene Products," 98 *Harv. L. Rev.* 713, 737–40 (1985); Paul Brest, "The Substance of Process," 42 *Ohio St. L. J.* 131 (1981).

12. 347 U.S. at 494.

13. See generally "Symposium: The Courts, Social Science and School Desegregation," 39 *Law and Contemp. Probs.* (Winter/Spring 1975).

14. Herbert Wechsler, "Toward Neutral Principles of Constitutional Law," 73 *Harv. L. Rev.* 1, 34 (1959).

15. See Louis Pollak, "Racial Discrimination and Judicial Integrity: A Reply to Professor Wechsler," 108 *U. Pa. L. Rev.* 1 (1959); Charles Black, "The Lawfulness of the Segregation Decisions," 69 *Yale L. J.*421 (1960).

16. Quoted in Kluger, *Simple Justice* at 684.

17. Quoted in id. at 688.

18. See Dworkin, discussed in text accompanying note 46, infra; see also Paul Gewirtz, "Remedies and Resistance," 92 *Yale L. J.* 585 (1983).

19. For elaboration of the impact of the Civil War on conceptions of social authority, both in the South and the North, see Chapter 6, infra.

20. William A. Dunning articulated this view in the first sentence of his influential history of the Reconstruction era, published in 1907: "Few episodes of recorded history more urgently invite thorough analysis and extended reflection than the struggle through which the southern whites, subjugated by adversaries of their own race, thwarted the scheme which threatened permanent subjugation to another race." *Reconstruction: Political and Economic, 1865–1877* 1 (New York: Harper & Bros., 1907).

21. See Chapter 6, infra, for a more extended account.

22. Ambassador Warren Austin, quoted by Arthur Hertzberg, "The Impasse over Israel," *New York Review of Books*, October 25, 1990, p. 47.

23. *Least Dangerous Branch* at 244.

24. Id. at 251.

25. Id. at 254.

26. Id. at 240.

27. See Chapter 8, infra, for an extended account.

28. *Least Dangerous Branch* at 266.

29. In his 1969 Holmes lectures at the Harvard Law School, Bickel said, "The Court is the place for principled judgment . . . and in constitutional adjudication, the place *only* for that, or else its insulation from the political process is inexplicable." Alexander Bickel, *The Supreme Court and the Idea of Progress* 87 (New York: Harper & Row, 1970) (emphasis added). Bickel reiterated this proposition throughout these lectures: "The methods of reason and principle . . . alone justify the exercise of supreme judicial power in a political democracy." Id. at 95. "The process of the coherent, analytically warranted, principled declaration of general norms alone justifies the Court's function." Id. at 96. "The judicial process is . . . principle-prone and principle-bound—it has to be, there is no other justification or explanation for the role it plays." Id. at 175.

30. This latter-day enforcement enterprise, Bickel claimed, invoked "not the judicial process, properly so-called, but the managerial talents of the judges . . . [in devising] more or less expedient" results where "principled

solutions are not probable." *Idea of Progress* at 165. Bickel was especially critical of the increasing attention in lower federal courts to *de facto* school segregation: "Present judicial attitudes . . . are not stable. All too many federal judges have been induced to view themselves as holding roving commissions as problem solvers." Id. at 134.

31. *Idea of Progress* at 7.

32. *Idea of Progress* at 99.

33. See Richard Hofstadter, *The Progressive Historians: Turner, Beard, Parrington* (New York: Knopf, 1968); Samuel Huntington, *American Politics: The Promise of Disharmony* (Cambridge: Harvard Univ. Press, 1981).

34. (San Diego: Harcourt Brace Jovanovich, 1955).

35. *Liberal Tradition,* frontispiece.

36. Id. at 62.

37. Id. at 130.

38. Id. at 85–86.

39. "It has rarely occurred to American thinkers that . . . there has been a classic solution to [this classic problem]: namely that when a nation is united on the liberal way of life the majority will have no interest in destroying it for the minority. Santayana, exploring America's 'unison,' caught at once the crucial fact that minorities on any issue could easily tolerate the outcome 'either way' [citing *Character and Opinion in the United States* (1924)]. But the American perspective has not been Santayana's, and so the very liberalism that restrains the majority has given rise to a vast neurotic fear of what the majority might do. What must be accounted one of the tamest, mildest, and most unimaginative majorities in modern political history has been bound down by a set of restrictions that betray fanatical terror. The American majority has been an amiable shepherd dog kept forever on a lion's leash." Id. at 129.

40. Id. at 9.

41. Indeed, Bickel explicitly relied on Hartz for this view (*Least Dangerous Branch* at 30): "Very probably, the stability of the American Republic is due in large part, as Professor Louis Hartz has eloquently argued, to the remarkable Lockeian consensus of a society that has never known a feudal regime: to a "moral unity" that was seriously broken only once, over the extension of slavery."

42. *Least Dangerous Branch* at 16, 18.

43. In *The Least Dangerous Branch,* Bickel concluded his theoretical account about the counter-majoritarian "deviancy" of judicial review by considering Lincoln's refusal to acquiesce in the *Dred Scott* decision and the conflict between North and South over the legitimacy of slavery. "On the supreme occasion," Bickel stated, "when the system is forced to find ultimate self-consistency, the principle of self-rule must prevail." *Least Dangerous Branch* at 261. Bickel's statement is, however, unintelligible in the context of this polar dispute.

44. Bickel's phrase, *Least Dangerous Branch* at 239.

45. The Court's phrase, 349 U.S. at 301.

46. "The adjudicative principle of integrity," Dworkin says, invoking his special formulation for the legal interpretative process, "instructs judges to identify legal rights and duties, so far as possible, on the assumption that they were all created by a single author—the community personified—expressing a coherent conception of justice and fairness." *Law's Empire* at 225.

47. *Idea of Progress* at 178.

48. Alexander Bickel, *The Morality of Consent* 19 (New Haven: Yale Univ. Press, 1975).

49. 4 *Collected Works* 271.

2. Madison's Institutional Answer

1. E. Goffman, *Relations in Public* 288 n.44 (New York: Basic Books, 1971).

2. D. Hume, "Of the First Principles of Government," in *David Hume's Political Essays* 24 (C. Hendel, ed.) (Indianapolis: Bobbs-Merrill, 1953).

3. Douglass Adair, " 'That Politics May Be Reduced to a Science': David Hume, James Madison, and the *Tenth Federalist*," 20 *Huntington Library Q.* 343 (1957).

4. See Gordon Wood, "Interests and Disinterestedness in the Making of the Constitution," in *Beyond Confederation* 85 (R. Beeman et al., eds.) (Chapel Hill: Univ. North Carolina Press, 1987): "Th[e] age-old distinction between gentlemen and others in the society had a vital meaning for the Revolutionary generation that we have totally lost. It was a horizontal cleavage that divided the social hierarchy into two unequal parts." See also Paul Kahn, "Community in Contemporary Constitutional Theory," 99 *Yale L. J.* 473, 512 (1989).

5. See Richard Hofstadter, *The Progressive Historians* 212–18 (New York: Knopf, 1968).

6. Foreword to Catherine Drinker Bowen, *Miracle at Philadelphia: The Story of the Constitutional Convention, May to September 1787* x (Boston: Little, Brown, 1986 ed.).

7. *New York Times*, May 7, 1987, at A1, col.5.

8. For examples of this accusation from diverse colonial sources, see Bernard Bailyn, *The Ideological Origins of the American Revolution* ix, 102, 107, 111, 119–20, 122, 125–26 (Cambridge: Harvard Univ. Press, 1967).

9. Samuel Johnson, "Taxation No Tyranny," in Donald L. Greene, ed., *Samuel Johnson's Political Writings* 454 (New Haven: Yale Univ. Press, 1977). See also Drew McCoy, *The Last of the Fathers: James Madison and the Republican Legacy* 263 (Cambridge: Cambridge Univ. Press, 1989).

10. Jefferson, *Notes on Virginia* 214 (1782), rpt. in 3 *Writings of Thomas Jefferson* 223–24 (P. Ford, ed.) (New York: G. P. Putnam, 1894).

11. Madison, June 6, 1787, *Notes of Debates in the Federal Convention of 1787* 76–77.

12. Madison's categorical framework was even more directly evident in unpublished working notes he wrote in 1791–92:

The danger of oppression to the minority from unjust combinations of the majority . . . is illustrated by various instances.
  By the case of Debtors & Creditors in Rome & Athens . . .
  By the Spartans & Helots
  By the case of Black slaves in Modern times
 By religious persecutions every where . . .
 By the conduct of Carthage towards Sicily &c—
  of Athens towards her colonies . . .
  of G. B towards Ireland
  of d[itt]o towards America.

Notes for the *National Gazette* Essays, ca. 19 December 1791–3 March 1792, 14 *Papers of Madison* 160 (Hutchinson et al., eds.) (Charlottesville: Univ. Virginia Press, 1981).

13. *Federalist* 49 at 315 (New York: New American Library, 1961 ed.).

14. Id. at 314–15.

15. *Notes on Virginia* at 298–99, in 4 *Jefferson Writings* 266–67.

16. *Notes* at 251–52, 4 *Writings* 243–44.

17. In describing the mood of the delegates, Madison later observed that "most of us carried into the Convention a profound impression . . . as to the necessity of binding the States together by a strong Constitution. . . . Nor was the recent and alarming insurrection, headed by Shays, in Massachusetts, without a very sensible effect on the public mind." Letter to John Jackson, December 27, 1821, 9 *Writings of James Madison* 71–2 (G. Hunt, ed.) (New York: G. P. Putnam's Sons, 1910).

18. "The real difference of interests [in the Union] lay, not between the large [and] small but between the N[orthern and] South[ern] States. The institution of slavery [and] its consequences formed the line of discrimination." Madison, July 14, 1787, *Notes of Debates* 295.

19. J. Locke, *The Second Treatise of Civil Government* 26 (J. Gough, ed.) (Oxford: Blackwell, 1946).

20. 6 *Writings of James Monroe* 13–14 (S. M. Hamilton, ed.) (New York: G. P. Putnam's Sons, 1902).

21. *Liberal Tradition* at 129.

22. New York Times v. Sullivan, 376 U.S. 254, 270 (1964).

23. Thus Madison observed in 1821, "It is true, as the public has been led to understand, that I possess materials for a pretty ample view of what passed in [the 1787 Convention]. It is true, also, that it has not been my intention that they should forever remain under the veil of secrecy. . . . In general, it had appeared to me that it might be best to let the work be a posthumous one, or, at least, that its publication should be delayed till the Constitution should be well settled by practice, and till a knowledge of the controversial

part of the proceedings of its framers could be turned to no improper account." Letter to Thomas Ritchie, September 15, 1821, 3 *Letters and Other Writings of James Madison* 228.

Senate consideration in 1795 of the Jay Treaty with Great Britain provides another measure of the vast distance separating our assumptions from the founders' regarding public deliberations. The Senate consented to ratification in executive session, without any public release of the text of the treaty. A Republican newspaper in Philadelphia obtained the text and published it only a week later; considerable public clamor then followed, urging President Washington to withhold his act of ratification. See Ruth Wedgwood, "The Revolutionary Martyrdom of Jonathan Robbins," 100 *Yale L. J.* 229, 261–62 (1990).

24. Richard Hofstadter clearly identified this attitude in George Washington's thinking: "[Washington's] intellectual confusion about the problem of government and opposition was altogether genuine and . . . it partook of an intellectual difficulty quite common among his contemporaries. He had on the one hand given a great part of his life to assuring the American people a popular republican form of government and a broad base of liberty. But he could not, at the same time, reconcile himself to the oppositional politics that liberty brought with it. His real goal was first the maintenance, and then the restoration, of that spirit of happy unanimity which had been manifested in his own election in 1788 and 1792. It was with keen gratification that he had written in 1790 that the government of the United States was already "one of the best in the world," and that he was grateful for the near "miracle that there should been so much unanimity, in such points of importance, among such a number of Citizens, so widely scattered, and so different in their habits" . . . . He was, of course, aware, as he wrote to Jonathan Trumbull early in 1797, that "in all free governments, contention in elections will take place . . . ." [But] the normal and proper thing would be unanimity—a word that recurs in his later letters. To avoid ruin from the war in Europe, he wrote to Benjamin Goodhue in 1798, American required "nothing . . . but unanimity," and less than four months before his death he was calling again for "more unanimity in our public councils." R. Hofstadter, *The Idea of a Party System: The Rise of Legitimate Opposition in the United States, 1780–1840* 99–100 (Berkeley: Univ. California Press, 1969).

25. Pursuit of this ideal was one expression of the founding generation's commitment to an overarching conception of "civic virtue" that Gordon Wood and J. G. A. Pocock have identified; see generally Wood, *The Creation of the American Republic, 1776–1787* (New York: Norton, 1969); Pocock, *The Machiavellian Moment: Florentine Political Thought and the Atlantic Republican Tradition* (Princeton: Princeton Univ. Press, 1975).

26. Quoted in Adrienne Koch, *Madison's "Advice to My Country"* 116 (Princeton: Princeton Univ. Press, 1966).

27. *Idea of Party System* at 29.

28. Id. at 212 et seq.

29. Id. at 16–17.

30. Id. at 24.

31. See Alpheus T. Mason, "The Federalist—A Split Personality," 57 *Amer. Hist. Rev.* 625 (1952); George Carey, "Publius—A Split Personality?" 46 *Review of Politics* 3 (1984).

32. See Douglass Adair's convincing verdict on all the disputed numbers of the *Federalist Papers* in Madison's favor, in *Fame and the Founding Fathers* 257–58 (New York: Norton, 1974).

33. See generally *Notes of Debates* at 131–36.

34. Id. at 137.

35. "The Farmer Refuted, &c.," February 23, 1775, 1 *Papers of Alexander Hamilton* 98–99 (H. Syrett, ed.) (New York: Columbia Univ. Press, 1961).

36. Jerrilyn Marston, *King and Congress: The Transfer of Political Legitimacy, 1774–1776* 27 (Princeton: Princeton Univ. Press, 1987). For similar, though more modulated, expressions of dependence on royal authority by Benjamin Franklin and James Wilson, see id. at 37–39.

37. "The Farmer Refuted," 1 *Hamilton Papers* 98. See Bailyn, *Ideological Origins* at 222–23, regarding the intellectual credence given to this proposition in England and, though less generally, in America immediately before the Revolution.

38. So Douglass Adair observed: "We mistake the significance of Hamilton's proposal of an elective monarch as a solution of the crisis of 1787 if we think of his plan as either original or unrepresentative of the thought of important segments of American opinion in 1787. [His proposal] . . . was the traditional . . . solution for the specific dangers of interclass and interstate conflict that were destroying the imperfect Union . . . [There were many] like Hamilton [who] had favored independence in 1776 but who had become disillusioned about ever achieving order and security in a republic. Add to this group the large bloc of old tories . . . and it is easy to see why Washington, Madison and other leaders were seriously alarmed that the Union would break up and that kings would reappear in the Balkanized segments. Furthermore, . . . leading members of the Convention . . . accepted the fact that an American monarchy was inevitable at some future date. As Mr. Williamson of North Carolina remarked on July 24, 'It was pretty certain . . . that we should at some time or other have a king; but he wished no precaution to be omitted that might postpone the event as long as possible.' . . . John Adams' Defense [of the Constitution of the United States, published earlier in 1787] contained the same sort of prophecy. . . . Gouvernor Morris is reported to have argued during the Convention that 'we must have a Monarch sooner or later . . . and the sooner we take him while we are able to make a Bargain with him, the better.' " Adair, *Fame and the Founding Fathers* at 117–18.

39. See Gerald Stourzh, *Alexander Hamilton and the Idea of Republican Government* 51 (Stanford: Stanford Univ. Press, 1970).

40. *Federalist* 49 at 315.

41. Bruce Ackerman claims to have heard this voice somewhat more frequently; see "Constitutional Politics/Constitutional Law," 99 *Yale L. J.* 453, 490–515 (1989). For consideration of his claim, see Chapter 7.

42. *Federalist* 9 at 75.

43. Introduction to *Federalist Papers* by Clinton Rossiter, xi.

44. For discussion of the many difficulties in this conventional usage, see Boris Bittker, "The Bicentennial of the Jurisprudence of Original Intent: The Recent Past," 77 *Calif. L. Rev.* 235, 270–73 (1989).

45. The same, of course, is true for Madison, who held views on the indivisibility of sovereignty diametrically opposed to Hamilton's and whose separate contributions to the *Federalist Papers* gave, as will be seen, a starkly different construction to the Constitution on this score.

46. *Federalist* 78 at 466.

47. Id. at 467–68.

48. Letters of Brutus, No. XV, March 20, 1788, in *The Antifederalists* 350 (C. Kenyon, ed.) (Indianapolis: Bobbs-Merrill, 1966). Yates had been a delegate from New York to the Constitutional Convention but left early because of his opposition to the apparent direction of the enterprise. Morris, *Witnesses* at 20, 211.

49. *Federalist* 78 at 465.

50. Id. at 465–66.

51. Id. at 469–70.

52. The issue remains unsettled to this day. See Robert A. Burt, "Inventing Judicial Review: Israel and America," 10 *Cardozo L. Rev.* 2013, 2093–94 (1989).

53. Purposeful manipulation of the Court's size was achieved immediately after the Civil War (see Chapter 6), and was proposed with near success by President Roosevelt in 1937 (see Chapter 7).

54. For discussion of such legislative proposals immediately after the Civil War, see Chapter 6.

55. Remarks of Mr. Gerry and Mr. King, *Notes of Debates,* June 4, at 61; Mr. L. Martin, id., July 21, at 340.

56. Id., August 15, 1787, at 481.

57. From the drafting history of Article V, there is good reason to believe that no invalidating authority over congressional acts by state or federal judges was specifically intended by the phrase "in Pursuance thereof"; see Frank Strong, "Bicentennial Benchmark: Two Centuries of Evolution of Constitutional Processes," 55 *North Carolina L. Rev.* 1, 35–36 (1976).

58. *Federalist* 78 at 467.

59. Addressing a draft provision authorizing Congress to tax importation of slaves in the interim before it might forbid such importation, Madison objected that it would be "wrong to admit in the Constitution the idea that there could be property in men." *Notes of Debates,* August 25, 1787, at 532. The provision was altered to refer obliquely to "such Persons as any of the

States now existing shall think proper to admit" (as it reads in the final version of Article I, section 9).

60. This speculation finds some support in Gouverneur Morris' later recollections of his service on the Committee of Style appointed to draft the final language of the Constitution: "Having rejected redundant and equivocal terms, I believed it to be as clear as our language would permit; excepting, nevertheless, a part of what relates to the judiciary. On that subject, conflicting opinions had been maintained with so much professional astuteness, that it became necessary to select phrases, which expressing my own notions would not alarm others, [and] not shock their selflove." Letter to Timothy Pickering, December 22, 1814, in M. Farrand (ed.), 3 *Records of the Federal Convention of 1787* 420. Among the four additional members of the Committee of Style were Hamilton and Madison. Morris, *Witnesses* at 221.

A letter written by James Monroe to Madison in November 1788 provides additional, though indirect, support. Reporting the deliberations of the Virginia House of Delegates on a court reorganization bill, just five months after Virginia had ratified the federal constitution, Monroe stated, "The arrangement of the Judiciary is the principal subject before the house. It has been agreed by all to pass by the question 'whether the Judiciary may declare a law, in their opinion agnst the Constitution, void,' as calculated to create heats & animosities that will produce harm." Letter of November 22, 1788, 11 *Papers of Madison* 361 (R. Rutland et al., eds.) (Charlottesville: Univ. Press of Virginia, 1977).

61. The appraisal is Richard Hofstadter's, favorably comparing Madison to Jefferson, *Party System* at 54.

62. *Notes of Debates* 539.

63. Letter to James Monroe, December 27, 1817, 3 *Letters and Other Writings* 56.

64. Madison's most direct reference to judicial review was in *Federalist* 39, where he discussed generally whether the proposed government was more national than state-based or vice versa. On the way to his conclusion that it was "neither wholly federal nor wholly national," Madison asserted that the constitutional limitation of national jurisdiction to "certain enumerated objects only . . . leaves to the several States a residuary and inviolable sovereignty over all other objects." *Federalist* 39 at 245–46. Madison immediately added this qualification: "It is true that in controversies relating to the boundary between the two jurisdictions, the tribunal which is ultimately to decide is to be established under the general government. But this does not change the principle of the case. The decision is to be impartially made, according to the rules of the Constitution . . . Some such tribunal is clearly essential to prevent an appeal to the sword and a dissolution of the compact; and that it ought to be established under the general rather than under the local governments, or, to speak more properly, that it could be safely established under the first alone, is a position not likely to be combated." In this passage,

Madison envisaged not simply that the federal judicial "tribunal" will invalidate state acts transgressing the "boundary between the two jurisdictions" but that it will police both sides of the boundary, for congressional as well as state infringements. This is vintage judicial review, and if Madison said nothing more (or nothing less) on the subject, we might count him as a proponent.

Even so, this passage is not a ringing endorsement of judicial review of congressional acts, since Madison introduced the passage as a qualification to his immediately preceding statement that the enumerated national powers in the Constitution protect the "residuary . . . inviolable sovereignty" of the states. Many years later, when South Carolina claimed authority to nullify congressional acts, Madison pointed to this passage in the *Federalist Papers* to establish the consistency of his position regarding the supremacy of national authority generally, and national judicial authority specifically, over state claims of sovereignty. See letter to Robert Hayne, April 3 or 4, 1830, 9 *Writings of James Madison* 393 (New York: Putnam, 1910).

65. Thus Sotirios Barber maintains with regard to judicial review specifically that " 'Publius' is who *The Federalist* implicitly says Publius is: Madison and Hamilton (in the main) together and therefore reconciled . . . ." "Judicial Review and *The Federalist*," 55 *U. Chi. L. Rev.* 836, 837 (1988).

66. *Federalist* 47 at 301, 307–08.

67. *Federalist* 48 at 308.

68. Id.

69. *Federalist* 49 at 313.

70. Id. at 315.

71. *Federalist* 50 at 317 (emphasis in original).

72. Id. (emphasis in original).

73. Madison's specific grounding for this conclusion has an ironically direct application to the current, and many past, workings of the Supreme Court: "Throughout the continuance of the council, it was split into two fixed and violent parties. . . . In all questions, however unimportant in themselves, or unconnected with each other, the same names stand invariably contrasted on the opposed columns. Every unbiased observer may infer . . . that, unfortunately, *passion*, not *reason*, must have presided over their decisions. When men exercise their reason coolly and freely on a variety of distinct questions, they inevitably fall into different opinions on some of them. When they are governed by a common passion, their opinions, if they are so to be called, will be the same." *Federalist* 50 at 319.

74. Id.

75. *Federalist* 51 at 320.

76. Id. at 322–23.

77. Id. at 323.

78. Id. at 323–24.

79. Ibid.

80. Rossiter, *Introduction to Federalist Papers* at viii. On April 3 Hamilton sent Madison the first bound volume of the *Federalist Papers* and newspaper clippings of later essays through number 77, with the observation that he was "too much engaged to make a rapid progress in what remains." 4 *Papers of Alexander Hamilton* 644 (New York: Columbia Univ. Press, 1962). On May 19, 1788, he sent Madison the second volume, which included new essays, numbers 78 through 85. Id. at 649–50.

81. Morris, *Witnesses* at 233, 248.

82. Letter by Madison to John Brown, October 1788, 1 *Letters and Other Writings of James Madison* 194 (W.C. Rives, ed.) (Philadelphia: J. B. Lippincott, 1865).

83. *Federalist* 78 at 467–68.

84. Note, in particular, the implications of this passage: "In framing a government which is to be administered by men over men, the great difficulty lies in this: you must first enable the government to control the governed; and in the next place oblige it to control itself." If Madison truly adhered to the popular idea of popular sovereignty, why would he claim that the "first" task in framing a government was to enable it "to control the governed"? But Madison was not eager to have his readers pause long over this question, for he immediately appended this observation: "A dependence on the people is, no doubt, the primary control on the government; but experience has taught mankind the necessity of auxiliary precautions." *Federalist* 51 at 322.

85. It is also possible that Madison had not crisply acknowledged in his own mind how far his thinking, as set out in *Federalist* 51, had carried him from the conventional premises of unitary sovereignty. In October 1787, a month after the end of the Philadelphia Convention and just as he was beginning to write his systematic exposition and defense of its work in his *Federalist* essays, Madison wrote a long letter to Thomas Jefferson, then Minister to France, about the Convention's work. In that letter, Madison lamented that the Convention had rejected his proposal for a general congressional veto of state laws and observed, "Without such a check in the whole over the parts, our system involves the evil of imperia in imperio. If a compleat supremacy some where is not necessary in every Society, a controuling power at least is so, by which the general authority may be defended against encroachments of the subordinate authorities, and by which the latter may be restrained from encroachments on each other." Letter to Jefferson, October 24, 1787, 10 *Papers of James Madison* 209 (Chicago: Univ. Chicago Press, 1977).

Later in this letter, however, Madison sketched the theory of the extended republican sphere that he was to develop in *Federalist* 10, and he stated, "Divide et impera, the reprobated axiom of tyranny, is under certain qualifications, the only policy, by which a republic can be administered on just principles." He then elaborated, "The great desideratum in Government is, so to modify the sovereignty as that it may be sufficiently neutral between different parts of the Society to controul one part from invading the rights of another, and at the same time sufficiently controuled itself, from setting up an interest adverse to that of the entire Society. . . . In the extended Republic of the United States, the General Government would hold a pretty even balance between the parties of particular States, and be at the same time sufficiently restrained by its dependence on the community, from betraying its general interests." Id. at 214. In this portion of his letter, Madison thus broke away from the conventional idea of unitary sovereignty: government should be based not on the tyrannous maxim "divide and conquer" but on the libertarian precept, "divide the conqueror."

86. Letter to Jefferson, October 17, 1788, 11 *Papers of James Madison* 298–99 (Charlottesville: Univ. of Virginia Press, 1977).

87. Letter of Jefferson to Madison, March 15, 1789, 14 *Papers of Thomas Jefferson* 659 (J. Boyd, ed.) (Princeton: Princeton Univ. Press, 1958).

88. Speech of June 8, 1789 to House of Representatives, 12 *Papers of James Madison* 206–07. Throughout this speech, Madison made clear that in sponsoring the amendments he was acting on "principles of amity and moderation" to defer to the wishes of others who remained "dissatisfied" with the Constitution; he stated that he would "not propose a single alteration which I do not wish to see take place, as intrinsically proper in itself, or proper because it is wished for by a respectable number of my fellow citizens." Id. at 198–99. See Ralph Rossum, " 'To Render These Rights Secure': James Madison's Understanding of the Relationship of the Constitution to the Bill of Rights," 3 *Benchmark* 4, 12 (1987).

89. For the conventional truncation of Madison's statement, see, e.g., Hugo Black, "The Bill of Rights," 35 *N. Y. Univ. L. Rev.* 865, 880 (1960); Irving Brant, "The Madison Heritage," 35 *N. Y. Univ. L. Rev.* 882, 899 (1960).

90. Speech of June 8, at 207.

91. Speech of June 18, 1789, to House of Representatives, 12 *Papers of James Madison* 238.

92. Perhaps Madison had a distinction in mind regarding the judicial role in constitutional provisions for interbranch divisions of authority and provisions, such as the Bill of Rights, withholding all subject-matter authority from the government. He did not explicitly draw this distinction, however, and it does not seem analytically justified since in both cases the basic issue is to determine the existence and extent of a constitutional limit on congressional authority.

93. See, e.g., George Carey, "James Madison on Federalism: The Search for Abiding Principles," 3 *Benchmark* 27 (1987).

94. See Lance Banning, "James Madison and the Nationalists, 1780–83," 40 *Wm. and Mary Q.* (3d series) 227 (1983), for a careful study of the earliest "nationalist" phase of Madison's career.

95. As Robert Wiebe has observed, "The steps [Madison] took . . . followed logically from his lifelong and almost obsessive commitment to the principle

of balance." *The Opening of American Society: From the Adoption of the Constitution to the Eve of Disunion* 56 (New York: Vintage Books, 1985).

96. *Federalist* 51 at 321–22.

97. See McCoy at 143.

98. *The Kentucky–Virginia Resolutions and Mr. Madison's Report of 1799* 2 (Richmond: Virginia Commission on Constitutional Government, 1960).

99. Id. at 12.

100. See U.S. Senate, 62d Cong., 2d Sess., *Alien and Sedition Laws: Debates in the Virginia House of Delegations, 1798* 140–48 (Document No. 873, Washington: Government Printing Office, 1912).

101. *Kentucky–Virginia Resolutions* at 13 (emphasis in original).

102. Virginia Commission, supra, at 79.

103. Letter to Jefferson, June 27, 1823, 3 *Letters and Other Writings of Madison* 325–26. Madison repeated almost verbatim this differentiation between federal–state and intra-branch federal conflicts over constitutional interpretation in his 1830 letter intended as a public refutation of the nullifiers' claim, Letter to Edward Everett, August 28, 1830, 9 *Writings of James Madison* 393–94. The consistency of Madison's conviction that individual states must not judge constitutional questions for themselves is apparent from the memorandum, "Vices of the Political System of the United States," which he prepared just before the Philadelphia Convention assembled in 1787. Madison warned then against this "evil": "As far as the Union of the States is to be regarded as a league of sovereign powers, and not as a political Constitution by virtue of which they are become one sovereign power, so far it seems to follow from the doctrine of compacts, that a breach of any of the articles of the confederation by any of the parties to it, absolves the other parties from their respective obligations, and gives them a right if they chuse to exert it, of dissolving the Union altogether." 9 *Papers of James Madison* 352–53 (R. Rutland, ed.) (Chicago: Univ. Chicago Press, 1975).

104. Virginia Commission, supra, at 79–80.

105. Virginia Commission, supra, at 79.

106. Letter of June 27, 1823, at 326.

107. Edward Pessen, *Jacksonian America: Society, Personality and Politics* 155 (Urbana: Univ. Illinois Press, 1985 ed.). A significant shift toward direct election did not come until just before the election of 1824, id.; by 1828 only two states, Delaware and South Carolina, retained the old scheme of state legislative selection of electors; from 1832 until after the Civil War, South Carolina stood alone. Kenneth Greenberg, *Masters and Statesmen: The Political Culture of American Slavery* 60–61 (Baltimore: Johns Hopkins Univ. Press, 1985).

108. Letter to Spencer Roane, June 29, 1821, 3 *Letters and Other Writings* 223. Madison enclosed a copy of this letter in his 1823 correspondence with Jefferson regarding the justification for federal judicial supremacy. Id. at 327.

109. Remarks on Bank bill, February 8, 1791, 13 *Papers of James Madison* 386.

110. Letter to Charles J. Ingersoll, June 25, 1831, 4 *Letters* 186.

111. Message of January 30, 1815, 8 *Writings* 327. Madison vetoed this bill on practical but not constitutional grounds; the following year he approved a revised bill creating the Second Bank of the United States. McCoy at 81. For a similar evolution of Madison's views regarding national expenditures for canals and roads, from his veto on constitutional grounds in 1817 to his reluctant but acquiescent reading of the approving "will of the nation" in 1825, see McCoy at 92–96 and Madison's letter to Jefferson, February 17, 1825, 3 *Letters* 483.

112. Madison reiterated his reluctance for moving "out of doors" to engage popular participation on constitutional issues in his 1823 letter to Jefferson, where he repeated his *Federalist* critique of Jefferson's proposal for regularized conventions and noted that if the judiciary specifically "abuse[d] its trust" in constitutional interpretation, he would "prefer a resort to the nation for an amendment of the tribunal itself to continual appeals from its controverted decisions to that ultimate arbiter." Letter of June 13, 1823, 3 *Letters* 325, 327.

113. In his 1823 letter to Jefferson he observed, "I am not unaware that the Judiciary career has not corresponded with what was anticipated. At one period, the Judges perverted the Bench of Justice into a rostrum for partisan harangues [apparently referring to federal judicial enforcement of the Sedition Act]. And latterly, the Court, by some of its decisions, still more by extra-judicial reasonings and *dicta,* has manifested a propensity to enlarge the general in derogation of the local, and to amplify its own jurisdiction, which has justly incurred the public censure." Id. at 327. Just two years later, reflecting on the repeated enactments of internal improvements bills by Congress, Madison suggested to Jefferson that he was "not sure that the Judiciary branch . . . is not a safer expositor of the power of Congress" regarding such appropriations measures "backed, and even pushed on, by [congressional] constituents." Letter of February 17, 1825, 3 *Letters* 483. Finally, in a letter to an unidentified correspondent in 1834, Madison suggested that the Court was "most familiar" to and "most engages the respect and reliance of the public as the surest expositor of the Constitution" generally. 4 *Letters* 349–50.

114. In his 1834 letter, Madison began with the observation, "As the Legislative, Executive, and Judicial departments of the United States are co-ordinate, and each equally bound to support the Constitution, it follows that each must, in the exercise of its functions, be guided by the text of the Constitution according to its own interpretation of it." 4 *Letters* 349. In his 1825 letter to Jefferson, though Madison expressed his preference for judicial review regarding the constitutionality of internal improvements expenditures, he concluded that he "must submit to [the] danger of oppression

as an evil infinitely less than the danger to the whole nation from a will independent of it." 3 *Letters* 483.

115. *Federalist* 9 at 75.

116. 5 *Annals of Congress, 1797–99* 3776; 1 Stat. 596.

117. *Federalist* 10 at 79–80.

118. *Federalist* 51 at 323–24. The differing attitudes of Madison and Hamilton toward social conflict pervaded their separate Federalist essays, as is apparent even from the differences in their vocabularies. In a meticulously detailed study conducted to resolve the authorship disputes regarding some essays, researchers found that, in the undisputed essays, Hamilton used the following words with significantly greater frequency than Madison: defensive, destruction, offensive, vigor(ous), adversaries, aid, choice, common, and danger; and Madison more frequently than Hamilton used: fortune(s), innovation(s), join(ed), language, same, violence, voice, asserted, decide(s)(ed)(ing), principle, and usage(s). F. Mosteller and D. Wallace, *Inference and Disputed Authorship: The Federalist* 244–48 (Reading, MA: Addison-Wesley, 1964).

119. See McCoy at 151: "During the final six years of his life . . . Madison could not get the nullifiers out of his mind. At times mental agitation issued in physical collapse. . . . Literally sick with anxiety, he began to despair of his ability to make himself understood by his fellow citizens."

3. Lincoln's Egalitarian Answer

1. Hofstadter, *Idea of a Party System* at 54.

2. Id. at 132.

3. Ibid.

4. See Potter, *The Secession Crisis* at 301, 321.

5. Hofstadter, *American Political Tradition* at 126.

6. Id. at 130.

7. Id. at 116.

8. Id. at 117 n.

9. Id. at 124.

10. *Least Dangerous Branch* at 65.

11. Id. at 68.

12. Gerald Gunther, "The Subtle Vices of the Passive Virtues," 64 *Colum. L. Rev.* 1, 3 (1964).

13. 4 *Collected Works* 268.

14. *Least Dangerous Branch* at 16, 18.

15. Peoria address, October 16, 1854, 2 *Collected Works* 265–66.

16. In his first inaugural address Lincoln alluded to this limitation; just before the passage I cited earlier, Lincoln stated, "A majority held in restraint by constitutional checks and limitations, and always changing easily with

deliberate changes of popular opinions and sentiments, is the only true sovereign of a free people." 4 *Collected Works* 268.

17. Address of January 27, 1838, 1 *Collected Works* 111.

18. Id. at 114.

19. Id. at 112.

20. 4 *Collected Works* 268.

21. Id. at 271.

22. Id. at 269.

23. Message to Congress in Special Session, July 4, 1861, 4 *Collected Works* 435–36.

24. 2 *Collected Works* 385. In a fragment written some time between 1858 and his inauguration, Lincoln expressed this priority by adapting the language of Proverbs 25:11 that "a word fitly spoken is like apples of gold in a setting of silver"; he wrote:

> The expression of that principle [of equality], in our Declaration of Independence, was most happy, and fortunate. Without this, as well as with it, we could have declared our independence of Great Britain; but without it, we could not, I think, have secured our free government, and consequent prosperity. No oppressed people will fight, and endure, as our fathers did, without the promise of something better, than a mere change of masters.
>
> The assertion of that principle, at that time, was the word "fitly spoken" which has proved an "apple of gold" to us. The Union, and the Constitution, are the picture of silver, subsequently framed around it. The picture was made, not to conceal, or destroy the apple; but to adorn, and preserve it. The picture was made for the apple—not the apple for the picture. 4 *Collected Works* 169.

25. This was Harry Jaffa's defense of Lincoln, against Hofstadter's charge: "Lincoln never ceased to summon the people to fidelity to the principle of equality, considered as the principle of abstract justice. He would not abandon equality, as Douglas had done, when equality proved unpopular or inconvenient. But neither would he abandon equality's other face, reflected in the opinion of the governed who made up the political community of the United States. Because of the requirement of consent, Lincoln felt a duty to adjust public policy to the moral sense of the community. In the tension between equality and consent, in the necessity to cling to both and abandon neither, but to find the zone between which advances the public good, is the creative task of the statesman." *Crisis of the House Divided* 377 (Garden City, NY: Doubleday, 1959). Bickel explicitly relied on Jaffa's analysis for his depiction of the Lincolnian "tension between principle and expediency," *Least Dangerous Branch* at 65, but he missed its full significance.

26. As he stated in an 1845 letter to an abolitionist supporter: "I hold it to be a paramount duty of us in the free States, due to the Union of the

States, and perhaps to liberty itself (paradox though it may seem), to let the slavery of the other States alone; while, on the other hand, I hold it to be equally clear that we should never knowingly lend ourselves, directly or indirectly, to prevent that slavery from dying a natural death—to find new places for it to live in, when it can not longer exist in the old." Letter to Williamson Durley, October 3, 1845, 1 *Collected Works* 348. Similarly, in his 1852 eulogy for Henry Clay, Lincoln stated, "Cast into life where slavery was already widely spread and deeply seated, [Clay] did not perceive, as I think no wise man has perceived, how it could be at once eradicated, without producing a greater evil, even to the cause of human liberty itself." 2 *Collected Works* 132.

27. Thus Lincoln stated: "We had slavery among us, we could not get our constitution unless we permitted them to remain in slavery, we could not secure the good we did secure if we grasped for more, and having by necessity submitted to that much, it does not destroy the principle that is the charter of our liberties." Address of July 10, 1858, 2 *Collected Works* 501.

28. In his debates with Douglas, Lincoln advocated restoration of the Missouri Compromise and reversal of the *Dred Scott* decision in order to return to "the plain unmistakable spirit of [1776] towards slavery, [which] was hostility to the PRINCIPLE, and toleration, ONLY BY NECESSITY." Address at Peoria, October 16, 1854, 2 *Collected Works* 275.

29. Lincoln distilled this argument in an undated "fragment" among his private papers:

If A. can prove, however conclusively, that he may, of right, enslave B.—why may not B. snatch the same argument, and prove equally, that he may enslave A.?—

You say A. is white, and B. is black. It is *color*, then; the lighter having the right to enslave the darker? Take care. By this rule, you are to be slave to the first man you meet, with a fairer skin than your own.

You do not mean *color* exactly?—You mean the whites are *intellectually* the superiors of the blacks, and, therefore have the right to enslave them? Take care again. By this rule, you are to be slave to the first man you meet, with an intellect superior to your own.

But, you say, it is a question of interest; and, if you can make it your *interest,* you have the right to enslave another. Very well. And if he can make it his interest, he has the right to enslave you. (2 *Collected Works* at 222.)

Lincoln adverted to this argument "discursively through the debates" with Douglas; see Jaffa at 336.

30. 2 *Collected Works* 461.

31. 5 *Collected Works* 537.

32. 5 *Collected Works* 48–49.

33. 5 *Collected Works* 388–89.

34. See McPherson at 498–99.

35. McPherson at 271.

36. See Potter, *Secession Crisis* at 371–75.

37. McPherson at 558.

38. McPherson at 510, 687.

39. Gideon Welles, "The History of Emancipation" 14 *Galaxy* 842–43 (December 1872), quoted in James McPherson, *Abraham Lincoln and the Second American Revolution* 83–84 (New York: Oxford Univ. Press, 1990).

40. Thus James McPherson observed that "despite the exclusion of top Confederate leaders from Lincoln's blanket offer of amnesty, his policy would preserve much of the South's old ruling class in power" and that by his offer Lincoln "hoped to set in motion a snowballing defection from the Confederacy and a state-by-state reconstruction of the Union." *Battle Cry of Freedom* at 700. Radicals such as Wendell Phillips, intent on "annihilating that Oligarchy which formed and rules the South and makes the war," were intensely critical of Lincoln's amnesty offer. "What McClellan was on the battlefield—'Do as little hurt as possible!' " Phillips said, "Lincoln is in civil affairs—'Make as little change as possible!' " Id. at 701.

41. Draft letter to Charles D. Robinson, August 17, 1864, 7 *Collected Works* 501.

42. Draft letter to Henry Raymond, August 24, 1864, 7 *Collected Works* 517.

43. Interview with Alexander W. Randall and Joseph T. Mills, August 19, 1864, 7 *Collected Works* 507.

44. John Nicolay and John Hay, 9 *Abraham Lincoln: A History* 211 (New York: 1890). See McPherson, *Lincoln and Second American Revolution* at 89.

45. Address on Colonization to a Deputation of Negroes, August 14, 1862, 5 *Collected Works* 371.

46. Quoted by David Brion Davis, "The White World of Frederick Douglass," *New York Review of Books,* May 16, 1991, at 12.

47. William McFeely, *Frederick Douglass* 229 (New York: W. W. Norton, 1991).

48. A. Stephens, 2 *A Constitutional View of the Late War between the States* 614, 617 (Philadelphia: National Publ. Co., 1870). James McPherson has observed that Stephens must have misunderstood Lincoln's recommendation for "prospective" ratification since Lincoln "was too good a lawyer to suggest [such] an impossibility." McPherson at 823 n.30. By my lights, however, the recommendation was unorthodox but not conceptually impossible.

49. 8 *Collected Works* 260–61.

50. *Federalist* 51 at 325.

51. *Federalist* 10 at 78. For incisive critiques to the same effect, see Bruce Ackerman, *Social Justice in the Liberal State* 327–48 (New Haven: Yale Univ. Press, 1980), and Martha Minow, *Making All the Difference: Inclusion, Exclusion, and American Law* 146–226 (Ithaca: Cornell Univ. Press, 1990).

52. 4 *Collected Works* at 268.

53. Don Fehrenbacher, *Lincoln in Text and Context* 20 (Stanford: Stanford Univ. Press, 1987).

54. 2 *Collected Works* 400–03.

55. *Least Dangerous Branch* at 16.

56. Bork, *Tempting of America* at 256, quoting Alisdair MacIntyre, *After Virtue* 6 (2d ed. 1984).

57. Bork, *Tempting of America* at 256–57.

4. The Marshall Court Conflicts

1. Cooper v. Aaron, 358 U.S. 1, 18 (1958).

2. Morris, *Witnesses,* at 37–38.

3. Id. at 24.

4. Comparing Hamilton and Jefferson in terms that also can be applied to Madison, Robert Wiebe has observed: "Jefferson the reputed democrat had [like Madison] a more deeply ingrained sense of hierarchy than Hamilton the reputed aristocrat. Hamilton used it; Jefferson [like Madison] lived it." *Opening of American Society* at 51.

5. Rhys Isaac, *The Transformation of Virginia, 1740–1790* (Chapel Hill: Univ. North Carolina Press, 1982), esp. 150, 264–66. See also Wood, *Creation of the American Republic* at 82 ("By 1776 . . . the Crown had become, in a word, a scapegoat for a myriad of American ills.")

6. The formulation is Carl Becker's, in *The History of Political Parties in the Province of New York, 1760–1776* 22 (Madison: Univ. Wisconsin Press, 1909).

7. See Isaac at 168.

8. Wiebe, *Opening* at 50.

9. 1 *Documents of American History* 155–56 (H. S. Commager, ed.) (Englewood Cliffs, NJ: Prentice-Hall, 9th ed., 1973).

10. Letter to John Jay, November 13, 1790, 7 *Papers of Alexander Hamilton* 149 (H. C. Syrett, ed.) (New York: Columbia Univ. Press, 1961).

11. See Wiebe, *Opening* at 85.

12. Hofstadter, *Party System* at 108.

13. Charles Warren, 1 *The Supreme Court in United States History* 164–67 (Boston: Little, Brown, 1922).

14. Hofstadter, *Party System* at 109.

15. See Wiebe, *Opening* at 86–87.

16. See Chapter 2, text accompanying notes 98–102.

17. Wiebe at 97.

18. James Iredall to Hannah Iredall, January 24, 1799, 2 *Life and Correspondence of James Iredall* 543 (G. McRee, ed.) (New York, 1858).

19. Wiebe at 97.

20. Hofstadter at 109.

21. As Douglass Adair observed, from the outset of the national govern-

ment in 1789, "every device that Hamilton used to win the loyalty of the propertied elite tended to confirm the suspicions of the yeoman farmers and middle-class groups" who originally either had opposed or been ambivalent toward the Constitution. Jefferson and Madison accordingly "serv[ed] American nationalism" by putting themselves "at the head of this potentially dangerous opposition and thus guarantee[ing] that it would remain loyal to the Union." *Fame and the Founding Fathers* at 138.

22. Wiebe at 110.

23. Letter to Gideon Granger, August 13, 1800, 9 *Works of Jefferson* 139 (Ford ed.).

24. Hamilton to Jay, May 7, 1800, 24 *Papers of Alexander Hamilton* 465 (H. C. Syrett, ed.) (New York: Columbia Univ. Press, 1976).

25. Letter from Hamilton to James Ross, December 29, 1800, 25 *Papers of Hamilton* 281.

26. Hofstadter at 133.

27. Ibid.

28. Jefferson, First Inaugural Address, March 4, 1801, 1 *Messages and Papers of the Presidents* 322 (J. Richardson, ed., 1898).

29. Jay to Adams, January 1801, rpt. in 1 *The Justices of the United States Supreme Court 1789–1969* 19 (L. Friedman and F. Israel, eds.) (New York, 1969).

30. 1 Warren at 175–76.

31. Leonard Baker, *John Marshall: A Life in Law* 355 (New York: Collier Macmillan, 1974).

32. Jefferson to John Dickinson, December 18, 1801. See R. Ellis, *The Jeffersonian Crisis: Courts and Politics in the Young Republic* 43–44 (New York: Norton, 1971).

33. See George Haskins, *Foundations of Power: John Marshall, 1801–15*, Pt. 1, 229–30, 239–42 (New York: Macmillan, 1981). Marshall appeared as a witness in the Senate trial on Chase's impeachment and according to a contemporary observer, "there was in his manner an evident disposition to accommodate [Chase's opponents]." Ellis at 98, quoting a memorandum by a Federalist Senator. The Republicans could find support for the legitimacy of using the impeachment power as an ideological weapon from Hamilton's *Federalist* 81 at 484–85: "The supposed danger of judiciary encroachments on the legislative authority . . . is in reality a phantom. . . . [Impeachment] is alone a complete security. There can never be danger that the judges, by a series of deliberate usurpations on the authority of the legislature, would hazard the united resentment of the body intrusted with it, while this body was possessed of the means of punishing their presumption by degrading them from their stations." So much for the "independent spirit in the judges which must be essential" for courts to serve "as the bulwarks . . . against legislative encroachments," which Hamilton had extolled in *Federalist* 78 at 469.

34. James Banner, *To the Hartford Convention: The Federalists and the Origins of Party Politics in Massachusetts, 1789–1815* 40–41 (New York: Knopf, 1970).

35. Regarding the grip of the ideal of transcendent civic virtue on the founding generation, see Wood, *Creation of the American Republic* esp. 65–70. On the "patriot king" conception of executive leadership, see Ralph Ketcham, *Presidents above Party: The First American Presidency, 1789–1829* (Chapel Hill: Univ. North Carolina Press, 1984) esp. 90–99 (regarding Washington and Adams) and 169–76 (regarding Jefferson).

36. See Ketcham at 188–214.

37. *Federalist* 51 at 322.

38. *Federalist* 10 at 80.

39. *Federalist* 10 at 82–83.

40. See Ketcham at 113–23.

41. See Lance Banning, "The Hamiltonian Madison: A Reconsideration," 92 *Va. Mag. Hist. and Biography* 3, 12–16 (1984).

42. Baker at 14.

43. Gordon Wood, "Interests and Disinterestedness in the Making of the Constitution," in *Beyond Confederation: Origins of the Constitution and American National Identity* 87 (R. Beeman et al., eds.) (Chapel Hill: Univ. North Carolina Press, 1987).

44. In 1808, for example, Marshall described Jefferson and his party as "always hostile to our constitution [and having] for some time rule[d] our country despotically." And Jefferson in 1810 spoke of the "rancourous hatred which Marshall bears to the government of his country, and . . . the cunning and sophistry with which he is able to enshroud himself." See Baker at 524–25.

45. Letter from Marshall to Pinckney, October 19, 1808, quoted in Baker at 527–28.

46. See, e.g., Marshall's letter to Joseph Story, September 22, 1832, 14 *Mass. Hist. Soc. Proc.,* 2d ser., 351 (1901). ("I yield slowly and reluctantly to the Conviction that our Constitution cannot last.")

47. See G. Edward White's observation: "Every effort to depart from the sovereign relationships embodied in the Constitution, or from its central purposes, or from its establishment of a Union represented [for Marshall] cultural disintegration, a return to the chaos of the pre-framing period. An image of chaos, and the ever-present potential for decay and dissolution, were the spectres against which Marshall's theory of sovereignty was erected." *The Marshall Court and Cultural Change, 1815–35* 592–93 (New York: Macmillan, 1988).

48. 5 U.S. (1 Cranch) at 179–180. See Eakin v. Raub, 12 Serg. & Rawle 330, 353 (Pa. 1825) (Gibson, J.).

49. Republican Senators explicitly portrayed the Court's initial action in *Marbury* granting the show cause order against Madison in these terms: "Senator Jackson of Georgia spoke of the 'attack of the Judges on the

Secretary of State.' 'The Judges have been hardy enough to send their mandatory process into the Executive Cabinet to examine its concerns. Does this in the Judges seem unambitious?' said Giles of Virginia. The granting of a rule is 'an assumption of jurisdiction,' said John Randolph of Virginia, and he added sarcastically, 'The Judges are said to be humble, unaspiring men! Their humble pretensions extend only to a complete exemption from Legislative control; to the exercise of an inquisitorial authority over the Cabinet of the Executive. . . . In the inquisitorial capacity, the Supreme Court . . . may easily direct the Executive by mandamus in what mode it is their pleasure that he should exercise his functions.' " 1 Warren at 207.

50. 5 U.S. (1 Cranch) at 162–63.

51. 1 *Messages and Papers of the Presidents* 322.

52. For an excellent discussion of these issues, see William van Alstyne, "A Critical Guide to *Marbury v. Madison*," 1969 *Duke L. J.* 1.

53. See van Alstyne, 1969 *Duke L. J.* 7–8 (constitutionally doubtful that cabinet officer could be sued).

54. For an illuminating exploration of the centrality of the commitment to "reason" in Marshall's thinking, see Paul Kahn, "Reason and Will in the Origins of American Constitutionalism," 98 *Yale L. J.* 449, 479–87 (1989).

55. A cottage industry of academic game theorists has recently arisen to explore the implications of these strategies, as in the classic model of the "prisoners' dilemma" in choosing between narrowly self-aggrandizing and more cooperative decisional modes. See Paul Seabright, "Social Choice and Social Theories," 18 *Philosophy and Public Affairs* 365 (1989).

56. These implications were clear to Jefferson even before Marbury filed his suit in 1801: "[Jefferson's] policy of conciliation was not even being well-received by the Federalists at whom it was directed. The initial response to the principles expressed in the inaugural address had been favorable, but disenchantment came about almost immediately because many [Federalists] chose to interpret the speech as a promise of no removals. Jefferson's nullification of the undelivered commissions and his indiscriminate removal of marshals, attorneys, and all midnight appointees came under scathing criticism. . . . To the Federalists, the President's [actions were] a signal for the beginning of a systematic course of persecution and revenge. Moreover, they were convinced that whatever moderation Jefferson had shown was the direct result of their intimidations, and therefore they were not hesitant to criticize him." Ellis, *Jeffersonian Crisis* at 37–39.

57. *Federalist* 10 at 79–80 (emphasis added).

58. Id. at 78.

59. Van Alstyne, 1969 *Duke L. J.* 13 n.24.

60. Stuart v. Laird, 5 U.S. (1 Cranch) 299 (1803).

61. Ellis, *Jeffersonian Crisis* at 104.

62. 17 U.S. (4 Wheat.) 316, 400–01 (1819).

63. Martin v. Hunter's Lessee, 14 U.S. (1 Wheat.) 304 (1816); United States v. Peters, 9 U.S. (5 Cranch.) 115 (1809).

64. Letter of February 2, 1817, *Correspondence of John Adams and Thomas Jefferson, 1812–1826* 155 (P. Wilstach, ed.) (Indianapolis: Bobbs-Merrill, 1925).

65. Inaugural address, March 4, 1817, 2 *Messages and Papers of the Presidents* 579.

66. *John Marshall's Defense of McCulloch v. Maryland* 155–56 (G. Gunther, ed.) (Stanford: Stanford Univ. Press, 1969).

67. 17 U.S. (4 Wheat.) at 402.

68. Id. at 421.

69. See the newspaper critique by "Hampden" (Judge Spencer Roane) in *John Marshall's Defense* at 128–30.

70. *John Marshall's Defense* at 186–87, citing 17 U.S. (4 Wheat.) at 423.

71. 17 U.S. (4 Wheat.) at 414.

72. Id. at 423.

73. Id. at 430.

74. Id. at 429–30.

75. Id. at 431–32.

76. 17 U.S. (4 Wheat.) at 417.

77. 17 U.S. (4 Wheat.) at 402.

78. Id. at 403.

79. Id. at 427.

80. Speaking generally of the course of the Court's "sovereignty decisions" between 1815 and 1835 regarding both its authority to review state court judgments and the constitutional limits on state legislative authority, G. Edward White observed, "The most nationalistic achievement of the Marshall Court . . . was its erection of a theoretical justification of its own power . . . . The great significance of coterminous [federal-state governmental] power theory in the Court's decisions was a rationale for unlimited federal judicial power, not unlimited federal legislative power." White at 594. White was wrong, however, to conclude that "the Court's decisions had by the 1830's cemented its place as the final interpreter of the Constitution" (id.); this role was by then embedded only in its own decisions and not yet generally accepted elsewhere.

81. Richard Ellis, *The Union at Risk: Jacksonian Democracy, State's Rights and the Nullification Crisis* 7–8, 75 (New York: Oxford Univ. Press, 1987).

82. Id. at 7.

83. Id. at 76.

84. Nullification Proclamation, December 10, 1832, 2 *Messages and Papers of the Presidents* 652.

85. 31 U.S. (6 Peters) 515 (1832).

86. Ellis, *Union* at 31–32.

87. Fourth Annual Message, December 4, 1832, 2 *Messages and Papers of the Presidents* 604.

88. Veto Message, July 10, 1832, 2 *Messages and Papers of the Presidents* 581.

89. Nullification Proclamation, supra at 648–50.

90. Id. at 647.

91. Message of January 16, 1833, 2 *Messages and Papers of the Presidents* 629.

92. Id. at 631; see Ellis, *Union* at 94.

93. See Ellis, *Union* at ix. ("Although no other state endorsed the [nullification] concept . . . there was considerable support among well-placed individuals throughout the South for the nullifiers.")

94. Id. at 152–53. In a book written after his presidency, and published five years after his death, Van Buren reiterated this view, arguing that section 25 of the Judiciary Act of 1789 giving Supreme Court authority to "reexamine [and] reverse" state supreme court judgments was unconstitutional. M. Van Buren, *Inquiry into the Origin and Course of Political Parties in the United States* 301 (New York: Hurd & Houghton, 1867).

95. Van Buren's report referred to "the memorable civil revolution of 1800," Ellis, *Union* 152, thus echoing Jefferson's claim that his election and its repudiation of nationalist authority epitomized by the Alien and Sedition Acts was a second American Revolution. See Wiebe, *Opening* at 110; Ellis, *Jeffersonian Crisis* at 274–75. At the time *McCulloch* was decided, Judge Spencer Roane of the Virginia Supreme Court, in a pseudonymous newspaper attack, explicitly based his criticism on the principles of the Virginia Resolution, thereby indicating its persistent ideological significance: "It [the Resolution] has often been called by an eloquent statesman [John Randolph] his political bible. . . . It was the Magna Charta on which the republicans settled down, after the great struggle in the year 1799. Its principles have only been departed from since by turn-coats and apostates." *John Marshall's Defense* at 113. Judge William Brockenbrough of Virginia, in his newspaper critique of *McCulloch*, similarly relied on the premises of the Resolution: "[There is] no tribunal superior to the authority of the parties [so that] the parties themselves must be the rightful judges in the last resort [regarding the constitutionality of congressional acts]." Id. at 61.

96. See Powell, "Original Understanding of Original Intent" at 934–35: "With remarkable speed [after 1800], the constitutional theory of the Virginia and Kentucky Resolutions established itself as American political orthodoxy. . . . Acceptance of the compact theory . . . spread throughout the country and, beyond the confines of John Marshall's Supreme Court, stood virtually unquestioned until the nullification crisis of 1828 through 1832."

97. Ellis, *Union* at 170–77.

98. For the compromise resolution of *Worcester*, and the role of the Jackson administration facilitating this compromise to extricate itself from the "extremely awkward position" created by the contemporaneous nullification controversy, see White at 737–39; see also Ellis, *Union* at 186–87.

99. J. Calhoun, *A Discourse on the Constitution and Government of the United States* 146 (New York: D. Appleton & Co., 1854). See generally Theodore R.

Marmor, *The Career of John C. Calhoun: Politician, Social Critic, Political Philosopher* (New York: Garland Publ. Co., 1988).

100. Thus in Cohens v. Virginia, 19 U.S. (6 Wheat.) 264, 412 (1821), Marshall observed that the states were "for some purposes sovereign, for some purposes subordinate."

101. Calhoun at 152.

102. "[State] sovereignty [would not be] confined to taxation. That is not the only mode in which it might be displayed. The question is, in truth, a question of supremacy; and if the right of the States to tax the means employed by the general government be conceded, the declaration that the constitution . . . shall be the supreme law of the land, is empty and unmeaning declamation." McCulloch, 17 U. S. (4 Wheat.) at 433.

103. See H. Jefferson Powell, "Joseph Story's Commentaries on the Constitution: A Belated Review," 94 *Yale L. J.* 1285, 1308–09 (1985).

104. J. Story, 1 *Commentaries on the Constitution of the United States* 256 (3d ed.) (Boston: Little, Brown, 1858).

105. Letter to Senator Robert Hayne, April 3 or 4, 1830, 9 *Writings of James Madison* 390.

106. "Strong in the support which his predecessors did not have, he tramples his personal enemies underfoot wherever he finds them, with an ease impossible to any previous President; on his own responsibility he adopts measures which no one else would have dared to attempt; sometimes he even treats the national representatives with a sort of disdain that is almost insulting; he refuses to sanction laws of Congress and often fails to answer that important body. He is a favorite who is sometimes rude to his master. Hence General Jackson's power is constantly increasing, but that of the President grows less. The federal government is strong in his hands; it will pass to his successor enfeebled." Alexis de Tocqueville, *Democracy in America* 393–94 (J. Mayer, ed.) (Garden City, NY: Anchor Books, 1969 ed.).

107. McCoy, *Last of the Fathers* at 158–59.

108. See Greenberg, *Masters and Statesmen* at 33–41; Steven Stowe, *Intimacy and Power in the Old South: Ritual in the Lives of the Planters* 21–22, 47–49 (Baltimore: Johns Hopkins Univ. Press, 1987).

109. Greenberg at 31–32; Stowe at 23–49.

110. "The character of Andrew Jackson was a political issue because so much of his political behavior seems to be explained by it. . . . That same readiness to resort to violence which led this man, prior to his accession to the Presidency, to threaten or actually to inflict physical punishment or death on almost every man who thwarted him or who had offended him with some fancied insult, was brought into play in his dealing with foreign governments as with domestic issues and personages. There may have been something democratic in his total unconcern with the stature of the men he challenged—although he was southern aristocrat enough to distinguish between pistol whipping, caning, or dueling, depending on the status of his enemy. But there was something infinitely disturbing in the judgment that could distort

picayune differences literally into issues of life and death. He killed one man over a racetrack argument, threatened to kill two others for calling him ambitious, and a Secretary of War for advising him, accurately, about rumors that connected him with Burr." Pessen, *Jacksonian America* at 321.

111. Wiebe, *Opening* at 130.

112. Pessen at 34: "Where typically in the 1820s fewer than 15,000 Europeans came here each year, between 1832 and 1850 the annual number fell below 50,000 only twice and was usually over 100,000. In the 1830s more than a half million immigrants from Great Britain, Ireland and Germany arrived in New York City alone." See also Paul Boyer, *Urban Masses and Moral Order, 1820–1920* 67–70 (Cambridge: Harvard Univ. Press, 1978).

113. Tocqueville at 508.

114. See generally Hofstadter, *Party System* at 212–52.

115. Pessen at 154–56.

116. "It is to be regretted that the rich and powerful too often bend the acts of government to their selfish purposes. . . . [W]hen the laws undertake . . . to make the rich richer and the potent more powerful, the humble members of society—the farmers, mechanics, and laborers—who have neither the time nor the means of securing like favors to themselves, have a right to complain of the injustice of their Government." Andrew Jackson, Bank Veto Message, July 10, 1832, 2 *Messages and Papers of the Presidents* 590. See Ketcham at 154: "This polarizing conception of politics, which presents the central issue as that of either defeating or succumbing to the evil of special privilege, after 1829 became the reigning one in American public life." Compare Pessen at 160, noting the Jacksonian Democrats' "fondness for invoking a political rhetoric 'designed to sound something like a class war,' and the Whig response of attacking this alleged Democratic agrarianism as though for all the world it was authentic" with Arthur Schlesinger, Jr., "The Ages of Jackson," in *N.Y. Review of Books,* December 7, 1989, at 51, maintaining the authenticity of the Jacksonian era "struggle between the business community and the rest of society over who should control the state."

117. For Jackson himself, "majority rule constitute[d] the only meaning of liberty . . . [thus] subvert[ing] the earlier notion of republicanism" and its reliance on "intermediate agencies to refine and alter the popular will." Robert Remini, *Andrew Jackson and the Course of American Democracy, 1833–1845* 339 (New York: Harper & Row, 1984). Jackson accordingly proposed abolition of the Electoral College, direct election of Senators, and replacement of the life-tenured judiciary with federal judges elected to renewable seven-year terms. Id. at 342–43.

5. The Black Race within Our Bosom

1. The 1787 Constitution, for example, almost exclusively addressed relations among whites; Indians were explicitly mentioned but only as excluded

people, and blacks were implicitly acknowledged as slaves. Article I, section 8, gave Congress authority to regulate commerce "with the Indian tribes"; Article I, section 2, apportioned electoral representation and direct taxes on the basis of "free Persons . . . excluding Indians not taxed, [and] three fifths of all other Persons." These "other Persons" were again euphemistically invoked in Article I, section 9, regarding congressional authority to ban the slave trade, and in Article IV, section 2, the fugitive slave clause.

2. On colonial relations with Indians see John Murrin, "A Roof without Walls: The Dilemma of American National Identity," in Beeman (ed.), *Beyond Confederation* 336: "Except in Quaker communities, the [colonial] settlers . . . adopted a ferocious style of waging war. For Europe's more limited struggles among trained armies, they substituted people's wars of total subjection and even annihilation. Their methods were deliberately terroristic. They, not the Indians, began the systematic slaughter of women and children, often as targets of choice." On the evolution of colonial slave relations, see Edmund Morgan, *American Slavery/American Freedom: The Ordeal of Colonial Virginia* (New York: Norton, 1975)

3. *Notes on Virginia* at 299–300, 4 *Jefferson's Writings* 267–68.

4. Letter to General William Henry Harrison, February 27, 1803, 10 *Jefferson's Writings* 370–71.

5. Letter to Colonel Benjamin Hawkins, February 18, 1803, id. at 363.

6. Cited in Michael Paul Rogin, *Fathers and Children: Andrew Jackson and the Subjugation of the American Indian* 128 (New York: Knopf, 1975).

7. Regarding Jefferson's "uncertain commitment" to abolition of slavery, see Davis at 169–84. Regarding his attitude toward Indians, see Richard Drinnon, *Facing West: The Metaphysics of Indian-Hating and Empire Building* 78–98 (Minneapolis: Univ. Minnesota Press, 1980).

8. Letter to Thomas L. McKenney, February 10, 1826, 3 *Letters and Other Writings* 516.

9. Drinnon at 88. In the manuscript of a speech prepared for delivery to Northwest Indian tribal representatives in 1796, George Washington first wrote "Brothers," then crossed out the word and addressed them as "my Children." Ernest Schusky, "Thoughts and Deeds of the Founding Fathers: The Beginning of United States and Indian Relations," in *Political Organization of Native North Americans* 26 (E. Schusky, ed.) (Washington, D.C.: Univ. Press of America, 1980).

10. Robert Remini, *Andrew Jackson and the Course of American Freedom, 1822–1832*, 269–71 (New York: Harper & Row, 1981).

11. Robert Remini, *Andrew Jackson and the Course of American Empire, 1767–1821*, 397–98 (New York: Harper & Row, 1977). Even Jackson's victory against the British was intertwined with his successful conquest of Indians. Just nine months before the Battle of New Orleans, he had won the climactic battle against the Creek Indians, who were allied with the British and Spanish in northern Florida. "More Indians fought and were killed in this battle than

in any other in the history of American-Indian warfare. . . . Jackson's victory over the Creeks was the turning point of his life. He achieved the American army's first dramatic military triumph." Rogin at 156.

12. By these means, Jackson effectively removed Indians from "almost one-third of Tennessee, three-fourths of Florida and Alabama, one-fifth of Georgia and Mississippi, and perhaps one-tenth (or slightly less) of Kentucky and North Carolina." Remini, *1767–1821* at 306. See Rogin at 202: "Jackson built his authority on the unconscious falsification of memory and experience. Jackson denied depredations by Tennessee troops against the Cherokees, although he had admitted them two years earlier; he invented a Cherokee agreement with Jefferson and reported Cherokee acknowledgements of that agreement contradicted by the written record; and he called 'the plain language of truth' his unsupported wish, conveyed as fact to the Chickawas, that Congress planned to take their Tennessee land if they did not cede it."

13. Rogin at 207.

14. See Remini, *1833–1845* at 314: "By the close of Jackson's eight years in office approximately 45,690 Indians had been relocated beyond the Mississippi River. In addition, a number of treaties had been signed and ratified (but not yet executed) that would raise that figure by several thousand. . . . Only about 9,000 Indians, mostly in the Old Northwest and New York, were without treaty stipulations requiring their removal when Jackson left office."

15. Id. at 302–03. The same fierce execution of removal treaties was directed against the Creek and Seminole tribes; see id. at 303–14.

16. Murray Wax, *Indian Americans: Unity and Diversity* 32 (Englewood Cliffs, NJ: Prentice-Hall, 1971). See also Rogin at 241: "War, disease, accident, starvation, depredations, murder, whiskey, and other causes of death from the extension of state laws through removal and resettlement had killed by 1844 one-quarter to one-third of the southern Indians."

17. Rogin at 212.

18. Remini, *1822–1832* at 259–63. In enacting the Removal Bill, the Senate rejected an amendment providing that the federal government should respect Indian political and property rights until the tribes had decided whether to remove. The vote split on sectional lines, with the opposition (which included every southern senator) coming from the states with significant tribal presence. Joseph Burke, "The Cherokee Cases: A Study in Law, Politics, and Morality," 21 *Stanford L. Rev.* 500, 507 (1969).

19. Remini, *1822–1832* at 269 (emphasis added). Jackson's address was widely disseminated in newspapers at the time. In a similarly publicized address to the Cherokees in 1835, Jackson more directly spelled out the practical reasons why state jurisdiction would destroy the Indian tribes: "You are liable to [state] prosecution for offenses, and to civil actions for a breach of any of your contracts. . . . Most of your people are uneducated, and are liable to be brought into collision at all times with your white neighbors. Your young men are acquiring habits of intoxication. With strong passions, and

without those habits of restraint which our laws inculcate and render necessary, they are frequently driven to excesses which must eventually terminate in their ruin. The game has disappeared among you, and you must depend upon agriculture, and the mechanic arts for support. And, yet, a large portion of your people have acquired little or no [state-recognized] property in the soil itself, or in any article of [state-recognized] personal property which can be useful to them. How, under these circumstances, can you live in the country you now occupy? Your condition must become worse and worse, and you will ultimately disappear, as so many tribes have done before you." Remini, *1833–1845* at 297–98.

20. Quoted by Remini, *1822–1832* at 279.

21. See Remini, *1822–1832* at 265.

22. Under the Articles of Confederation, congressional authority to regulate commerce was restricted to Indians who were "not members of any of the states." As Madison observed in *Federalist* 42 at 269, "What description of Indians are to be deemed members of a State is not yet settled, and has been a question of frequent perplexity and contention in the federal councils. And how the trade with Indians, though not members of a State, yet residing within its legislative jurisdiction can be regulated by an external [national] authority, without so far intruding on the internal [state] rights of legislation, is absolutely incomprehensible. This is not the only case in which the Articles of Confederation have inconsiderately endeavored to accomplish impossibilities; to reconcile a partial sovereignty in the Union, with complete sovereignty in the States; to subvert a mathematical axiom by taking away a part and letting the whole remain."

23. 21 U.S. (8 Wheat.) 543 (1823).

24. Id. at 587.

25. Id. at 584.

26. Id. at 591–92.

27. Id. at 590.

28. Id. at 591.

29. Id. at 590.

30. 30 U.S. (5 Peters) 1 (1831).

31. Id. at 17.

32. For consideration of the strategic elements in Marshall's approach in *Cherokee Nation*, see White at 723–30 and Burke, passim.

33. Marshall's resistance to state authority over Indian tribes in *Worcester* was foreshadowed in his observation in *Cherokee Nation* that the tribes were "so completely under the sovereignty and dominion of the United States, that any attempt [by foreign governments] to acquire their lands, or to form a political connexion with them, would be considered by all as an invasion of our territory, and an act of hostility," 30 U.S. (5 Peters) at 17–18.

34. See White at 712–14.

35. A few cases involving aspects of slave status came before the Supreme

Court during Marshall's tenure, and he was notably disinclined to provoke any controversy. See generally White at 688–703. Marshall's attitude is best revealed in a letter to Justice Story, noting the public acrimony produced by Justice Johnson's circuit ruling that overturned a South Carolina statute imposing detention on all free black sailors entering state ports. Marshall observed that, in another circuit case, he "might have considered [the] constitutionality" of a similar Virginia statute, "but it was not absolutely necessary, and, as I am not fond of butting against a wall in sport, I escaped on the construction of the act." Letter of September 26, 1823, quoted in 1 Warren at 626. He was equally circumspect in Supreme Court rulings. For example, in The Antelope, 23 U.S. (10 Wheat.) 66, 120–21 (1825), Marshall stated that, although the slave trade violated "natural right," nonetheless "the usages, the national acts, and the general assent of [the relevant] portion of the world [testified] in favor of the legality of the trade." In an earlier circuit court ruling, Justice Story had freed captive blacks on a ship seized in American waters based on the illegality of the slave trade, United States v. La Jeune Eugenie, 26 F.Cas. 832 (No. 15,551) (C.C.Mass. 1822). Though Marshall's statement in The Antelope appeared inconsistent with this ruling, his opinion steered a cautious course regarding the proof necessary to establish that blacks on seized ships were slaves and thus should not be freed. See generally Donald Roper, "In Quest of Judicial Objectivity: The Marshall Court and the Legitimation of Slavery," 21 *Stanford L. Rev.* 532 (1969). Jackson was more openly hostile to any challenges to slavery than Marshall, and as President he supported the institution on the few occasions when public controversy required action, such as his support for legislation authorizing federal censorship of abolitionist mailings to the South. See Remini, *1833–1845* at 258–63.

36. Davis at 87, 89, 197.

37. Robert McColley, *Slavery and Jeffersonian Virginia* 71–73 (Urbana: Univ. Illinois Press, 1978 ed.). In 1806 the Virginia legislature specified that any subsequently freed slave in the state one year after manumission would forfeit "his or her right to freedom . . . and may be apprehended and sold by the overseers of the poor." This law was, however, only sporadically enforced; in 1837, in apparent recognition of this fact, the legislature provided that slaves freed after 1806 could remain in the state only after specific judicial certification of their "peaceable, orderly and industrious" character. Paul Finkelman, *The Law of Freedom and Bondage* 114–15 (New York: Oceana Publications, 1986); Benjamin Klebaner, "American Manumission Laws and the Responsibility for Supporting Slaves," 63 *Va. Mag. Hist. and Biography* 443, 449 (1955).

38. "Prior to the 1830s, black subordination was the practice of white Americans, and the inferiority of the Negro was undoubtedly a common assumption, but open assertions of *permanent* inferiority were exceedingly rare." George Frederickson, *The Black Image in the White Mind: The Debate on*

Afro-American Character and Destiny, 1817–1914 at 43 (New York: Harper & Row, 1971).

39. Id. at 74–90. See also Willie Lee Rose, *Slavery and Freedom* 25 (New York: Oxford Univ. Press, 1982): "New laws restricting [slaves'] movement and eliminating their education indicate blacks were categorized as *a special and different kind of humanity,* as lesser humans in a dependency assumed to be perpetual. In earlier . . . times, they had been seen as luckless, unfortunate barbarians. Now they were to be treated as children expected never to grow up." (Emphasis in original.) In one reflection of this changed attitude, after 1830 "one state after another closed off manumissions altogether." Eugene Genovese, *Roll, Jordan, Roll: The World the Slaves Made* 399 (New York: Pantheon Books, 1974).

40. William Freehling, *The Road to Disunion: Secessionists at Bay, 1776–1854* 150–52 (New York: Oxford Univ. Press, 1990).

41. See Frederickson at 5–6.

42. See Freehling at 193: "All Virginians in the 1830s, even [those] who flirted with slavery-blessed-for-all-races, hoped the Upper South would someday contain no more slaves—and only the white race."

43. See Freehling at 150–51 (regarding 1819 Missouri Compromise debate), 421–23 (regarding 1845 Texas annexation debate).

44. Morgan at 312.

45. In 1795, St. George Tucker observed: "This abominable law continued to stain our code, and to corrupt the morals of the people of Virginia until the year 1788. In that year, I, for the first time since my acquaintance with courts, saw a white man tried and *convicted* for the murder of a slave by excessive whipping, and he was hanged accordingly. Unfortunately, in the new edition of our laws, the legislature thought it sufficient to expunge the former act, without inserting the latter. I fear it may have an ill consequence; for there is nothing like holding up a warning in view of bad men." Letter to Dr. Belknap, June 29, 1795, 3 *Collections of the Mass. Hist. Soc.,* 5th ser., 407. Tucker was professor of law at William and Mary College where he edited the standard American edition of Blackstone and subsequently served on the Virginia Court of Appeals from 1804 to 1811 and as United States District Judge from 1813 to 1825.

46. 13 N.C. 263 (1828).

47. Id. at 265–66.

48. Id. at 266. Ruffin continued, id. at 267–68: "We are [also] happy to see that there is daily less and less occasion for the interposition of the Courts [to protect slaves against masters' power.] The protection already afforded by . . . that all-powerful motive, the private interest of the owner, the benevolences towards each other, seated in the hearts of those who have been born and bred together, the frowns and deep execrations of the community upon the barbarian who is guilty of excessive and brutal cruelty to his unprotected slave, all combined, have produced a mildness of treatment

and attention to the comforts of the unfortunate class of slaves, greatly mitigating the rigors of servitude and ameliorating the condition of the slaves."

49. See Mark Tushnet, *The American Law of Slavery 1810–1860: Considerations of Humanity and Interest* 62 (Princeton, NJ: Princeton Univ. Press, 1981).

50. See Genovese at 686 n.33.

51. 20 N.C. 365 (1839).

52. Id. at 368–69.

53. See Tushnet, *American Law of Slavery* at 188–228.

54. Chapter 107, section 29, Revised Code of North Carolina, (1855), rpt. in J. B. White, *The Legal Imagination: Studies in the Nature of Legal Thought and Expression* 445 (Boston: Little, Brown, 1973).

55. Chapter 15, Penal Code, Laws of Alabama (1843), rpt. in White at 442–43.

56. Section 16, Slave Code, Laws of Alabama (1843), rpt. in White at 440.

57. For example, Chapter 107, section 31, North Carolina Revised Code (1853), provided "It shall not be lawful for any slave to be insolent to a free white person . . . nor for any male slave to have sexual intercourse, or indulge in any grossly indecent familiarities with a white female; . . . nor to raise any horses, cattle, hogs, or sheep; nor to teach, or attempt to teach, any other slave or free negro to read or write, the use of figures excepted; nor to sell any spiritous liquor or wine; nor to play at any game of cards, dice, or nine pins . . . ; nor to preach or exhort in public . . . at any prayer-meeting . . . where slaves of different families are collected together." Rpt. in White at 445–46.

58. Rose at 24.

59. For example, the Alabama Constitution provided that "any person, who shall maliciously dismember or deprive a slave of life, shall suffer such punishment as would be inflicted in case the like offence had been committed on a free white person, and on the like proof, except in case of insurrection of such slave." Chapter 92, section 44, of the Mississippi Laws (1840) imposed fines on "any master . . . who shall inflict . . . cruel or unusual punishment, or shall authorize or permit the same to be inflicted." See also Tushnet at 68.

60. Chapter 107, section 27, Revised Code of North Carolina (1855). This provision had an ingenious enforcement scheme; if a slave "who shall appear not to have been properly clothed and fed" stole produce or livestock, the "injured person" (that is, the farmer) was given a civil damages action against the slave's owner. See generally Rose at 23.

61. See Genovese at 38–39: "When whites did find themselves before the bar of justice, especially during the late antebellum period, they could expect greater severity than might be imagined. The penalties seldom reached the extreme or the level they would have if the victim had been white; but neither did they usually qualify as a slap on the wrist. If one murderer in

North Carolina got off with only eleven months in prison in 1825, most fared a good deal worse. Ten-year sentences were common, and occasionally the death penalty was invoked." Judge Ruffin's own court, just six years after his ruling in *Mann*, held that a slave who was wounded by and, in response, killed his overseer could claim self-defense, even though the overseer could not have been criminally prosecuted for his action under the *Mann* holding. State v. Will, 18 N.C. 121 (1834). Ruffin himself silently concurred in this holding, notwithstanding its problematic relation to *Mann*. In 1849 the North Carolina Supreme Court, over Ruffin's vigorous dissent, held that a slave who killed a white man engaged in assaulting another slave was guilty only of manslaughter, not murder. State v. Caesar, 31 N.C. 391 (1849). Judge Pearson, for the majority, stated that "we [are] forced, in spite of stern policy, to admire, even in a slave, the generosity, which incurs danger to save a friend. The law requires a slave to tame down his feelings to suit his lowly condition, but it would be savage, to allow him, under no circumstances, to yield to a generous impulse." Id. at 406. Echoing his concerns in *Mann*, Ruffin rejoined, id. at 427–28, "It seems to me dangerous to the last degree to hold the doctrine, that negro slaves may assume to themselves the judgment as to the right or propriety of resistance, by one of his own race, to the authority taken over them by the whites. . . . First denying their general subordination to the whites, it may be apprehended that they will end in denouncing the injustice of slavery itself, and, upon that pretext, band together to throw off their common bondage entirely."

62. Rose at 27.

63. Cong. Globe, 25th Cong., 2d Sess., Appendix at 61–62 (January 10, 1838).

64. Tocqueville at 358.

65. The South could cite distinguished precedent for this practice: in the Declaration of Independence, the final injury charged to George III was that "he has excited domestic insurrections amongst us, and has endeavored to bring on the inhabitants of our frontiers the merciless Indian savages, whose known rule of warfare is an undistinguished destruction of all ages, sexes, and conditions." See Gary Wills, *Inventing America: Jefferson's Declaration of Independence* 71–75, 377 (Garden City, NY: Doubleday, 1978).

66. See Remini, *1833–1845* at 258–62.

67. Id. at 405–06.

68. See generally Freehling at 308–352.

69. Robert M. Cover, *Justice Accused: Antislavery and the Judicial Process* 161 (New Haven: Yale Univ. Press, 1975)

70. Id. at 162.

71. 41 U.S. 539 (1842).

72. See Story's circuit opinion in United States v. La Jeune Eugenie, discussed note 35 supra; Cover at 239–40.

73. 41 U.S. at 609.

74. Id. The conviction was affirmed "pro forma" by the Pennsylvania

Supreme Court, which led Justice McLean to observe in his dissent that "the case has been made up merely to bring the question before this Court." Id. at 673.

75. Act of February 12, 1793, Chap. 7, 1 Stat. 302 (1793).

76. 41 U.S. at 620, 666–67.

77. Id. at 623–24.

78. Id. at 624.

79. So Justice McLean observed in his dissent, id. at 669.

80. Id. at 624.

81. Id. at 622.

82. Id. at 613.

83. Id. at 609. See Paul Finkelman, *An Imperfect Union: Slavery, Federalism and Comity* 138–39 (Chapel Hill: Univ. North Carolina Press, 1981).

84. Story's justification is almost ludicrously one-sided: "The [fugitive slave] clause manifestly contemplated the existence of a positive, unqualified right on the part of the owner of the slave . . . . The slave is not to be discharged from service or labour, in consequence of any state law or regulation. Now, certainly, without indulging in any nicety of criticism upon words, it may fairly and reasonably be said, that any state law or state regulation, which interrupts, limits, delays, or postpones the right of the owner to the immediate possession of the slave . . . operates, pro tanto, a discharge of the slave therefrom." 41 U.S. at 612.

85. Cover at 240–41.

86. 13 N.C. 263, 267 (1828).

87. See David Potter, *The Impending Crisis, 1848–1861* at 137–39 (New York: Harper & Row, 1976), noting "substantial evidence that a considerable segment of northern opinion was willing, for the sake of the [Constitutional] Compromise [regarding slavery] to accept [enforcement of fugitive slave laws . . . and that there] is no convincing evidence that a preponderant majority in the North were prepared to violate or nullify the law."

88. See Genovese at 398–413.

89. In 1853, for example, a Mississippi Senator recalled that New York and Pennsylvania had once been slave states but then sent many blacks southward and ultimately freed the rest. "Virginia, Maryland, and the border states" he observed, "are now undergoing the same process." A Georgia Senator privately wrote John Calhoun in 1849 that heretics "are to be found in all the southern states [and] will be encouraged, at no distant day, to hoist the antislavery banner. . . . Then it will soon be recorded—the slaveholding states, *were*." Freehling at 473–74. Southern secessionists dreaded the prospect, according to Freehling, that "northerners could just hem slavery in [and then] southern allies, bolstered by national patronage and prestige, might draw southern [anti-slavery] dissent out of hiding." Id. at 472.

90. For a modern statement of this rule mandating use of state procedures in federal litigation, see Guarantee Trust v. York, 326 U.S. 99 (1945).

91. In conventional modern formulations, this constitutional ruling could

be conceptualized as a vindication of state autonomy protected by the Tenth Amendment. Though the leading modern case for the proposition, National League of Cities v. Usery, 426 U.S. 833 (1976), has been overruled by Garcia v. San Antonio Metropolitan Transit Authority, 469 U.S. 528 (1985), there is a more limited version of state autonomy that might still survive. This version more directly tracks Madison's own concerns, not with state autonomy as such but with the more generally applicable principle of institutional equality in the interpretation of the Constitution. Just as John Marshall could insist in *Marbury* that the judiciary had an equal interpretive claim when the Congress enlisted its active assistance, so the states could claim equal authority to interpret the constitutional jury guarantees when Congress sought direct state assistance in fugitive slave cases. For a modern, post-*Garcia* judicial articulation of this concern, see Bowen v. American Hospital Ass'n, 476 U.S. 610, 643–45 (1986); compare Federal Energy Regulatory Commission v. Mississippi, 456 U.S. 742 (1982).

92. For a modern application of this judicial strategy, see Kent v. Dulles, 357 U.S. 116 (1958), discussed in Bickel, *Least Dangerous Branch* at 164–67.

93. For elaboration of this proposition, and consideration of its relationship to more conventional justifications for judicial interventions on issues such as the death penalty and abortion, see generally Chapter 9, infra.

94. Chief Justice Taney thus stated in his separate opinion, "According to the opinion just delivered [by Justice Story], the state authorities are prohibited from interfering for the purpose of protecting the right of the master and aiding him in the recovery of his property. I think the states are not prohibited; and that, on the contrary, it is enjoined upon them as a duty to protect and support the owner . . . . In many of the states there is but one [federal] district judge, and there are only nine states which have judges of the Supreme Court residing within them. The fugitive will frequently be found by his owner in a place very distant from the residence of either of these judges; and would certainly be removed beyond his reach, before a warrant could be procured from the judge to arrest him . . . . [This] show[s] how ineffectual and delusive is the remedy provided by Congress, if state authority is forbidden to come to its aid." 41 U.S. at 627, 630–31.

95. 60 U.S. (19 How.) 393 (1857).

96. See Paul Finkelman, "*Prigg v. Pennsylvania* and Northern State Courts: Anti-Slavery Use of a Pro-Slavery Decision," 25 *Civil War Hist.* 5, 21–22 (1979).

97. Just after *Prigg* was decided, Story privately recommended a more devious route to this same end. In a letter to a Senator from Georgia, Story wrote that "it might be unwise to provoke debate" by enacting legislation that explicitly referred to fugitive slave rendition; and he proposed instead that federal judges be authorized to appoint commissioners in each state to "exercise all the powers" under "any Law" of the United States. This "general" provision, Story suggested, "would meet the practical difficulty now

presented by the refusal of State Magistrates" to enforce the 1793 Act "without creating the slightest sensation in Congress." Letter to John McPherson Berrien, April 29, 1842, quoted in Finkelman, *"Prigg"* at 16.

The 1850 Act provided a summary administrative proceeding and rejected every procedural safeguard that the northern abolitionist bar had sought: no jury trial before extradition (or afterward, in southern courts, as Henry Clay unsuccessfully proposed), no access to habeas corpus review in federal or state courts, no rights for the alleged fugitive to testify or confront adverse witnesses. Freehling at 500–01.

98. See Cover at 175–191. The Supreme Court forcefully rebuffed the Wisconsin officials in Ableman v. Booth, 62 U.S. (21 How.) 506 (1858), discussed in Chapter 6, infra. Regarding the general pattern of enforcement under the 1850 act, David Potter, *Impending Crisis* at 138, concluded that the North did not readily comply, since "it must be remembered that it was impossible to secure convictions of members of mobs who had taken fugitives from custody, that slaves were often recovered only at great public expense and with major display of official force, and that the law was defied primarily by spiriting slaves away before officers found them, rather than by resisting officers directly. Yet, the picture of overwhelming northern defiance must be qualified. There were, after all, in the first six years of the law, only three cases of forcible and successful rescue. During the same time, it is estimated that two hundred Negroes were arrested. Perhaps a third of these were taken back to the South without trial, while of the remaining two-thirds, eight were released, twelve were rescued, and the rest were remanded to slavery."

99. Potter, *Impending Crisis* at 18–22.

100. Cong. Globe, 1st sess., appendix, p. 686 (1848).

101. The Texas and New Mexico Act, 9 Stat. 446 (1850); the Utah Act, 9 Stat. 453 (1850).

102. Wallace Mendelson, "Dred Scott's Case—Reconsidered," 38 *Minn. L. Rev.* 16, 27 n.53 (1953) (quoting Senator Corwin). Henry Clay similarly declared, "We cannot settle the question [of authority over territorial slavery] because of the great diversity of opinion which exists." Cong. Globe, 31 Cong., 1 Sess. (June 7, 1850): Appendix, 1155.

103. 10 Stat. 227 (1854).

104. Potter, *Impending Crisis* at 199–215.

105. See id. at 272–73.

106. McPherson, *Battle Cry of Freedom* at 171–73. Justice Nelson of New York had prepared the early, narrow-gauged opinion for the Court; but when the decision was finally rendered, only he adhered to this position. 60 U.S. at 457.

107. See Don Fehrenbacher, *The Dred Scott Case: Its Significance in American Law and Politics* 559–60 (New York: Oxford Univ. Press, 1978).

108. 60 U.S. at 454–55.

109. 6 *Messages and Papers of the Presidents* 2962.

110. A standard criticism of *Dred Scott,* first articulated in Justice Curtis's dissent, has been that its ruling on the Missouri Compromise was obiter dicta because the citizenship holding wholly disposed of the case. Technically speaking, this criticism is erroneous, since the invalidation of the Missouri Compromise was in effect an alternative basis to reach the conclusion that Scott was not a citizen for federal court jurisdictional purposes; if, that is, the Missouri Compromise were invalid, then Scott remained a slave and as such was indisputably not a federal citizen even if free blacks were eligible for this status. See Burt, "What Was Wrong with *Dred Scott,* What's Right about *Brown,*" 42 *Wash. and Lee L. Rev.* 1, 12–13 (1985). This only means, however, that it was technically permissible for the Court majority to address the constitutionality of the Missouri Compromise in considering Scott's citizenship status, not that the majority was required or was wise to do so. For my evaluation of the internal coherence generally of the legal reasoning in the majority and dissenting opinions in the case, see id. at 4–11.

111. Congress was forbidden, Taney said, to treat territories as "colonies . . . to be ruled and governed at its own pleasure" but must instead ensure that all territories will ultimately become states "upon an equal footing with the other [original] States" which under the Constitution had possessed unqualified, independent authority to determine their own policies toward slavery. 60 U.S. at 446–47.

112. Cong. Globe, 36th Cong., 1st Sess. 658 (February 1860). Davis was reiterating here the position he had taken at least a year earlier; see McPherson at 195, 214.

113. See McPherson at 214–16, 223.

114. For statements of this view, see, e.g., Robert Jackson, *The Struggle for Judicial Supremacy* 327 (New York: Knopf, 1949); Stanley Kutler, *The Dred Scott Decision: Law or Politics* xvii (Boston: Houghton Mifflin, 1967); Potter, *Impending Crisis* at 291–93.

115. See Aileen Kraditor, *Means and Ends in American Abolitionism: Garrison and His Critics on Strategy and Tactics, 1834–1850* at 195–216 (New York: Pantheon, 1969); Cover at 168, 175.

116. Tocqueville at 508.

117. Id. at 317.

118. Id. at 324.

119. See, e.g., Mechal Sobel, *The World They Made Together: Black and White Values in Eighteenth-Century Virginia* (Princeton: Princeton Univ. Press, 1987); James Axtell, *The European and the Indian: Essays in the Ethnohistory of Colonial North America* 39–86, 272–315 (New York: Oxford Univ. Press, 1981).

120. Michael Paul Rogin, *Ronald␣Reagan, the Movie, and Other Episodes in Political Demonology* 154 (Berkeley: Univ. California Press, 1987).

121. Second Annual Message, December 6, 1830, 2 *Messages and Papers of the Presidents* 521.

122. March 4, 1825, 2 *Messages and Papers of the Presidents* 862.

123. Annual Message to Congress, December 6, 1825, id. at 881. See generally Ketcham at 130–40.

124. This essence of Adams's views was distilled by one grandson, Brooks Adams, in his introduction to a book by another grandson, Henry Adams, *The Degradation of the Democratic Dogma* 22–32 (New York: Macmillan, 1919).

125. Ketcham at 155–56; Remini, *1833–1845* at 406, 441–42.

126. See Eric Foner, *Free Soil, Free Labor, Free Men: The Ideology of the Republican Party before the Civil War* 11–51 (New York: Oxford Univ. Press, 1970).

127. Id. at 66–69.

128. On the vast scale of Civil War destruction, see Chapter 6, text accompanying notes 32–36, infra.

6. The Civil War Rules

1. See David Potter, *Lincoln and His Party in the Secession Crisis* 8–19 (New Haven: Yale Univ. Press, 1942).

2. See McPherson at 317.

3. In re Booth, 3 Wis. 1, 23–24 (1854).

4. Ableman v. Booth, 62 U.S. 506, 525 (1859).

5. Id. at 519.

6. This is the full passage from the Court's opinion: "As the final appellate power in all such questions [regarding the constitutionality of congressional acts] is given to this court, controversies as to the respective powers of the United States and the States, instead of being determined by military and physical force, are heard, investigated, and finally settled, with the calmness and deliberation of judicial inquiry. And no one can fail to see, that if such an arbiter had not been provided, . . . internal tranquillity could not have been preserved; and if such controversies were left to arbitrament of physical force, our Government, State and national, would soon cease to be Governments of laws, and revolutions by force of arms would take the place of courts of justice and judicial decisions. Id. at 520–21.

7. 4 *Collected Works* 264.

8. Walter Murphy, "Who Shall Interpret? The Quest for the Ultimate Constitutional Interpreter," 48 *Review of Politics* 401, 405 (1986). Lincoln's supportive reasoning in his inaugural address reads like a judge's opinion (or a lawyer's brief):

Perpetuity is implied, if not expressed, in the fundamental law of all national governments. It is safe to assert that no government proper ever had a provision in its organic law for its termination . . .

Again, if the United States be not a government proper, but an association of States in the nature of contract merely, can it as a contract be peaceably unmade by less than all the parties who made it? One party to a contract may violate it—break it, so to speak; but does it not require all to lawfully rescind it?

Descending from these general principles, we find the proposition that in legal contemplation the Union is perpetual confirmed by the history of the Union itself. The Union is much older than the Constitution. It was formed, in fact, by the Articles of Association in 1774. It was matured and continued by the Declaration of Independence in 1776. It was further matured, and the faith of all the then thirteen States expressly plighted and engaged that it should be perpetual, by the Articles of Confederation in 1778. And, finally, in 1787 one of the declared objects for ordaining and establishing the Constitution was "to form a more perfect Union." . . .

It follows from these views that no State upon its own mere motion can lawfully get out of the Union; that resolves and ordinances to that effect are legally void; and that acts of violence, within any State or States, against the authority of the United States, are insurrectionary or revolutionary, according to circumstances. 4 *Collected Works* 264–65.

9. See McPherson at 235.

10. Luther v. Borden, 48 U.S. (7 How.) 1 (1849).

11. The Prize Cases, 67 U.S. (2 Black) 635 (1863).

12. In June 1861, Chief Justice Taney, acting alone as Circuit Justice, had overridden Lincoln's suspension of the writ of habeas corpus in Ex Parte Merryman, in part relying on the absence of congressional authorization for such suspension. See 2 Warren at 368–74.

13. For an astute discussion of the ways in which the internal organization of the Congress provided the southern states with an effective veto, both before the Civil War and then again after the end of Reconstruction, and thus had "functionally" achieved Calhoun's formal goal of requiring concurrent sectional majorities even though neither Calhoun nor the later southern secessionists acknowledged this fact, see David Potter, *The South and the Concurrent Majority* 6–8 (Baton Rouge: Louisiana State Univ. Press, 1972).

14. For a brief sketch of the plausible constitutional arguments available in 1861 to support the secession right, see David Currie, "The Constitution in the Supreme Court: Civil War and Reconstruction, 1865–1873," 51 *U. Chi. L. Rev.* 131, 163–65 (1984). See also Tocqueville's reflection of views commonly held in 1831: "If today one of [the] states wished to withdraw its name from the [constitutional] contract, it would be hard to prove that it could not do so. In resisting it the federal government would have no obvious source of support either in strength or in right" (at 369). Note, too, that in an 1861 letter to former President Franklin Pierce, Chief Justice Taney wrote that he hoped both North and South would see that "a peaceful separation, with free institutions in each section, is far better than the union of all the present states under a military government, and a reign of terror preceded

too by a civil war with all its horrors." Letter of June 12, 1861, cited in C. G. Haines and F. H. Sherwood, *The Role of the Supreme Court in American Government and Politics* 465 (Berkeley: Univ. of California Press, 1957).

15. See Currie, 51 *U. Chi. L. Rev.* 144.

16. 71 U.S. (4 Wall.) 2, 126–27 (1866).

17. Ex parte Vallandigham, 68 U.S. (1 Wall.) 243 (1864) (finding no jurisdiction for direct Supreme Court review of a military commission judgment). See Ex parte Merryman, supra, note 12.

18. 2 Warren at 374, 423.

19. Ex parte Garland, 71 U.S. (4 Wall.) 333 (1867).

20. See Currie, 51 *U. Chi. L. Rev.* 144–68.

21. See Gordon v. United States, 69 U.S. (2 Wall.) 561 (1865) (invalidating Supreme Court appellate jurisdiction over the Court of Claims); Reichart v. Felps, 73 U.S. (6 Wall.) 160 (1868) (invalidating congressional authority to nullify land titles); The Alicia, 74 U.S. (7 Wall.) 571 (1869) (invalidating original Supreme Court jurisdiction in naval blockade seizure cases). For immediately subsequent decisions provoking greater political controversy, see Hepburn v. Griswold, 75 U.S. (8 Wall.) 603 (1870) (invalidating congressional act substituting paper money for species notes) *reversed by* Legal Tender Cases, 79 U.S. (12 Wall.) 457 (1871); United States v. Klein, 80 U.S. (13 Wall.) 128 (1872) (invalidating congressional act construing legal consequences of presidential pardons for participation in rebellion).

22. McCulloch v. Maryland, 17 U.S. (4 Wheat.) at 401.

23. Ableman v. Booth, 62 U.S. (4 How.) at 521.

24. Cong. Globe, 39th Cong., 1st Sess. 1033–34 (1866).

25. Representative Thaddeus Stevens, who reported the new version to the House, plainly revealed the concern that led the Joint Committee away from its previous reliance on enhanced congressional authority: "Unless the Constitution should restrain them [the rebel] States will all, I fear, keep up th[eir race] discrimination, and crush to death the hated freedmen. Some answer, 'Your civil rights bill secures the same things.' That is partly true, but a law is repealable by a majority. And I need hardly say that the first time that the South with their copperhead allies obtain the command of Congress it will be repealed." Cong. Globe, 39th Cong. 1st Sess. 2459 (May 8, 1866).

During the February House debate, Representative Hotchkiss had faulted the first draft of the Amendment for failing to provide safeguards against this eventuality. Id. at 1095 (February 28, 1866).

26. Cong. Globe, 39th Cong., 1st Sess. 2462 (May 8, 1866).

27. Cong. Globe, 39th Cong., 2d Sess. 502 (January 16, 1867).

28. Ibid.

29. See Eric Foner, *Reconstruction: America's Unfinished Revolution, 1873–1877* 272 (New York: Harper & Row, 1988).

30. Madison's *Notes*, August 15, 1787, at 481.

31. Sigmund Freud, *Civilization and Its Discontents* 13 (J. Strachey, ed.) (New York: W. W. Norton, 1961).

32. The number of southern civilian casualties is a "fair estimate," but less reliable than the estimates of uniformed deaths. See McPherson at 619 n.53, 854. American military deaths in all other wars total approximately 656,600. See Phillip Paludan, *"A People's Contest": The Union and Civil War, 1861–1865* 316 (New York: Harper & Row, 1988), and *Information Please Almanac, 1989* 313 (Boston: Houghton Mifflin Co., 1989).

33. M. Small and J. D. Small, *Resort to Arms: International and Civil Wars, 1816–1980* 224 (Beverly Hills, CA: Sage Publications, 1982). T. H. Williams, *The Selected Essays of T. Harry Williams* 33 (Baton Rouge: Louisiana State Univ. Press, 1983).

34. Paludan at 316–17.

35. McPherson at 742–43 (emphasis in original).

36. *Mary Chesnut's Civil War* 411–12 (C. Vann Woodward, ed.) (New Haven: Yale Univ. Press, 1981).

37. 8 *Writings* 330–31.

38. Foner, *Reconstruction* at 119.

39. *Mary Chesnut's Civil War* at 198–99.

40. See Litwack at 193–212.

41. *4 Collected Works* 271.

42. See especially the recent works of Foner and Litwack.

43. William Dunning, *Reconstruction: Political and Economic, 1865–1877* 3 (New York: Harper & Bros., 1907).

44. Litwack at 370.

45. Dunning at 59.

46. See Foner at 208–210.

47. Stevens continued, "If impartial [black] suffrage is excluded in the rebel States then every one of them is sure to send a solid rebel representation to Congress, and cast a solid rebel electoral vote. They, with their kindred Copperheads of the North, would always elect the President and control Congress." Quoted in C. Vann Woodward, *The Burden of Southern History* 95 (Baton Rouge; Louisiana State Univ. Press, 1968 ed.).

48. Id. at 97.

49. Foner at 425.

50. See Foner at 438, 443: "On paper, the new state governments did take decisive steps, outlawing going about in disguise, raising the penalties for assault, murder, and conspiracy [and other such measures]. Yet when it came to enforcing these laws, Republican leaders vacillated. . . . [The] violence underscored yet again the 'abnormal' quality of Reconstruction politics. Before the war, Democrats and Whigs had combated fiercely through the South, but neither party . . . advised its supporters 'to drive out, to starve and to perish' its political opponents. Corrupt election procedures, political chicanery, and even extralegal attempts to oust the opposition party from office were hardly unknown in the North, but not pervasive political violence."

51. Foner at 458.
52. Foner at 32–33.
53. See McPherson at 606–11, 816.
54. Foner at 309.
55. See Litwack at 374–79.
56. See Foner at 512–17.
57. Id. at 523.
58. See C. Vann Woodward, *Reunion and Reaction: The Compromise of 1877 and the End of Reconstruction* 21 (Boston: Little, Brown, 1951): "Debates became angrier on Capitol Hill and members began to arm themselves. Scenes on the floor of the two Houses reminded old-timers of the days of 1860–61. . . . Memories of those days were always present in this crisis." P. Haworth, *The Hayes–Tilden Disputed Presidential Election of 1876* 168 (1906): "More people [expected civil war in 1876] than had anticipated a like outcome to the secession movement of 1860–61." Dunning at 319: "The Democratic half of the population believed that Tilden had been elected president, and many were professing a determination to place him in the White House by force, if necessary; the Republican half were no less convinced and resolute in their claims for Hayes."
59. 4 *Collected Works* 269.
60. Henry Adams, *The Education of Henry Adams* 226 (New York: Modern Library, 1931 ed.).
61. Id. at 229.
62. Id. at 277.
63. Charles Fairman, "Mr. Justice Bradley," in *Mr. Justice* 69 (A. Dunham and P. Kurland, eds.) (Chicago: Univ. of Chicago Press, 1956).
64. Bradley himself observed, "I know that it is difficult for men of the world to believe this, but I know it, and that is enough for me." Id. at 83.
65. See Woodward, *Reunion* at 155–62.
66. See C. Vann Woodward, *Origins of the New South, 1877–1913* 45, 48 (Baton Rouge: Louisiana State Univ. Press, 1951), citing Republican editorialist charges in 1878 that "the spirit of rebellion still lives [in the South] and is liable at any moment to be again entrenched in arms."
67. Address on Colonization to a Deputation of Colored Men, August 14, 1862, 5 *Collected Works* 371.
68. Foner at 49; McPherson at 852.
69. See C. Vann Woodward, *The Strange Career of Jim Crow* (New York: Oxford Univ. Press, rev. ed. 1957), which, though overstating the gap between immediate and later post-Reconstruction policies, nonetheless correctly pointed to considerable differences in degree. See generally Woodward's later essay, "The Strange Career of a Historical Controversy" in C. Vann Woodward, *American Counterpoint: Slavery and Racism in the North–South Dialogue* 234–60 (Boston: Little, Brown, 1971). See also David Potter, *History and American Society* 162–79 (New York: Oxford Univ. Press, 1973).
70. Woodward, *Origins* at 51: "The politics of Redemption belonged there-

fore to the romantic school, emphasizing race and tradition and deprecating issues of economics and self-interest." See also id. at 79–80, 105–06, 154–57, 209–10, 321.

71. 17 U.S. (4 Wheat.) at 410.

72. See generally William Nelson, *The Fourteenth Amendment: From Political Principle to Judicial Doctrine* 40–148 (Cambridge: Harvard Univ. Press, 1988).

73. See generally Michael Les Benedict, "Preserving Federalism: Reconstruction and the Waite Court," 1978 *Sup. Ct. Rev.* 39.

74. United States v. Reese, 92 U.S. 214 (1876), United States v. Cruikshank, 92 U.S. 542 (1876).

75. 109 U.S. 3 (1883).

76. Id. at 25.

77. Ex parte Siebold, 100 U.S. 371 (1880); Ex parte Clarke, 100 U.S. 399 (1880); Ex parte Yarbrough, 110 U.S. 651 (1884).

78. Strauder v. West Virginia, 100 U.S. 303 (1880); Ex parte Virginia, 100 U.S. 339 (1880).

79. Slaughter-House Cases, 83 U.S. (16 Wall.) 36 (1873).

80. Id. at 82.

81. Id. at 78.

82. Id. at 82.

83. Id. at 78. The majority was inescapably aware of the irregularities of the ratification process involving the defeated southern states, which themselves clouded the traditionally conceived legitimacy of the process. See generally Bruce Ackerman, "Constitutional Politics/Constitutional Law," 99 *Yale L. J.* 500–03.

84. 83 U.S. at 81.

85. Id. at 74. See Burt, 1969 *Sup. Ct. Rev.* 85–86.

86. This parallel with *Dred Scott* was not, however, unnoticed at the time; Justice Field adroitly alluded to it in his dissenting opinion, id. at 94–95. See also L. H. LaRue, "The Continuing Presence of *Dred Scott*," 42 *Wash. and Lee L. Rev.* 57, 59–61 (1985).

87. 83 U.S. at 82.

88. Corfield v. Coryell, 6 Fed. Case. 546, 552 (C.C.E.D.Pa. 1823), quoted by Justice Field, 83 U.S. at 97.

89. 83 U.S. at 110–11.

90. 94 U.S. 113 (1877).

91. Id. at 140.

92. See Robert Wiebe, *The Search for Order, 1877–1920* 10 (New York: Hill & Wang, 1967).

93. 94 U.S. at 126.

94. See Nelson at 165–75.

7. Reconstructing the Constitution

1. Davidson v. New Orleans, 96 U.S. 97, 104 (1877).

2. See Howard Jay Graham, "The 'Conspiracy Theory' of the Fourteenth Amendment," 47 *Yale L. J.* 371, 48 *Yale L. J.* 171 (1938). Justices Black and Douglas maintained that the Court should not have ruled that corporations were "persons" protected by the Fourteenth Amendment in Santa Clara County v. Southern Pacific R.R., 118 U.S. 394 (1886); see their dissents in Connecticut General Life Ins. Co. v. Johnson, 303 U.S. 77 (1938) and Wheeling Steel Corp. v. Glander, 337 U.S. 562 (1949).

3. Charles Beard, *An Economic Interpretation of the Constitution of the United States* (New York: Macmillan, 1913).

4. See Burt, 1969 *Sup. Ct. Rev.* 86–90.

5. Cong. Globe, 39th Cong., 1st Sess. 1034 (1866). Bingham had been so intent on identifying the substantive guarantees of the amendment with preexisting constitutional language that an earlier draft he proposed in committee contained explicit parenthetical references to Article IV, section 2, and the Fifth Amendment in the text of the proposal. See Horace Flack, *The Adoption of the Fourteenth Amendment* 62–63 (Gloucester, MA: P. Smith Co., 1965 ed.).

6. Cong. Globe at 2642.

7. Alexander Bickel, "The Original Understanding and the Segregation Decision," 69 *Harv. L. Rev.* 1, 25 (1955).

8. *Federalist* 10 at 84.

9. In his letter to Jefferson immediately after the Convention adjourned, Madison extensively criticized the omission of the generalized congressional veto; in particular, he stated, "A constitutional negative on the laws of the States seems . . . necessary to secure individuals against encroachments on their rights. The mutability of the laws of the States is found to be a serious evil. The injustice of them has been so frequent and so flagrant as to alarm the most steadfast friends of Republicanism. I am persuaded I do not err in saying that the evils issuing from these sources contributed more to that uneasiness which produced the Convention, and prepared the public mind for a general reform, than those which accrued to our national character and interest from the inadequacy of the Confederation to its immediate objects. A reform therefore which does not make provision for private rights, must be materially defective. The restraints against paper emissions, and violations of contracts [specified in Article I, section 10 of the Constitution] are not sufficient. Supposing them to be effectual as far as they go, they are short of the mark. Injustice may be effected by such an infinitude of legislative expedients, that where the disposition exists it can only be controuled by some provision which reaches all cases whatsoever." Letter of October 24, 1787, 10 *Papers of Madison* 212.

10. It can be argued that the shift in terminology from the first draft's

reference to "equal protection in the rights of life, liberty and property" to the second, and final, draft's reference to "equal protection of the laws" meant that Bingham intended to narrow the substantive scope of the amendment. Some congressmen indeed had criticized the latitude of the first draft; but Bingham never explained whether his second draft was responsive to or dismissive of this criticism. In the debates on the second draft, Bingham described it at some times as a generalized protection against injustice and at other times as a protection against unequal treatment. See Nelson at 114–123. Bingham may have thought, however, that these two formulations were identical. All legislation necessarily creates inequalities by putting some people in different categories from others; to prohibit all legislative inequalities would accordingly forbid all legislation. Bingham and his colleagues stated that their draft prohibited only "unreasonable" differentiations, but this formula is tantamount to a generalized review authority for determining the reasonableness of all conceivable legislation. Even if, moreover, the equal protection clause in the second draft was intended to be narrower than in the first, the reiterated reference to privileges and immunities itself implies generalized review authority over state laws.

11. *Federalist* 51 at 323. "This, at best," he continued, "is but a precarious security; because a power independent of the society may as well espouse the unjust views of the major as the rightful interest of the minor party, and may possibly be turned against both parties." Id. at 324.

12. Id. at 324.

13. *Federalist* 51 at 325.

14. 163 U.S. 537 (1896).

15. 198 U.S. 45 (1905).

16. 158 U.S. 564 (1895). For identifying the centrality of the *Debs* case in the jurisprudence of the Fuller Court, I am indebted to Owen Fiss and his forthcoming volume of the Holmes Devise, *The Supreme Court and the Rise of the Modern State: 1888–1910.*

17. David Brewer, "The Nation's Safeguard," *N. Y. State Bar Assn., Proc.* 39 (New York: Stumpf & Steurer, 1893).

18. Id. at 40.

19. Id. at 41.

20. Id. at 44.

21. Id. at 46–47.

22. Id. at 47.

23. Wiebe, *Order* at 90.

24. Robert Higgs, *Crisis and Leviathan: Critical Episodes in the Growth of American Government* 92 (New York: Oxford Univ. Press, 1987).

25. Robert Fogelson, *America's Armories: Architecture, Society, and Public Order* 55–62 (Cambridge: Harvard Univ. Press, 1989).

26. Id. at 157–64.

27. Quoted id. at 75.

28. "Although even a downturn as severe [as the 1893 depression] did not significantly alter the nature of the conflict, it carried a far more jolting impact than had the milder decline of the eighties. Loosening tongues and feeding fears, it added a sharp sense of urgency to the debates. The very presence of entire agricultural districts impoverished, of perhaps one-quarter of the cities' unskilled without jobs, of over six hundred banks closed before autumn, meant concrete evidence for everyone's predictions of disaster." Weibe, *Order* at 91.

29. *New York Times,* July 5, 1894, quoted in Almont Lindsey, *The Pullman Strike: The Story of a Unique Experiment and of a Great Labor Upheaval* 175 (Chicago: Univ. of Chicago Press, 1942).

30. 158 U.S. at 597.

31. Though this (so-called "dormant") use of the commerce clause could find precedential support in a dictum by John Marshall in Brown v. Maryland, 25 U.S. (12 Wheat.) 419 (1827), it had only recently become prominent in the Court's jurisprudence; see Wabash, St. Louis & Pacific Rlwy. v. Illinois, 118 U.S. 557 (1886), Leisy v. Hardin, 135 U.S. 100 (1890).

32. 158 U.S. at 581, citing Article III, section 2, of the Constitution.

33. 158 U.S. at 581–82.

34. Id. at 583.

35. Id. at 598.

36. Id. at 597–98.

37. Id. at 597.

38. Id. at 597–98.

39. *Proceedings* at 46.

40. 158 U.S. at 598.

41. Id. at 581.

42 *Proceedings* at 39. He elaborated this danger in a further passage: "There are to-day ten thousand million of dollars invested in railroad property, whose owners in this country number less than two million persons. Can it be that whether that immense sum shall earn a dollar, or bring the slightest recompense to those who have invested perhaps their all in that business, and are thus aiding in the development of the country, depends wholly upon the whim and greed of that great majority of sixty millions who do not own a dollar. It may be said that that majority will not be so foolish, selfish and cruel as to strip that property of its earning capacity. I say that so long as constitutional guarantees lift on American soil their buttresses and bulwarks against wrong, and so long as the American judiciary breathes the free air of courage, it cannot." Id. at 41.

43. 7 *Harv. L. Rev.* 129 (1893).

44. Id. at 144.

45. Id. at 136–37 n.1.

46. Id. at 156. To this observation, Thayer appended a footnote quoting from a recent book on the British judicial system: "The popular will: this is,

in free countries of the ancient and the New World, the source and the end of all power. When this will is sane, nations prosper in spite of imperfections and gaps in their institutions; if good sense is in default, if passions rule, the most perfect constitutions, the wisest laws, are powerless." Le Compte de Franqueville, 1 *Le Systeme Judiciare de la Grande Bretagne* 25 (Paris: J. Rothschild, 1893).

47. *Proceedings* at 47. He also advocated "strengthen[ing] the judiciary" in state governments by replacing popularly elected with life-tenured judges. Id. at 44.

48. Id. at 46.

49. Id. at 47.

50. Reagan v. Farmers' Loan & Trust Co., 154 U.S. 362, 420 (1894); Smyth v. Ames, 169 U.S. 466 (1898). These decisions effectively overruled the deferential review of rate regulations mandated by the Waite Court in Munn v. Illinois, 94 U.S. 113 (1877).

51. Pollock v. Farmers' Loan & Trust Co., 157 U.S. 429 (1895), rev'd on rehearing, 158 U.S. 601 (1895). The ostensible ground for invalidation was that the tax was not equally apportioned among the respective state populations; but the Court majority's underlying animus against even the mild redistributive character of the tax was implicitly revealed in Justice Harlan's dissent: "Undue and disproportioned burdens are placed upon the many [by the Court's decision], while the few, safely entrenched behind the rule of apportionment among the States on the basis of numbers are permitted to evade their share of responsibility," 158 U.S. at 685, and explicitly trumpeted by Justice Field in his separate opinion: "Where is the course of usurpation to end? The present assault upon capital is but the beginning. It will be but the stepping-stone to others, larger and more sweeping, till our political contests will become a war of the poor against the rich; a war constantly growing in intensity and bitterness," 157 U.S. at 607.

52. Holden v. Hardy, 169 U.S. 366 (1898) (miners); Lochner v. New York, 198 U.S. 45 (1905) (bakers); Muller v. Oregon, 208 U.S. 412 (1908) (women); Adair v. United States, 208 U.S. 161 (1908) (union members).

53. Turner v. Williams, 194 U.S. 279 (1904) (upholding federal deportation order against radical labor organizer); Patterson v. Colorado, 205 U.S. 454 (1907) (upholding state contempt conviction against newspaper publisher for criticizing court opinion).

54. Williams v. Mississippi, 170 U.S. 213 (1898).

55. 158 U.S. at 571.

56. See generally Henry Monaghan, "Of 'Liberty' and 'Property,'" 62 *Cornell L. Rev.* 405 (1977).

57. *Proceedings* at 39.

58. *Proceedings* at 40–41.

59. See generally Donald Nieman, "Republicanism, the Confederate Constitution, and the American Constitutional Tradition," in *An Uncertain Tra-*

dition: Constitutionalism and the History of the South 201–24 (K. Hall and J. Ely, eds.) (Athens: Univ. of Georgia Press, 1989).

60. C. B. Macpherson, *The Political Theory of Individualism: Hobbes to Locke* 93 (1962).

61. See Charles Lofgren, *The Plessy Case: A Legal-Historical Interpretation* 5 (New York: Oxford Univ. Press, 1987).

62. As C. Vann Woodward observed, "The [southern] paternalistic order under bourgeois custody had been insecure for some years, and by [1900] the collapse of the 'traditional harmony' and the political alliance that sustained it was almost complete. . . . The top people of the South . . . were frightened by the white lower class, not by the blacks . . . [which led to the] upper class desertion of the blacks and capitulation to racist demagogues and their ruthless program of proscription, disfranchisement, and segregation." *American Counterpoint* at 258–59.

63. 163 U.S. at 540.

64. This was evident even in Justice Harlan's passionate dissent: "The white race," he said, "deems itself to be the dominant race in this country. And so it is, in prestige, in achievements, in education, in wealth, and in power. So, I doubt not, it will continue to be for all time, if it remains true to its great heritage, and holds fast to the principles of constitutional liberty." 163 U.S. at 559.

65. See 14 *Madison Papers* 160, discussed at text accompanying note 12, Chapter 2, supra.

66. *Notes of Debates in the Federal Convention* at 132, discussed at text accompanying note 33, Chapter 2, supra.

67. "Law and the Court," Speech at the Harvard Law School Association of New York, February 15, 1913, rpt. in *The Mind and Faith of Justice Holmes* 390 (Max Lerner, ed.) (New York: Modern Library, 1943).

68. Ibid.

69. On the formative significance for Holmes of his military service in the Civil War, where he was wounded three times and almost died, see Saul Touster, "In Search of Holmes from Within," 18 *Vanderbilt L. Rev.* 437 (1965); Mark deWolfe Howe, *Justice Holmes: The Shaping Years, 1841–1870* (Cambridge: Harvard Univ. Press, 1957). The seeds of Holmes' agnostic deference to majority will in his judicial philosophy are apparent in a letter he wrote to his father on December 1862, as he lay in an army hospital recovering from dysentery: "I never . . . have shown . . . any wavering in my belief in the right of our cause—it is my disbelief in our success by arms in which I differ from you. . . . I don't think . . . you realize the unity or determination of the South. I think you are hopeful because (excuse me) you are ignorant. But if it is true that we represent civilization . . . and if civilization and progress are the better things, why they will conquer in the long run . . . and will stand a better chance in their proper province—peace—than in war, the brother of slavery—brother, it is slavery's parent, child and sustainer at

once." Quoted in Howe at 138. Holmes' war experience seemed to have made him prematurely world-weary, and accordingly unwilling to engage in battle for any ideal against a united or determined adversary. Cf. Howe's puzzled criticism of Holmes' refusal to re-enlist in the Union army at the expiry of his term in July 1864, id. at 171–74. Thus does war become "slavery's parent, child and sustainer at once."

70. See generally William Forbath, "The Shaping of the American Labor Movement," 102 *Harv. L. Rev.* 1109 (1989).

71. See Wiebe, *Search for Order* at 293–302.

72. See generally id. at 164–223.

73. See Laurence Tribe, *American Constitutional Law* 567–68 (Mineola, NY: Foundation Press, 2d ed., 1988).

74. Panama Refining Co. v. Ryan, 293 U.S. 388 (1935) (invalidating petroleum code under National Industrial Recovery Act); Railroad Retirement Board v. Alton R.R. Co., 295 U.S. 330 (1935) (invalidating compulsory railroad retirement plan); Schechter Poultry Corp. v. United States, 295 U.S. 495 (1935) (invalidating NIRA); United States v. Butler, 297 U.S. 1 (1936) (invalidating Agricultural Adjustment Act); Carter v. Carter Coal Co., 298 U.S. 238 (1936) (invalidating coal mining hours and wage regulation).

75. Potter, *The South and the Concurrent Majority* at 19.

76. Schechter Poultry Corp. v. United States, 295 U.S. 495 (1935).

77. The statement was made to Thomas Corcoran and conveyed to Harry Hopkins, who subsequently recorded it in "Statement to Me by Thomas Corcoran Giving His Recollection of the Genesis of the Supreme Court Fight," April 3, 1939, quoted in Arthur Schlesinger, Jr., *The Politics of Upheaval* 280 (Boston: Houghton Mifflin, 1960).

78. See, e.g., United States v. Carolene Products Co., 304 U.S. 144 (1938), United States v. Darby, 312 U.S. 100 (1941), Wickard v. Filburn, 317 U.S. 111 (1942), North American Co. v. SEC, 327 U.S. 686 (1946).

79. Lincoln Federal Labor Union v. Northwestern Iron & Metal Co., 335 U.S. 525, 535 (1949).

80. Felix Frankfurter and Nathan Greene, *The Labor Injunction* 205 and n.7 (New York: Macmillan, 1930). In a private memorandum to President Roosevelt in 1935, urging support for the Wagner Act, Frankfurter invoked the same premise, that "the day of industrial absolutism is done" and that, although employers' willingness to "give a square deal to unorganized labor . . . has been precluded by the pressure of immediate self-interest," once labor's organizational rights were statutorily protected and "the employer has ungrudgingly accepted the process of collective bargaining with the freely chosen representatives of his employees, differences as to wages and hours are more readily reconciled by negotiation or arbitration. Reasonableness begets reasonableness." *Roosevelt and Frankfurter: Their Correspondence, 1928–1945* 604–05 (M. Freedman, ed.) (Boston: Atlantic Monthly Press, 1967).

81. Robert Jackson, *The Struggle for Judicial Supremacy: A Study of a Crisis in American Power Politics* 320–21 (New York: Knopf, 1941).

82. See Steve Fraser, "The Labor Question" in *The Rise and Fall of the New Deal Order, 1930–1980* 62 (S. Fraser and G. Gerstle, eds.) (Princeton: Princeton Univ. Press, 1989), describing the progressive ideology, prevalent particularly among the architects of the second New Deal, of "industrial democracy, the Marxism of the professional middle class, wise to the class antinomies of industrial society but sanguine enough to believe in their pacific supersession by science and abundance." Compare the observations in 1935 of Sidney Hillman, head of the CIO–Amalgamated Clothing Workers Union, that under the New Deal "organized labor, with the full feeling that it 'belongs' and that everyone recognizes it as an essential part in industry, will cooperate to make it more efficient, more productive, more humane." Cited in Ronald Radosh, "The Corporate Ideology of American Labor Leaders from Gompers to Hillman," in *For a New America: Essays in History and Politics from "Studies on the Left," 1959–1967* 145–46 (New York: Random House, 1970). See generally Thomas Ferguson, "Industrial Conflict and the Coming of the New Deal: The Triumph of Multinational Liberalism in America," in *The Rise and Fall of the New Deal Order* (S. Fraser and G. Gerstle, eds.) at 3–31. See also Wiebe, *Search for Order* at 164–223.

83. NLRB v. Jones & Laughlin Steel Co., 301 U.S. 1 (1937).

84. See Fraser, "The Labor Question" at 77: "The common ground for a close collaboration between modern management and centralized industrial unionism emerged clearly by the end of the [1930s] decade." There is controversy about the extent to which this attitude spread beyond labor leaders and their elite political allies. Compare Irving Bernstein, *A Caring Society: The New Deal, the Worker, and the Great Depression* 296–307 (Boston: Houghton Mifflin, 1985) with Karl Klare, "Judicial Deradicalization of the Wagner Act and the Origins of Modern Legal Consciousness, 1937–1941," 62 *Minn. L. Rev.* 265, 289–90 (1978). But however many post-New Deal rank-and-file workers continued to view industrial relations as fundamentally combative, the Roosevelt Justices did not; see Klare at 330–31.

85. Ackerman, Constitutional Law/Constitutional Politics," 99 *Yale L. J.* 490–97, 510–15.

86. For my speculations about the temperamental bases for Frankfurter's inclination, and the significance of his attitude toward his status as a foreign-born Jew specifically, see *Two Jewish Justices* at 38–61.

87. United States v. Carolene Products, 304 U.S. 144, 152 (1938).

88. Id. at 152–53, n.4 (citations omitted).

8. An Egalitarian Response

1. Missouri ex rel. Gaines v. Canada, 305 U.S. 337 (1938). McReynolds observed that an integrated law school would "damnify both races." Id. at 353.

2. See McCabe v. Atchison, T. & S.F. Ry. Co., 235 U.S. 151 (1914) (requiring equal, though separate, transportation facilities); Buchanan v. Warley, 245 U.S. 60 (1917) (overturning racially exclusionary residential zoning law); Nixon v. Herndon, 273 U.S. 536 (1927), Nixon v. Condon, 286 U.S. 73 (1932) (invalidating exclusion of blacks from state election primaries).

3. Cumming v. Board of Education, 175 U.S. 528 (1899). The Court unanimously reaffirmed the constitutionality of school segregation in Gong Lum v. Rice, 275 U.S. 78 (1927).

4. G. Myrdal, *An American Dilemma: The Negro Problem and Modern Democracy* 3 (New York: Harper & Row, 1944) (emphasis in original).

5. Id. at 4.

6. Id. at lxxi (emphasis omitted).

7. Id. at lxxii–lxxiii (emphasis omitted).

8. Id. at 1023.

9. Id. at 1024.

10. 347 U.S. at 495 and n.11.

11. 347 U.S. at 489. The Court was widely criticized for this apparent reliance. See generally "Symposium, The Courts, Social Science and School Desegregation," 39 *Law and Contemp. Probs.* (Winter/Spring 1975). Within the Court, William Rehnquist sent a memorandum to Justice Jackson, for whom he was then law clerk, that echoed Holmes's famous quip in his *Lochner* dissent: "If the Fourteenth Amendment did not enact Spencer's *Social Statics*," Rehnquist wrote, "it just as surely did not enact Myrdal's *American Dilemma*" (quoted in Schwartz, 1988 *Sup. Ct. Rev.* 246. Rehnquist also wrote that *Plessy* "was right and should be re-affirmed," though he subsequently maintained that this was not his view; see Chapter 1, n.8, supra).

12. "A competent Negro social scientist, who has recently been studying conditions in the Upper South . . . confides that he expects the outbreak of serious race riots in the South within the year.

The situation is grave. . . . But regardless of what happens, we do not believe that this is a turn for the worse in race relations in the South. Even if there are going to be serious clashes and even if their short-run effects will be devastating to the Negroes involved and, perhaps, to Negroes in the whole region, we believe that the long-run effect of the present opinion crisis in the South, because it is a catharsis for the whites, will be a change toward increased equality for the Negro." Myrdal at 1014.

13. This reasoning recalls Frankfurter's prediction to President Roosevelt in 1935 regarding the likely impact of the enactment of the NLRA on

industrial conflict: "Employers as a class cannot be relied upon, voluntarily and out of the goodness of their hearts, to give a square deal to unorganized labor; . . . [but] once the employer has ungrudgingly accepted the process of collective bargaining with the freely chosen representatives of his employees, differences as to wages and hours are more readily reconciled by negotiation or arbitration. Reasonableness begets reasonableness." *Roosevelt and Frankfurter: Their Correspondence* at 604–05, discussed supra, Chapter 7, text accompanying n.80.

14. In his article in the 1988 *Supreme Court Review,* Bernard Schwartz quotes extensively from this draft, the original of which is in the *Brown* file, Robert H. Jackson Papers, Library of Congress. Professor Schwartz generously provided me with a copy of Jackson's draft, from which I have drawn quotations throughout this chapter.

15. "Education of Negroes was almost nonexistent, and practically all of the race were illiterate [when the Fourteenth Amendment was adopted]. In fact, any education of Negroes was forbidden by law in some states. Today, in contrast, many Negroes have achieved outstanding success in the arts and sciences as well as in the business and professional world. . . . Today, education is perhaps the most important function of state and local governments. . . . It is the very foundation of good citizenship. Today it is a principal instrument in awakening the child to cultural values, in preparing him for later professional training, and in helping him to adjust normally to his environment. . . . Such an opportunity, where the state has undertaken to provide it, is a right which must be made available to all on equal terms." 347 U.S. at 490, 493.

16. In *Plessy* itself, the state statute had mandated "equal but separate accommodations," 163 U.S. at 540, but the Court gave no special significance to this requirement, ruling simply that separate transportation facilities were not inherently unequal under the Fourteenth Amendment. In 1914 the Court reinterpreted *Plessy* to require that separate facilities be equal in fact, McCabe v. Atchison, T. & S.F. Rly. Co., 235 U.S. 151, 160. See Benno Schmidt, "Principle and Prejudice: The Supreme Court and Race in the Progressive Era" (pt. 1), 82 *Colum. L. Rev.* 444, 468–69, 485–94 (1982). Beginning with the Missouri law school case in 1938, the Court pressed the "equality" side of the "separate but equal" formula in public schools.

17. Brown v. Board of Education (*Brown II*), 349 U.S. 294, 300 (1955).

18. Schwartz, 1988 *Sup. Ct. Rev.* 253, citing notes by Justices Frankfurter and Burton of the 1953 conference deliberations following the reargument in *Brown I.*

19. As Bernard Schwartz, 1988 *Sup. Ct. Rev.* 253, observed, "Jackson started his [1953] conference presentation by noting, 'Cardozo said the work of this Court is partly statutory construction and partly politics. This is a question of politics.' What he meant by this is shown by the Jackson gloss on

the Cardozo statement in a posthumous work: 'Of course [Cardozo] uses 'politics' in no sense of partisanship but in the sense of policy-making.'" Jackson, *The Supreme Court in the American System of Government* 54 (1955).

20. Statement of May 19, 1862, 5 *Collected Works* 223.

21. 358 U.S. 1 (1958).

22. See Robert McKay, "'With All Deliberate Speed': A Study of School Desegregation," 31 *N.Y. Univ. L. Rev.* 991, 1076–77 (1956). Cf. United States v. Cox, 342 F.2d 167, 171 (5th Cir.), cert. denied sub nom. Cox v. Hauberg, 381 U.S. 935 (1965) (courts may not direct Attorney General to initiate criminal prosecutions).

23. So Chief Justice Warren believed from his contacts with Eisenhower; see Earl Warren, *Memoirs* 289, 291–92 (Garden, City, NY: Doubleday, 1977).

24. See "Radio-Television Address by President Eisenhower, September 24, 1957," rpt. in Benjamin Muse, *Ten Years of Prelude* 141 (New York: Viking Press, 1964).

25. 358 U.S. at 18–19.

26. Dennis Hutchinson, "Unanimity and Desegregation: Decisionmaking in the Supreme Court, 1948–1958," 68 *Georgetown L J.* 1, 80 (1979).

27. Williams v. Lee, 358 U.S. 217, 218–19 (1959).

28. 358 U.S. at 19–20.

29. Missouri ex rel. Gaines v. Canada, 305 U.S. 337, 353 (1938).

30. Smith v. Allright, 321 U.S. 649 (1944) (invalidating exclusion of blacks from primary elections); Morgan v. Virginia, 328 U.S. 373 (1946) (overturning, as burden on interstate commerce, Virginia law requiring segregation on interstate carriers); Steele v. Louisville & Nashville R.R., 323 U.S. 192 (1944) (Railway Labor Act requires recognized labor organization to represent employees without racial discrimination); Shelley v. Kraemer, 334 U.S. 1 (1948) (judicial enforcement of covenant was impermissible state action); Sweatt v. Painter, 339 U.S. 629 (1950) (racially separate state law schools inherently unequal); McLaurin v. Oklahoma State Regents, 339 U.S. 637 (1950) (segregation of black student from whites enrolled in same graduate school program inherently unequal).

31. For a detailed account of these efforts, see Hutchinson, 68 *Georgetown L. J.* 4–30.

32. Letter of May 20, 1954, quoted in Hutchinson, 68 *Georgetown L. J.* 43 n.344.

33. As Dennis Hutchinson observed, based on conference notes of the Justices' deliberations on *Brown II*: "Despite the diversity of views over general and specific issues, the Court appeared to be united on one point. The final opinion, if at all possible, should be unanimous—as the opinion the year before had been. Four Justices expressly stated their hope for unanimity: Black ("If humanly possible, will do everything possible to achieve unanimous result"); Burton ("Unanimous action of the Court is of primary importance"); Minton ("Ought to be unanimous"); and Harlan ("Vital to be

unanimous"). The statements at conference by Warren and Frankfurter suggest that they shared that desire. The remaining Justices—Reed, Douglas, and Clark—said nothing at the conference to indicate they harbored particular views that would lead them to write separately, especially in the face of what was a growing and strongly held goal for the rest of the Court." 68 *Georgetown L. J.* 55–56.

34. See Elman, 100 *Harv. L. Rev.* 824, 828–29.

35. 347 U.S. at 495.

36. Goss v. Board of Education, 373 U.S. 683 (1963).

37. Griffin v. County School Board, 377 U.S. 218 (1964)

38. Green v. County School Board, 391 U.S. 430, 439 (1968) (emphasis in original).

39. See Kluger at 339, 342, 381–82, 391–94.

40. Speech at Holt Street Baptist Church, Montgomery, Alabama, December 5, 1955, rpt. in *Eyes on the Prize: America's Civil Rights Years—A Reader and Guide* 45 (Claybourne Carson et al., eds., 1987). See generally Randall Kennedy, "Martin Luther King's Constitution: A Legal History of the Montgomery Bus Boycott," 98 *Yale L. J.* 999 (1989).

41. Letter of June 8, 1953, quoted in Schwartz, 1988 Sup. *Ct. Rev.* 252. For discussion of the hesitancies within the Truman Administration regarding its amicus brief for overruling *Plessy*, see Elman, 100 *Harv. L. Rev.* at 825–27.

42. Transcript of oral argument, 22 *U.S. Law Week* 3161 (1953).

43. Brown v. Board of Education, Order for Reargument, 345 U.S. 972 (1953).

44. "The Court can strike down legislation which supports educational segregation, but any constructive policy for abolishing it must come from Congress. Only Congress can enact a policy binding on all states and districts, and it can delegate its supervision to some administrative body provided with standards for determining the conditions under which sanctions should apply. It can make provisions for federal funds where changes required are beyond the means of the community, for mixing the races will require extensive changes in physical plants and will impose the largest burden on some of the nation's lowest income regions. Moreover, Congress can lift the heavy burden of private litigation from disadvantaged people and make the investigation and administrative proceedings against recalcitrant districts the function of some public agency that would secure enforcement of the policy.

A Court decision striking down state statutes or constitutional provisions which authorize or require segregation will not produce a social transition, nor is the judiciary the agency to which the people should look for that result." Jackson Draft Memorandum at 13–14.

45. Hutchinson, 68 *Georgetown L. J.* 79 n.671. Clark noted on the draft he returned to Brennan, "*Leave out about Congress.* Close with hoopla—remind nation what issues are involved here." Id. (emphasis in original).

46. See Alexander Bickel's observation in 1962: "The presidential campaign of 1960 marked the assumption of political responsibility for the principle of racial integration. And there has since been a world of difference between the tone of the Kennedy Administration on this subject and that of its predecessor, and a difference as well in the vigor and imagination of the litigating activity undertaken by the Department of Justice." *Least Dangerous Branch* at 268.

47. Griffen v. Maryland, certiorari granted, 370 U.S. 935 (1962), reargument ordered, 373 U.S. 920 (1963).

48. Bell v. Maryland, 378 U.S. 226, 243–45 (1964).

49. Bell v. Maryland, 378 U.S. at 243.

50. Bell v. Maryland, 387 U.S. at 243–45.

51. Bell v. Maryland, 378 U.S. at 242.

52. See David Garrow, *Protest at Selma: Martin Luther King, Jr., and the Voting Rights Act of 1965* 89–110, 126–32 (New Haven: Yale Univ. Press, 1978).

53. Earl Black and Merle Black, *Politics and Society in the South* 110 (Cambridge: Harvard Univ. Press, 1987). See also David Goldfield, *Black, White and Southern: Race Relations and Southern Culture, 1940 to the Present* 145 (Baton Rouge: Louisiana State Univ. Press, 1990):

> [The 1964 Act's] impact on the South was remarkably swift. . . . Andrew Young recalled returning to a St. Augustine motel five days after the act's passage. Just the previous week, a waitress had poured hot coffee over Young and his group, who were seeking service in the motel restaurant, and the manager had laced the swimming pool with hydrochloric acid just as Young prepared to wade in. "We went back to that same restaurant," Young related "and those people were just wonderful. They were apologetic. They said, 'We were just afraid of losing our business. We didn't want to be the only ones to be integrated. But if everybody's got to do it, we've been ready for it a long time. We're so glad the president signed this law and now we can be through these troubles.'"

54. Black and Black at 96, 154.

55. U.S. Bureau of the Census, Statistical Abstract of the United States 124 (1974).

56. Griffen v. County School Board, 377 U.S. 218 (1964).

57. See Samuel Lubell, *White and Black: Test of a Nation* 140–45 (New York: Harper & Row, 1966); Philip Hauser, "Demographic Factors in the Integration of the Negro," 94 *Daedalus* 847, 850–53 (1965).

58. See *Nat'l Advisory Comm'n on Civil Disorders, Report 35–108* (New York: Bantam Books, 1968).

59. 384 U.S. 641 (1966).

60. See Burt, 1969 Sup. Ct. Rev. 101–04 for consideration of the narrower grounds available.

61. See id. at 114–18.

62. In upholding the central provisions of the 1964 and 1965 Civil Rights Acts, the Supreme Court was notably generous in construing the reach of congressional authority; see Katzenbach v. McClung, 379 U.S. 294 (1964), South Carolina v. Katzenbach, 383 U.S. 301 (1966).

63. 392 U.S. 409 (1968).

64. See Gerhard Casper, "Jones v. Mayer: Clio, Bemused and Confused Muse," 1968 *Sup. Ct. Rev.* 89, 99.

65. Id. at 415.

66. 392 U.S. at 478–90.

67. 358 U.S. at 20.

9. Atavistic Reaction

1. See, e.g., Miranda v. Arizona, 384 U.S. 436 (1966) (requiring warning and appointed counsel for criminal suspects in police custody); Watkins v. United States, 354 U.S. 178 (1957) (restricting congressional committee authority to inquiry into Communist party affiliations); School District v. Schempp, 374 U.S. 203 (1963) (prohibiting public school prayer requirement); Griffen v. Illinois, 351 U.S. 12 (1956) (requiring free transcripts for indigent appeals from criminal convictions); Levy v. Louisiana, 391 U.S. 68 (1968) (invalidating wrongful death statute discrimination against illegitimate children).

2. Martin Luther King, Jr., *Why We Can't Wait* 37 (New York: New American Library, 1964).

3. 388 U.S. 307, 320–21 (1967).

4. The text of King's speech appeared as an appendix to the Court's opinion, 388 U.S. at 323–24.

5. 388 U.S. at 349.

6. Goffman at 288 n.44.

7. Bernard Schwartz, *The Unpublished Opinions of the Burger Court* 153 (New York: Oxford Univ. Press, 1988).

8. United States v. Nixon, 418 U.S. 683 (1974).

9. See Gerald Gunther, "Judicial Hegemony and Legislative Autonomy: The *Nixon* Case and the Impeachment Process," 22 *UCLA L. Rev.* 30, 35–38 (1974).

10. See 418 U.S. at 688–90.

11. The Court stated, "To require a President [to follow the traditional route for obtaining appellate review of the subpoena] would be unseemly, and would present an unnecessary occasion for constitutional confrontation between two branches of the Government." 418 U.S. at 691–92.

12. For a similar critique, comparing the Court to "compulsive gamblers

unable to resist a piece of the action, or . . . knights in shining armor tempted to ride to the rescue in every situation of distress," see Gunther, 22 *UCLA L. Rev.* 33.

13. 418 U.S. at 684.

14. See Nixon v. Fitzgerald, 457 U.S. 731 (1982); Harlow v. Fitzgerald, 457 U.S. 800, 822 (1982) (concurring opinion); Butz v. Economou, 438 U.S. 478, 517 (1978) (dissenting opinion).

15. 418 U.S. at 706.

16. 418 U.S. at 703, quoting 5 U.S. (1 Cranch) at 177.

17. 418 U.S. at 694–95 and n. 8.

18. For a detailed exposition of the contemporary Court's grappling with capital punishment, see Robert A. Burt, "Disorder in the Court: The Death Penalty and the Constitution," 85 *Mich. L. Rev.* 1741 (1987).

19. Against Eighth Amendment challenges in the nineteenth century, it upheld death by shooting in Wilkerson v. Utah, 99 U.S. 130 (1879), and by electrocution in *In re* Kemmler, 136 U.S. 436 (1890); in Powell v. Alabama, 287 U.S. 45 (1932), the Court required appointed counsel in all state capital cases—its first significant incursion not only in the death penalty but in state criminal law administration generally. The first indication that some Justices were receptive to general systemic challenges to the death penalty did not appear until 1963, in a dissent from a denial of certiorari by Justice Goldberg, joined by Justices Douglas and Brennan, maintaining that death was a disproportionate and therefore "cruel and unusual" punishment for rape. Rudolph v. Alabama, 375 U.S. 889 (1963). This dissent was instrumental in prompting attorneys at the NAACP Legal Defense Fund to launch a litigative campaign against capital punishment, not only in its racially discriminatory aspects but generally. See Michael Meltsner, *Cruel and Unusual: The Supreme Court and Capital Punishment* 30–35 (New York: Random House, 1973). Justice Goldberg subsequently disclosed that he had preceded his public dissent with a private memorandum circulated within the Court arguing that prohibition of capital punishment for rape should be an initial step toward ultimate judicial abolition of the death penalty generally. See Arthur Goldberg, "Memorandum to the Conference Re: Capital Punishment, October Term, 1963," 27 *S. Tex. L. J.*493 (1986).

20. 391 U.S. 510, 512 (1968).

21. 391 U.S. at 520 n.17, quoting Arthur Koestler, *Reflections on Hanging* 166–67 (1956).

22. 391 U.S. at 515, 522 n.21 (emphasis omitted).

23. 391 U.S. at 538.

24. Meltsner at 123.

25. 391 U.S. at 519–20.

26. 91 U.S. at 520 n.16.

27. See Neil Vidmar and Phoebe Ellsworth, "Public Opinion and the Death Penalty," 26 *Stanford L. Rev.* 1245, 1249–50 (1974).

28. Lauren Reskin, "LawPoll," 71 *Amer. Bar Assoc. J.* 44 (April 1985). In 1936, the effective beginning of the modern era of opinion polling, 62% of the American public supported capital punishment. Erskine, "The Polls: Capital Punishment," 34 *Pub. Opinion Q.* 290 (1970).

29. From their analysis of the polling data, Zimring and Hawkins concluded, "The most striking finding was that those who either strongly or very strongly favored the death penalty were, with few exceptions, unswayed by the information presented. . . . [This] almost complete indifference . . . suggests very strongly that support for the death penalty is generally not a matter of cognition (that is, knowing something), or of evaluation (that is, determining the worth, value, or utility of something). . . . [What appears to be] involved is not judgment based on empirical evidence or ethical argument but rather such mental states as are connoted by terms like "faith," "belief," or "conviction," or even such affective conditions as "allegiance" or "loyalty." This is precisely what would be expected if . . . the appeal of the death penalty derives not from its function as a particularly effective or appropriate penal method, but rather from its symbolic significance." Franklin Zimring and Gordon Hawkins, *Capital Punishment and the American Agenda* 18–19 (Cambridge: Cambridge Univ. Press, 1986).

30. 402 U.S. 183 (1971).

31. 402 U.S. at 208, 204.

32. 402 U.S. at 213.

33. 402 U.S. at 252.

34. In a law review article, Justice Brennan identified "a certain lofty conservatism" in Harlan's jurisprudence generally that was "premised on . . . a conviction that there are limits to what heights we should reasonably expect people and society to ascend." William Brennan, "Constitutional Adjudication and the Death Penalty: A View from the Court," 100 *Harv. L. Rev.* 313, 319 (1986). See also Bourgignon, "The Second Mr. Justice Harlan: His Principles of Judicial Decision Making," 1979 *Sup. Ct. Rev.* 251.

35. 408 U.S. 238 (1972).

36. 100 *Harvard L. Rev.* at 321.

37. Id. at 322.

38. Id. at 323.

39. 408 U.S. at 309–10.

40. 408 U.S. at 313.

41. 408 U.S. at 248 and n.11

42. For Douglas's views on the limited role of precedent in constitutional adjudication, see William Douglas, "Stare Decisis," 49 *Columbia L. Rev.* 735, 736–37 (1949). See generally Earl Maltz, "Some Thoughts on the Death of Stare Decisis in Constitutional Law," 1980 *Wisc. L. Rev.* 467. The quickest (and much-criticized) reversal in the Court's history had been in the *Legal Tender* cases, Knox v. Lee, 79 U.S. (12 Wall.) 457 (1871), overruling Hepburn v. Griswold, 75 U.S. (8 Wall.) 603 (1870).

43. 100 *Harv. L. Rev.* at 321.

44. Gregg v. Georgia, 428 U.S. 153 (1976); Proffitt v. Florida, 428 U.S. 242 (1976); Jurek v. Texas, 428 U.S. 262 (1976); Woodson v. North Carolina, 428 U.S. 280 (1976); Roberts v. Louisiana, 428 U.S. 325 (1976).

45. *Gregg,* 428 U.S. at 196 n.47. Stewart acknowledged "substantial tension" with *McGautha,* however, and favorably cited Brennan's dissent there, id. and at 195 n.45.

46. *Gregg,* 428 U.S. at 179.

47. *Gregg,* 428 U.S. at 183.

48. Thus Stewart found that a mandatory statute "may well exacerbate the . . . jury's willingness to act lawlessly," *Woodson,* 428 U.S. at 303, and "plainly invites the jurors to disregard their oaths and choose a verdict for a lesser offense whenever they feel the death penalty is inappropriate," *Roberts,* 428 U.S. at 335.

49. *Gregg,* 428 U.S. at 232.

50. *Furman,* 408 U.S. at 370 n.163.

51. *Furman,* 408 U.S. at 344.

52. Robert Weisberg, "Deregulating Death," 1983 *Sup. Ct. Rev.* 305 n.1.

53. Coker v. Georgia, 433 U.S. 585 (1977).

54. Enmund v. Florida, 458 U.S. 782 (1982).

55. Lockett v. Ohio, 438 U.S. 586 (1978).

56. Gardner v. Florida, 430 U.S. 349 (1977).

57. As Justice Stevens acidly observed in 1981, death penalty "questions have not been difficult for three Members of the Court [since] Justice Brennan and Justice Marshall have invariably voted to set aside the death penalty and, if my memory serves me correctly, Justice Rehnquist has invariably voted to uphold the death penalty." Coleman v. Balkcom, 451 U.S. 949, 951 and n.2 (1981).

58. Barefoot v. Estelle, 463 U.S. 880 (1983).

59. Barclay v. Florida, 463 U.S. 939, 990 (1983).

60. Pulley v. Harris, 465 U.S. 37 (1984).

61. Wainright v. Witt, 469 U.S. 412 (1985).

62. Jack Greenberg, "Capital Punishment as a System," 91 *Yale L. J.* 908, 917–18 (1982). Of the 247 death sentence cases decided by the Florida Supreme Court from 1972 until March 1984, 116 or 47% were set aside. M. Vandiver and M. Radelet, "Post-*Furman* Death Sentences in Florida" (1984) (unpub. ms., available from Capital Punishment Project, Sociology Department, University of Florida). A 1985 study found a similar proportion of death sentence reversals among the states generally. NAACP Legal Defense Fund, Inc., *Death Row, U.S.A.* (October 1985). See also Justice Marshall's dissent in Barefoot v. Estelle, 463 U.S. 880, 915 (1983), citing "an extraordinary number" of reversals by federal appeals courts on claims that had been "unsuccessful in the state courts, that this Court in its discretion has decided not to review on certiorari, and that a federal district judge has rejected."

63. Witherspoon v. Illinois, 391 U.S. 510, 517 (1968).

64. Lockhart v. McCree, 476 U.S. 162, 178 (1986).

65. 476 U.S. at 185.

66. 481 U.S. 279 (1987).

67. *Furman,* 408 U.S. at 364–66. Justice Brennan did not mention race discrimination in his *Furman* opinion, but the extent to which his expressed concern there about "arbitrary" inflictions, 408 U.S. at 295, referred implicitly to racial bias was made explicit in his subsequent dissenting opinion in Pulley v. Harris, 465 U.S. 37, 65 (1984).

68. *Furman,* 408 U.S. at 310.

69. See Hans Zeisel, "Race Bias in the Administration of the Death Penalty: The Florida Experience," 95 *Harv. L. Rev.* 456 (1981).

70. See Richard Lempert, "Capital Punishment in the '80s: Reflections on the Symposium," 74 *J. Crim. Law and Criminology* 1101, 1110 (1983).

71. See Samuel Gross, "Race and Death: The Judicial Evaluation of Evidence of Discrimination in Capital Sentencing," 18 *U.C. Davis L. Rev.* 1275, 1279–82 (1985).

72. McCleskey v. Zant, 580 F. Supp. 338, 366 table 2 (N.D. Ga. 1984).

73. McCleskey v. Kemp, 753 F.2d 877, 887 (11th Cir. 1985).

74. 580 F. Supp. at 379.

75. 481 U.S. at 291 n.7.

76. See South Carolina v. Katzenbach, 383 U.S. 301, 313 (1966).

77. See Spaziano v. Florida, 468 U.S. 447, 464 (1984).

78. See Grigsby v. Mabry, 569 F.Supp. 1273, 1293–94 (E.D. Ark. 1983).

79. *New York Times,* April 4, 1990, A16.

80. 410 U.S. 113 (1973).

81. 402 U.S. 62 (1971).

82. 402 U.S. at 71.

83. See Schwartz, *Unpublished Opinions of the Burger Court* at 113–17.

84. Id. at 141–43. In a covering memorandum accompanying his draft opinion, Blackmun had observed: "Knocking out the Texas statute [on vagueness grounds] . . . will invalidate the abortion laws in a *majority* of our States. Most States focus only on the preservation of the life of the mother. *Vuitch,* of course, is on the books, and I had assumed that the Conference, at this point, has no intention to overrule it. It is because of *Vuitch's* vagueness emphasis and a hope, perhaps forlorn, that we might have a unanimous court in the Texas case, that I took the vagueness route." Id. at 92.

85. Id at 144.

86. In doctrinal terms, Blackmun's opinion in *Roe* most resembled the opinions of Justices Brennan and Marshall in *Furman* in their novel, if not tenuous, extensions beyond prior precedential contexts. The closest prior application for *Roe's* constitutional "privacy" right had been to invalidate statutes restricting the use or distribution of contraceptives. Griswold v. Connecticut, 381 U.S. 479 (1965); Eisenstadt v. Baird, 405 U.S. 438 (1972). But such statutes did not address conduct that directly affected others, such

as was plausibly claimed for abortion restrictions to protect fetal life. For capital punishment, there had been no prior invalidating application of the constitutional guarantee against "cruel and unusual punishment," even in the grisly circumstance when a first electrocution had failed and the state undertook to repeat the event. Louisiana *ex rel.* Francis v. Resweber, 329 U.S. 459 (1947). See also Chief Justice Warren's observation in 1958 that "the death penalty has been employed throughout our history, and, in a day when it is still widely accepted, it cannot be said to violate the constitutional concept of cruelty." Trop v. Dulles, 356 U.S. 86, 99 (1957) (plurality opinion).

87. See Zimring and Hawkins at 26–47, for an illuminating discussion of the previous trend and the public backlash against *Furman.*

88. See Kristin Luker, *Abortion and the Politics of Motherhood* 127, 137 (Berkeley: Univ. California Press, 1984).

89. See Laurence Tribe, *Abortion: The Clash of Absolutes* 143–47 (New York: Norton, 1990).

90. See Luker at 95–101.

91. See Tribe at 46–50.

92. For different guesses, compare Glendon at 48–50 with Tribe at 49–51.

93. United States v. Guest, 383 U.S. 745, 758 (1966).

94. This result would be inconsistent with the Court's action in Maher v. Roe, 432 U.S. 464 (1977) and Harris v. McRae, 448 U.S. 297 (1980), approving denial of state and federal health care benefits for abortions. But these rulings were themselves accommodations to the legislative backlash against *Roe v. Wade;* and for the moment I am imagining that *Roe* had been decided differently.

95. See Shapiro v. Thompson, 394 U.S. 618 (1969).

96. For a similar approach to the abortion dispute—criticizing *Roe* for failing to recognize "the values on the losing side as real and significant," and identifying the equality ideal as preferable to constitutional "privacy" both in comprehending the issues at stake and in working toward an accommodation of the conflicting perspectives in the dispute—see Guido Calabresi, *Ideals, Beliefs, Attitudes, and the Law: Private Law Perspectives on a Public Law Problem* 101–14 (Syracuse: Syracuse Univ. Press, 1985).

97. Only Justice Scalia has clearly espoused this result; see Webster v. Reproductive Health Services, 109 S.Ct. 3040, 3064 (1989). Chief Justice Rehnquist's opinion in this case strongly suggests, however, that at least three other members of the Court are similarly inclined.

10. A Constitutional Resolution

1. See Ely, "The Wages of Crying Wolf: A Comment on *Roe v. Wade,*" 82 *Yale L. J.* 920 (1973).

2. *Least Dangerous Branch* at 152.

3. Luker at 94.

4. *Least Dangerous Branch* at 155.

5. Poe v. Ullman, 367 U.S. 497 (1961). Immediately following this decision, the state prosecutor changed the factual context of the dispute by obtaining a criminal conviction under this statute against a physician who had prescribed contraceptives for use by a married couple. The Court found this case to be ripe for adjudication and overturned the statute on constitutional privacy grounds in Griswold v. Connecticut, 381 U.S. 479 (1965).

6. Rust v. Sullivan, 59 *U.S. Law Week* 4451 (May 23, 1991).

7. The Court admitted that the statute itself was "ambiguous" and that it had not been administratively interpreted to forbid abortion counseling until eighteen years after its enactment. 59 *U.S. Law Week* at 4454.

8. *Least Dangerous Branch* at 181, 216. "The method of the colloquy," Bickel observed, was "calling the political institutions to draw near the bench, for all the world like counsel in a lawsuit tried to a jury, there to be drawn out on their deliberate purposes, to be urged to clarify them and thus perhaps to reduce the issue, all 'out of the hearing of the jury,' which is to say outside the framework of the final, binding process of judgment." Id. at 156.

9. Frontiero v. Richardson, 411 U.S. 677 (1973).

10. Craig v. Boren, 429 U.S. 190, 197 (1976).

11. See, e.g., Mississippi University v. Hogan, 458 U.S. 718 (1982) (overturning exclusion of men from state nursing school); Kirchberg v. Feenstra, 450 U.S. 455 (1981) (overturning statute permitting husband alone to dispose of jointly owned marital property); Orr v. Orr, 440 U.S. 268 (1979) (overturning statute limiting alimony to divorced women); Michael M. v. Sonoma County Superior Court, 450 U.S. 464 (1981) (upholding imposition on men of criminal liability for sexual intercourse with females under 18); Rostker v. Goldberg, 453 U.S. 57 (1981) (upholding congressional act excluding women from military draft registration).

12. See, e.g., Justice Stevens' concurrence in Craig v. Boren, 429 U.S. at 213 n.5; his dissent in Michael M. v. Sonoma County Superior Court, 450 U.S. at 501; Justice Blackmun's opinion for the Court in Califano v. Westcott, 443 U.S. 76, 88 (1979); Justice O'Connor's opinion for the Court in Mississippi University for Women v. Hogan, 458 U.S. at 724–25.

13. 17 U.S. (4 Wheat.) 414, 423 (1819).

14. See Gerald Gunther, "Foreword: In Search of Evolving Doctrine on a Changing Court: A Model for a Newer Equal Protection," 86 *Harv. L. Rev.* 1 (1972), for an early appreciation of promising potential in this doctrinal innovation.

15. City of Cleburne v. Cleburne Living Center, 473 U.S. 432, 445–46 (1985).

16. 473 U.S. at 448–50.

17. Brown v. Board of Education, 892 F.2d 851, 866 (10th Cir. 1989).

18. Board of Education v. Brown, No. 89–1681, petition for certiorari filed, 58 *U.S. Law Week* 3725 (April 26, 1990).

19. Board of Education of Okla. City Public Schools v. Dowell, 111 Sup.Ct. 630, 637, 638 n.2 (1991).

20. Freeman v. Pitts, certiorari granted, 111 S.Ct. 949 (1991).

21. The characteristic example of this sequence was Regents of the University of California v. Bakke, 438 U.S. 265 (1978). Four Justices voted to invalidate a racial quota for minority admission to medical school, on the ground that Congress had embraced "color-blindness" in the 1964 Civil Rights Act; four voted to affirm the school's policy as an appropriate, even if not required, measure for equalizing minority status in the medical profession; and the swing vote, Justice Powell, found that an explicitly numerical quota was unconstitutional but a less rigidly administered preference in the service of "educational diversity" would pass muster.

22. City of Richmond v. J. A. Croson Co., 488 U.S. 469, 493 (1989). In this same Term, the Court imposed an increased evidentiary burden on those claiming racial discrimination in employment. Compare Wards Cove Packing Co. v. Atonia, 490 U.S. 642 (1989) with Griggs v. Duke Power Co., 401 U.S. 424 (1971).

23. The ordinance in the Richmond case was so bizarrely formulated that it could readily be invalidated using middle-tier standards of clarity and precision. In particular, the ordinance extended preferences to "Spanish-speaking, Oriental, Indians, Eskimos, or Aleuts" minority groups, even though—as the Court noted—"there is *absolutely no evidence* of past discrimination [against such groups in Richmond, and] it may well be that Richmond has never had an Aleut or Eskimo citizen." 488 U.S. at 506 (emphasis in original). It seems most likely that these groups were included in the Richmond scheme because they had been favored in a federal public works statute which the Court had previously approved, Fullilove v. Klutznick, 448 U.S. 448 (1980). Unlike Richmond, of course, the United States clearly does have Aleut and Eskimo citizens; but Richmond's plagiarism, whether thoughtless or cynically opportunistic, cannot satisfy middle-tier requirements for particularistic, fact-based, contextually relevant judgments in sensitive, contentious matters, such as the use of gender or race criteria.

24. Metro Broadcasting, Inc. v. Federal Communications Comm'n, 110 Sup.Ct. 2997 (1990).

25. "Historic Case on Rights Is Reopened in Topeka," *New York Times,* October 7, 1986, at A22, col. 2.

26. The Court committed a similar error in 1974 when it ruled that whites could flee from political relations with blacks, out of range of any judicial remedial actions, simply by moving across jurisdictional lines separating cities from suburbs. Milliken v. Bradley, 418 U.S. 717 (1974).

27. For discussion of the significance of this goal as the basis for judicial actions on behalf of disabled people, see Burt, "Constitutional Law and the Teaching of the Parables," 93 *Yale L. J.* 455, 489–502 (1984). Regarding the importance of social relationships in formulating an adequate conception of legal rights, see generally Minow, *Making All the Difference.*

Works Cited

Ackerman, Bruce. *We the People: Foundations.* Cambridge: Harvard Univ. Press, 1991.
——— "Constitutional Politics/Constitutional Law," 99 *Yale L. J.* 453 (1989).
——— "Beyond Carolene Products," 98 *Harv. L. Rev.* 713 (1985).
——— *Social Justice in the Liberal State.* New Haven: Yale Univ. Press, 1980.
Adair, Douglass. *Fame and the Founding Fathers.* New York: Norton, 1974.
——— "'That Politics May Be Reduced to a Science': David Hume, James Madison, and the *Tenth Federalist,*" 20 *Huntington Library Q.* 343 (1957).
——— "The Authorship of the Disputed Federalist Papers," 1 *Wm. & Mary Q.* 97 (1944).
Adams, Brooks. Introduction to Henry Adams. *The Degradation of the Democratic Dogma.* New York: Macmillan, 1919.
Adams, Henry. *The Education of Henry Adams.* New York: Modern Library, 1931.
Axtell, James. *The European and the Indian: Essays in the Ethnohistory of Colonial North America.* New York: Oxford Univ. Press, 1981.

Bailyn, Bernard. *The Ideological Origins of the American Revolution.* Cambridge: Harvard Univ. Press, 1967.
Baker, Leonard. *John Marshall: A Life in Law.* New York: Collier MacMillan, 1974.
Banner, James. *To the Hartford Convention: The Federalists and the Origins of Party Politics in Massachusetts, 1789–1815.* New York: Knopf, 1970.
Banning, Lance. "The Hamiltonian Madison: A Reconsideration," 92 *Va. Mag. of Hist. and Biography* 3 (1984).
——— "James Madison and the Nationalists, 1780–83," 40 *Wm. & Mary Q.* (3d series) 227 (1983).
Barber, Sotirios. "Judicial Review and *The Federalist,*" 55 *U. Chi. L. Rev.* 836 (1988).
Beard, Charles. *An Economic Interpretation of the Constitution of the United States.* New York: Macmillan, 1913.

Becker, Carl. *The History of Political Parties in the Province of New York, 1760–1776.* Madison: Univ. Wisconsin Press, 1968.

Benedict, Michael Les. "Preserving Federalism: Reconstruction and the Waite Court," 1978 *Sup. Ct. Rev.* 39.

Bernstein, Irving. *A Caring Society: The New Deal, the Worker, and the Great Depression.* Boston: Houghton Mifflin, 1985.

Bickel, Alexander. *The Morality of Consent.* New Haven: Yale Univ. Press, 1975.

———— *The Supreme Court and the Idea of Progress.* New York: Harper & Row, 1970.

———— *The Least Dangerous Branch: The Supreme Court at the Bar of Politics.* Indianapolis: Bobbs-Merrill Co., 1962.

———— "The Original Understanding and the Segregation Decision," 69 *Harv. L. Rev.* 1 (1955).

Bittker, Boris. "The Bicentennial of the Jurisprudence of Original Intent: The Recent Past," 77 *Cal. L. Rev.* 235 (1989).

Black, Charles. "The Lawfulness of the Segregation Decisions," 69 *Yale L. J.* 421 (1960).

Black, Earl, and Merle Black. *Politics and Society in the South.* Cambridge: Harvard Univ. Press, 1987.

Black, Hugo. "The Bill of Rights," 35 *New York Univ. L. Rev.* 865 (1960).

Bork, Robert. *The Tempting of America: The Political Seduction of the Law.* New York: Free Press, 1990.

Bourgignon, Henry. "The Second Mr. Justice Harlan: His Principles of Judicial Decision Making," 1979 *Sup. Ct. Rev.* 251.

Boyer, Paul. *Urban Masses and Moral Order, 1820–1920.* Cambridge: Harvard Univ. Press, 1978.

Brandeis, Louis. *Business—A Profession.* Boston: Small, Maynard & Co., 1914.

Brant, Irving. "The Madison Heritage," 35 *N.Y.U. L. Rev.* 882 (1960).

Brennan, William. "Constitutional Adjudication and the Death Penalty: A View from the Court," 100 *Harv. L. Rev.* 313 (1986).

Brest, Paul. "The Substance of Process," 42 *Ohio St. L. J.* 131 (1981).

Brewer, David. "The Nation's Safeguard," *New York State Bar Ass'n Proceedings.* New York: Stumpf & Steurer, 1893.

Burger, Warren. Foreword to Catherine Drinker Bowen, *Miracle at Philadelphia: The Story of the Constitutional Convention, May to September 1787.* Boston: Little, Brown, 1986.

Burke, Joseph. "The Cherokee Cases: A Study in Law, Politics, and Morality," 21 *Stanford L. Rev.* 500 (1969).

Burt, Robert. "Inventing Judicial Review: Israel and America," 10 *Cardozo L. Rev.* 2013 (1989).

———— *Two Jewish Justices: Outcasts in the Promised Land.* Berkeley: Univ. Calif. Press, 1988.

———— "Disorder in the Court: The Death Penalty and the Constitution," 85 *Michigan L. Rev.* 1741 (1987).

———— "What Was Wrong with *Dred Scott*, What's Right about *Brown*," 42 *Wash. & Lee L. Rev.* 1 (1985).

———— "Constitutional Law and the Teaching of the Parables," 93 *Yale L. J.* 455 (1984).

———— "Miranda and Title II: A Morganatic Marriage," 1969 *Sup. Ct. Rev.* 81.

Calabresi, Guido. *Ideals, Beliefs, Attitudes, and the Law: Private Law Perspectives on a Public Law Problem.* Syracuse: Syracuse Univ. Press, 1985.

Calhoun, John. *A Discourse on the Constitution and Government of the United States.* New York: D. Appleton & Co., 1854.

———— *Works of John C. Calhoun.* Ed. R. Cralle. New York: D. Appleton & Co., 1854.

Carey, George. "James Madison on Federalism: The Search for Abiding Principles," 3 *Benchmark* 27 (1987).

———— "Publius—A Split Personality?" 46 *Rev. of Politics* 3 (1984).

Casper, Gerhard. "Jones v. Mayer: Clio, Bemused and Confused Muse," 1968 *Sup. Ct. Rev.* 89.

Chesnut, Mary. *Mary Chesnut's Civil War.* Ed. C. Vann Woodward. New Haven: Yale Univ. Press, 1981.

Cover, Robert. "The Origins of Judicial Activism in the Protection of Minorities," 91 *Yale L. J.* 1287 (1982).

———— *Justice Accused: Antislavery and the Judicial Process.* New Haven: Yale Univ. Press, 1975.

Currie, David. "The Constitution in the Supreme Court: Civil War and Reconstruction, 1865–1873," 51 *U. Chi. L. Rev.* 131 (1984).

Davis, David Brion. *The Problem of Slavery in the Age of Revolution, 1770–1823.* Ithaca: Cornell Univ. Press, 1975.

De Tocqueville, Alexis. *Democracy in America.* Ed. J. Mayer. Garden City, NY: Anchor Books, 1969.

Douglas, William. "Stare Decisis," 49 *Colum. L. Rev.* 735 (1949).

Drinnon, Richard. *Facing West: The Metaphysics of Indian-Hating and Empire Building.* Minneapolis: Univ. Minnesota Press, 1980.

Dunning, William. *Reconstruction: Political and Economic, 1865–1877.* New York: Harper & Bros., 1907.

Dworkin, Ronald. *Law's Empire.* Cambridge: Harvard Univ. Press, 1986.

Ellis, Richard. *The Union at Risk: Jacksonian Democracy, States' Rights and the Nullification Crisis.* New York: Oxford Univ. Press, 1987.

———— *The Jeffersonian Crisis: Courts and Politics in the Young Republic.* New York: Norton, 1971.

Elman, Philip. "The Solicitor General's Office, Justice Frankfurter, and Civil Rights Litigation, 1946–1960: An Oral History," 100 *Harv. L. Rev.* 817 (1987).

Ely, John Hart. *Democracy and Distrust: A Theory of Judicial Review.* Cambridge: Harvard Univ. Press, 1980.

—— "The Wages of Crying Wolf: A Comment on *Roe v. Wade,*" 82 *Yale L. J.* 920 (1973).

Fairman, Charles. *The Oliver Wendell Holmes Devise History of the Supreme Court of the United States: Reconstruction and Reunion, 1864–88,* pt. 1. New York: Macmillan, 1971.

—— "Mr. Justice Bradley." In *Mr. Justice.* Eds. A. Dunham & P. Kurland. Chicago: Univ. Chicago Press, 1956.

Fehrenbacher, Don. *Lincoln in Text and Context.* Stanford: Stanford Univ. Press, 1987.

—— *The Dred Scott Case: Its Significance in American Law and Politics.* New York: Oxford Univ. Press, 1978.

Ferguson, Thomas. "Industrial Conflict and the Coming of the New Deal: The Triumph of Multinational Liberalism in America." In *The Rise and Fall of the New Deal Order.* Eds. S. Fraser and G. Gerstle. Princeton: Princeton Univ. Press, 1989.

Finkelman, Paul. *An Imperfect Union: Slavery, Federalism and Comity.* Chapel Hill: Univ. N. Car. Press, 1981.

—— "*Prigg v. Pennsylvania* and Northern State Courts: Anti-Slavery Use of a Pro-Slavery Decision," 25 *Civil War History* 5 (1979).

Fiss, Owen. *The Supreme Court and the Rise of the Modern State: 1888–1910.* (forthcoming).

—— "Foreword: The Forms of Justice," 93 *Harv. L. Rev.* 1 (1979).

Flack, Horace Edgar. *The Adoption of the Fourteenth Amendment.* Baltimore: The John Hopkins Press, 1908.

Fogelson, Robert. *America's Armories: Architecture, Society, and Public Order.* Cambridge: Harvard Univ. Press, 1989.

Foner, Eric. *Reconstruction: America's Unfinished Revolution, 1873–1877.* New York: Harper & Row, 1988.

—— *Politics and Ideology in the Age of the Civil War.* New York: Oxford Univ. Press, 1980.

—— *Free Soil, Free Labor, Free Men: The Ideology of the Republican Party before the Civil War.* New York: Oxford Univ. Press, 1970.

Forbath, William. "The Shaping of the American Labor Movement," 102 *Harv. L. Rev.* 1109 (1989).

Fox-Genovese, Elizabeth. *Within the Plantation Household: Black and White Women of the Old South.* Chapel Hill: Univ. N. Car. Press, 1988.

Frankfurter, Felix. "Mr. Justice Roberts," 104 *U. Pa. L. Rev.* 311 (1955).

Frankfurter, Felix, and Nathan Greene. *The Labor Injunction.* New York: Macmillan, 1930.

Fraser, Steve. "The 'Labor Question.'" In *The Rise and Fall of the New Deal*

Order, 1930–1980. Eds. S. Fraser and G. Gerstle. Princeton: Princeton Univ. Press, 1989.

Frederickson, George. *The Black Image in the White Mind: The Debate on Afro-American Character and Destiny, 1817–1914*. New York: Harper & Row, 1971.

Freedman, Max, ed. *Roosevelt and Frankfurter: Their Correspondence, 1928–1945*. Boston: Little, Brown, 1967.

Freehling, William. *The Road to Disunion: Secessionists at Bay 1776–1854*. New York: Oxford Univ. Press, 1990.

Freud, Sigmund. *Civilization and Its Discontents*. Ed. J. Strachey. New York: W. W. Norton, 1961.

Friedman, L., and F. Israel, eds. *The Justices of the United States Supreme Court 1789–1969*. New York, 1969.

Froman, Lewis. *The Congressional Process: Strategies, Rules, and Procedures*. Boston: Little, Brown, 1967.

Garrow, David. *Protest at Selma: Martin Luther King, Jr., and the Voting Rights Act of 1965*. New Haven: Yale Univ. Press, 1978.

Genovese, Eugene. *Roll, Jordan, Roll: The World the Slaves Made*. New York: Pantheon Books, 1974.

Gewirtz, Paul. "Remedies and Resistance," 92 *Yale L. J.* 585 (1983).

Glendon, Mary Ann. *Abortion and Divorce in Western Law*. Cambridge: Harvard Univ. Press, 1987.

Goffman, Erving. *Relations in Public*. New York: Basic Books, 1971.

Goldberg, Arthur. "Memorandum to the Conference Re: Capital Punishment, October Term, 1963," 27 *S. Tex. L. J.* 493 (1986).

Goldfield, David. *Black, White and Southern: Race Relations and Southern Culture, 1940 to the Present*. Baton Rouge: Louisiana State Univ. Press, 1990.

Graham, Howard Jay. "The 'Conspiracy Theory' of the Fourteenth Amendment," 47 *Yale L. J.* 371, 48 *Yale L. J.* 171 (1938).

Greenberg, Jack. "Capital Punishment as a System," 91 *Yale L. J.* 908 (1982).

Greenberg, Kenneth. *Masters and Statesmen: The Political Culture of American Slavery*. Baltimore: Johns Hopkins Univ. Press, 1985.

Grey, Thomas. "Do We Have an Unwritten Constitution?" 27 *Stanford L. Rev.* 703 (1975).

Gross, Samuel. "Race and Death: The Judicial Evaluation of Evidence of Discrimination in Capital Sentencing," 18 *U. C. Davis L. Rev.* 1275 (1985).

Gunther, Gerald. "Judicial Hegemony and Legislative Autonomy: The *Nixon* Case and the Impeachment Process," 22 *UCLA Law Rev.* 30 (1974).

——— "Foreword: In Search of Evolving Doctrine on a Changing Court: A Model for a Newer Equal Protection," 86 *Harv. L. Rev.* 1 (1972).

——— "The Subtle Vices of the Passive Virtues," 64 *Colum. L. Rev.* 1 (1964).

Haines, C. G., and F. H. Sherwood. *The Role of the Supreme Court in American Government and Politics*. Berkeley: Univ. Calif. Press, 1957.

Hamilton, Alexander. *Papers of Alexander Hamilton.* Ed. H. Syrett. New York: Columbia Univ. Press, 1961.

Hamilton, Alexander, James Madison, and John Jay. *Federalist Papers.* New York: New American Library, 1961.

Hartz, Louis. *The Liberal Tradition in America.* San Diego: Harcourt Brace Jovanovich, 1955.

Haskins, George. *The Oliver Wendell Holmes Devise History of the United States Supreme Court: Foundations of Power: John Marshall, 1801–15,* pt. 1. New York: Macmillan, 1981.

Hauser, Phillip. "Demographic Factors in the Integration of the Negro," 94 *Daedalus* 847 (1965).

Higgs, Robert. *Crisis and Leviathan: Critical Episodes in the Growth of American Government.* New York: Oxford Univ. Press, 1987.

Hofstadter, Richard. *The Idea of a Party System: The Rise of Legitimate Opposition in the United States, 1780–1840.* Berkeley: Univ. Calif. Press, 1969.

—— *The Progressive Historians: Turner, Beard, Parrington.* New York: Knopf, 1968.

—— *The American Political Tradition and the Men Who Made It.* New York: Knopf, 1948.

Holmes, Oliver Wendell. *The Mind and Faith of Justice Holmes.* Ed. Max Lerner. New York: Modern Library, 1943.

Howe, Mark deWolfe. *Justice Holmes: The Shaping Years, 1841–1870.* Cambridge: Harvard Univ. Press, 1957.

Hume, David. "Of the First Principles of Government." In *David Hume's Political Essays.* Ed. C. Hendel. Indianapolis: Bobbs-Merrill, 1953.

Huntington, Samuel. *American Politics: The Promise of Disharmony.* Cambridge: Harvard Univ. Press, 1981.

Hutchinson, Dennis. "Unanimity and Desegregation: Decisionmaking in the Supreme Court, 1948–1958," 68 *Georgetown L. J.* 1 (1979).

Isaac, Rhys. *The Transformation of Virginia, 1740–1790.* Chapel Hill: Univ. N. Car. Press, 1982.

Jackson, Robert. *The Struggle for Judicial Supremacy: A Study of a Crisis in American Power Politics.* New York: Knopf, 1941.

Jaffa, Harry. *Crisis of the House Divided.* Garden City, NY: Doubleday, 1959.

Jefferson, Thomas. *Papers of Thomas Jefferson.* Ed. J. Boyd. Princeton: Princeton Univ. Press, 1958.

—— "Notes on Virginia (1782)." Reprinted in *Writings of Thomas Jefferson,* vol. 3. Ed. P. Ford. New York: G. P. Putnam, 1894.

Kahn, Paul. "Community in Contemporary Constitutional Theory," 99 *Yale L. J.* 473 (1989).

———— "Reason and Will in the Origins of American Constitutionalism," 98 *Yale L. J.* 449 (1989).

Kennedy, Randall. "Martin Luther King's Constitution: A Legal History of the Montgomery Bus Boycott," 98 *Yale L. J.* 999 (1989).

Ketcham, Ralph. *Presidents above Party: The First American Presidency, 1789–1829.* Chapel Hill: Univ. N. Car. Press, 1984.

King, Martin Luther, Jr. *Why We Can't Wait.* New York: New American Library, 1964.

Klare, Karl. "Judicial Deradicalization of the Wagner Act and the Origins of Modern Legal Consciousness, 1937–1941," 62 *Minn. L. Rev.* 265 (1978).

Kluger, Richard. *Simple Justice: The History of Brown v. Board of Education and Black America's Struggle for Equality.* New York: Knopf, 1976.

Koch, Adrienne. *Madison's "Advice to My Country".* Princeton: Princeton Univ. Press, 1966.

Kraditor, Aileen. *Means and Ends in American Abolitionism: Garrison and His Critics on Strategy and Tactics, 1834–1850.* New York: Pantheon, 1969.

Kutler, Stanley. *Judicial Power and Reconstruction Politics.* Chicago: Univ. Chicago Press, 1968.

———— *The Dred Scott Decision: Law or Politics.* Boston: Houghton Mifflin, 1967.

LaRue, L. H. "The Continuing Presence of *Dred Scott*," 42 *Wash. & Lee L. Rev.* 57 (1985).

Lempert, Richard. "Capital Punishment in the '80s: Reflections on the Symposium," 74 *J. Crim. Law & Criminology* 1101 (1983).

Levinson, Sanford. *Constitutional Faith.* Princeton: Princeton Univ. Press, 1988.

Levy, Leonard. *The Law of the Commonwealth and Chief Justice Shaw.* New York: Oxford Univ. Press, 1957.

Lincoln, Abraham. *Collected Works.* Ed. Roy Basler. New Brunswick: Rutgers Univ. Press, 1953.

Lindsey, Almont. *The Pullman Strike: The Story of a Unique Experiment and of a Great Labor Upheaval.* Chicago: Univ. Chicago Press, 1942.

Litwack, Leon. *Been in the Storm So Long: The Aftermath of Slavery.* New York: Vintage Books, 1979.

Locke, John. *The Second Treatise of Civil Government.* Ed. J. Gough. Oxford: Blackwell, 1946.

Lofgren, Charles. *The Plessy Case: A Legal-Historical Interpretation.* New York: Oxford Univ. Press, 1987.

Lubell, Samuel. *White and Black: Test of a Nation.* New York: Harper & Row, 1966.

Luker, Kristin. *Abortion and the Politics of Motherhood.* Berkeley: Univ. Calif. Press, 1984.

Macpherson, C. B. *The Political Theory of Possessive Individualism: Hobbes to Locke*. Oxford: Clarendon Press, 1962.

Madison, James. *Papers of James Madison*. Eds. W. Hutchinson et al. Charlottesville: Univ. Virginia Press, 1981.

—— *Papers of James Madison*. Eds. R. Rutland et al. Charlottesville: Univ. Press of Virginia, 1977.

—— *Notes of Debates in the Federal Convention of 1787 Reported by James Madison*. New York: Norton, 1969.

—— *Writings of James Madison*. Ed. G. Hunt. New York: G. P. Putnam's Sons, 1910.

—— *Letters and Other Writings of James Madison*. Ed. W. C. Rives. Philadelphia: J. B. Lippincott, 1865.

Maltz, Earl. "Some Thoughts on the Death of Stare Decisis in Constitutional Law," 1980 *Wisconsin L. Rev.* 467.

Marmor, Theodore. *The Career of John C. Calhoun: Politician, Social Critic, Political Philosopher*. New York: Garland, 1988.

Marshall, John. *John Marshall's Defense of McCulloch v. Maryland*. Ed. G. Gunther. Stanford: Stanford Univ. Press, 1969.

Marston, Jerrilyn. *King and Congress: The Transfer of Political Legitimacy, 1774–1776*. Princeton: Princeton Univ. Press, 1987.

Mason, Alpheus T. "The Federalist—A Split Personality," 57 *Amer. Hist. Rev.* 625 (1952).

—— *Brandeis: A Free Man's Life*. New York: Viking, 1946.

McColley, Robert. *Slavery and Jeffersonian Virginia*. Urbana: Univ. Illinois Press, 1978.

McCoy, Drew. *The Last of the Fathers: James Madison and the Republican Legacy*. Cambridge: Cambridge Univ. Press, 1989.

McPherson, James. *Abraham Lincoln and the Second American Revolution*. New York: Oxford Univ. Press, 1990.

—— *Battle Cry of Freedom: The Civil War Era*. New York: Oxford Univ. Press, 1988.

Meltsner, Michael. *Cruel and Unusual: The Supreme Court and Capital Punishment*. New York: Random House, 1973.

Mendelson, Wallace. "Dred Scott's Case—Reconsidered," 38 *Minn. L. Rev.* 16 (1953).

Michelman, Frank. "Law's Republic," 97 *Yale L. J.* 1493 (1988).

—— "Foreword: Traces of Self-Government," 100 *Harv. L. Rev.* 4 (1986).

Miller, John C. *The Wolf by the Ears: Thomas Jefferson and Slavery*. New York: Free Press, 1977.

Monaghan, Henry. "Of 'Liberty' and 'Property,'" 62 *Cornell L. Rev.* 405 (1977).

Monroe, James. *Writings of James Monroe*. Ed. S. M. Hamilton. New York: G. P. Putnam's Sons, 1902.

Morgan, Edmund. *American Slavery/American Freedom: The Ordeal of Colonial Virginia*. New York: Norton, 1975.

Morris, Richard. *Witnesses at the Creation: Hamilton, Madison, Jay, and the Constitution*. New York: New American Library, 1985.

Mosteller, F., and D. Wallace. *Inference and Disputed Authorship: The Federalist*. Reading, MA: Addison-Wesley, 1964.

Murphy, Walter. "Who Shall Interpret? The Quest for the Ultimate Constitutional Interpreter," 48 *Rev. of Politics* 401 (1986).

Murrin, John. "A Roof without Walls: The Dilemma of American National Identity." In *Beyond Confederation*. Eds. R. Beeman et al. Chapel Hill: Univ. N. Car. Press, 1987.

Muse, Benjamin. *Ten Years of Prelude*. New York: Viking Press, 1964.

Myrdal, Gunnar. *An American Dilemma: The Negro Problem and Modern Democracy*. New York: Harper & Row, 1944.

Nat'l Advisory Comm'n on Civil Disorders. *Report*. New York: Bantam Books, 1968.

Nelson, William. *The Fourteenth Amendment: From Political Principle to Judicial Doctrine*. Cambridge: Harvard Univ. Press, 1988.

Nieman, Donald. "Republicanism, the Confederate Constitution, and the American Constitutional Tradition." In *An Uncertain Tradition: Constitutionalism and the History of the South*. Eds K. Hall and J. Ely. Athens: Univ. Georgia Press, 1989.

Paludan, Phillip. *"A People's Contest": The Union and Civil War, 1861–1865*. New York: Harper & Row, 1988.

Perry, Michael. *The Constitution, The Courts, and Human Rights*. New Haven: Yale Univ. Press, 1982.

Pessen, Edward. *Jacksonian America: Society, Personality and Politics*. Urbana: Univ. Illinois Press, 1985.

Pocock, J. G. A. *The Machiavellian Moment: Florentine Political Thought and the Atlantic Republican Tradition*. Princeton: Princeton Univ. Press, 1975.

Pollak, Louis. "Racial Discrimination and Judicial Integrity: A Reply to Professor Wechsler," 108 *U. Pa. L. Rev.* 1 (1959).

Potter, David. *The Impending Crisis, 1848–1861*. New York: Harper & Row, 1976.

——— *History and American Society*. New York: Oxford Univ. Press, 1973.

——— *The South and the Concurrent Majority*. Baton Rouge: Louisiana State Univ. Press, 1972.

——— *Lincoln and His Party in the Secession Crisis*. New Haven: Yale Univ. Press, 1942.

Powell, H. Jefferson. "Joseph Story's Commentaries on the Constitution: A Belated Review," 94 *Yale L. J.* 1285 (1985).

——— "The Original Understanding of Original Intent," 98 *Harv. L. Rev.* 885 (1985).

Radosh, Ronald. "The Corporate Ideology of American Labor Leaders from Gompers to Hillman." In *For a New America: Essays in History and Politics from Studies on the Left, 1959–1967*. New York: Random House, 1970.

Remini, Robert. *Andrew Jackson and the Course of American Democracy, 1833–1845*. New York: Harper & Row, 1984.

——— *Andrew Jackson and the Course of American Freedom, 1822–1832*. New York: Harper & Row, 1981.

——— *Andrew Jackson and the Course of American Empire, 1767–1821*. New York: Harper & Row, 1977.

Richardson, J., ed. *Messages and Papers of the Presidents*. Washington: Government Printing Office, 1898.

Roark, James. *Masters without Slaves: Southern Planters in the Civil War and Reconstruction*. New York: W. W. Norton, 1977.

Rogin, Michael Paul. *Ronald Reagan, the Movie, and Other Episodes in Political Demonology*. Berkeley: Univ. Calif. Press, 1987.

——— *Fathers and Children: Andrew Jackson and the Subjugation of the American Indian*. New York: Knopf, 1975.

Roper, Donald. "In Quest of Judicial Objectivity: The Marshall Court and the Legitimation of Slavery," 21 *Stanford L. Rev.* 532 (1969).

Rose, Willie Lee. *Slavery and Freedom*. New York: Oxford Univ. Press, 1982.

Rossum, Ralph. "'To Render These Rights Secure': James Madison's Understanding of the Relationship of the Constitution to the Bill of Rights," 3 *Benchmark* 4 (1987).

Scalia, Antonin. "Originalism: The Lesser Evil," 57 *U. Cincinnati L. Rev.* 849 (1989).

Schlesinger, Arthur, Jr. "The Ages of Jackson." In *New York Review of Books*, Dec. 7, 1989, p. 51.

——— *The Politics of Upheaval*. Boston: Houghton Mifflin, 1960.

Schmidt, Benno. "Principle and Prejudice: The Supreme Court and Race in the Progressive Era," pt. 1, 82 *Colum. L. Rev.* 444 (1982).

Schusky, Ernest. "Thoughts and Deeds of the Founding Fathers: The Beginning of United States and Indian Relations." In *Political Organization of Native North Americans*. Ed. E. Schusky. Washington, DC: Univ. Press of America, 1980.

Schwartz, Bernard. "Chief Justice Rehnquist, Justice Jackson, and the *Brown* Case," 1988 *Sup. Ct. Rev.* 245.

——— *The Unpublished Opinions of the Burger Court*. New York: Oxford Univ. Press, 1988

Seabright, Paul. "Social Choice and Society Theories," 18 *Philosophy & Public Affairs* 365 (1989).

Simon, James. *The Antagonists: Hugo Black, Felix Frankfurter and Civil Liberties in Modern America.* New York: Simon & Schuster, 1989.

Small, M., and J. D. Small. *Resort to Arms: International and Civil Wars, 1816–1980.* Beverly Hills, CA: Sage Publications, 1982.

Sobel, Mechal. *The World They Made Together: Black and White Values in Eighteenth-Century Virginia.* Princeton: Princeton Univ. Press, 1987.

Stephens, Alexander. *A Constitutional View of the Late War between the States.* Philadelphia: Nat'l Publ. Co., 1870.

Story, Joseph. *Commentaries on the Constitution of the United States.* Boston: Little, Brown, 1858.

Stourzh, Gerald. *Alexander Hamilton and the Idea of Republican Government.* Stanford: Stanford Univ. Press, 1970.

Stowe, Steven. *Intimacy and Power in the Old South: Ritual in the Lives of the Planters.* Baltimore: John Hopkins Univ. Press, 1987.

Strong, Frank. "Bicentennial Benchmark: Two Centuries of Evolution of Constitutional Processes," 55 *N. Car. L. Rev.* 1 (1976).

Strum, Philippa. "Brandeis and the Living Constitution." In *Brandeis and America.* Ed. N. Dawson. Lexington: Univ. Press of Kentucky, 1989.

Sunstein, Cass. "Beyond the Republican Revival," 97 *Yale L. J.* 1539 (1988).

——— "Interest Groups in American Public Law," 38 *Stanford L. Rev.* 29 (1985).

Thayer, James Bradley. "The Origin and Scope of the American Doctrine of Constitutional Law," 7 *Harv. L. Rev.* 129 (1893).

Tise, Larry. *Proslavery: A History of the Defense of Slavery in America, 1701–1840.* Athens: Univ. Georgia Press, 1987.

Touster, Saul. "In Search of Holmes from Within," 18 *Vanderbilt L. Rev.* 437 (1965).

Tribe, Laurence. *Abortion: The Clash of Absolutes.* New York: Norton, 1990.

——— *American Constitutional Law.* 2nd ed. Mineola, NY: Foundation Press, 1988.

Tushnet, Mark. *Red, White and Blue.* Cambridge: Harvard Univ. Press, 1989.

——— *The American Law of Slavery 1810–1860: Considerations of Humanity and Interest.* Princeton: Princeton Univ. Press, 1981.

Van Alstyne, William. "A Critical Guide to *Marbury v. Madison,*" 1969 *Duke L. J.* 1.

Van Buren, Martin. *Inquiry into the Origin and Course of Political Parties in the United States.* New York: Hurd & Houghton, 1867.

Vidmar, Neil, and Phoebe Ellsworth. "Public Opinion and the Death Penalty," 26 *Stanford L. Rev.* 1245 (1974).

Virginia Comm'n on Constitutional Government. *The Kentucky-Virginia Resolutions and Mr. Madison's Report of 1799.* Richmond: Virginia Comm'n on Constitutional Government, 1960.

Warren, Charles. *The Supreme Court in United States History.* Boston: Little, Brown, 1922.

Warren, Earl. *Memoirs.* Garden City, NY: Doubleday, 1977.

Wax, Murray. *Indian Americans: Unity and Diversity.* Englewood Cliffs, NJ: Prentice-Hall, 1971.

Wechsler, Herbert. "Toward Neutral Principles of Constitutional Law," 73 *Harv. L. Rev.* 1 (1959).

Wedgwood, Ruth. "The Revolutionary Martyrdom of Jonathan Robbins," 100 *Yale L. J.* 229 (1990).

Weisberg, Robert. "Deregulating Death," 1983 *Sup. Ct. Rev.* 305.

Wellington, Harry. "The Nature of Judicial Review," 91 *Yale L. J.* 486 (1982).

White, G. Edward. *The Oliver Wendell Holmes Devise History of the United States Supreme Court: The Marshall Court and Cultural Change, 1815–35.* New York: Macmillan, 1988.

White, James Boyd. *The Legal Imagination: Studies in the Nature of Legal Thought and Expression.* Boston: Little, Brown, 1973.

Wiebe, Robert. *The Opening of American Society: From the Adoption of the Constitution to the Eve of Disunion.* New York: Vintage Books, 1985.

——— *The Search for Order, 1877–1920.* New York: Hill & Wang, 1967.

Williams, T. Harry. *The Selected Essays of T. Harry Williams.* Baton Rouge: Louisiana State Univ. Press, 1983.

Wills, Gary. *Inventing America: Jefferson's Declaration of Independence.* Garden City, NY: Doubleday, 1978.

Wood, Gordon. "Interests and Disinterestedness in the Making of the Constitution." In *Beyond Confederation.* Eds. R. Beeman et al. Chapel Hill: Univ. N. Car. Press, 1987.

——— *The Creation of the American Republic, 1776–1787.* New York: Norton, 1969.

Woodward, C. Vann. *American Counterpoint: Slavery and Racism in the North–South Dialogue.* Boston: Little, Brown, 1971.

——— *The Burden of Southern History.* Baton Rouge: Louisiana State Univ. Press, 1968.

——— *The Strange Career of Jim Crow.* New York: Oxford Univ. Press, 1957.

——— *Origins of the New South, 1877–1913.* Baton Rouge: Louisiana State Univ. Press, 1951.

——— *Reunion and Reaction: The Compromise of 1877 and the End of Reconstruction.* Boston: Little, Brown, 1951.

Yates, Robert (Brutus). In *The Antifederalists.* Ed. C. Kenyon. Indianapolis: Bobbs-Merrill, 1966.

Zeisel, Hans. "Race Bias in the Administration of the Death Penalty: The Florida Experience," 95 *Harv. L. Rev.* 456 (1981).

Zimring, Franklin, and Gordon Hawkins. *Capital Punishment and the American Agenda.* Cambridge: Cambridge Univ. Press, 1986.

Acknowledgments

For their gifts of friendship and critical scrutiny of the manuscript of this book, I thank Bruce Ackerman, Milner Ball, Les Benedict, Lee Bollinger, Owen Fiss, Charlie Halpern, Paul Kahn, Jay Katz, Tony Kronman, John Langbein, Sandy Levinson, Ted Marmor, Robert Post, Mark Rose, Austin Sarat, Paul Schwartz, and Harry Wellington. Steve Sowle generously gave the same gifts, as well as research assistance over two summers while he was a student at Yale Law School. After Steve graduated, Adam Aronson was invaluable in helping me bring the manuscript into finished form. I am also grateful to Aida Donald at Harvard University Press for her caring attention to the book and to Susan Wallace for astute, sympathetic editorial advice. Finally, I am indebted to Warren Weiswasser for his guidance and support, and to Linda Burt for being with me through it all.

Robert A. Burt
Woodbridge, Connecticut
September 1991

Index